Padraic Wall

8467409

Corporate
Financial Distress

Corporate Financial Distress

A Complete Guide to Predicting, Avoiding, and Dealing with Bankruptcy

EDWARD I. ALTMAN

A Wiley-Interscience Publication

JOHN WILEY & SONS

New York • Chichester • Brisbane • Toronto • Singapore

Library of Congress Cataloging in Publication Data:

Altman, Edward I., 1941–
  Corporate financial distress

  (Wiley professional banking and finance series)
  "A Wiley-Interscience publication."
  Includes bibliographical references and index.
  1. Bankruptcy—United States. I. Title. II. Series.

HG3766.A66 1982   658.1′5   82-16103
ISBN 0-471-08707-6

Printed in the United States of America

10 9 8 7 6 5

For my mother, Florence,
and in memory of my father, Sidney.

Series Preface

The worlds of banking and finance have changed dramatically during the past few years, and no doubt this turbulence will continue through the 1980s. We have established the Wiley Professional Banking and Finance Series to aid in characterizing this dynamic environment and to further the understanding of the emerging structures, issues, and content for the professional financial community.

We envision three types of book in this series. First, we are commissioning distinguished experts in a broad range of fields to assemble a number of authorities to write specific primers on related topics. For example, some of the early handbook-type volumes in the series concentrate on the Stock Market, Investment Banking, and Financial Depository Institutions. A second type of book attempts to combine text material with appropriate empirical and case studies written by practitioners in relevant fields. An early example is a forthcoming volume on The Management of Cash and Other Short-Term Assets. Finally, we are encouraging definitive, authoritative works on specialized subjects for practitioners and theorists.

It is a distinct pleasure and honor for me to assist John Wiley & Sons, Inc. in this important endeavor. In addition to banking and financial practitioners, we think business students and faculty will benefit from this series. Most of all, though, we hope this series will become a primary source in the 1980s for the members of the professional financial community to refer to theories and data and to integrate important aspects of the central changes in our financial world.

EDWARD I. ALTMAN

Professor of Finance
New York University,
Schools of Business

Preface

As I am writing this preface, the corporate bankruptcy phenomenon in the United States has been propelled into national prominence because of the record number of business failures. Within the last month, four companies with liabilities of at least $0.5 billion have filed for protection under the bankruptcy code and two, Wickes, Inc. and Braniff Airlines, have liabilities exceeding $1 billion. The business failure rate in 1982 is likely to exceed the rate of any year since 1933! Indeed, the bankruptcy "business" is booming, and it is more important than ever to understand the characteristics and implications of corporate demise.

When I began my research into the bankruptcy phenomenon in the mid-1960s, there were virtually no academics or researchers interested in the subject. The realm of bankruptcy and reorganization was left to the legal and economic specialists who worked within the confines of courts and bank workout departments. Even after the famous Penn Central debacle of 1970, the number of large firms which appeared to be vulnerable to financial distress was relatively few. When my first book, *Corporate Bankruptcy in America* (1971), was published, it seemed to me that business failure analysis was a fertile area of conceptual, empirical, and case-oriented research. Today, the bankruptcy topic is a subject of international concern and analysis. Indeed, researchers in at least 10 countries are currently exploring the efficacy of building models to explain and predict business failures.

As well as studying the explosion in number and size of bankrupt firms, academics in the world of finance have expended an increasing amount of time and effort in attempting to gain a better understanding of market imperfections and questions related to optimum capital structure, agency costs, and the dynamics of business demise. There has been a continual flow of failure prediction models, both here and abroad.

I decided to write another book in the bankruptcy area since so much has happened in the last decade. For one thing, the bankruptcy act was completely revamped, resulting in the new Bankruptcy Reform Act of

1978, which went into effect in October 1979, followed by the Bankruptcy Tax Bill of 1980. Practitioners and researchers are still trying to understand and gauge the impact of this new legislation. We explore the new code in Chapter 1 as well as the background statistics on failures and bankruptcies. The Appendix to Chapter 1 discusses a case, analyzed under the old Chapter X, but whose principles of reorganization remain essentially unchanged under the new code. In Chapter 2, we examine the statistical association between aggregate economic phenomena and business failure in order to understand how macroeconomic conditions effect the marginal firm's ability to survive. The central theme of the book is bankruptcy prediction. In addition to the original Z-score model's (1968) discussion, we present, in Chapter 3, a model which does not rely on stock market data. Hence, it is applicable, I believe, to the privately held firm. The material in this book is the first presentation of this extension. Chapter 4 explores the "second generation" failure model (ZETA) and the attempts by others in the United States to build models that classify and predict bankruptcy among industrial and nonindustrial firms.

The most relevant sections of the book for business practitioners can be found in Chapters 5 through 10. There we explore the implications of failure prediction models for various industries and professions. In Chapter 5, I discuss the commercial banking sector; in Chapter 6, the managerial implications for distressed firms; in Chapter 7, the public accounting sector; in Chapter 8, the legal arena; in Chapters 9 and 10, the investor implications; in Chapter 11, failure models for nonindustrial firms (i.e., railroads, S&Ls, commercial banks, and broker-dealers), and, in Chapter 12, the results of an exhaustive survey and analysis of those efforts to build failure prediction models outside of the United States.

I am particularly interested in the reaction of business practitioners and advisors to the material presented in Chapter 6 on "Managing a Financial Turnaround." Here we report on the successful attempt of one chief executive officer to use a failure prediction model to help him manage his firm back to health after being on the brink of bankruptcy.

This book is written for two primary audiences. First, there are the many practitioners who increasingly need to understand the analysis and prediction of business bankruptcy. It is to be hoped that the book will be relevant for commercial bankers, investment specialists, legal analysts, accounting auditors, and business consultants. It is also my objective that managers of operating companies will find the concepts and techniques of real use in managing their firms. Second, there are the academics and students of business. Specialized courses in business schools, bank and accounting training programs, and perhaps law schools will, I hope, utilize these concepts and techniques in their programs. Since bankruptcy is a worldwide phenomenon, I expect foreign practitioners and scholars will find the work relevant to their specific needs.

Over the last decade, there have been an extraordinary number of academics, business practitioners, graduate assistants, and editorial assistants who have assisted me. I am indebted to a number of foreign researchers who assisted in the international survey (Chapter 12). These include Professors Bilderbeek (Netherlands), Cahill (Ireland), Castagna and Matolcsy (Australia), Fischer (West Germany), Izan (Australia), Lavallee (Canada), Ribeiro-Dias (Brazil), Taffler (the United Kingdom), Takahashi (Japan), van Frederikslust (Netherlands), and von Stein (West Germany).

Among business and journalist practitioners, I have benefited from discussions with P. Barrett and K. Alberti (Avis, Inc.), S. Cunningham and R. Stollman (*Business Week*), N. Follrath (First National Bank of Chicago), R. Grimmig and C. Oppenheimer (Chemical Bank), R. Goeltz (Jos. Seagrams), L. Goodman (Chase), D. Kaplan (Kaplan & Smith), J. La-Fleur (GTI Corp.), J. McWilliams (Continental Bank), K. McWilliams (PruCapital, Inc.), B. Loris (NASD), R. Metz (*The New York Times*), P. Narayanan and D. Raj (Chase Manhattan Bank), R. Roussey and F. Koster (Arthur Andersen & Co.) and B. Siegel (Drexel Burnham). Of special mention should be my work with R. Haldeman (ZETA Services, Inc.) and P. Narayanan (Chase), both in the development of the ZETA model and in our continued professional interface.

Many academic colleagues, notably R. Avery, R. Eisenbeis, and J. Sinkey, deserve special credit for stretching the analytical quality of the work. I would also like to thank the National Science Foundation (NSF Grant #5-283-040) and Arthur Andersen & Co. for their generous support of sections of the research.

At New York University, I have been particularly fortunate to have the assistance of talented graduate students including J. Byrom, P. Ho, J. Ko, P. Narayanan, B. Rothberg, A. Sohn, B. Silverman, C. S. Tsai, P. Tsang, and K. Yon. Also at NYU, the indispensable typing and editorial assistance of L. Cohen, D. Daniels, E. Kaplan, J. Marks, and L. Scott are sincerely appreciated.

One cannot write a book of this type and duration without the support and enthusiasm of his loved ones. My wife Elaine and nine-year-old son Gregory learned to tolerate my perverse enthusiasm for such a negative subject as bankruptcy. Thanks for your patience and understanding.

EDWARD I. ALTMAN

New York, New York
October 1982

Contents

Tables

Chapter 12

List of Charts

Chapter 5

Chapter 6

List of Figures

Corporate
Financial Distress

1 Bankruptcy and Reorganization: Background

Business failure, including the legal procedures of corporate bankruptcy liquidation and reorganization, is a sobering economic reality reflecting the uniqueness of the American way of corporate death. The business failure phenomenon has received a great deal of exposure during the 1970s and especially in 1980 to 1982. Between 1972 and 1979, 29,500 to 35,200 firms a year petitioned the courts to liquidate or to reorganize under the protection of the nation's bankruptcy laws. In fiscal 1980 and 1981, the number increased 55% and 30% respectively over that posted in 1979 and 1980. The bankruptcy rate continued to rise significantly in fiscal 1982 (year-end June 30). The business failure rate for the first 8 months of 1982 is running at the highest level since 1933! Although business failures occur worldwide, this section concentrates on bankruptcy in the United States. The reasons for the dramatic increase in bankruptcies will be discussed at a later point in this chapter.

Corporate failure is no longer the exclusive province of the small, undercapitalized business but occurs increasingly among the large industrial and financial corporations. The decade of the 1970s was a watershed in this respect: the $5-billion Penn Central bankruptcy (in 1970) heralded the new wave of larger firm failures, and we witnessed the $12-billion all-but-bankruptcy of the Chrysler Corp. and its subsequent government bailout beginning in 1979. Table 1-1 lists the 36 largest U.S. bankruptcies—all of which took place during or since 1970. The list does not include financial organizations such as commercial banks and savings and loan associations but does include real estate investment trusts (REITs). Certainly, inflation helps account for the increase in size of all firms, including those that go bankrupt, but the astounding increase in the average liability of business failures (next subsection) goes beyond inflationary influences.

Table 1-1 The Largest U.S. Bankruptcies*a* (in Terms of Dollar Liabilities) as of October 1982.

	Total Liabilities ($ Millions)	Bankruptcy Petition Date	Filed under
1. Penn Central Transportation Co.	3,300	June 1970	Chapter VIII, Section 77
2. Wickes	2,000	April 1982	Chapter 11
3. Itel	1,700	January 1981	Chapter 11
4. Braniff Airlines	1,100	May 1982	Chapter 11
5. Manville Corp.	1,116	August 1982	Chapter 11
6. W.T. Grant Co.	1,000	October 1975	Chapter XI
7. Seatrain Lines	785	February 1981	Chapter 11
8. Continental Mortgage Investors	607	March 1976	Chapter XI-X
9. United Merchants & Manufacturing	552	July 1977	Chapter XI
10. AM International	510	April 1982	Chapter 11
11. Saxon Industries	461	April 1982	Chapter 11
12. Commonwealth Oil Refining Co.	421	March 1978	Chapter XI
13. W. Judd Kassuba	420	December 1973	Chapter XI
14. Erie Lackawanna Railroad	404	June 1972	Chapter VIII, Section 77
15. White Motor Corp.	399	September 1980	Chapter 11
16. Investors Funding Corp.	379	October 1974	Chapter X
17. Sambo's Restaurants	370	June 1981	Chapter 11

18. Food Fair Corp.	347	October 1978	Chapter XI
19. Great American Mortgage & Trust	326	March 1977	Chapter XI
20. McLouth Steel	323	December 1981	Chapter 11
21. U.S. Financial Services	300	July 1973	Chapter XI
22. Chase Manhattan Mortgage & Realty Trust	290	February 1979	Chapter XI
23. Daylin, Inc.	250	February 1975	Chapter XI
24. Guardian Mortgage Investors	247	March 1978	Chapter XI
25. Revere Copper & Brass	237	October 1982	Chapter 11
26. Chicago, Rock Island & Pacific	221	March 1975	Chapter VIII, Section 77
27. Equity Funding Corp. of America	200	April 1973	Chapter X
28. Interstate Stores, Inc.	190	May 1974	Chapter XI
29. Fidelity Mortgage Investors	187	January 1975	Chapter XI
30. Omega, Alpha Corp.	175	September 1974	Chapter X
31. Lionel Corp.	165	February 1982	Chapter 11
32. Reading Railroad	158	November 1971	Chapter VIII, Section 77
33. Boston & Maine Railroad	148	December 1975	Chapter VIII, Section 77
34. Westgate-California	144	February 1974	Chapter X
35. Colwell Mortgage & Trust	142	February 1978	Chapter XI
36. Pacific Far East Lines	132	January 1978	Chapter XI
37. Allied Supermarkets	124	June 1977	Chapter XI
38. Penn Dixie Co.	122	April 1980	Chapter 11

*Does not include commercial banking entities.

Among the 36 largest bankruptcies, in terms of assets and liabilities, are seven retailers, six REITs, and four railroads. Prior to 1980, few large manufacturers are evident, but even this sector appears increasingly vulnerable with the near failure of Chrysler (as of June 1982) and the recent Wickes, AM International, Saxon Industries, and White Motor Co. failures. Wickes is the largest bankruptcy filed thus far ($2 billion in liabilities—see Table 1-1) under the Bankruptcy Reform Act of 1978, which went into effect in October 1979.

BANKRUPTCY AND REORGANIZATION THEORY

In any economic system, the continuous entrance and exit of productive entities are natural components. Since there are costs to society inherent in the failure of these entities, laws and procedures have been established (1) to protect the contractual rights of interested parties, (2) to provide for the orderly liquidation of unproductive assets, and (3) when deemed desirable, to provide for a moratorium on certain claims, to give the debtor time to become rehabilitated and to emerge from the process as a continuing entity. Both liquidation and reorganization are available courses of action in most countries of the world and are based on the following premise: If an entity's intrinsic or economic value is greater than its current liquidation value, then from both the public policy and entity ownership viewpoints, the firm should attempt to reorganize and continue. If however, the firm's assets are worth more dead than alive—that is, if liquidation value exceeds economic value—liquidation is the preferable alternative.

The theory of reorganization in bankruptcy is basically sound and has potential economic and social benefits. The process is designed to enable the financially troubled firm to continue in existence and maintain whatever goodwill it still possesses, rather than to liquidate its assets for the benefit of its creditors. Justification of this attempt is found in the belief that continued existence will result in a healthy going concern worth more than the value of its assets sold in the marketplace. Since this rehabilitation process often requires several years, the time value of money should be considered explicitly through a discounted cash flow procedure. If, in fact, economically productive assets continue to contribute to society's supply of goods and services above and beyond their opportunity costs, the process of reorganization has been of benefit, to say nothing of the continued employment of the firm's employees. These benefits should be weighed against the costs of bankruptcy to the firm and to society.

The primary groups of interested parties are the firm's creditors and owners. The experience of these parties is of paramount importance in the evaluation of the bankruptcy-reorganization process, although the laws governing reorganization reflect the legislators' concern for overall societal welfare. The primary immediate responsibility of the reorganization process is to relieve the burden of the debtor's liabilities and realign the capital structure so that financial problems will not recur in the foreseeable future.

COSTS OF BANKRUPTCY

From the firm's standpoint, bankruptcy includes direct and indirect costs. Direct bankruptcy costs are the tangible, out-of-pocket expenses of either liquidating or attempting a reorganization of the ailing enterprise. These include bankruptcy filing fees and legal, accountant, and other professional service costs. Some analysts include in the direct cost category the costs involved with lost managerial time, a difficult "expense" to measure empirically. I prefer to include lost managerial time with other intangible opportunity costs or indirect costs. The primary indirect cost is the lost sales and profits of the firm due to the perceived potential bankruptcy—primarily from customer reluctance to buy from a firm that may fail. This cost was dramatically illustrated when sales of Chrysler products dropped during the 1978–1980 financial crisis.

Continuing research in this area centers on trying to quantify the magnitude of these direct and indirect costs to permit their comparison with the tax benefit that a firm receives from additional leverage. Many theorists believe that the increasing bankruptcy possibility, due to increased leverage, and the attendant costs of bankruptcy, help explain why firms seek some optimal capital structure; in other words, an optimal mix of debt and equity capital.

DEFINING CORPORATE PROBLEMS

The unsuccessful business enterprise has been defined in numerous ways in attempts to depict the formal process confronting the firm and/or to categorize the economic problems involved. Three generic terms that are commonly found in the literature are *failure, insolvency,* and *bankruptcy.* Although these terms are sometimes used interchangeably, they have distinctly different meanings.

Failure, by economic criteria, means that the realized rate of return on invested capital, with allowances for risk considerations, is significantly and continually lower than prevailing rates on similar investments. Somewhat different economic criteria have also been utilized, including insufficient revenues to cover costs and cases of the average return on investment being below the firm's cost of capital. These economic situations make no positive statements about the existence or discontinuance of the entity. Normative decisions to discontinue operations are based on expected returns and the ability of the firm to cover its variable costs. It should be noted that a company may be an economic failure for many years, yet never fail to meet its current obligations because of the absence or near absence of legally enforceable debt. When the company can no longer meet the legally enforceable demands of its creditors, it is sometimes called a legal failure. The term legal is somewhat misleading because the condition, as just described, may exist without formal court involvement.

The term business failure has also been adopted by Dun & Bradstreet (D&B)—a leading supplier of relevant statistics on unsuccessful enterprises—to describe various unsatisfactory business conditions. Business failures include businesses that cease operation following assignment or bankruptcy; those that cease with loss to creditors after such actions as execution, foreclosure, or attachment; those that voluntarily withdraw leaving unpaid obligations, or have been involved in court actions such as receivership, reorganization, or arrangement; and those that voluntarily compromise with creditors. In actuality, business failures as defined by D&B are a fraction, although a significant one, of the enterprises that are discontinued each year.

Insolvency is another term depicting negative firm performance and is generally used in a more technical fashion. The state of technical insolvency exists when a firm cannot meet its current obligations, signifying a lack of liquidity. Another term used to describe the same situation is insolvency in an equity sense. Walter (1957) discussed the measurement of technical insolvency and advanced the theory that net cash flows relative to current liabilities should be the primary criterion used to describe technical insolvency, not the traditional working capital measurement. Technical insolvency may be a temporary condition, although it often is the immediate cause of formal bankruptcy declaration.

Insolvency in a bankruptcy sense is more critical and indicates a chronic rather than temporary condition. A firm finds itself in this situation when its total liabilities exceed a fair valuation of its total assets. The real net worth of the firm is, therefore, negative. Technical insolvency is easily detectable, whereas the more serious bankruptcy insolvency condition requires a comprehensive valuation analysis, which is usually not undertaken until asset liquidation is contemplated. Insolvency, as it relates to the formal bankruptcy process, is defined explicitly in Section 101, Clause 26, of the Bankruptcy Reform Act of 1978.

Finally, we come to *bankruptcy* itself. One type of bankruptcy is described above and refers to the net worth position of an enterprise. A second, more observable type is a firm's formal declaration of bankruptcy in a federal district court, accompanied by a petition to either liquidate its assets or attempt a recovery program. The latter procedure is legally referred to as a bankruptcy reorganization and is discussed later. The judicial reorganization is a formal procedure that is usually the last measure in a series of attempted remedies.

INSOLVENCY TESTS AND CORPORATE DISTRIBUTIONS

Corporate distributions to shareholders involve the transfer of money or other property (except its own shares) or the incurrence of indebtedness, whether by cash dividend or share repurchase. The revised Model Business Corporation Act specifies that the board of directors may authorize and the corporation may make distributions except where (1) the corporation would be unable to pay its debts as they become due in the usual course of its business, or (2) the corporation's total assets would be less than its total liabilities, sometimes known as the balance sheet test. The former test describes equity insolvency and the latter describes bankruptcy insolvency. No longer are the terms par value, stated value, or capital surplus of any relevance to a firm's payment of dividends or share repurchase.

Whether a firm would be insolvent as a result of a proposed distribution is to be determined by the board of directors based on its collective business judgment. This is stipulated to involve judgments as to the future course of the corporation's business, including an analysis of the firm's ability to generate sufficient funds from operations or from the orderly disposition of its assets, to satisfy its existing and reasonably anticipated obligations as they come due.

Discussion of these and other provisions can be found in "Changes in the Model Business Corporation Act—Amendments to Financial Provisions" (*Business Lawyer,* Vol. 34, July 1979). The question of corporate solvency is now explicit and fundamental to the concept of shareholder return on investment.

EVOLUTION OF THE BANKRUPTCY PROCESS IN THE UNITED STATES

The Constitution empowers the U.S. Congress to establish uniform laws regulating bankruptcy. By virtue of this authority, various acts and amendments have been passed, starting with the Bankruptcy Act of 1898. Several bankruptcy acts have been passed in this century, and in 1978 Congress enacted the Bankruptcy Reform Act of 1978, which is the current standard. To appreciate the bankruptcy process, it is necessary to review the previous statutes and codes that have helped to form the present system.

Equity Receiverships

The Bankruptcy Act of 1898 provided only for a company's liquidation and contained no provisions allowing corporations to reorganize and thereby remain in existence. Reorganization could be effected, however, through equity receiverships. Although the basic theory of corporate reorganization is sound, the equity receivership procedure proved to be ineffective. It was developed to prevent disruptive seizures of property by dissatisfied creditors who were able to obtain liens on specific properties of the financially troubled concern. Receivers were appointed by the courts to manage the corporate property during financial reorganization. The procedure presented serious problems, however, and essentially was replaced by provisions of the bankruptcy acts of 1933 and 1934. Receivership in equity is not the same as receivership in bankruptcy. In the latter case, a receiver is a court agency that administers the bankrupt's assets until a trustee is appointed. While receivership is still available to companies, it has been almost entirely replaced by reorganization under the new act.

Equity receivership was extremely time-consuming and costly, as well as being susceptible to severe injustices. The courts had little control over the reorganization plan, and the committees set up to protect security holders were usually made up of powerful corporate insiders who used the process to further their own interests. The initiative for equity receivership was usually taken by the company in conjunction with some friendly creditor. There was no provision made for independent, objective review of the plans that were invariably drawn up by a biased committee or friendly receiver. Since ratification required majority creditor support, it usually meant that companies offered cash payoffs to powerful dissenters to gain their support. This led to long delays and charges of unfairness. Because of these disadvantages, the procedure was ineffective, especially when the number of receiverships skyrocketed during the Depression years.

The Chandler Act of 1938

In 1933 a new bankruptcy act with a special Section 77 (for railroad reorganizations) was hastily drawn up and enacted. The following year Section 77B was enacted, to provide for general corporate reorganizations. The act was short-lived: in 1938 it underwent a comprehensive revision and was thereafter known as the Chandler Act. This legislation was the result of the joint efforts of the National Bankruptcy Conference, the Securities and Exchange Commission (SEC), which had embarked on its own study of reorganization practices, and various other interested committees and associations.

For our purposes, the two most relevant chapters of the Chandler Act were those related to corporate bankruptcy and to subsequent attempts at reorganization. Chapter XI arrangements applied only to the unsecured creditors of corporations and removed the necessity to get all creditor types to agree on a plan of action. A Chapter XI arrangement was a voluntary proceeding that could be initiated by corporate or noncorporate entities or persons. The court had the power to appoint an independent trustee or receiver to manage the corporate property or, in many instances, to permit the old management team to continue its control during the proceedings. The bankrupt's petition for reorganization usually contained a preliminary plan for financial relief. The prospect of continued management control and reduced financial obligations made Chapter XI particularly attractive to present management. During the proceedings, a referee called the creditors together to go over the proposed plan and any new amendments that had been proposed. If a majority in number and amount of each class of unsecured creditors consented to the plan, the court could confirm the arrangement and make it binding on all creditors. Usually, the plan provided for a scaled-down creditor claim, composition of claims, and/or extension of payment over time. New financial instruments could be issued to creditors in lieu of their old claims.

In addition to the advantages noted above, Chapter XI placed the bankrupt's assets strictly in the custody of the court and made them free from any prior pending court proceeding. Also, the debtor could borrow new funds that had preference over all unsecured indebtedness. Although the interest rate on such new credit was expectedly high, it still enabled the embarrassed firm to secure an important new source of financing. As in all corporate reorganizations, the assets were protected by the court during these proceedings. Also, the Chapter XI arrangements, if successful, were of relatively short duration compared to the more complex Chapter X cases, since administrative expenses were a function of time. Chapter XI was usually less costly than proceedings that involved all security holders. Successful out-of-court settlements, however, were usually even less costly. Finally, the arrangement was binding in all states of the country.

The least common but most important type of corporate bankruptcy reorganization was the Chapter X proceeding. The importance of this bankruptcy form is clearly illustrated by the dollar amount of liabilities involved, the size and importance of the petitioning companies, and the fact that most of the empirical data utilized in bankruptcy analysis involved Chapter X bankrupts.

Chapter X proceedings applied to publicly held corporations except railroads, and to those that had secured creditors. This bankruptcy process could be initiated voluntarily by the debtor or involuntarily by three or more creditors with total claims of $5,000 or more. It was generally felt that Section 77B of the 1934 act was too liberal to the small creditors, since only $1,000 in claims was required. The bankruptcy petition had to contain a statement of why adequate relief could not be obtained under Chapter XI. The aim of this requirement was to make Chapter X proceedings unavailable to corporations having simple debt and capital structures. On the other hand, the court had the right (and exercised it on several occasions) to refuse to allow a Chapter XI proceeding and to require that a reorganization be processed under Chapter X. This usually happened when a substantial public interest was deemed present by the court or by the SEC, and the firm had originally filed a Chapter XI voluntary petition. The SEC on particular occasions filed motions in Chapter XI proceedings to force companies into Chapter X because Chapter XI could not adequately handle the case when a substantial public interest was involved.

In most cases, a Chapter XI was preferred by the debtor because Chapter X automatically provided for the appointment of an independent, disinterested trustee or trustees to assume control of the company for the duration of the bankruptcy proceeding. Actually the act provided for the appointment of the independent trustee in every case in which indebtedness amounted to $250,000 or more. Where the indebtedness was less than $250,000, the judge could either continue the debtor in possession or appoint a disinterested trustee. The only prescribed qualification of the trustee, in addition to disinterestedness, was competence to perform the duties.

The independent trustee was charged with the development and submission of a reorganization plan that was "fair and feasible" to all the parties involved. The Interstate Commerce Commission (ICC) was charged with this task in the case of railroad bankruptcies. Invariably, this plan involved all the creditors as well as the preferred and common stockholders. This important task was in addition to the day-to-day management responsibilities, although the trustee usually delegated the latter authority to the old management or to a new management team. New management was often installed, since management incompetence, in one form or another, was by far the most common cause of corporate failure. In most contemporary Chapter X bankruptcies, the trustee was aided by various experts in the development and presentation of reorganization plans, as well as by committees representing the various creditors and stockholders. This practice will no doubt continue under the new act. At the outset, the creditors, indenture trustees, and stockholders were permitted to file answers controverting the allegations of a voluntary or involuntary petition. While bankruptcy initiation action was curtailed by the 1938 act, the ability to answer was enhanced.

Another extremely important participant in Chapter X proceedings was the SEC. This is clearly not the case under the current code, which all but eliminates the role of the SEC. Although the commission did not possess any decision-making authority, its involvement, via the SEC advisory reports, was in my opinion a powerful objective force in the entire process. The SEC was charged with rendering its advisory report if the debtor's liabilities exceeded $3 million, but the court could ask for SEC assistance regardless of liability size.

The advisory reports usually took the form of a critical evaluation of the reorganization plan submitted by the trustee and an opinion on the fairness and feasibility of the plan. This involved a comprehensive valuation of the debtor's existing assets in comparison with the various claims against the assets. In the event of a discrepancy between the SEC evaluation and that of the trustee, the former usually suggested alternative guidelines. Ultimately, the decisions on (1) whether the firm was permitted to reorganize and (2) the submission of the plan for final acceptance rested with the federal judge (and with the new bankruptcy judge under the 1978 bankruptcy act).

The Chandler Act provided that the reorganization plan, after approval by the court, be submitted to each class of creditor and stockholder for final approval. Final ratification required approval of two-thirds of each class of stockholder. Of course, if the plan, as accepted by the court, completely eliminated a particular class, such as the common stockholders, this excluded group had no vote in the final ratification, although it could always file suits on its own behalf. Common stockholders were eliminated when the firm was deemed insolvent in a bankruptcy sense, that is, when the liabilities exceeded a fair valuation of the assets. Regardless of whether the old stockholders were permitted to participate in the reorganized enterprise, the plan invariably entailed a restructuring of the old capital accounts as well as plans for improving the productivity of the debtor. This will no doubt be the case in the future, as well.

The entire bankruptcy reorganization process, including those relevant features and conditions of the bankruptcy code of 1978, is summarized in Table 1-2, which follows the discussion of liquidation and the new code.

Liquidation

When, either through a court petition or a trustee decision, it is deemed that there is no hope for rehabilitation or if prospects are so poor as to make it unreasonable to invest further efforts, costs, and time, the only alternative remaining is liquidation. Economically, liquidation is justified when the value of the assets sold individually exceeds the capitalized value of the assets in the marketplace. Usually, the key variables are time and risk. For instance, it may be estimated that the absolute economic value of the firm will exceed the liquidation value but the realization of the economic benefits is subject to uncertainty, because of time and subjective probability estimates, resulting in a lower discounted value. In this case, final liquidation may take the form of an assignment or a formal bankruptcy liquidation.

An assignment is a private method whereby assets are assigned to a trustee, usually selected by the creditors, to be liquidated by him. The net liquidation value realized is equal to the funds received less the creditor claims against the company. Rarely are the funds sufficient to pay off all creditors in full. All creditors must agree to the settlement. Since the assignment is generally handled in good faith, it is customary for the creditors to release the debtor from further liability. This process is usually faster and less costly than the more rigid bankruptcy procedure, but it is not feasible when the debtor has a complicated liability and capital structure.

The expanded Act (1938) continued to provide for the orderly liquidation of an insolvent debtor under court supervision. Regardless of who filed the petition, liquidations were handled by referees who oversaw the operation until a trustee was appointed. The latter liquidated the assets, made a final accounting, and paid the liquidating dividends—all subject to referee approval. Payments of receipts usually entailed the so-called absolute priority doctrine, under which claims with priority must be paid in full before less prior, or subordinated, claims can receive any funds at all.

The liquidation fate is primarily observed in the small firm. The large bankrupt firm is more likely to attempt a reorganization and/or a merger with another entity. Sometimes, however, the basis for merger terms while a corporation is in bankruptcy is the net liquidating value of the company, not its capitalized income value. This was precisely the basis for negotiation in the ICC hearings on the Penn Central–New York New Haven & Hartford Railroad merger in 1968.

Although larger firms usually attempt to reorganize or merge in bankruptcy, the result is often not successful, and liquidation eventually occurs. In an earlier study (Altman, 1971), I showed that a large percentage of firms are not successfully reorganized and as much as 56% of the cases resulted in a total loss to common stockholders. A glaring example of a recent failure to reorganize successfully was the billion-dollar W.T. Grant case. The firm filed under Chapter XI in 1975 and attempted to reorganize, but was forced to liquidate several months later in 1976. This is in contrast to several more recent, large, successful reorganizations, including the billion-dollar (in assets) United Merchants & Manufacturing Chapter XI proceeding in July 1977. The firm was reorganized and emerged as a going concern in less than one year.

The delays caused by court action to determine whether a firm should file under Chapter X or Chapter XI were often costly and took time to settle because of the ambiguity in the Chandler Act. One could argue that in both the W.T. Grant and United Merchants cases, a large public interest was involved and parties other than unsecured creditors were affected. Still, persuasive pressures were brought to bear by the debtors and their legal counsels, and the courts ruled that these cases could be handled more efficiently, without adverse effects to other interested parties, under Chapter XI. Under the new bankruptcy code, the old Chapters X and XI are combined under a new reorganization title, Chapter 11, and this no longer is an issue.

THE BANKRUPTCY REFORM ACT OF 1978

Rationale for the New Act

Forty years after the passage of the Chandler Act, Congress enacted the Bankruptcy Reform Act of 1978, which revised the administrative and, to some extent, the procedural, legal, and economic aspects of corporate and personal bankruptcy filings in the United States. The complete text of the new act can be found in Bankruptcy Law Reports, No. 389, October 26, 1978, Part II, published by the Commerce Clearing House, Chicago, Illinois.

The following reasons were presented in 1970 in a joint Congressional resolution to create a commission to look into the nation's bankruptcy laws (S.J.R. 88, 91st Congress, 1st Session, July 24, 1970). An accompanying report from the Committee on the Judiciary Report No. 91–230, strongly endorsed the proposal.

1 In the 30 years since the last major revision, there has probably been even greater change in the social and economic conditions of the country than in the 40 years prior to the enactment of the 1938 Act.

2 Population has increased by 70 million people, while installment credit has skyrocketed from about $4 billion to $80 billion. The number of total bankruptcies has risen to an annual rate of more than 200,000 from a rate of 110,000 in 1960. By far, the major increase has been in personal bankruptcies.

3 More than one-quarter of the referees in bankruptcy have problems in the administration of their duties and have made suggestions for substantial improvement in the Act.

4 There is little understanding by the federal government and the commercial community in evaluating the need to update the technical aspects in the Act.

I served as an advisor to the Commission on the Bankruptcy Laws of the United States. Charles Seligson, a member of the commission, enumerated some current problems in "Major Problems for Consideration By the Commission on the Bankruptcy Laws of the United States" (*American Bankruptcy Law Journal,* Winter 1977, pp. 73–112).

In 1979 the problems under the old act were even more acute. The long-term worldwide problems of inflation and recession had further increased the number of bankruptcy filings in the U.S. court system. Transitions in credit policies—for example, greater reticence to delay default proceedings in large corporations, and other not so definable changes—had contributed to making the old bankruptcy laws awkward and the 1978 code desirable. Whether the structure of the new code will alleviate pressures and make the system more efficient will be determined empirically as the new code is implemented. One thing is certain: the new code is being tested immediately as the number of filings increase in the face of the 1980–1982 recession and record interest rates.

The new act, which went into effect on October 1, 1979, is divided into four titles, with Title I containing the substantive and much of the procedural law of bankruptcy. This part, known as "the code," is divided into eight chapters: 1, 3, 5, 7, 9, 11, 13, 15. Chapter 1 (General Provisions),

Chapter 3 (Case Administration), and Chapter 5 (Creditors, the Debtor and the Estate) apply generally to all cases, and Chapter 7 (Liquidation), Chapter 9 (Adjustment of Municipality Debt), Chapter 11 (Reorganization), Chapter 13 (Adjustment of Debts of Individuals with Regular Income), and Chapter 15 (U.S. Trustee Program) apply to specific debtors and procedures. For an informative review of the new code, see Duberstein, "A Broad View of the New Bankruptcy Code" (*Brooklyn Barrister,* April 1979). The major provisions of the new act are discussed below.

Bankruptcy Filings

The debtor must reside or have a domicile or place of business or property in the United States. Liquidation cases of banks and insurance companies engaged in business in this country are excluded. A foreign bank or foreign insurance company that is not engaged in business in the United States but does have assets here may become a debtor under the code, but an involuntary petition cannot be filed against a foreign bank even if it has property here. The debtor may file a petition for liquidation or reorganization. The filing of the petition constitutes what is known as "an order for relief." An involuntary case may be commenced only under Chapter 7, dealing with liquidation, or Chapter 11, dealing with reorganization. This route is not permitted for municipalities under Chapter 9, nor in Chapter 13 cases. An involuntary petition is prohibited against farmers, ranchers, and charitable institutions.

Claims and Protections

The provision for an involuntary Chapter 11 case is a change from the old law: involuntary cases were permitted under Chapter X, dealing with corporate reorganization, and Chapter XII, dealing with real property arrangements, but not under a Chapter XI arrangement. Acts of bankruptcy are no longer the criteria for the commencement of an involuntary case. Instead, it will be necessary to show that the debtor is generally not paying its debts as such debts become due, or that within 120 days before the filing of the petition, a custodian (e.g., an assignee for the benefit of creditors) was appointed and took possession of the debtor's assets. If the debtor has more than 12 creditors, three creditors must join in the involuntary petition whose claims must aggregate at least $5,000. If there are fewer than 12 creditors, two creditors or a single creditor holding claims of at least $5,000 may file. An indenture trustee representing the holder of a claim against the debtor may be a petitioning creditor.

Section 10, Paragraph (4) of the code defines "claim." The effect of the definition is a significant departure from the old act, which never defined "claim" in straight bankruptcy. The term was simply used, along with the concept of provability, to limit the kinds of obligations that were payable in a bankruptcy case. The new definition adopts a broader meaning: a claim is any right to payment, whether or not reduced to judgment, liquidation, unliquidated, fixed, contingent, matured, unmatured, disputed, undisputed, legal, equitable, secured, or unsecured. The definition also includes as a claim an equitable right to performance that does not give rise to payment. The use of the term throughout the act seems to imply that all legal obligations of the debtor, no matter how remote or contingent, will be dealt with in a bankruptcy case.

One of the most important parts of the code deals with stays of secured and unsecured creditor action and the right of the debtor to continue to use the creditor's collateral in his business. The automatic stay is one of the fundamental debtor protections provided by the bankruptcy laws. It gives the debtor a breathing spell from creditors. It stops all collection efforts, all harassment, and all foreclosure actions. It permits the debtor to attempt a repayment or reorganization plan, or simply to be relieved of the financial pressures that drove the firm into bankruptcy.

Sections 361–64 remove some of the uncertainty concerning the rights of secured creditors. The basic requirement that secured creditors be afforded "adequate protection" is not formally defined, but some guidelines are offered in Section 361, which suggests that such protection might include cash payments, additional collateral, or replacement collateral, but would not include the simple giving of any priority.

Lessor Claims

Under the old bankruptcy act, a lessor was entitled to a claim on unpaid rents of a maximum of one year of lease or rental payments in a straight bankruptcy liquidation and a maximum of three years in a reorganization. Under the new code's Section 502 b(7), a formula replaces the one-to-three-year rule for both liquidations and reorganizations. In essence the claim for damages resulting from the termination of a lease of real property is now the greater of one year of payments, or 15%, not to exceed three years, of the remaining term of the lease, plus any unpaid rent due under such lease. Such terms start the earlier of (1) the petition date or (2) the date on which the lessor repossessed the leased property, or the lessee surrendered it.

Section 365 of the code deals with executory contracts and unexpired leases and specifies under what provisions a trustee, or the court, can assume continuance of a lease while in reorganization. Essentially, the code specifies that lessors must be cured or compensated for their claims or that adequate assurance of prompt compensation be given. The trustee must assume a lease or executory contract within 60 days of the petition date.

Priorities

The concept of provability of claims, apparently troublesome under the previous act, has been discarded in favor of simple sections (501–503) dealing with the allowance of claims; among other things, these sections require that contingent or unliquidated claims be estimated. Many of the familiar priorities for claims remain, but significant changes have been made to protect employees. The new act expands and increases the wage priority. The amount entitled to priority is raised from $600 to $2000. The priority is expanded to cover fringe benefits, which is new (Section 507). A new priority has been established for consumer creditors who have deposited money in connection with the purchase, lease, or rental of property, or the purchase of services, for their personal, family, or household use, when such properties or services are not delivered or provided.

Bank Setoffs

Banks may specify that, in the event of bankruptcy, all existing balances of the debtor will be set off against the outstanding claim of the bank and the balance of the loan will be included among general creditor claims. One can argue that this is unfair to the debtor, since once a loan is made, the proceeds can be used in any manner that the borrower chooses. The banks can argue, on the other hand, that the balances are a type of "security" against repayment of the loan. In any event, the new act provides for the continuation of setoffs, but the court must ratify them in a manner that is more formal than in the past.

As in the old law, the right of setoff is unaffected except when the creditor's claim is disallowed by the court or the creditor has acquired the claim, other than from the debtor, during a 90-day period preceding the case at a time when the debtor was insolvent. An exception to the right of setoff is the automatic stay provided for in Section 362 of the code. The automatic stay refers to an injunction against the creditor and prohibits any action to further set off the loan after the petition is filed.

The code does contain an additional limitation on the rights of creditors who have offset a mutual debt on or within 90 days before the filing of a petition when the creditor receives a preferential payment. For example, assume that a debtor owes a bank $150,000 and has $50,000 on deposit 90 days prior to the filing. If the bank exercises its right of setoff 30 days before filing, when the debtor owes $75,000, the bank will recover all but

$75,000 of the amount owed to it by the debtor; if the bank had set off the amount 90 days before bankruptcy, on the other hand, it would have received $50,000. Thus by waiting 60 days before exercising its right of setoff, the bank recovered an additional $25,000 and therefore improved its position by that amount. This $25,000 is the amount that the trustee may recover for the debtor under Section 553 (b).

The setoff section operates only in the case of prefiling setoffs, thus encouraging creditors to work with the debtor rather than attempting to recover as much as appears possible at the time. In any case, a default must exist before there is a setoff right. It appears that the right of setoff is somewhat constrained under the new code compared to the old law. Still, we can expect that financial institutions and others will continue the practice and it will be up to the trustee to recover the funds.

Chapter 11 Reorganizations

An extremely important change in the new act appears in Chapter 11, which is a consolidated chapter for business rehabilitations. It adopts much of the old Chapter XI arrangement and incorporates a good portion of the public protection of the old Chapter X and also a major part of Chapter XII real property arrangements.

Under Chapter 11, the debtor continues to operate the business unless the court orders a disinterested trustee for cause shown, or if it would be in the best interests of the creditors and/or the owners. "Cause" includes fraud, dishonesty, incompetence, or gross mismanagement, either before or after commencement of the case. For an excellent discussion of Chapter 11, see Weintraub (1980).

Creditors Committee.   After the petition for a Chapter 11 rehabilitation has been filed, the court, or a U.S. Trustee where available, appoints a committee of unsecured creditors. Chapter 11 is permitted to affect secured debts and equity security holders and, upon request of a party in interest, the court may order the appointment of additional committees of creditors or of equity security holders. Ordinarily, committees consist of the holders of the seven largest claims or interests to be represented, if they are willing to serve. The number of members can exceed 7, especially in large, complex cases. A recent case involves 19 different creditors. The code permits continuation of a committee selected before the case is filed if the committee is fairly chosen and is representative of the different kinds of claims to be represented. A designated committee of equity security holders ordinarily consists of the persons willing to serve who hold the seven largest amounts of shares of the debtor. On the request of a party in interest, the court is authorized to change the size of membership of the creditors or the equity security holders' committee if the membership is not representative of the different claims or interests.

Reorganization Plan Filing. The essence of the reorganization process is the plan of reorganization for financial and operating rehabilitation. The new code gives the debtor, or its trustee if appointed, the exclusive right for 120 days to file a plan. The debtor has up to 180 days after the reorganization petition is filed to receive the requisite consents from the various creditors and owners (if relevant). The court, however, is given the power to increase or reduce the 120- and 180-day periods. For example, in the current Itel Corp. case, the debtor received several additional 120 extensions before filing a plan. If the debtor fails to meet either of these deadlines or others established by the court, creditors and other interested parties may file a plan for approval.

Role of the Securities and Exchange Commission. The SEC may raise and be heard on any issue but may not appeal from any judgment order or decree. Greater expediency for completing reorganization and alleged uneven performance of the SEC in past cases are reasons that have been given for the virtual exclusion of the SEC. Although any interested party can still petition the courts and appeal any perceived inequities, the role of the SEC as the public's representative has been greatly diminished. For example, the SEC had often petitioned to change a Chapter XI arrangement to a Chapter X reorganization. There is no need for such a petition under the new code. Despite the SEC's performance in Chapter X cases, it has issued some excellent commentary and suggestions in its reorganization reports, particularly on the valuation process.

Reorganization Valuation. The reorganization plan has as its centerpiece the valuation of the debtor as a continuing entity. Traditionally, valuation is based on the capitalization of future earnings flows, which involves a forecast of expected after tax earnings and the attachment of an appropriate capitalization rate (discount rate). The capitalized value can then be adjusted for excess working capital and tax and other considerations. If the resulting value is greater than the liquidation value of the assets, reorganization is justified. If the value is less than the allowed claims, the firm is insolvent in a bankruptcy sense and the old shareholders are usually eliminated. Typically, the creditors become the new shareholders along with any new shareholders that might purchase shares. A discussion of the valuation is given in the Appendix to this chapter.

Absolute Priority of Claims.   Since the inception of the bankruptcy laws, most reorganization plans have been guided by the so-called absolute priority doctrine. This "doctrine" stipulates that creditors should be compensated for their claims in a certain hierarchical order and that the more senior claims must be paid in full before a less senior claim can receive anything. In fact, however, plans are often based on a combination of absolute and relative priorities whereby lesser claimants receive partial payment even though a claim that is more senior is "not made whole" (not paid off completely). This arrangement is often expedient, and it permits compromise with creditors who are likely to vote against the plan unless some satisfactory payment to them is forthcoming.

Creditors are frequently compensated for their claims with a combination of cash and securities different from the original securities. It is quite common for the old debtholders to become the new stockholders. For example, the old debtholders of the Penn Central Transportation Co. received a combination of new series debt securities, new preferred stock, and shares of the common stock, while the old stockholders received but a fraction of their old shares; one for each 25 shares owned.

The objective of the reorganization plan is to provide for a fair and feasible rehabilitation. The term "fair" refers to the priority of claims, and "feasible" implies that the recapitalized company will be structured so that the new fixed cost burden will realistically be met without a recurrence of default. The reorganization plan must therefore provide the cash flow analysis necessary to make that assessment. The costs involved with negotiations for restructuring—both in bankruptcy or what takes place out of reorganization, that is, a quasi-reorganization, are referred to as agency costs and represent a deadweight loss to the firm, a loss that is not someone else's gain in society.

Priorities are spelled out in Section 507 of the code. Expenses and claims have priority in the following order:

1 Administration expenses of the bankruptcy, such as legal and accounting fees and trustee fees.

2 Unsecured claims arising in the ordinary course of the debtor's business or financial affairs after the commencement of the case, for example, supplier claims on goods delivered and accepted, with some exceptions as spelled out in Section 502(f).

3   Unsecured claims for wages, salaries, or commissions, including vacation, severance, and sick leave pay earned by an individual within 90 days before the filing of the petition or the date of the cessation of the debtor's business but only to the extent of $2,000 per individual.

4   Unsecured claims for contributions to employee benefit plans, with the same limitations noted in item 3.

5   Unsecured claims to individuals up to $900 arising from the deposit, before bankruptcy, of money in connection with the future use of goods or services from the debtor.

6   Unsecured claims of governmental units, that is, taxes on income, property, and employment, and excise and tax penalties.

7   Secured debts, that is, debt that has specific assets as collateral, has priority over the funds received in the liquidation of that asset. To the extent that the funds received are insufficient to cover the entire allowed claim, the balance is owed by the debtor and is considered part of the remaining unsecured claims.

8   Senior debt has priority over all debt that is specified as subordinated to that debt but has equal priority with all other unsecured debt. The terms of most loan agreements spell out these priorities.

9   Remaining unsecured claims.

10 After the unsecured claims are satisfied, the remaining "claimants" are the equity holders of the firm—preferred and common stockholders, in that order. As noted earlier, these individuals should not receive any payment or securities in the new firm if the value of the firm's assets is less than the allowed claims.

Execution of the Plan.   A plan must provide adequate means for its execution. It may provide for the satisfaction or modification of any lien, the waiver of any default, and the merger or consolidation of the debtor with one or more entities. The issuance of nonvoting equity securities is prohibited, and the plan must provide for distribution of voting powers among the various classes of equity securities. It may impair, or leave unimpaired, a class of claims, secured or unsecured; provide for the assumption or rejection of executory contracts or unexpired leases not previously rejected; and propose the sale of all or substantially all of the estate property and the distribution of the proceeds among creditors and equity security holders, making it a liquidating plan.

Confirmation of the Plan.   A plan may place a claim in a particular class if such claim is substantially similar to other claims of the class. Con-

Table 1-2 Financial Rehabilitation Procedures.

Function	Chapter X	Chapter XI	Section 77 (1933 Act)	Chapter 11 (New Code)
1. Initiation of proceedings	1. *a.* Voluntary by the debtor *b.* Involuntary—three or more creditors with claims totaling $5,000 or more	1. *a.* Voluntary only *b.* Noncorporate and corporate *c.* Affects only unsecured creditors	1. *a.* Railroad only *b.* Voluntary *c.* Involuntary by creditors representing 5% or more of total indebtedness	1. *a.* Voluntary by debtor *b.* Involuntary—by three creditors with claims of at least $5,000 (where more than 12 creditors exist); fewer than three creditors with $5,000 or more in claims where less than 12 creditors exist
2. Custody of property	2. Court appoints disinterested trustee (mandatory if debts exceed $250,000) *a.* Cannot be officer or employee *b.* Cotrustee from previous management to aid in operation	2. Court may or may not appoint receiver or trustee	2. Trustees appointed who act as operating managers	2. Court may or may not appoint a trustee; trustee may or may not act as operating manager

3. Creditor protection	3. Committees representing each class of creditors and stockholders are formed	3. Court conducts meetings; may use advisory creditors' committee	3. Committee for each class of creditor	3. Creditors' committee comprises seven largest creditors plus any others sanctioned by the court
4. Reorganization plan	4. *a.* Trustee creditors, or creditors' committee prepares plan; confers with committees *b.* Court hearings on plan *c.* SEC renders advisory report (mandatory if debts over $3 million)	4. Debtor proposes arrangement	4. Presented by one of the following: *a.* Trustee *b.* Debtor *c.* Holders of 10% or more of each security	4. Debtor proposes plan within 120 days; adequate approval required within 180 days of petition; if deadline not met, any interested party may submit a plan
5. Court review	5. Court approves plan if it is: *a.* Fair *b.* Feasible	5. Court holds hearings	5. *a.* Hearings before Interstate Commerce Commission *b.* ICC submits plan to court *c.* Court approval	5. Court holds hearings on the plan and will approve if fair and feasible
6. Reorganization plan	6. Provides for *a.* Provision for exchange of securities	6. Composition—claims of unsecured creditors scaled down, or extension in time of	6. Same as Chapter X	6. Provides for any or all aspects of old Chapters X, XI, and XII

(Continued)

23

Table 1-2 (*Continued*)

Function	Chapter X	Chapter XI	Section 77 (1933 Act)	Chapter 11 (New Code)
6. Reorganization plan (*Continued*)	*b.* Provision for selection of new management *c.* Adequate means for execution of plan	payment, or both		
7. Approval	7. Two-thirds of each class of creditors by value; majority of stockholders (unless total liabilities exceed total assets)	7. Majority in number and amount of each class	7. Same as Chapter X	7. Two-thirds in amount and one-half in number of the allowed claims. Where an equity exists, two-thirds in amount of outstanding shares actually voted; "cramdown" provision possible (i.e., court may approve plan despite dissatisfied creditors). In all cases, creditors must receive an amount that is greater than if the firm was liquidated
8. Execution of plan	8. Court confirms plan	8. Receiver, trustee, or disbursing agent to carry out arrangement	8. Plan executed by ICC	8. Plan is confirmed by the court and executed by U.S. trustee or by the court

firmation of a plan requires that every claimant or holder of an interest accept the plan, or, if it is not accepted by all classes, the creditors must receive or retain under the plan an amount that is not less than the amount that they would receive or retain if the debtor were liquidated on the date of the plan. At least one class of creditors must accept the plan. Thus, for example, if the only class affected by the plan comprises a mortgagee, the plan cannot be confirmed without the mortgagee's consent. A plan is deemed accepted by a class of creditors if at least two-thirds in amount and more than one-half in number of the allowed claims of the class that are voted are cast in favor of the plan. Shareholders are deemed to have accepted the plan if at least two-thirds in amount of the outstanding shares actually voted are cast for the plan. These terms are reviewed in Table 1-2.

The code deals with the impairment of claims, which is a new concept. A plan may be confirmed over the dissent of a class of creditors. If all the requirements for confirmation of the plan are satisfied, except that a class of impaired claimants or shareholders has not accepted it, the court may nevertheless confirm the plan if the plan does not discriminate unfairly and is "fair and equitable" with respect to each class of claims or interests impaired.

This is the new code's version of the "cram down" clause, which appeared in Chapters X and XII. The test for what is "fair and equitable" with regard to a class of secured claimants impaired under a plan is met, in general, if the plan provides (1) that said class will retain its lien on the property whether the property is retained by the debtor or transferred, (2) that the property will be sold and the lien transferred and the secured creditor will receive deferred cash payments of at least the allowed amount of the claims of the value on the date of confirmation, and (3) that the secured class will realize the "indubitable equivalent" of its claims under the plan. If a class of unsecured claims that are impaired under the plan will receive property or payment equal to the allowed amount of the claims, or if the holders of the claims junior to such class will receive nothing under the plan, the plan has met the "fair and equitable" test of the code.

Reorganization Time in Bankruptcy.   One of the important goals of the new act is to reduce the time it takes for a firm to go through the reorganization process and devise a plan for restructuring its capital financing and rehabilitating its operations. The new act, in and of itself, will certainly not provide any novel solutions to the typical problems that cause firms to fail. But the requirement that the debtor submit a reorganization plan within 120 days is likely to speed up the initial process. One wonders whether large, complicated cases are amenable to the four-month time frame; only time will tell.

The attempt to reduce reorganization time is important, since there is a positive correlation between the time spent in reorganization and the direct costs of bankruptcy. The latter include legal and accounting fees, trustee and filing fees, and any other tangible costs involved with the bankruptcy process. In a study of almost 90 reorganizations, I found that the average industrial reorganization took 27 months, with the median period being 20 months. Another study concentrating on more complex railroad bankruptcies (Chapter 7 of the same source) concluded that the average and median Section 77 reorganization took slightly more than seven years. A more recent study (Warner, 1977) found that railroad reorganizations took even longer. Clearly, it would be desirable to reduce the time needed to reorganize entities.

Changes in the Judiciary and Procedure.   The code creates a U.S. Bankruptcy Court in each of the present districts where there is a U.S. District Court. The new court will be established April 1, 1984. The bankruptcy judges will be appointed by the president, with the advice and consent of the Senate, for a term of 14 years. The established bankruptcy courts are to continue from October 1, 1979, to March 31, 1984.

The code eliminates the present jurisdictional dichotomy between summary and plenary jurisdiction; the bankruptcy court is given exclusive jurisdiction of the property of the debtor wherever it is located. All cases under the code and all civil actions and proceedings arising from its enforcement will be held before the bankruptcy judge unless he decides to abstain from hearing a particular proceeding that is already pending in the state court or in another court that he believes to be more appropriate.

Appeals from the bankruptcy judge will go to the district judge, except that if the circuit counsel of the circuit court so orders, the chief judge of the circuit shall designate panels of three bankruptcy judges to hear appeals in the bankruptcy court. The panel may not hear an appeal from an order entered by a panel member. An appeal from the panel will go directly to the U.S. Court of Appeals. An appeal can go directly from the bankruptcy court to the court of appeals if the parties so agree.

U.S. Trustee Program.   To aid bankruptcy judges in avoiding involvement in many administrative functions, and to allow them to devote more time to the area of judicial determination, the code establishes a five-year trial pilot program of U.S. trustees that will be operative in only 10 geographical areas of the country, covering 18 present judicial districts. It will include the Southern District of New York (but not the Eastern District), the Districts of Delaware and New Jersey, the Central District of California (which includes Los Angeles), and the Northern District of Illinois (which includes Chicago). The program will run to April 1, 1984, at which time Congress will decide whether to implement the U.S. trustee system fully. The U.S. trustees will not be serving the bankruptcy courts either as assistants to the bankruptcy judges or as arms of the court, but will be under the supervision of the attorney general, who will appoint them.

BANKRUPTCY TAX ISSUES

The Bankruptcy Reform Act of 1978 completely rewrote the laws that govern bankruptcy procedures and principles but was essentially silent with respect to tax considerations. In bankruptcy proceedings, the government acts both as a creditor and as a force to aid in the rehabilitation of an entity. The two roles are not easy to reconcile, and the tax laws that are relevant present considerable problems and are the subject of much debate. A proposed tax bill contemporaneous with the new bankruptcy code was so controversial, for solvent as well as nonsolvent firms, that it never was voted on by Congress; instead, the Bankruptcy Tax Bill of 1980 (H.R. 5043) was evaluated by the House Ways and Means Committee and passed by the House of Representatives on March 24, 1980. As a consequence, the nation was governed for a period of time by a bankruptcy code that had no relevant tax law. The tax bill of 1980 was finally passed and went into effect in early 1981. Copies of the bill are available from the Commerce Clearing House, Chicago, Illinois, 60646.

The new bill deals with all aspects of bankruptcy and reorganization and, indeed, affects solvent firms as well, especially on the repurchase of outstanding debt. Three issues of the reorganization process will be discussed: (1) the discharge or reduction in outstanding debt, (2) exchange of equity for debt, and (3) tax loss carry-forwards. All are common to almost every bankruptcy reorganization and are often important elements in the estimation of the value of an emerging company—on an aftertax basis.

Discharge of Indebtedness

In Public Law 95–598, Congress repealed provisions of the old bankruptcy act governing income tax treatment of a discharge of indebtedness in bankruptcy for cases filed on or after October 1, 1979. The Bankruptcy Tax Bill of 1980 fills this vacuum by providing that no amount of debt discharge is to be included in income for federal income tax purposes if the debtor is insolvent. Instead, the amount of debt reduction can be applied at the debtor's election first to reduce the debtor's depreciable asset basis. This policy can, however, affect reported income in the future, and the government will eventually be rewarded for its "generosity" if the firm becomes a profitable, going concern. In essence, the government is helping to provide a fresh start but is not totally forgiving the benefits for all time.

If the debtor does not choose to apply the reduction to depreciable assets, the amount is applied to reduce the taxpayer's tax attributes in the following order:

1   Net operating losses and carryovers.
2   Carryovers of investment tax credits and other tax credits.
3   Capital losses and carryovers.
4   The basis of the taxpayer's assets.

The reduction in each category of carryovers is made in the order of taxable years in which the items would be used, with the order based on the year of discharge and the taxes that would have been paid. After reduction of the specified carryover, any remaining debt discharge is applied to reduce the debtor's asset basis, but not below the amount of the taxpayer's remaining undischarged liabilities. Finally, any remaining debt discharge is disregarded; see page 10 of the Bankruptcy Tax Bill of 1980, as reported in *Bankruptcy Law Reports*.

For example, assume that a debtor borrows $1 million on a short-term note and later issues $600,000 worth of stock in cancellation of the note. Under the old bankruptcy law, the creditor recognized a $400,000 loss, but the debtor neither recognized income nor reduced tax attributes. Under the new bill, the creditor can still recognize the loss, but the debtor corporation must account for a debt discharge of $400,000. This ruling, which applies to all corporations, was the subject of heated debate because it was viewed as an attempt by the Treasury Department to eliminate an alleged tax loophole and recover an estimated $500 million a year in taxes (B. Greene, "What Big Teeth You Have, Grandma," *Forbes,* February 4, 1980). Therefore, solvent companies will have to pay income taxes on profits made when they buy back their own bonds at a discount. For companies being reorganized in bankruptcy, the "gain" on an exchange of the type noted above will be treated as a debt discharge and will be subject to the tax rules as specified above.

Recapture Rule

To ensure that the debt discharged amount eventually will result in ordinary income, the bill provides that any gain on a subsequent sale of an asset that had been reduced in value, by virtue of the provisions of the bill, will be subject to "recapture" under rules similar to standard recapture tax law.

Exchange of Equity for Debt

One of the most common provisions of a recapitalization plan in a bankruptcy reorganization is a compensation arrangement involving the exchange of stock in the reorganized firm for all or part of the outstanding indebtedness of the debtor-bankrupt. In essence, the old creditors become the new owners. If a debtor issues stock to its creditor for an outstanding security, such as a bond, there is no debt discharge amount. Thus there are no consequences of the type discussed above. There will be no recognition of a gain or loss for the creditors. If stock is issued for other debts, such as a supplier claim or short-term note, the debtor is treated as having satisfied the claim with an amount of money equal to the stock's value. A value can be placed on the stock either by the bankruptcy court in a proceeding in which the IRS had the right to intervene or in an out-of-court agreement in which the debtor and creditor had adverse interests in the tax consequences of the valuation. The new tax bill provides that the special limitations on net operating loss carryovers generally will not apply to the extent that creditors receive stock in exchange for their claims. See Section 382 of the Internal Revenue Code for more details.

If both stock and other property are issued to satisfy a debt, the stock is treated as issued for a proportion of the debt equal to its proportion of the total value exchanged. For example, if $20 million in cash and $30 million in stock are issued for a claim of $100 million, the cash is to be treated as satisfying $40 million of the debt and the stock for the other $60 million, with no income resulting nor attribute reduction required.

Some recent stock-for-debt exchanges in large firm reorganization plans involved Equity Funding of America (1976), Interstate Stores (1978), King Resources (1978), and Daylin Corp. (1979). Debt is not always replaced by equity, however, as witnessed by the reorganization plans of Penn Central Co. [combination of debt and equity but mostly debt (1978)] and United Merchants and Manufacturing (1978). For a discussion and evaluation of the postbankruptcy performance of reorganization plan securities, see "A Caveat on Successful Reorganizations" (Chapter 9).

Tax Loss Carry-Forwards

Tax loss carry-forwards are an extremely important element in any reorganization, especially if the value of the new firm is relevant, as it almost always is. Tax loss questions are irrelevant, of course, in a straight liquidation. Theoretically, the value of a firm is equal to the discounted present value of its future earnings after taxes. Since tax loss carrybacks or carry-forwards will affect taxes paid, they have a potentially powerful impact on the earnings to be discounted. The most appropriate procedure is to discount the expected aftertax earnings projection and then add the present value of tax loss carry-forwards to arrive at the net overall value.

Under the Chapter X, tax-free transfers of corporate assets to a successor corporation were generally provided for. But no reference was made to the carryover of tax losses, and this caused considerable confusion. Certain cases established the clean-slate rule, which held that a firm emerging from bankruptcy that had discharged its old debts was precluded from using losses from the "old" business.

Other cases ruled on the so-called continuity of business doctrine, and allowed carryovers of losses when there was a continuity of interest and of the business. When the principal purpose of a merger (in or out of bankruptcy) was tax avoidance, carryovers were disallowed (see Section 269 of the Internal Revenue Code). In practice, this has come to mean that the tax loss carryover is not allowed when a greater than 50% change in ownership or a change in business occurs after the transfer of assets. This highly subjective test probably has not been very effective in curbing takeovers for tax purposes. In addition, the debtor or creditor could petition for a favorable IRS ruling in a bankruptcy-merger reorganization plan that was the only feasible alternative to liquidation.

The new bill introduces a category of tax-free reorganization, known as a "G" reorganization, which is more flexible than other types and is, in the belief of the Congress, a means to facilitate the rehabilitation of a problem firm. For instance, a "G" does not require a statutory merger (type A), nor does it require that the financially distressed corporation receive solely stock of the acquiring corporation in exchange for its assets (type C), and former shareholders do not have to be in control of a "split-off" company (type D). This new type of reorganization is intended to facilitate the reorganization of bankrupt companies. In light of the debt discharge rules of the bill, which adjust tax attributes of a reorganized corporation to reflect changes in debt structure, the statutory rule regarding loss carryovers will apply in "G" reorganizations.

Since "G" reorganizations are subject to the same rules on security exchanges for shareholders and other security holders that apply generally to reorganizations, any party receiving new securities whose principal value is greater than that of the securities surrendered is taxed on the excess, and vice versa. Money or other property received in a "G" will be subject to the dividend equivalency tests (as to whether the property is a return on capital), which apply to reorganizations generally. Likewise, securities transferred to creditors based on claims attributable to accrued or unpaid interest on securities surrendered will be subject to tax as if interest income were received.

Triangular Reorganization

The new bill permits a firm to purchase a company in bankruptcy in exchange for stock of the parent company of the acquiring firm rather than its own stock. This is known as a triangular reorganization. In addition, the creditors of the insolvent company are permitted to exchange their claims for voting stock of the surviving company when the stock received equals at least 80% of the value of the debts of the insolvent firm.

Modification of the Absolute Priority Rule

The House Ways and Means Committee report made it clear that the continuity of interest rule would be clarified with regard to creditors. The report also advised that the absolute priority rule should be modified to permit junior creditors and shareholders to retain an interest in the reorganized business even when senior creditors do not receive full settlement; that is, it favored relative priority rules. Junior and senior claims should be considered as proprietary interests for purposes of the continuity of interest test.

BUSINESS FAILURE

Bankruptcy and Business Failure Statistics

The two primary sources of aggregate business failure and bankruptcy statistics in the United States are Dun & Bradstreet Corp. and the Administrative Office of the U.S. Courts, Division of Bankruptcy. Dun & Bradstreet has been compiling failure statistics since 1857 and presents annual

Table 1-3 Number of Bankruptcy Cases Filed and Number of Business Failures and Failure Rates Reported Since 1950.

Year	Number of Business Bankruptcies[a]	Number of Business Failures[b]	Business Failure Rate per 10,000 Firms[b]	Average Liability per Failure[b]
1950	8,352	9,162	34	$ 27,099
1951	7,387	8,058	31	32,210
1952	6,542	7,611	29	37,224
1953	6,772	8,862	33	44,477
1954	8,888	11,086	42	41,731
1955	9,185	10,969	42	40,968
1956	9,748	12,686	48	44,356
1957	10,144	13,739	52	44,784
1958	11,403	14,964	56	48,667
1959	11,729	14,053	52	49,300
1960	12,284	15,445	57	60,772
1961	15,241	17,075	64	63,843
1962	15,644	15,782	61	76,898
1963	16,303	14,274	56	94,100
1964	16,510	13,501	53	98,454
1965	16,910	13,514	53	97,800
1966	16,430	13,061	52	106,091
1967	16,600	12,364	49	102,332
1968	16,545	9,636	39	97,654
1969	15,430	9,154	37	124,767
1970	16,197	10,748	44	175,638
1971	19,103	10,326	42	185,641
1972	18,132	9,566	38	209,099
1973	17,490	9,345	36	245,972
1974	20,747	9,915	38	307,931
1975	30,130	11,432	43	383,150
1976	35,201	9,628	35	312,762
1977	32,189	7,919	28	390,872
1978	30,528	6,619	24	401,270
1979	29,500	7,564	28	353,000
1980	45,841[c]	11,742	42	394,744
1981	66,006[d]	17,041	61	n.a.
1982	77,503[e]	19,170[f]	88[f]	n.a.

[a]From the U.S. Administrative Bankruptcy Courts, Washington, D.C., 1980. Statistical year ends June 30.

[b]From Dun & Bradstreet, *Failure Record, 1981*. (Failures include businesses that ceased operations following assignment or bankruptcy, with loss to creditors, and

32

data in the *Business Failure Record* publication and monthly data in *News from D&B, Monthly Failures.* The bankruptcy division source assembles summary reports from the 96 U.S. district courts and breaks down bankruptcy filings by chapter filed, whether business or personal, and by sector of the economy.

Table 1-3 combines information from the two sources just named, presenting data for 1950–1981. Column 2 indicates that the number of business bankruptcy filings has increased dramatically since 1950, with major increases registered in 1975 and 1976 and most dramatically in 1980 and 1981. The aftermath of the 1974–1975 recession saw bankruptcy filings rise to a record, over 35,000. This record was recently surpassed with a great increase in 1980 to over 36,000 individual company filings, and again in 1981. A continuation into 1982 appeared likely (see my forecast in *Business Week,* March 27, 1982, p. 20). The current rise reflects recessionary activity, a relatively tight money and credit market in response to inflationary pressures, high interest rates, and increased financial risk profiles of U.S. companies.

The most continuous time series bankruptcy statistic is D&B's business failure rate. This index, which records the number of failures recorded per 10,000 firms that D&B covers, is an excellent barometer of relative changes in business "exiting" in the United States and Canada. Column 4 of Table 1-3 shows that the failure rate has been relatively low in recent years, with less than 0.5% of the firms followed actually ceasing operations in a given year, following assignment or bankruptcy, loss to creditors, receivership, reorganization, or arrangement. D&B data do not include certain industries, including railroads, most financial enterprises, real estate companies, and many small service firms. The data are also

---

voluntarily withdrew, leaving unpaid obligations, or were involved in court actions such as receivership, reorganization, or arrangement.) Certain industries such as financial enterprises, railroads, insurance, real estate companies, and many small services are not represented. Failure liabilities do not include publicly held debt, nor most long-term liabilities and as such underestimate average liabilities.

'Includes 9,308 joint husband and wife filings; individual business bankruptcies were 36,433 in 1980.
ᵈIncludes 18,512 joint husband and wife filings; individual bankruptcies were 47,414 in 1981.
ᵉIncludes 21,080 joint husband and wife filings.
ᶠThrough first 40 weeks 1982.
Note: n.a. = not available.

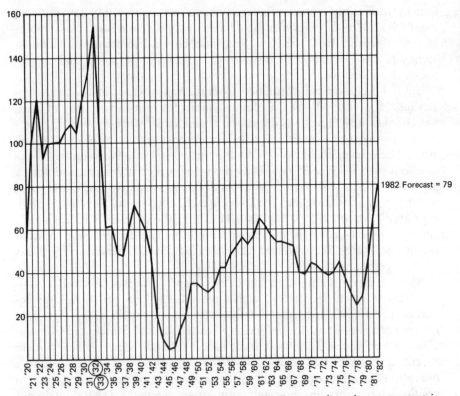

Chart 1-1 Dun's Failure Index (1920–1982). 1982 Forecast based on econometric model (see Chapter 2).

less than comprehensive, since far fewer business failures (column 3) are recorded than business bankruptcy filings (column 2).

Just as we saw in bankruptcies, the business failure rate has jumped dramatically in 1980 and 1981. If the rate reaches at least 79 per 10,000 in 1982, as I estimated, it will be the highest since 1933! (See Chart 1-1.) As of October, 1982 the failure rate had increased to 88 per 10,000.

The three final columns of Table 1-3 show that although there has not been a noticeable trend in business failures or failure rates, the average liability per failure has been moving steadily upward since 1950, with a peak of over $400,000 in 1978. This can be explained only partially by inflation, since the average size of U.S. firms, and the consequent liabilities, have grown with price level increases. As noted earlier, however, I feel that the major change in the profile of business failures in the United States is the susceptibility of the larger firm to total demise. The last column of Table 1-3 does not include any long-term publicly held debt and

Table 1-4   Outstanding Publicly Traded Debt of Bankrupt Firms (1970–1982).

Year	Number of Firms	Amount of Default ($ Millions)
1970	1	686.6
1971	1	50.1
1972	1	291.4
1973	2	60.5
1974	6	234.1
1975	5	335.4
1976	1	40.4
1977	3	144.8
1978	5	138.4
1979	1	107.8
1980	2	45.2
1981	2	304.8
1982	6[a]	516.9[a]
Total	36	2955.9

[a]First ten months of 1982. This list is based only on bankrupt firm data where liabilities exceeded $75 million. Also, only publicly traded debt is included; hence the totals are not inclusive of all long-term debt defaults.

primarily reflects short-term claims. As such, it understates failure claims—in some years, for example, 1975 and 1977—significantly. Table 1-4 lists the publicly traded long-term debt defaults since 1970 based on bankrupt firms only.

Tables 1-5 and 1-6 list the nation's bankruptcy filings by chapter of the bankruptcy act (prior to 1980) and by type of business. "Straight bankruptcy," whether voluntary or involuntary, means that the firm had to liquidate its assets and repay its creditors in some manner reflecting their priorities. This filing, now known as Chapter 7 straight bankruptcies, encompasses individuals as well as companies. Personal bankruptcies are discussed at the end of this section in the context of the new bankruptcy code.

If we compare the number of Chapter X and XI (or new Chapter 2) filings with the total number of business bankruptcies, it appears that the combined total is a small percentage (slightly over 10%) of all business filings and is relatively insignificant. Nothing could be further from the truth, however: the size, complexity, and public policy issues involved far outweigh the relatively small number that represents the remaining bankruptcies. To my knowledge, no accurate combined or separate compilation of Chapter X and XI liabilities existed, nor are the new Chapter 11 liabilities recorded.

Table 1-5   Filings by Chapter of the Bankruptcy Act since 1950.

Fiscal Year	Total	Voluntary Straight Bankruptcy	Involuntary Straight Bankruptcy	IX	X	11	XII	XIII	Section 77 (1933 Act)
1950	33,392	25,263	1,369	4	134	583	31	6,007	0
1951	35,193	26,594	1,099	3	88	459	22	6,924	0
1952	34,873	25,890	1,059	15	74	413	21	7,397	0
1953	40,087	29,815	1,064	0	86	437	15	8,670	0
1954	53,136	41,335	1,398	2	104	649	12	9,634	0
1955	59,404	47,650	1,249	1	73	547	19	9,864	0
1956	62,086	50,655	1,240	1	40	597	15	9,535	0
1957	73,761	60,335	1,189	0	65	599	24	11,549	0
1958	91,668	76,048	1,417	2	67	720	23	13,391	0
1959	100,672	85,502	1,288	3	78	787	21	12,993	0
1960	110,034	94,414	1,296	0	90	622	12	13,599	0
1961	146,643	124,386	1,444	0	112	947	31	19,723	0
1962	147,780	122,499	1,382	1	77	903	37	22,880	0
1963	155,493	128,405	1,409	0	128	1,188	33	24,329	0
1964	171,719	141,828	1,339	0	125	1,088	47	27,292	0
1965	180,323	149,820	1,317	0	88	1,022	49	28,027	0
1966	192,354	161,840	1,173	2	93	909	75	28,261	1
1967	208,329	173,884	1,241	1	138	1,033	68	31,963	1
1968	197,811	164,592	1,001	3	128	953	69	31,065	0
1969	184,930	154,054	946	0	87	867	66	28,910	0
1970	194,399	161,366	1,085	0	115	1,262	58	30,510	3
1971	201,352	167,149	1,215	2	179	1,782	120	30,904	1
1972	182,869	152,839	1,094	1	105	1,361	92	27,374	3
1973	173,197	144,929	985	0	101	1,458	92	25,632	0
1974	189,513	156,962	1,009	1	163	2,172	172	29,019	15
1975	254,484	208,064	1,266	0	189	3,506	280	41,178	1
1976	246,549	207,926	1,141	2	141	3,235	525	33,579	0
1977	214,399	180,062	1,132	1	96	3,046	640	29,442	0
1978	202,951	167,776	995	2	75	3,266	650	30,185	2
1979	226,476	182,344	915	1	63	3,042	669	39,442	0
1980	360,960	—	—	a	a	5,637	a	a	—
1981	519,063	—	—	a	a	8,752	a	a	—
1982	527,342	—	—	a	a	12,385	a	a	—

Source: U.S. Bankruptcy Courts, Administrative Office of the President, Table of Bankruptcy Statistics, 1980.

ªNew bankruptcy act, Chapter 11 replaced old Chapters X and XI.

Table 1-6 Number of Bankruptcy Cases Filed by Occupations in the Business and Nonbusiness Groups for Fiscal Years 1950–1981.

Fiscal Year	Nonbusiness			Business						Grand Total	National Population
	Employee	Others Not in Business	Total	Merchants	Manu-facturers	Farmers	Profes-sionals	Others in Business	Total		
1950	22,933	2,107	25,040	2,565	803	290	126	4,568	8,352	33,392	151,667,000
% of total	68.7	6.3	75.0	7.7	2.4	0.8	0.4	13.7	25.0	100.0	
1951	25,984	1,822	27,806	2,360	522	205	127	4,173	7,387	35,193	154,360,000
% of total	73.8	5.2	79.0	6.7	1.5	0.6	0.4	11.8	21.0	100.0	
1952	26,527	1,804	28,331	2,319	532	196	137	3,358	6,542	34,873	156,981,000
% of total	76.1	5.2	81.3	6.6	1.5	0.6	0.4	9.6	18.7	100.0	
1953	31,253	2,062	33,315	2,402	518	214	140	3,498	6,772	40,087	159,696,000
% of total	78.0	5.1	83.1	6.0	1.3	0.5	0.4	8.7	16.9	100.0	
1954	40,889	3,359	44,248	3,191	745	322	154	4,476	8,888	53,136	162,409,000
% of total	77.0	6.3	83.3	6.0	1.4	0.6	0.3	8.4	16.7	100.0	
1955	46,163	4,056	50,219	3,317	750	386	217	4,515	9,185	59,404	165,248,000
% of total	77.7	6.8	84.5	5.6	1.3	0.6	0.4	7.6	15.5	100.0	
1956	48,784	3,824	52,608	3,155	730	400	212	4,981	9,478	62,086	168,091,000
% of total	78.6	6.2	84.8	5.1	1.2	0.6	0.3	8.0	15.2	100.0	
1957	59,053	4,564	63,617	3,160	665	405	204	5,710	10,144	73,761	171,191,000
% of total	80.1	6.2	86.3	4.3	0.9	0.5	0.3	7.7	13.7	100.0	
1958	73,379	6,886	80,265	3,504	758	332	284	6,525	11,403	91,668	174,000,000
% of total	80.1	7.5	87.6	3.8	0.8	0.4	0.3	7.1	12.4	100.0	
1959	81,516	7,427	88,943	3,400	634	408	430	6,857	11,729	100,672	177,128,000
% of total	81.0	7.4	88.4	3.4	0.6	0.4	0.4	6.8	11.6	100.0	

(Continued)

Table 1-6 (Continued)

Fiscal Year	Nonbusiness			Business						Grand Total	National Population
	Employee	Others Not in Business	Total	Merchants	Manu- facturers	Farmers	Profes- sionals	Others in Business	Total		
1960	89,639	8,111	97,750	3,157	624	453	495	7,555	12,284	110,034	180,670,000
% of total	81.4	7.4	88.8	2.9	0.6	0.4	0.4	6.9	11.2	100.0	
1961	119,117	12,285	131,402	4,244	790	546	623	9,038	15,241	146,643	182,868,000
% of total	81.2	8.4	89.6	2.9	0.5	0.4	0.4	6.2	10.4	100.0	
1962	120,742	11,383	132,125	4,295	735	548	771	9,306	15,655	147,780	186,482,000
% of total	81.8	7.7	89.5	3.0	0.4	0.4	0.5	6.2	10.5	100.0	
1963	127,156	12,034	139,190	4,271	859	554	753	9,866	16,303	155,493	189,278,000
% of total	81.8	7.7	89.5	2.7	0.6	0.4	0.5	6.3	10.5	100.0	
1964	141,550	13,659	155,209	5,064	819	565	785	9,277	16,510	171,719	191,851,000
% of total	82.4	8.0	90.4	2.9	0.5	0.3	0.5	5.4	9.6	100.0	
1965	148,965	14,448	163,413	4,856	852	589	780	9,833	16,910	180,323	193,818,000
% of total	82.6	8.0	90.6	2.7	0.5	0.3	0.4	5.5	9.4	100.0	
1966	160,299	15,625	175,924	4,683	747	551	632	9,817	16,430	192,354	196,843,000
% of total	83.3	8.2	91.5	2.4	0.4	0.3	0.3	5.1	8.5	100.0	
1967	174,205	17,524	191,729	4,929	729	443	704	9,732	16,600	208,329	199,118,000
% of total	83.6	8.4	92.0	2.4	0.4	0.2	0.3	4.7	8.0	100.0	
1968	162,879	18,387	181,266	4,567	749	567	1,087	9,575	16,545	197,811	200,996,000
% of total	82.3	9.3	91.6	2.3	0.4	0.3	0.5	4.9	8.4	100.0	
1969	150,235	19,265	169,500	3,969	680	606	1,301	8,874	15,430	184,930	203,216,000
% of total	81.3	10.4	91.7	2.1	0.4	0.3	0.7	4.8	8.3	100.0	

Year										Total	Population
1970	156,397	21,805	4,413	178,202	858	658	1,304	8,964	16,197	194,399	205,395,000
% of total	80.5	11.2	2.3	91.7	0.4	0.3	0.7	4.6	8.3	100.0	
1971	156,143	26,106	5,113	182,249	1,160	788	1,474	10,568	19,103	201,352	207,006,000
% of total	77.5	13.0	2.5	90.5	0.6	0.4	0.7	5.3	9.5	100.0	
1972	139,466	25,271	4,757	164,737	801	631	1,562	10,381	18,132	182,869	208,837,000
% of total	76.2	13.8	2.6	90.1	0.4	0.3	0.9	5.7	9.9	100.0	
1973	131,153	24,554	4,851	155,707	746	431	1,452	10,010	17,490	173,197	209,724,000
% of total	75.7	14.3	2.8	90.0	0.4	0.2	0.9	5.7	10.0	100.0	
1974	141,930	26,836	5,634	168,766	809	308	1,587	12,409	20,747	189,513	211,909,000
% of total	74.9	14.2	3.0	89.1	0.4	0.2	0.8	6.5	10.9	100.0	
1975	184,178	40,176	6,345	224,354	938	550	2,547	19,750	30,130	254,484	213,466,000
% of total	72.4	15.8	2.4	88.2	0.4	0.2	1.0	7.8	11.8	100.0	
1976	166,499	44,849	6,417	211,348	740	672	2,813	24,559	35,201	246,549	214,988,000
% of total	67.5	18.2	2.6	85.7	0.3	0.3	1.1	10.0	14.3	100.0	
1977	144,840	37,370	6,881	182,210	849	736	2,685	21,038	32,189	214,399	216,168,000
% of total	67.6	17.4	3.2	85.0	0.4	0.3	1.3	9.8	15.0	100.0	
1978	139,910	32,513	5,759	172,423	907	751	2,353	20,758	30,528	202,951	217,916,000
% of total	68.9	16.0	2.8	85.0	0.4	0.4	1.2	10.2	15.0	100.0	
1979	164,150	32,826	4,306	196,967	653	592	2,249	21,700	29,500	226,476	219,759,000
% of total	72.5	14.5	1.9	87.0	0.3	0.3	0.9	9.6	13.0	100.0	
1980	n.a.	n.a.	n.a.	314,875	n.a.	n.a.	n.a.	n.a.	45,841	360,960	228,497,100[a]
% of total				87.2					12.8	100.0	
1981	n.a.	n.a.	n.a.	453,057	n.a.	n.a.	n.a.	n.a.	66,006	519,063	230,667,000[a]
% of total				87.2					12.8	100.0	

Source: U.S. Bankruptcy Courts, Administrative Office of the President, Table of Bankruptcy Statistics, 1980.

[a]Calendar year population. All other totals are June 30 fiscal year.

The breakdown of filings by sector indicates that merchants and professional service firms account for a large proportion, but the total is dominated by "Others in Business." Certain financial and real estate firms make up the bulk of the "other" category. This explains why the number of bankruptcy filings exceeds D&B's number of business failures, since the latter source does not include them. A more complete breakdown of failures by sector can be found in Dun & Bradstreet's *Failure Record*, published annually.

Causes of Business Failure

The overwhelming cause of individual firm failures is managerial incompetence. In 1980, over 94% of all failures were identified with the lack of experience or unbalanced experience (50%), or just plain incompetence (44%). The remaining causes are categorized as neglect (0.8%), fraud (0.5%), and reasons unknown (3.5%). These statistics represent the opinions of informed creditors and information from D&B reports for over 17,000 business failures. Of course, if debtors' management were asked why businesses fail, the category of inexperience and incompetence would receive much lower significance. Causes of failure are discussed in Argenti (1976). Argenti's narrative is persuasive; it is his view that collapse of firms occurs not suddenly, but with clear signposts of impending disaster. Many of these indicators are management oriented (not quantifiable).

New Business Formation and Age of Business Failures

The rate of business formation can affect the failure rate in subsequent periods, since it is well documented that there is a greater propensity for younger firms to fail than for more mature companies. Table 1-7 shows this propensity and breaks down failures by age for different sectors and for all concerns. Note that more than 53% of all firms that failed did so in the first five years of their life. This percentage has been remarkably stable over the years, with the rate between 53 and 60% since 1952. Before 1952 an even higher percentage of younger firms failed.

Although almost 28% of the firms that failed did so in their first three years, only about 1% failed in the first year. This is not surprising: it takes time to fail! Even when a firm is in its worst competitive situation (i.e., when it starts out), there is usually sufficient capital to keep it going for a period of time, and default on loans is usually not immediate. Because of this phenomenon, any model observing the association between new business formation and changes in failure rates must attempt to exploit this sequence. See the discussion in Chapter 2.

Table 1-7 Age of Failed Businesses by Function—1980.

Age in Years	Manu-facturing	Whole-sale	Retail	Construc-tion	Service	All Concerns
One Year or Less	0.7%	0.9%	1.1%	0.5%	1.3%	0.9%
Two	8.3	8.5	11.7	5.3	11.2	9.6
Three	14.6	13.4	18.2	11.1	14.6	15.3
Total Three Years or Less	23.6	22.8	31.0	16.9	27.1	25.8
Four	12.3	16.1	16.6	15.7	14.2	15.4
Five	11.4	11.5	13.3	12.8	10.6	12.4
Total Five Years or Less	47.3	50.4	60.9	45.4	51.9	53.6
Six	9.3	8.6	8.7	9.5	8.6	8.9
Seven	6.7	5.9	5.5	7.9	6.8	6.3
Eight	4.8	5.5	4.7	6.2	5.8	5.2
Nine	5.0	4.4	3.1	5.4	5.4	4.3
Ten	3.0	4.3	2.9	4.1	3.1	3.4
Total Six–Ten Years	28.8	28.7	24.9	33.1	29.7	28.1
Over Ten Years	23.9	20.9	14.2	21.5	18.4	18.3
Total	100.0%	100.0%	100.0%	100.0%	100.0%	100.0%
Number of Failures	1,599	1,284	4,910	2,355	1,594	11,742

Source: Dun & Bradstreet, *Failure Record,* 1980, p. 10.

CAUSES OF THE RECENT INCREASE IN BANKRUPTCIES

Aggregate Measures of Increased Corporate Financial Vulnerability

Chart 1-2 illustrates the dramatic increase in the number of business bankruptcy filings in the United States, especially since 1978. In my opinion, the fact that the new bankruptcy code went into effect in October 1979 *cannot* explain the record number of bankruptcy filings. It is the result, however, of two fundamental, negative powerful forces combining in 1980 through 1982 to cause the greatest threat to firm viability since the great depression of the 1930s. I refer to the economic malaise of the economy since 1980 that has continued, virtually without abatement, to this present day (June 1982), combined with the deterioration in firm liquidity, in-

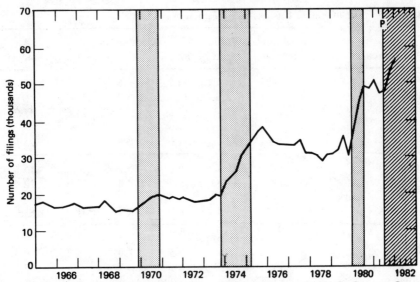

Chart 1-2 Business Bankruptcies. (Nonpersonal filings with U.S. Courts. Quarterly data at annual rates, seasonally adjusted by Federal Reserve. Latest data are for 1982, first quarter.)

creased leverage, and dramatically reduced coverage of financial payments of interest and principal.

Charts 1-3 to 1-6 illustrate the above arguments. Many of these charts were compiled by J. Charles Partee, for his recent statement before the Subcommittee on Domestic Monetary Policy of the Committee on Banking, Finance and Urban Affairs (U.S. House of Representatives, May 26, 1982). Liquid assets as a percentage of current liabilities have decreased from a 1976 high of approximately 30% to just above 20% in 1982 (Chart 1-3). The ratio of liabilities to total assets (Chart 1-4) has increased over this same period from a low of 54% in 1976 to over 57% in 1982. Perhaps the most revealing trend is indicated in Chart 1-5 where we observe that net interest payments as a percentage of income for nonfinancial corporations have increased from approximately 20 cents for every dollar of income in 1978 to over 40 cents per dollar in 1981. No doubt the primary cause of this increase is the record high interest rates that firms are paying in recent years.

If the average firm pays out in interest over 40% of every dollar earned before interest and taxes, no wonder so many marginal firms are succumbing to the economic reality of bankruptcy.

The small and young firm is particularly vulnerable today. The firm

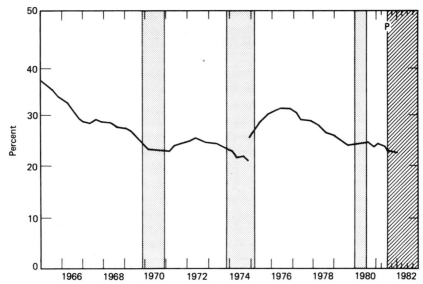

Chart 1-3 Liquid Assets as a Percent of Current Liabilities—Nonfinancial Corporations. (Flow of Funds, quarterly data for nonfinancial corporations at seasonally adjusted annual rates. Data for 1982, first quarter, are preliminary. Shaded areas denote recessions as defined by NBER; asterisk indicates break in series.)

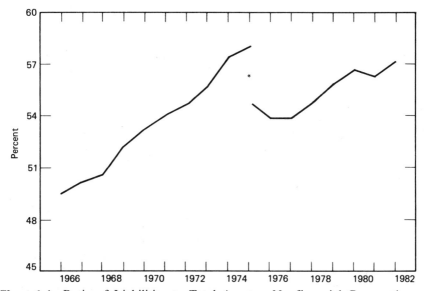

Chart 1-4 Ratio of Liabilities to Total Assets—Nonfinancial Corporations. (Flow of Funds, year-end data. Values of assets and liabilities are based on historical costs. Asterisk indicates break in series.)

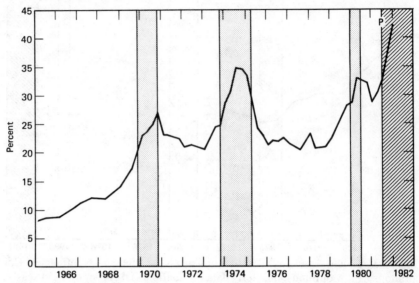

Chart 1-5   Net Interest Payments as a Percent of Capital Income—Nonfinancial Corporations. (Capital income is economic profits before tax plus net interest payments. Department of Commerce, National Income and Product Accounts, quarterly data at seasonally adjusted annual rates. Data for 1982, first quarter, are preliminary and based on estimates of net interest payments by the Federal Reserve Board staff. Shaded areas denote recessions as defined by NBER.)

which financed its early growth with debt capital in the mid- to late 1970s has been faced with the unfortunate necessity of refinancing its short-term loans with new loans at record interest rates. The small firm does not typically have access to the long-term debt markets or even the equity markets. Chart 1-6 shows that, for all firms, the ratio of short-term debt to total debt has increased from a low of under 35% in 1976 to about 42% in 1982. Most short-term loans are part of a revolving or line of credit agreement with financial institutions where the interest rate charged is on a floating rate basis (e.g., prime rate +3%). A loan costing 10% in 1976 and 1977 (7% + 3% premium for a risky loan) is costing (in 1982) approximately 20% and has even reached the 23-25% level in recent years. No wonder we have record levels of bankruptcies and business failures! Even more difficult is the *real* rate of interest that firms are now paying. Whereas the real rate (nominal rate—inflation rate) was close to zero from 1976 through 1978, it is now perhaps as high as 10 to 15%. Firms simply do not have the ability to pass along their cost increases as they once did. The diminution in the inflation rate is a mixed blessing to some segments of the economy, particularly the small firm.

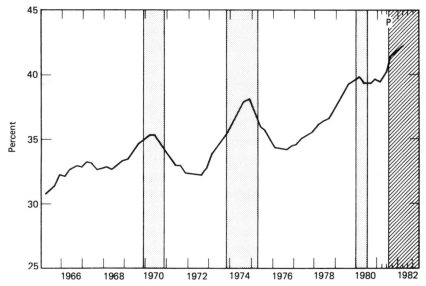

Chart 1-6 Short-term Debt as a Percent of Total Debt—Nonfinancial Corporations. (Flow of Funds, quarterly data at seasonally adjusted annual rates. Data for 1982, first quarter, are preliminary. Shaded areas denote recessions as defined by NBER.)

In 1982, banks are more frequently requiring a string of loan covenants if continued credit is to be extended to small- and medium-size entities. These include controls over management's investment decisions, more frequent financial reports, extra collateral, and increasingly restrictive working capital and debt/equity ratios. These conditions, however, are seen as necessary in order for loans to be restructured and for small firms to be permitted to stay in business. Banks have even on occasion suspended or reduced interest payments and lengthened short-term loans as competition for the small and "middle market" gets intense. Banks can usually recoup these reductions through increased fees and continued receipt of principal repayments. The essence is that the business failure rate would be even higher in 1982 if financial institutions felt that they would be better off forcing small firms into liquidation.

Failure Rate By Age and New Business Formation

An important factor to consider that is particularly related to the small, young entity, is the failure propensity of firms according to their age. Dun & Bradstreet's statistics show that the highest failure propensity is between 2-5 years of a firm's existence, with the peak in the third and fourth

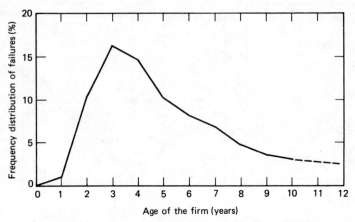

Chart 1-7   Frequency Distribution of Failures versus Age of the Firm.

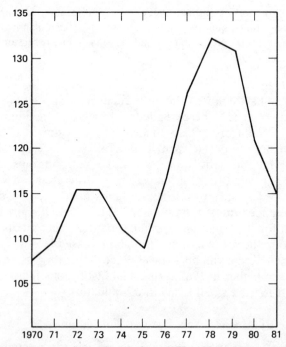

Chart 1-8   Index of Net Business Formation, 1970–1981. (*Source:* Department of Commerce, Bureau of Economic Analysis, and Dun and Bradstreet, Inc.)

years (Chart 1-7). During the 2-5 year age period, over 50% of all failures occur.

Chart 1-8 depicts the index of net business formation from 1970-1981. Note that the years 1977–1979 were particularly high business formation years with new business incorporations rising to about 525,000 in 1979 from 375,000 in 1976. Using the failure propensity by age relationships discussed above, the 1977–1979 business expansion should result in an increasing number of small firm failures in the period 1980–1984.

I have utilized many of the aforementioned aggregate economic influences on business failures in order to construct an econometric failure prediction model. The model incorporates the following aggregate series in order to explain historical movement in business failure rates:

1 Change in real GNP—a measure of overall economic activity
2 Change in money supply ($M2$ and $M1$-B)—a measure of overall credit availability
3 Change in the S&P 500 stock index—a measure of investor expectations and firm cost of equity capital
4 Change in new business formation

For a full discussion of this model, see Chapter 2.

PERSONAL BANKRUPTCY

The New Personal Bankruptcy Rules

The Bankruptcy Reform Act of 1978 made sweeping changes in the rules that govern the personal bankruptcy filings in the United States. In fact, the changes were so dramatic that the number of filings jumped considerably after the act went into effect on October 1, 1979. For the first six months of 1980, the number of personal bankruptcies increased more than 75% over the comparable period in 1979. Total bankruptcy filings in 1980 exceeded 360,000, with 314,875 filings in the personal sector. Chart 1-9 shows the trend in personal filings since 1950 (see also Table 1-6). Total personal bankruptcy filings in 1981 were approximately the same as in 1980 (313,500 vs. 314,875).

Note that, as expected, the number of personal filings increases during recessionary periods and, in all but the 1974–1975 recession, the increase tends to continue for a short time after the recession has ended. Also, with the exception of 1968–1969, 1972–1973, and 1976–1978, the number of filings has been consistently increasing, and we can expect the trend to continue in the 1980s.

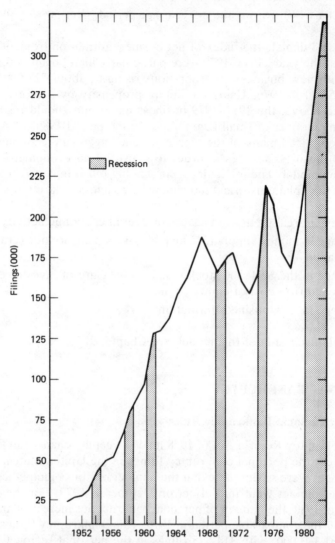

Chart 1-9 Personal Bankruptcy Filings in the United States (1950–1981). (*Source:* Administrative Office of the U.S. District Courts, Bankruptcy Divisions, *Table of Statistics,* Washington, D.C., 1981.)

There are two reasons for the great increase in personal filings under the new code (1980 and beyond): (1) the recession and the attendant credit restraints, which had harsh effects on the individual, and (2) the increased liberality of the new code, particularly in the exemptions that are available. See "The New Rules About Bankruptcy," *Changing Times,* May 1979 for details of the new code related to personal filings.

Personal bankruptcy rationale is based on the premise that individuals should have the opportunity to work out a liquidation or repayment schedule that is feasible and be able to get a fresh start. The new code creates a broad set of federal exemptions that normally apply to debtors in all states. In states that provide more liberal allowances, a debtor can opt for them. Also, states can pass laws prohibiting the use of federal exemptions, and many of them have done so since the new act went into effect.

Exempt Property

The following property is exempted by the federal code:

1 Up to $7,500 in equity in a home or burial plot. Some states (e.g., New York) permit up to $10,000.
2 An individual's interest up to $1,200 in a motor vehicle.
3 An individual's interest up to $200 for any single item in household goods, furnishings, clothes, appliances, books, animals, crops, and musical instruments.
4 Up to $500 in jewelry.
5 Any property worth up to $400 plus any unused part of the household exemption (item 1 above).
6 Up to $750 worth of implements, books, or tools of trade.
7 Any professionally prescribed health aids.
8 Protection includes social security and veterans' benefits, unemployment compensation, alimony and child support, and pension and profit-sharing payments.

If husband and wife file for bankruptcy jointly, the dollar limit doubles. The new code is far more liberal in its exemptions. For example, under the old act the federal homestead exclusion was only $2,000.

Just because property falls into an exempt category, however, a bankrupt cannot necessarily keep it. If a person owns the property completely, he can keep it. Property that is security for a purchase or a loan can be repossessed, regardless of whether it is exempted. Once repossessed, the property is sold to satisfy the debt; if there is something left over, in the case of exempt property, the debtor can then list the asset's value under the exclusion categories noted above (e.g., $7,500 for a home). The court might, however, invalidate certain repossessable property in favor of the debtor for such items as furniture, tools of trade, and other necessities. In addition, the law limits a creditor's claim against certain property to the value of the property, regardless of how much is still owed. So if a washing machine that cost $500 on credit has $300 still outstanding but the repossessed value was only $200, the debtor could pay the store the $200 and the remaining $100 of the debt would be eliminated.

Chapter 13 Repayment Plans

Chapter 13 of the new bankruptcy code deals with the small business debtor and the individual. Whereas previously the law was limited to "wage earners," now it is possible for any individual with regular income to file a Chapter 13 if he has unsecured debts of less than $100,000 and secured debts of less than $350,000.

The debtor has the right to propose a repayment plan that may provide for payments over a period of up to three years, with the court having the power to extend a repayment period up to five years. The debtor may make his payments from future income only or from a combination of future income and a liquidation of his assets. A repayment plan may modify the rights of secured creditors, but not claimants who hold a security interest in real property that is the debtor's principal residence. A plan may not be confirmed unless each secured creditor accepts the plan, or the plan provides that the creditor retain the lien securing his claim and that he receive property valued at no less than the allowed amount of his claim. There is no requirement that unsecured creditors vote on or accept a plan.

The key aspect of a Chapter 13 repayment plan is the monthly budget, listing expected revenues and expenses for the debtor. Any surplus then becomes the basis for the repayment schedule over the three-to-five-year repayment period. It is not uncommon for the debtors to petition for and receive confirmation on very low repayment schedules including the so-called 1% (of liabilities) or $5 (a month) plans.

Chapter 13 offers several advantages over straight bankruptcy liquidation (Chapter 7) filings. The major one is that people can discharge, or obtain release from a wider range of debts. Student loans as well as loans obtained through false financial statements can be discharged depending on expected disposable income available. Nondischargeable debts, however, still include alimony and child support and long-term debts such as mortgages.

Codebtor Clause and Refiling Restrictions

The court now extends its protection to codebtors or guarantors of a loan. Under the old act, if a person filed a Chapter XIII plan, a creditor had no problem in seeking repayment from a loan guarantor. The new code stipulates that creditors cannot try to collect from a codebtor as long as the repayment plan is in effect. Under Chapter 13, there is no limit to when one may file again for bankruptcy as long as the debtor repays at least 70% of the debts. Under Chapter 7 (liquidation), however, one must wait six years before filing for bankruptcy again.

Chapter 7: Straight Bankruptcy Liquidation

Chapter 7 of the code deals with liquidation procedures, which are similar to those that existed under the old act. The new code provides for the court, or the U.S. trustee, to appoint an interim trustee to liquidate the debtor's assets and pay off the claims in their order of priority (see the material on absolute priority, above). At the first meeting, creditors holding at least 20% in amount of claims may elect a trustee. At least 20% in amount of claims must actually vote, and the candidate who receives the majority of the amount of the claims is elected. A creditors' committee comprises no fewer than three nor more than 11 creditors for the purpose of consulting with the trustee and making recommendations to him respecting the administration of the estate.

Section 727 of the code provides for the discharge of all remaining debts after the estate is liquidated except when certain infractions of the individual debtor preclude it. Essentially, when one goes bankrupt, the court takes the property, sells it, splits the proceeds among the creditors, and erases any remaining debt. The broad set of exemptions discussed earlier for Chapter 13 apply for the most part to Chapter 7 as well.

Filing Costs and Lawyer Fees

Personal bankruptcy is not costless. The filing fee for individuals is $60, up from $50 under the old act. In 1980 the range of lawyer fees was usually from $150 to $400. Although the majority of individuals hire a bankruptcy lawyer, this is not necessary; the requisite forms can be purchased in stationery stores for less than $10 (in 1980).

APPENDIX TO CHAPTER 1

UNDERSTANDING THE BANKRUPTCY REORGANIZATION PROCESS (CASE STUDY—SELF-TEACHING AND CRITIQUE)

INTRODUCTION AND BACKGROUND

Chapter 1 discussed the objectives and procedures of a Chapter 11 corporate bankruptcy reorganization. Although several aspects of the reorganization procedure have been modified under the new Chapter 11, the basic valuation methodology and criteria for achieving an acceptable reorganization plan of the old Chapters X and XI are unchanged. The achievement of a plan which will lead to a rehabilitated going concern and which is fair to the various creditors and owners is the primary goal. The difficulty of distinguishing between a Chapter XI plan of arrangement and a public interest Chapter X reorganization is now eliminated, and the parties involved are more certain as to the procedures which will be followed.

The purpose of this appendix is to explore the reorganization process from the viewpoint of a case analysis. Source documents from an actual case will be utilized to complement the issues identified and discussed earlier. Before presenting the case materials and asking for the reader's own analysis and critique, it might be helpful to spell out again the main steps involved in a reorganization plan.

1 The voluntary debtor or another petitioner files for reorganization in bankruptcy in a U.S. district court (Bankruptcy Court after 1984).

2 Upon acceptance of the petition, either the court or a U.S. trustee may assign a trustee or trustees to take over the running of the business and be responsible for devising a reorganization plan. The old management may continue to operate the firm, however. There is an immediate automatic stay of execution on secured and unsecured creditor action.

3 The court, or trustee, forms a creditors' committee to represent the major creditors of the debtor.

4 The trustee or debtor has 120 days to file a plan, and has 60 days to obtain acceptances of the plan, although appeals for extensions can be made. The SEC may comment on the plan but may not appeal from any judgment or decree. Under the old Chapter X, the SEC had to

comment on all reorganizations of substantial size (greater than $3 million in liabilities). In the following case analysis, we will utilize much of the SEC commentary on the case. It is regrettable, in my opinion, that documents such as these will not necessarily be forthcoming in the future under Chapter 11.

5 The plan is analyzed by the bankruptcy judge with the assistance of expert witness, creditor committees, and other interested parties. If the plan is acceptable to a designated percentage of each creditor (and possibly owner) class, the plan will usually be sanctioned by the court. It is still possible that an unpopular plan may be "crammed down" and accepted by the court. Appeals from any relevant party are still possible.

THE DUPLAN CORPORATION CASE

Introduction and Instructions

The following case illustrates a thoughtful but somewhat controversial bankruptcy reorganization case. Due to insufficient experience under the new act, we utilize an old Chapter X reorganization, the Duplan Corp. The main source documents reproduced in part are the *SEC's Corporate Reorganization Release* No. 323 dated May 2, 1980, excerpts from a *Women's Wear Daily* article dated July 31, 1980, and the plan of confirmation. The reorganization plan was finally confirmed in June 1981, almost five years after the initial petition. A great deal has been written and discussed concerning this case, and the material presented is particularly informative and useful for pedagogic purposes.

Of particular interest is the fact that the SEC document discusses an amended plan submitted on October 2, 1979 and further amended by a letter dated January 17, 1980. The *Woman's Wear Daily* article commented on operating and financial results up to June 30, 1980. Hence, more up-to-date information is available to you in assessing the reorganization plan, and this data might conceivably impact on the valuation analysis for Duplan.

Questions for Discussion

You are asked to comment on the reorganization plan and the proposed compromise settlement amongst the creditors. Please evaluate the *valuation analysis* performed by the primary expert witness in the case as to the valuation of Duplan. Consider in your analysis, as well, the most recent performance of the firm. In essence, you are asked to present a *re-*

vised valuation for Duplan which should include, at a minimum, (1) capitalized value of earnings; (2) present value of tax loss carryover and litigation recovery; (3) cash available for distribution. The date of your own analysis should be as of the end of the fiscal year, *September 1980.*

How does your valuation compare with that of the reorganization plan's? In view of your answer, is there any remaining equity in the reorganized firm? (That is, is the firm insolvent in a bankrupt sense?) How would you recapitalize the company to make the plan fair as well as feasible?

Article From *Women's Wear Daily,* Thursday, July 31, 1980

Duplan Earnings Leap 232.4% for Quarter

New York (FNS)—Duplan Corp.'s net income (including all operating and non-operating results, ed. note) for the 3 months ended July 1 soared a whopping 232.4 percent over the same period in 1979, according to Alfred P. Slaner, the firm's Chapter X trustee.

His report shows earnings of $2,214,000 in the latest period compared with $666,000. This represents a 6.8 percent rise in net sales to $12,524,000 from $11,728,000.

For the nine months, net income jumped to $5,379,000, a 28.6 percent increase over $4,183,000. The earnings were generated on net sales of $32,303,000, against $30,251,000, a 6.5 percent increase.

Duplan has sold its fabric operation since going into Chapter X in October, 1976. Wundies, Inc., is a wholly owned subsidiary, and Rochester Button is a division.

As for coming out of Chapter X, Slaner said he is waiting for U.S. District Court Judge Kevin T. Duffy to approve the plan for paying creditors before solicitiations of creditors can begin.

CORPORATE REORGANIZATION
Release No. 323/May 2, 1980 (Excerpted)
UNITED STATES DISTRICT COURT
SOUTHERN DISTRICT OF NEW YORK
THE DUPLAN CORPORATION,
DUPLAN FABRICS, INC.
ADVISORY REPORT OF THE SECURITIES AND EXCHANGE
COMMISSION ON PROPOSED PLAN OF REORGANIZATION

This advisory report is submitted by the Securities and Exchange Commission ("Commission"). We conclude that the Trustee's plan is feasible but it is not fair and equitable to Duplan's creditors. The plan can be made fair and equitable by relatively modest amendments.

On August 31, 1976. Duplan and Fabrics filed original petitions under Chapter XI of the Act in the United States District Court for the Southern District of New York. On October 5, 1976, the Bankruptcy Court granted the Commission's motion to transfer the cases to Chapter X.

The Trustee, Alfred Slaner, filed his report of investigation dated May 22, 1978. He filed a plan on August 15, 1979, subsequently amended on October 2, 1979, and further amended by a letter agreement dated January 17, 1980, embodying a proposed settlement of claims of the four bank creditors and counterclaims by the Trustee and the present indenture Trustee for the 5-1/2% convertible subordinated debentures.

I. THE DEBTORS

Duplan was incorporated in 1917 in Delaware, succeeding predecessors originating in 1898. The present name, The Duplan Corporation, was adopted in 1941. Its common stock and debentures were traded on the New York Stock Exchange. As of 12/5/79, there were 5,712 holders of record of common stock and 1.156 holders of record of the convertible debentures. These convertible debentures and common shares were suspended from trading on the New York Stock Exchange at the close of trading on August 16, 1976, and subsequently delisted. Trading has continued on the over-the-counter market.

Until the mid-1970's, Duplan was generally profitable and was an innovator and leader in the development of new textile products and in the use of new yarns. The 1965 acquisition followed a decline in Duplan's profits. At that time, the company was engaged in the texturing of synthetic yarns and conventional yarn throwing.

In 1967, Duplan embarked on a program of diversification and acquisition. Between April 1967 and June 1970, 17 acquisitions were made at a total cost of approximately $64 million for cash and securities. In 1969 Duplan sold publicly $15 million of 5-1/2% convertible subordinated debentures, due February 1, 1994; and 400,000 shares of common stock were sold in 1970 for $10.3 million. More securities were issued in acquisitions. During the years 1967 through 1971, Duplan also spent approximately $40 million for new equipment, additional manufacturing plants, improvement and expansion of existing facilities and internal diversification.

These investments provided Duplan with increased capabilities in its existing operations, and gave it entree into the apparel and apparel components markets. New lines of yarn, production of bonded fabrics, dyeing of yarns and piece goods, carpet manufacturing, manufacturing of textile machinery, wholesaling of men's medium priced double knit suits, and the retailing of home crafts items and fabrics, were among the items added to Duplan's operations. By 1969, Duplan plants increased from 3 in 1965 to 43, and it had increased its employees from 1,200 to 6,000. Sales had grown from $25 million in 1965 to $113 million in 1969.

As indicated by the number of plants acquired, Duplan still faced a major task of consolidation and integration. Over the next few years, it liquidated or sold parts of its acquisitions and new projects of its own that did not succeed and its earnings and credit drastically deteriorated, as the following Table I shows:

TABLE I
THE DUPLAN CORPORATION
Summary of Consolidated Income
Fiscal Years Ended September 30
(in millions)

	1970	1971	1972	1973	1974	1975
Sales	$107	$128	$131	$147	$151	$116
Cost of sales	84	103	109	121	130	106
Selling, general and admin.	10	13	18	19	19	17
*Profit (loss)	$13	$12	$4	$7	$2	$(7)
Discontinued operations	(1)	(1)	(1)	(1)	(2)	1
Other income-net	1	1	1	1	1	—
Interest	(4)	(2)	(3)	(4)	(6)	(6)
Income tax provision	(4)	(4)	—	(1)	1	—
Profit after tax	$5	$6	$1	$2	$(4)	$(12)
Write-offs					(14)	
Losses on assets sold					(1)	(1)
Net income	$5	$6	$1	$2	$(19)	$(13)

*As restated through 1975 to eliminate operations of divisions discontinued.

In retrospect, this dramatic turn in the fortunes of the Debtors can be attributed primarily to losses incurred in its textile operations as a result of the collapse of the double knit textile boom. Prior to the 1960's the double knit industry was small. By the end of 1968, double knitting was an industry in its own right. However, its dynamic growth capacity proved vulnerable. By early 1974, when capacity had reached its highest point, a recession was in progress in the United States. The recession and the Arab oil embargo had a severe adverse effect on the double knit industry. The petroleum based raw materials rose in price. Knitters were forced to sell their goods, which had been produced at all time high costs, at record low prices. By early 1975, the industry, which had approximately 25,000 machines available for production, was able to operate only one-half that number and fabric prices often failed to cover much more than variable costs. As the double knit boom collapsed, Duplan also suffered severe operating losses in the textile segment of its business.

Duplan had, at this time, National Credit Organization's ("NCO") highest rating. But in January 1975, NCO withdrew that rating and at the same time recommended to its subscribers that the extension of trade credit to Duplan be reduced to a limit of $250,000. Shortly thereafter, Dun and Bradstreet refused to rate the credit worthiness of Duplan and NCO withdrew the qualified rating as a result of "the magnitude of the recent past losses coupled with projected unfavorable results".

Duplan relied heavily on bank financing, which grew from $5 million under its 1967 credit agreement to $34.5 million under its 1972 credit agreement. At the end of 1974, the present credit agreement, on a secured basis, was substituted. Duplan was unable to meet the terms of these loans and the agreement was repeatedly amended. The March 31, 1975 amendment authorized borrowing another $10 million on accounts receivable, and was implemented by a factoring agreement with Chemical Bank New York Trust Company, ("Chemical Bank"), one of the lending banks. During this period, Duplan was discussing recapitalization with the lending banks.

In June 1976, management submitted a formal proposal to its bank creditors for a recapitalization. Discussions continued through July 1976 during which time the payment of subordinated indebtedness was delayed. Subordinated notes in the principal sum of $861,000 came due on August 4, 1976.

The interest payment on Duplan's 5¹/₂% convertible subordinated debentures due on August 1, 1976, was not paid. This constituted an event of default under the indenture as well as other loan agreements. Duplan was unable to cure the default within the permissable 30 day period, and this bankruptcy case was commenced on August 31, 1976.

II. THE TRUSTEE'S ADMINISTRATION

When the petition was filed, Duplan included, as divisions, the Rochester Button Company ("RBD"), Duplan Yarn, and the following wholly-owned subsidiaries: Fabrics, Andrex Industries Corp. (which also owned 50% of Complex Industries Corp.), an apparel manufacturer, Laga Industries, Ltd., Wundies, Inc., Kickaway Corporation, Kitchener Button Industries, Ltd. and Lady Suzanne Foundations, Inc.

The product lines at August 31, 1976 were broadly classifiable into four categories: fabrics, yarn, apparel and apparel components. The fabric business consisted of the design, manufacture and sale of fabrics knitted from synthetic yarn and from blends of synthetic and natural fibers. The manufacturing processes encompassed single, double or warp knitting, dyeing and finishing. The fabric business also included the operation of fifteen retail stores engaged in the sale of fabrics and sewing notions and the design and distribution of printed fabrics.

The yarn operation consisted of the mechanical texturing of synthetic bulk yarns which produce a stable woven or knitted fabric used throughout the apparel industry. The apparel business consisted of the manufacture and sale of ladies' and children's underwear and children's sleepwear. The apparel component business consisted principally of the manufacture and sale of a wide variety of plastic buttons for use on apparel.

The Trustee undertook a comprehensive analysis of the textile operations and instituted programs to eliminate duplicate functions and to reduce overhead and, through centralized marketing efforts, to eliminate overlapping lines and to explore alternative markets. Convinced that the textile segment could not be salvaged, all components of the textile and yarn operations were discontinued or liquidated, and the plant and equipment used therein has been disposed of pursuant to court order.

III. ASSETS AND LIABILITIES

Appendix A sets forth the Debtor's assets and liabilities as reflected in its September 30, 1979, audited consolidated balance sheet, summarizes the effect of the liquidations completed after that date, and of the proposed settlement and plan.

About half of the $61.6 million of the consolidated assets is cash or equivalent which will be distributed to creditors. The balance consists of about $26.3 million of assets of the two operating divisions, Wundies and RBD, $2.2 million of deferred payments for properties sold, and not reflected on the balance sheet and related tax benefits.

Table II summarizes the Trustee's operations.

TABLE II
THE DUPLAN CORPORATION
Summary of Consolidated Income
Fiscal Years 1976–1979
(000 omitted)

	10-03-76	10-02-77	10-01-78	09-30-79
Sales-discontinued operations	$75,512	$22,759	$19,200	$13,753
Continuing Operations:				
Net sales	$37,739	$32,686	$37,361	$41,833
Cost of sales	$26,495	$25,671	$27,334	$30,416
Selling, general &				
administrative	8,659	7,558	7,199	7,831
Total	$2,585	$(543)	$2,828	$3,586
Income tax provision[1]	(195)	28	(2,515)	(2,649)
Current interest	(200)[2]	(203)	(151)	(139)
Net	$2,190	$(718)	$162	$798
Interest on long-term[2]	(4,764)	—	—	—
Interest income	416	609	994	2,203
Other adjustments	1,446[3]	—	1,200	—
Discontinued operations	(9,225)	(540)	(794)	1,483
Write-down & sales	(24,353)	1,200	(662)	(291)
Operating loss adjustment	—	—	2,200	3,189
Net income (loss)	$(34,290)	$551	$3,100	$7,382
[1]Current income taxes:				
Discontinued operations	$4	$(507)	$(194)	480
Continuing operations	195	(28)	2,515	2,657
Total	$199	$(535)	$2,321	$3,137
Operating loss adjustment	—	—	(2,200)	(3,189)
Net	$199	$(535)	$121	$(52)

[2]Accrual of interest on most debt ceased on filing this case. We have estimated the comparable portion of 1976 interest.
[3]Gain on repurchase of debentures, December 1975.

The principal cause of action is a lawsuit Duplan began in 1969 against Deering Milliken, Inc., and against a French company, and subsidiaries of each, manufacturers of textile machinery. The plaintiffs were successful on the issue of liability, the court finding that plaintiffs had proven a horizontal antitrust conspiracy. It also found that seven patents were invalid and that the antitrust violation precluded recovery of royalties on others. The issue of damages remains to be tried. Duplan relies primarily on about $4 million of royalty payments it made to defendants. It asserts triple damages and attorney fees under the antitrust laws, estimated at about $14 million. Defendants deny that there are recoverable damages.

The major liabilities are represented by the term bank loans amounting to $38.4 million principal. The subordinated notes, which are privately held, total $6.1 million. They were issued by Duplan in connection with acquisitions. The subordinated debentures, publicly held, amounted to $19.2 million. Total funded debt was as follows:

	Principal	(000 omitted) Pre-bankruptcy Interest	Book Total
Term bank loans	$38,500	$614	$39,114*
Subordinated notes	6,045	60	6,105
5½% convertible sub-ordinated debentures	19,198	616	19,814
	$63,743	$1,290	$65,033

The subordinated notes are subordinated to the bank debt. The debentures are subordinated to both. Claims of trade creditors are estimated at $2.6 million, of which an estimated $500,000 are classified as small claims. The notes and debentures are not subordinated to the trade claims, and the trade claims are not subordinated to anyone.

Duplan has outstanding 2,653,551 shares of common stock. It also has outstanding 8,319 shares of $4 convertible preferred stock, with a liquidation preference of $831,900. As the debtor is insolvent, the plan makes no provision for the preferred and common shares.

In addition to the setoffs, the bank claims that their loans are secured by a security interest through a pledge of stock and security interests in specified real estate and equipment. The $5,021,000 of restricted certificates of deposit, included as cash in Appendix A, represent net proceeds of property sold prior to the balance sheet date, and substituted for the claimed liens.

The banks commenced an adversary proceeding in this case to establish these security interests. Objections were filed by the Reorganization Trustee and the Indenture Trustee for the subordinated debentures. Aside

---

*Reduced to $38,385,000 by allowance of $728,987 of setoffs under the settlement.

from questions of detail, they charged that security interests were invalid or fraudulent conveyances, challenged the banks' status on equitable grounds, and asserted counterclaims. The case has not been tried, and the parties have proposed a compromise, which is included in the Trustee's plan.

IV. SUMMARY OF PLAN

Duplan, as reorganized, will consist, as it is now constituted, of the apparel business (Wundies and Kickaway) and of apparel components (RBD and Kitchener). The reorganized company will be managed by a board of directors consisting of seven members designated by the trustee and subject to court approval.

Administrative costs, principally allowances of compensation to be determined by the court, and tax claims are to be paid in cash from $30 million in cash available for distribution. The balance of the cash, estimated at about $27.6 million, will be distributed to creditors, along with all the common stock valued for purposes of the plan at $27.2 million, at $10 per share. *Since assets are valued at substantially less than $69 million of allowable debt, no participation is provided for the stock. Postbankruptcy interest has not been included.* About four years of post-bankruptcy interest is involved. For solvency purposes, about $100 million in value would be required to provide an equity for the stock. *Consolidated Rock Products Co.* v. *DuBois*, 312 U.S. 510, 527 (1941).

Trade creditors with allowed claims of $3,000 or less, including those who elect to reduce their claims to that amount are to be paid in cash. All other trade creditors will receive cash and stock, as indicated below. Trade creditors of Fabrics are treated as Duplan creditors. That is commonly known as "substantive consolidation". Since they were guaranteed by Duplan, the Fabrics trade claims are contractual claims against Duplan.

The plan incorporates the proposed settlement of the adversary proceeding. The salient features of the compromise are a release of the claimed security interests, and an offer of $6 million (about one-third in cash and two-thirds in new stock), from the banks' agreed share of the estate, to those debenture holders who release their claims against the banks. The banks will retain the pro rata share of the $6 million of those debenture holders who do not execute a release.

Table III below shows the distribution of cash and stock to the creditors. It reflects also the settlement with the banks.

TABLE III
THE DUPLAN CORPORATION
DISTRIBUTION PURSUANT TO TRUSTEE'S PLAN

	No of Creditors	Allowed Claims	Cash Amount	Percent of Claim	Stock Amount	Percent of Claim	Total Amount	Percent of Claim
Bank term loan	4	$38,385	$24,261[1]	63.2	$9,124	23.8	$33,385	87.0
Less: Chemical Bank cession[2]					(1,000)	(2.6)	(1,000)	(2.6)
Net		$38,385	$24,261	63.2	$8,124	21.2	$32,385	84.4
Trade creditors	125*	2,100*	858	40.8	860	41.0	1,718	81.8
Small claims	1,200*	500*	500	100.0			500	100.0
Subordinated notes	24	6,104	—	—	6,104	100.0	6,104	100.0
Subordinated debentures	1,200	19,814	—	—	8,093	40.8	combined below	
Settlement[2]		—	1,981	10.0	4,019	20.3	14,093	71.1
Total		66,903	$27,600	41.3	$27,200	40.6	$54,800	81.9
Reserve for costs			2,200					
Tax claims			200					
Total			$30,000					

*Estimates

[1]Includes $1,773,000 held by Chemical Bank as a claimed setoff.

[2]See text.

V. FAIRNESS AND FEASIBILITY

Chapter X requires that to approve or confirm a plan the court must find the plan "fair, equitable and feasible." There is no question of feasibility in this case. Fairness in this case requires a comparison of the rights of creditors as measured by their claims and what they receive in cash and new securities in exchange for their claims.

Consideration of value is usually an essential part of the issue of fairness. The scope of the necessary valuation depends on the specific issue of fairness that must be resolved. In this case about half of the estate is cash available for distribution which does not require valuation. It is the stock of the reorganized company, valued at $10 per share, that is being used to meet the conflicting claims of four creditor subclasses.

The noteholders have claims totaling about $6.1 million, and under the plan they are to receive common stock valued at that amount, at $10 per share and no cash. It is their contention that the stock is worth less and that a larger percentage of the stock would be required to satisfy their claims. Any additional stock would be necessarily obtained from the debenture holders who are subordinate to them. The noteholders also contend that as paramount or senior creditors they should receive, in lieu of an equivalent amount of stock, $1.98 million in cash that the plan provides for the debenture holders.

A. Valuation

The "value" of a business or property is based on expectations of profit. As the late Judge Frank of the United States Court of Appeals for the Second Circuit observed, "Value is the present worth of future anticipated earnings. It is not directly dependent on past earnings; these latter are important only as a guide in the prediction of future earnings." Thus, to arrive at the value of a debtor's business, prospective earnings are capitalized at a rate derived from market yields on comparable businesses. The Supreme Court has stated that the application of this standard:

> requires a prediction as to what will occur in the future, an estimate, as distinguished from mathematical certitude is all that can be made. But that estimate must be based on an informed judgment which embraces all facts relevant to future earning capacity and hence to present worth, including, of course, the nature and condition of the properties, the past earnings record,

and all circumstances which indicate whether or not that record is a reliable criterion of future performance.*

Bear Stearns & Co., an investment banking firm, was employed by the estate in valuing the debtors. The First Manhattan Company, another investment banker, was retained by a group of subordinated noteholders to review Bear Stearns' report and to form an opinion as to the fair market value of the proposed new common stock. Babian, Coyle & Company ("Coyle"), an accounting firm, was employed by the same group to examine the management forecasts on which Bear Stearns relied, and the tax loss carryover. Irving L. Schwartz, a retired partner of an accounting firm, presently a corporate advisor, was the third expert employed by this group, assigned to value the continuing operations.

All of the testimony relating to going concern value and tax loss was based on forecasts, discussed in Appendix B, of the two operating divisions, Wundies and RBD, prepared by their respective managements. The consolidated forecasts, which exclude nonoperating assets and other extraordinary items, such as costs of this case, may be summarized as follows:

(000's omitted)

12 months ended Sept. 30	Projected Sales	Projected Income	
		before Tax	after Tax†
1980	$44,775	$3,695	$1,995
1981	$51,700	$5,095	$2,750
1982	$58,000	$5,910	$3,190
1983	$64,500	$6,705	$3,620

Bear Stearns concluded that the four-year average of management's projected after-tax earnings of $2,890,000 would be a reasonable estimate of the reorganized company's earning power. The forecast for 1980 allows for an anticipated recession, 1981 is treated as a normal year, and 1982 and 1983 reflect Wundie's expectations of entry into new products. Bear Stearns was impressed by the market positions of both divisions and merchandising concepts of the present operating management of both companies.

To determine the appropriate multiplier, Bear Stearns analyzed the financial and operating results of 15 selected textile/apparel companies for

*Consolidated Rock Products Co. v. Dubois, supra, 312, U.S. at 526.
†Federal income tax.

the years 1974–1978. It characterized the selected companies as having been generally profitable but with volatile earnings, with modest growth in most cases and all in sound financial condition.

The companies selected did not include a company principally engaged in button manufacturing since there appears to be no significant public company of this character. Diversified textile companies manufacture many products, including apparel components, like buttons, sold primarily to apparel manufacturers. The expert's overriding consideration was the selection of a broad range of textile and apparel companies whose historical performance would be relevant to an investor considering an investment in a reorganized Duplan.

For each of the years 1974–1978, Bear Stearns divided the average of the annual high and low market prices of the common shares by the annual earnings per share for each of the 15 companies. For 1979, market quotations through August 31, 1979, and the latest available twelve months earnings were used. A ratio was also computed for the September 10, 1979, market price. The result, produced 80 annual ratios, three of which exceeded ten and two of which are less than three. The average ratios of all companies for each year ranged from 5.1 to 6.3.

At the hearing, Bear Stearns' representative testified that he made allowance for the fact that several of the companies were larger and stronger, with more assets, more efficient plants, and greater diversity and fewer things to go wrong that would affect them as a whole. He stated that the House of Ronnie, with an average ratio 4.9, a direct competitor of Wundies, was more comparable to Duplan. It was Bear Stearns' judgement that a reasonable range of a multiple for Duplan would be four to five times earnings. Applying a multiplier of five to the estimate of annual foreseeable earnings of $2,890,000, Bear Stearns determined that the continuing operations of Duplan had a value of $14,450,000.

The two witnesses for the subordinated noteholders took somewhat different approaches to going-concern valuation. Coyle limited its attention to the earnings projections. It concluded that total after tax earnings for the five years 1979–1983 would be in excess of $3 million less than the projections. The $3 million was apparently based on recomputing the income for both divisions on the assumption that rates of sales growth and ratios of gross profit and overhead expenses to sales, would correspond to historical patterns for 1974–1978, producing pre-tax income reductions of about $3 million for Wundies and $3.2 million for RBD.

Coyle also questioned whether the forecasts for 1980 correctly gauged the duration of the recession and pointed out that costs for the additional facilities which Wundies will require to meet its expected enlarged business after 1981 have not been allowed for. Coyle similarly criticized the omission of interest costs for Wundies recurrent inventory loans. First Manhattan was of the view that the forecasts should not be considered. It valued the going businesses by multiplying 1979 projected earnings, $2,120,000 by five, producing a value of $10.6 million rather than $14.4 million.

B. Tax Loss Carryover and Lawsuit

The tax loss carryover, the subject of an Internal Revenue Service letter ruling, dated January 11, 1980, is estimated at $28,355,000. Duplan also has an investment tax credit carry forward of $448,000. The expiration dates of carryovers, under present law, are:

(000 omitted)

Fiscal Year	Operating Loss Carryover	Investment Tax Credit		
1980	$6,622	1980–1982		$294*
1983	9,475	1983	$50	
1984	6,651	1984	13	
1985	5,607	1985	16	
	$28,355	1986	75	154
				$448

These tax benefits produce value only to the extent that taxable income is realized. The actual saving from operating loss deductions is a percentage of the deduction, i.e., the applicable statutory tax rate at the time it is used, assumed to be 46%. The investment tax credit produces a 100% savings when used.

The Trustee's forecast of the reorganized company's income and income taxes for the years 1980–1983 are:

Year	Income before Taxes	Federal Taxes (46%)	Carry-over Used	Tax Saving
1980	$3,695	$1,700	$3,695	$1,700
1981	5,095	2,345	5,095	2,345

*This credit can be used only if there is a tax, so the $294,000 will probably be lost. A tax savings of $154,000 would be available in 1983 under the forecasts.

Year	Income before Taxes	Federal Taxes (46%)	Carry-over Used	Tax Saving
1982	5,910	2,720	5,910	2,720
1983	6,705	3,085	4,117	1,900
Total	$21,405	$9,850	$18,817	$8,655
Extraordinary items:				
Laga dividend—1980	4,100		4,100	
Deering Milliken recovery	6,500		6,500	
Total	$32,005		$29,417	

Bear Stearns assumed a recovery of $8 million after two years in the Deering Milliken suit less $1.5 million for counsel fees, or a net of $6.5 million before taxes. It used $6.5 million of Duplan's tax loss carry forward to eliminate income taxes on the assumed recovery. At a 15% discount, the present value of that recovery is $5 million (rounded off).

Since the amount of the loss carry forward was subsequently revised to $28,355,000, an adjustment of Bear Stearns' computation is needed.

	(000 omitted)			
Bear Stearns	Income Forecast	Carryover Used	Tax Saving	Present Value
Litigation—1982	$6,500	$6,500	$2,900	$2,261
1980–1983 income	21,405	18,817	8,655	6,130
Revision of carryover		(1,062)	(489)	(280)
Investment tax credit			154	101
Total	$27,905	$24,255	$11,310	$8,212
Laga Dividend—1980	4,100	4,100		
Total carryover	$32,005	$28,355		

The actual benefit to the reorganized company of a taxable litigation recovery is the amount after deduction of taxes. The $6.5 million assumed to be recovered in 1982 would produce $3,510,000 after taxes. The present value of $3,510,000 is $2,654,000, which we will round to $2.7 million.

The trial on damages in the antitrust suit has already been ordered, so Bear Stearns' assumption that it will be resolved by 1982 is not unrealistic. The effect of any delay or reduction in recovery would be to make the realization of the tax savings depend more on operating income. This would not change the amount of the saving, except for the possible loss of $50,000 of the investment tax credit expiring in 1983. It would increase the discount as to the present value by up to $700,000 if no recovery occurred until 1984. Conversely, a settlement in 1980 or 1981 would accelerate realization of the savings and reduce the discount. Valuation of a pending law suit is not amenable to analytical techniques. It is usually avoided by plan provisions for a separate distribution of the recovery, when realized. In this case, we see no particular advantage to that technique.

A case in which a final judgement on liability has already been entered against substantial defendants cannot be dismissed as too speculative or contingent to consider. Debtor's asserted actual damages of about $4 million seem to be germane to the legal theories which led to the affirmed finding that defendants were guilty of an unlawful conspiracy involving misuse of patents. It would be rash to leap to the conclusion that $12 million of treble damages are practically money in the bank. Another trial lies ahead involving inevitable delay and possible surprises. But inclusion of a tax adjusted and discounted $2.7 million in the assets expected to accrue to the new stockholders appears to be a sufficient allowance for the remaining contingencies.

C. Value of Duplan (Reorganized)

The following table shows the value of the reorganized company as arrived at by Bear Stearns and First Manhattan.

	(000 omitted) Bear Stearns	Adjusted	First Manhattan
Capitalized Earnings	$14,450	$14,450	$10,600
Tax Savings	6,130	8,212*	5,000
Long-term receivables	1,610	1,610	1,300
	$22,190	$24,272	$16,900
Deering Milliken suit	5,000	2,700*	zero to
Total	$27,190	$26,972	$2.5 million

The valuation of the ongoing business and of the prospective tax savings must be considered together, since both depend on the income forecasts. We discuss those forecasts in some detail in Appendix B, and our conclusion as to the reorganized company's consolidated earnings poten-

*Our corrections are explained in the prior two tables.

tial does not differ significantly from that of Bear Stearns. We accept Bear Stearns' conclusion as to both an annual after tax earnings of about $2.9 million and its computation of the related tax savings, as stated above.

The capital value of Duplan's common stock is expressed as a times-earnings multiple of income. A multiple of five, for example, means a 20% annual return or yield on the investment. The expected yield differs according to the kind and quality of the investment, since it reflects the risks and uncertainties as to what the actual earnings will be.

The times-earnings multiplier is linked to actual market values by looking to the relationship between market price and earnings of comparable investments, as Bear Stearns did. Here again, the reorganization valuation process conforms to standard methods of investment decision making. Prices actually being paid for equivalent commodities are the best evidence of the yield that should be employed in determining current capital values of projected income.

We do not agree with Bear Stearns' choice of a multiple of five for the reorganized company. Of the 15 companies surveyed, only three indicated price/earnings ratios persistently below that level, and nine were above during the six years examined. Bear Stearns' conclusion that this table, which showed a 1974–1978 industry range of 5.4 to 6.3, "indicates a remarkably stable price/earnings ratio for the textile/apparel companies of about five times earnings," is correct as to the stability but, on its face, the words "about five times" are used rather loosely.

Its qualitative comments about the reorganized company are not in harmony with its decision to place it close to the bottom. Bear Stearns testified:

> "You have a comparison of textile companies which suggest that five times would be that for a normal textile company, but this isn't a normal textile company. First it is a company with no debt; secondly, its a company that is going to generate a lot of cash because it does not have any capital expenditures to make; it is going to generate a lot of cash because it has non-operating assets, which is going to bring cash back over the next few years."

Its report stated, (p. 6):

> "We were impressed by the market positions of both Rochester Button and Wundies, the business strategy and merchandising concepts of the present operating managements of both companies, and based on their continuation the achievement of the projections appear reasonable."

Another factor to which Bear Stearns refers, is the essentially debt free capital structure of the reorganized company. Price/earnings ratios for common stock assign a market value to a company's common equity. If its capital structure includes a significant amount of senior securities, the value of the enterprise is not identical with the value of its common stock. The senior securities obviously have to be taken into account in determining how much the business is worth, and the amount and kind of senior securities have a direct effect on the quality of the common stock and on its price/earnings ratio.

Careful attention to capital structure is, therefore, an elementary part of valuation technique in industries, such as railroads, utilities and real estate, where senior financing is a significant feature of the business. Bear Stearns reviewed the structure of each of the comparable companies, and found varying levels of funded debt. Eight had debt in the 24–34% range, four in the 13–19% range and only two below 10%. Bear Stearns' qualitative conclusion that this is one of the strengths of reorganized Duplan is firmly based on the record. But it failed to implement that conclusion in its choice of the multiple.

One method of assessing the effect of senior securities is to add debt and common stock value (price x number of shares), and express this sum as a multiple of interest and net income, and then compare this multiple with the common stock price/earnings ratio. Our computation (Appendix C) indicates a reasonably consistent company by company variation when senior capital is taken into account:

	Average		
	1976	1977	1978
Multiple (Value ÷ Total Return)	7.2	7.2	6.5
Price/earnings	6.1	5.7	5.4

First Manhattan, as witness for the subordinated noteholders, has taken an entirely different view of valuation by shifting the focus to the market value of the new Duplan stock. It would apply a multiple of five, not to prospective earnings but only to 1979 historical income. If the reorganization occurs in 1980, only the 1979 income will be available to the market. First Manhattan states that, if values are to reflect prospective earnings in subsequent years, then such future earnings should be discounted to their present worth.

This approach, which would make historical income and its reflection in the market place the foundation of reorganization values, is contrary to established criteria, under which, as announced by the Supreme Court, reorganization values rest on prospective earnings. A debtor, by definition, enters the bankruptcy court in distressed condition. Drastic changes are often made, as in the case of Duplan, and the plan of reorganization is the promise of its financial rehabilitation. The value of its new securities, in this case Duplan's common stock, must be based on its prospective income as a reorganized company.

In bankruptcy reorganization, if a creditor is offered new securities, fairness "requires a comparison of the new securities allotted to him with the old securities which he exchanges to determine whether the new are the equitable equivalent of the old." When a creditor exchanges his claim for stock, whose equivalence in value reflects current yields, the capitalized value of the stock represents the investment value of an income stream that the reorganized company may be expected to produce. It is not meant to be the cash equivalent to be measured by the market price of the stock which has yet to be issued by a debtor about to take its leave of the bankruptcy court.

The Deering Milliken suit recovery will be cash and income for the new stock when it is received. Since both the amount and time of recovery are uncertain, it is not now the kind of asset that can be readily translated into stock market prices. But the recovery itself, whatever the amount, will present no such difficulties. Bear Stearns made very liberal allowances for the contingency and delay and valued it, after taxes, at $1 a new share.

In light of the foregoing, we are satisfied that Bear Stearns' valuation of the reorganized company, except its earnings multiplier, gave adequate weight to all relevant factors. The record supports a multiplier of six rather that five, a change which would increase the value of the new stock to about $30 million.

As we said, the issue before the court is the fairness and equity of the plan and of the proposed settlement it embodies. The substantive significance of the value of the reorganized company in this case arises in a complicated way from the interrelationships of the various groups of creditors. Those relationships in turn are affected by the proposed settlement, which is expressly conditioned on a specific assumption of $10 per share. We conclude, as indicated below, that two features of the proposed settlement require revision. The necessary amendments to the plan will have to be negotiated and presumably will take the form of a revision of the proposed distributions of both the cash and the stock. It is the substantive fairness of such distributions, not the method of computation, on which the court is required to rule.

D. Settlements and Distribution under the Plan

The plan allocates available cash and the new stock for distribution to creditors. After payment of estimated costs of administration, tax claims and small claims ($2.9 million), the proposed net distribution to creditors is $27.1 million in cash and 2,720,000 shares of stock, valued at $10 per share, or 27.2 million. This total distribution of $54.3 million to creditors is for allowed and settled claims of $66.4 million. The distribution in cash and stock, as a percentage of allowed and settled claims, is as follows:

	Percent		
	Cash	Stock	Total
Banks	63.2	21.2	84.4
Trade creditors	40.8	41.0	81.8
Subordinated noteholders	—	100.0	100.0
Subordinated debenture holders	10.0	61.1	71.1

The overall distribution amounts to 41.3% of the claims in cash and 40.6% in new stock.

The plan, as noted, assumes $27.1 million cash will be available for the four groups of unsecured creditors. The record indicates the availability of about $2 million in additional cash. This, among other things, should permit, as discussed below, eliminating unfairness of the settlement by substitution of some cash for stock allotted to the subordinated noteholders.

The Trustee has accumulated, largely as a result of the liquidation of several divisions, over $30 million in cash. This sum includes about $6.8 million, including the factoring account held by Chemical Bank, in which security interests are claimed by the banks but which are made available for unsecured creditors under the proposed compromise. The pro forma cash at September 30, 1979, is $30,643,000, including the factoring account. The working balances of the operating divisions were $1,227,000, leaving $29,416,000 available for distribution. All of the available cash is in interest bearing accounts or certificates, at rates ranging in January 1980 from 10% to 14-1/4%.

Since, as shown in Appendix B, the operating divisions are self supporting, none of the accumulated cash is required as working capital for these divisions. This includes the interest income which will be earned on the deposits before consummation. Interest income for the 6 months ended March 31, 1980 is forecast at $1,677,000. Earnings on the January balances were estimated at the rate of $300,000 a month. Allowing for compounding and the interest on the installment receivables, about $2.6

million will be added from this source by June 30, 1980. Adding the $2.6 million of post September 30, 1979 interest to the $29.4 million of September 30, 1979, cash and equivalent, produces $32 million of available cash, rather than $30 million proposed by the plan.

E. Disputed Claims and Proposed Settlements

Compromises are a normal and essential part of the reorganization process, and as such also require an informed, independent determination by the District Judge that each compromise is fair and equitable. In this context, fairness and equity require the exercise of judgment as to the strengths and weaknesses of the claims being compromised, the probabilities of success, and the benefits and risks flowing to all affected interests from the proposed settlement. But, although the court must apprise itself of the probabilities of ultimate success should disputed issues be litigated, the court is not required to pass on the ultimate merit of those issues.

It must be noted that of the parties affected by the proposed compromise, only the four members of the bank group have actually assented to the terms. The trade creditors and debenture holders are numerous and unanimous agreement by them is most unlikely, and the noteholders have, so far, actively opposed the settlement. Judicial review of the issues is essential.

Effect of the Settlement

The settlement extends to all issues in the case. The range of recovery or distribution to the banks, as noted, was between 68% and 100%, depending on their total victory or defeat in the controversies raised by their claims. The settlement proposes a compromise at about midway between these limits, at 84.4%. The banks waive their security interests. The Trustee abandons the preference claims and counterclaims and recognizes the banks' setoffs for $728,987 out of $2.5 million claimed by the banks, and Chemical Bank waives its claims to setoff $1,773,000 held in the factoring accounts. The banks, including Chemical Bank, are offering the debenture holders $6 million in settlement of their claims for breach of trust to them. The subordination agreements relating to the status of the bank claims remain in effect and are recognized for determining the distribution under the plan.

The overall distribution proposed by the plan, giving effect to the settlement, is as follows:

In Millions

	Bank Claims	Trade Claims	Subor- dinated Notes	Subor- dinated Deben- tures	Total
Allowed claim	$38.4	$2.1	$6.1	$19.8	$66.4
%	57.83	3.16	9.19	29.82	100.0
Pro rata distribution	$31.4	1.7	$5.0	$16.2	$54.3
Subordination adjustment	7.0	—	1.1	(8.1)	—
Proposed offer to debenture holders	(6.0)			6.0	—
Total	$32.4	$1.7	$6.1	$14.1	$54.3

The subordination clauses do not affect the trade creditors. The subordinated noteholders, with claims of $6.1 million, are compensated in full. Since the debenture holders are subordinated to them as well as to the banks, the debenture holders' pro rata distribution is reduced by amounts necessary to pay them in full. The offer by the banks to the debenture holders reduces the net distribution to the banks from $38.4 million to $32.4 million.

The plan in this case provides for distribution of cash and common stock, so subordination has special effects upon the distribution. When the value of the estate is sufficient to provide a participation for subordinated creditors, the effect of that subordination is to capture for the senior or paramount creditors the cash distribution that, without subordination, creditors would share, pro rata, as equals. The senior creditors retain so much of the stock as is required for full compensation. Any excess is reallocated to the subordinated noteholders, to whom the debenture holders are subordinated (absolute priority doctrine).

The previous table of distribution under the plan is here restated to reflect the distribution in terms of cash and stock.

In Millions

	Bank Claims	Trade Claims	Subor- dinated Notes	Subor- dinated Deben- tures	Total
Cash pro rata	$15.7	$0.8	$2.5	$8.1	$27.1
Subordination	10.6		(2.5)	(8.1)	—
Total	$26.3	0.8	—	—	$27.1

In Millions

	Bank Claims	Trade Claims	Subor- dinated Notes	Subor- dinated Deben- tures	Total
Stock pro rata	15.7	0.9	2.5	8.1	27.2
Excess over claim	(3.6)		(3.6)	—	
Total	$38.4	$1.7	$6.1	$8.1	$54.3
% of claim	100.0	81.8	100.0	40.9	81.8
Settlement:					
Total distribution	$38.4	$1.7	$6.1	$8.1	$54.3
Offer to debentures	(6.0)			6.0	—
	32.4	1.7	6.1	14.1	54.3
% of claim	84.4	81.8	100.0	71.2	81.7

The banks are the largest group of creditors. In the settlement they have made major concessions by their waiver of liens and setoffs and concessions to the debenture holders consisting of $2 million in cash and $4 million in stock (as shown in Table III). The settlement agreement, as noted, is an offer by the banks for a release of the personal claims asserted against them by the successor indenture Trustee on behalf of the debenture holders. We note only that the debenture holders would receive the $4 million in stock even if some of the stock was treated as part of a settlement of the estate's claims against the banks.

The banks are allotted $7 million of the debenture holders pro rata share of the new stock by virtue of the debenture holders' subordination, as tabulated above. Assuming arguendo that their return of $4 million of that stock to the debenture holders should be attributed solely to the defenses asserted by the Reorganization Trustee, neither the subordinated noteholders nor the trade creditors would have any basis for sharing therein. The noteholders were not adversely affected by the enforcement of the subordination. On the contrary, they receive and keep $1.1 million of stock from the debenture holders on the same basis to cover their full deficiency. And the trade creditors receive their full pro rata share of the estate, not being involved in any phase of the subordination.

The treatment of the subordinated noteholders under the settlement is nonetheless unfair. As shown above, their subordination had no effect on their total distribution. But it had a radical effect on their interest in the available cash, reducing their pro rata share of $2.5 million, 41% of their claims, to zero. The proposed settlement is based on continued full enforcement of the subordination by the banks against the noteholders. As to them it is tantamount to total abandonment of the estate's claims, rather than a settlement.

In fairness to the subordinated noteholders, the settlement should be renegotiated to provide for some appropriate cash distribution to them. As we have noted, there is about $2 million in cash available for distribution in addition to the $30 million for which the plan provides.

The plan, however, should be amended as it relates to dissenters. If debenture holders holding two-thirds in amount of the claims vote for the plan, the plan is binding upon the entire class, including those who did not vote or voted against the plan. These dissenters will receive only their share of the $8.1 million in common stock that the plan provides for them as creditors of Duplan, but, their share of the $6 million settlement would be kept by the banks. This in effect would be a forfeiture of the recovery by anyone who fails to sign an acceptance for whatever reason.

Such a forefeiture is not necessary or justified. The banks are entitled to protection against suit. But when a substantial majority votes for the plan, suit by a minority of dissenters is highly unlikely. Nonetheless, they are entitled to be free from mischief and nuisance, against which a release provides immediate immunity. Deferral of distribution to those who fail to supply the release is proper until that protection is otherwise supplied. For that purpose, forfeiture is too strong a remedy. Distribution to dissenters when the time for bringing suit is legally at an end should be sufficient.

APPENDIX A
THE DUPLAN CORPORATION
Consolidated Balance Sheet
September 30, 1979
(000 omitted)

	Consolidated	Liquidations[1]	Adjustments[2]	Cash Distribution	Unpaid Claims	New Stock
Cash & Equivalent	$27,547[1]	$1,323	$1,773[2]	$(30,000)		
Receivables	8,876					
Inventories	9,527					
Pre-paid expenses	253					
Continuing operations	$46,203					
Current assets-discontinued	1,483	(1,483)	—			
Property held for sale	732	(732)	—			
Other receivables & deposits	2,269	—	—			
Plant & equipment-net	5,103		—			
Other assets	235	(4)	—			
Bank setoffs	2,502	—	(2,502)[2]			
Acquisition adjustments	1,586	—	—			
Deferred costs of case	1,263	—	(1,263)			
Debenture discount	249		(249)			
Total assets	$61,625	$(896)	$(2,241)	$(30,000)		
Current liabilities	$3,496	$(307)	$—	$—		
Reserves:						
Administrative costs	500	—	1,700	(2,200)		
Discontinued operations	161	(161)	—	—		

(Continued)

APPENDIX A (Continued)

	Consolidated	Liquidations[1]	Adjustments[2]	Cash Distribution	Unpaid Claims	New Stock
Long-term debt-Wundies	1,909	—	—	—		
Unaffected liabilities	$6,066	$(468)	$1,700	$(2,200)		
Liabilities deferred by case:						
Taxes	143		57	(200)		
Small claims	—		500	(500)		
Other trade creditors	2,567		(467)	(858)	$(1,242)	860
Term bank loans	39,114		(729)[2]	(24,261)	(14,124)	8,124
Subordinated notes	6,105		—	—	(6,105)	6,104
Subordinated debentures	19,814		—	(1,981)	(17,833)	12,112
Inter-company	—		—	—	—	—
Total liabilities	$73,809	$(468)	$1,061	$(30,000)	$(39,304)	$27,200
Equity (deficit)	$(12,184)	(428)	(3,302)	—	39,304	—
Total	$61,625	$(896)	$(2,241)	$(30,000)	$0	$27,200

[1] As computed by Bear Stearns.
[2] As computed by the Commission.

APPENDIX B

DESCRIPTION OF CONTINUING OPERATIONS

1. Wundies Inc. and Kickaway Corporation

Wundies, founded in 1948, and acquired by Duplan in 1968, manufactures women's and children's panties and children's sleepwear, and has recently begun to produce a line of thermal undergarments for women and children. Wundies' products are manufactured for approximately 500 retailers located throughout the United States. Customers are primarily discount stores, chain stores, department stores and mail order houses. K-Mart is the largest customer and accounted for 12% of the consolidated sales for fiscal 1979. Management believes that Wundies is one of the largest domestic manufacturers of children's underwear and sleepwear, and that it is the largest single supplier of girls' underwear to the discount stores.

There are presently approximately 770 employees. Although there is relatively little seasonality to the manufacturing operation, inventories of finished goods reach a peak prior to the back-to-school season.

Competition is keen and comes from both domestic and foreign sources, although the latter is not considered a serious threat primarily because the imported garments are limited as to choice of fabrics and trim utilized. Management believes that its recently expanded manufacturing facilities and anticipated expansion to meet production goals beyond 1981, will enable Wundies to maintain or increase its position in its established lines, and to substantially expand its production and sales in the women's and children's thermal underwear market.

The following table shows actual results of operations for the four years ended September 30, 1979, and projected results for the four years ended September 30, 1983, as prepared by Duplan. The historical data was adjusted to eliminate an intercompany charge based on a percentage of net assets. We have computed the percentages shown.

Management projected annual results assuming compound inflation factors of 6% for sales and 7% for selling, general and administrative expenses. Projected gross profit margins of approximately 20.5% were assumed based on experience prior to 1978.

During the plan hearings in October 1979, Banner, Wundies' chief executive, testified that, considering the possibility of recession, he felt that the projected sales of $24 million for 1980 might be reduced by 10% and that as a result net income for that year would be reduced 20%. He said, however, he would reassess his opinions during January. During the hearing in January, he stated that for the first quarter of fiscal 1980 actual sales were 8% above the original budget and 15% above the like quarter of the prior year. Based on these results, he felt that the original projected sales of $24 million would be achieved.

For the first three months of the current fiscal year, reported sales were 22.4% above the like period of the prior year. Net income for the 1980 period was 22.2% higher than the prior year period, due primarily to the increased sales.

WUNDIES AND KICKAWAY
SALES AND INCOME
(000 omitted)

Fiscal Year	Net Sales	Gross Profit		Selling General & Administrative Expenses		Interest, Income & Expenses— Net	State Income Tax	Income before Taxes
		Amount	Percent	Amount	Percent			
Actual								
1976	$14,186	$2,905	20.5	$1,663	11.7	$6	$(79)	$1,169
1977	15,142	3,019	19.9	1,767	11.7	33	(77)	1,208
1978	18,272	4,178	22.9	2,362	12.9	84	(104)	1,796
1979	21,014	4,707	22.4	2,211	10.5	105	(101)	2,500
Projected								
1980	$24,000	$4,926	20.5	$2,331	9.7		$(160)	$2,435
1981	27,000	5,541	20.5	2,594	9.6		(180)	2,767
1982	31,000	6,373	20.6	2,859	9.2		(215)	3,299
1983	35,000	7,193	20.6	3,158	9.0		(250)	3,785

APPENDIX C

COMPARISON OF HISTORICAL PRICE/EARNINGS RATIOS[1] AND ENTERPRISE MULTIPLIERS[2] OF SELECTED TEXTILE/APPAREL COMPANIES[3], 1976—1978

	Debt Ratio Percent	1976		1977		1978	
		P/E Ratio	Firm Multi-plier	P/E Ratio	Firm Multi-plier	P/E Ratio	Firm Multi-plier
Adams Mills	13	8.2	9.7	5.1	6.4	8.6	9.2
Belding Hemingway	25	9.1	9.7	10.1	10.5	6.3	7.1
Collins & Aikman	10	7.9	7.6	6.2	8.6	5.6	7.2
Dan River	32	4.5	7.0	6.2	8.5	5.6	7.4
Fab Industries	4	4.0	4.7	3.4	3.8	3.8	3.5
Guilford Mills	28	3.4	5.0	3.9	5.2	3.0	3.1
House of Ronnie	8	6.1	7.1	4.8	6.1	4.4	5.4
Riegel Textile	26	4.6	5.3	5.9	6.8	6.0	7.2
Spring Mills	15	6.9	9.0	6.1	8.9	5.1	8.1
Average P/E Ratios Multipliers		6.1	7.2	5.7	7.2	5.4	6.5

[1]As computed by Bear Stearns.

[2]As computed by the Commission.

[3]Bear Stearns' selection consisted of 15 companies. For the purpose of this schedule the following have been excluded for lack of comparability: Burlington Industries, Stevens (J.P.) and West Point-Pepperell (huge size and brand diversification); Concord Fabrics, M. Lowenstein and National Spinning (record of losses during test period).

2 Aggregate Influences on Business Failure Rates

INTRODUCTION

The business failure phenomenon has received increased attention in the literature in the last decade. As we discussed in Chapter 1, in recent years, over 40,000 firms per year petitioned the courts to liquidate or to reorganize under the bankruptcy act. A good deal of the recent interest in business failures has resulted from the number of large firms which have succumbed to this negative economic reality. Prior to 1970, firms with assets of more than $25 million almost never failed. Since 1970, more than 35 nonfinancial firms with assets over $125 million have failed, topped by the Penn Central debacle. The costs to society of large firm bankruptcies have been cited and debated in the popular press; frequently mentioned are Chrysler Corp.'s problems and government loan guarantees (1979–81), and more recently the International Harvester crisis.

The importance of microeconomic issues and the attendant large number of analytical studies (see Chapters 3 and 4) have obscured the relevance and influence of macroeconomic influences on the business failure phenomenon. It is argued, however, that certain aggregate measures and macroeconomic conditions are closely associated with the causes of business failure and contribute to the fact that marginally continuing enterprises are forced to declare bankruptcy or are unable to continue as going concerns.

The primary purpose of this chapter is to examine the aggregate economic influences on business failure experience. We will primarily be concerned with the failure rate in the United States, that is, the number of business failures recorded per 10,000 firms covered by Dun & Bradstreet (the most comprehensive and continuous failure time series). A quarterly, first difference, distributed lag regression model is constructed to achieve our objectives. In doing so, we will be guided by some rather intuitive economic relationships and the work performed by the National Bureau of Economic Research in the area of business cycle analysis and economic indicators. Business failure had been classified as a fairly consistent leading indicator of recessions and somewhat less reliable, but still leading, for recovery periods. However, it no longer is considered one of the nation's leading indicators. The work discussed in this chapter has formed the basis of my econometric business failure rate forecasts found in *Business Week,* (March 24, 1980, p. 98, and April 29, 1982, p. 20).

I am aware of just a few published studies relating to macroeconomic influences on bankruptcies in the United States: Noto and Zimmerman (1980, 1981), and, for Britain and Japan, Cumming and Saini (1981). For more details of the work discussed below, see Altman (1980).

VARIABLE SPECIFICATION

We will attempt to analyze the change in aggregate business failure experience in the United States. Our dependent variable will be the change in the business failure rate (BFR) as compiled by D&B over the period 1951–1978. For statistical reasons, discussed later, we specify the model in a first difference form.

The primary theme which will guide us in our choice of explanatory variables is exacerbating pressures on the marginal firm, that is, what

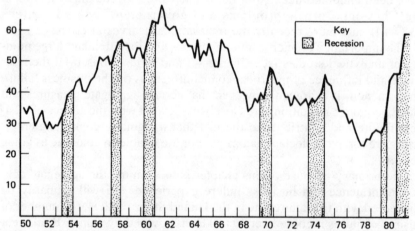

Chart 2-1   Business Failure Rate per 10,000 Firms: Quarterly 1950–1981. (*Source:* Dun & Bradstreet, *Business Failure Record* and *Dun's Review.*)

conditions, at the aggregate level, can be expected to impact upon a firm's propensity to continue. The following categories of aggregate economic behavior are specified as potentially revealing indicators of business failure:

1   Economic growth activity
2   Credit availability or money market activity
3   Capital market activity
4   Business population characteristics
5   Price level changes

Economic Growth

Interest in business failure is usually heightened during periods of economic stress. Stress is most devastating to vulnerable entities, and we can expect that business failure and low or negative economic growth are closely associated economic series. Chart 2-1 presents quarterly business failure rates from 1950 through the last quarter of 1981. Recessionary periods are indicated as well, and we observe increases in failure rates during these phases.

Sales and earnings of individual enterprises are directly related to overall business activity, and we should expect a negative correlation between series which reflect the nation's economic health and business failures. A related factor is the timing specification between economic activity and failure. On the one hand, we might specify that business failures will lead to changes in aggregate activity since the failure rate has often been referred to as a leading indicator of business cycle changes. On the other hand, we would also expect that the accumulation of negative aggregate activity will heighten pressures on all firms, particularly on those most vulnerable. Therefore, a distributed-lag model could provide a more effective structural specification.

The two series chosen to reflect economic growth are real GNP and corporate profits. Both are aggregate series which indicate total sales and profit experience of the individual entities which make up the market. Growth in GNP is traditionally viewed as an overall indicator of national economic health and an important measuring tool for economic analysts. The relationship between corporate profits and failures is well documented in business cycle measurement. Conditions leading to a change in profits are logically related to failures since a slight drop in profits to the marginal firm is often critical to its continued existence.

Money Market and Credit Conditions

One of the more lively current economic debates concerns the effect that the nation's monetary stock has on our economic conditions. In the case of the potential failing firm the argument is quite clear. Money, or more specifically credit availability and its cost, most certainly does matter. The typical chain of events in a failing firm begins with operating difficulties manifesting in losses and/or deteriorating market share. The firm's vulnerability is often magnified by relatively high financial and/or operating leverage structures. Since the capital markets are usually unavailable to firms whose solvency is threatened (see discussion below), and suppliers may be reluctant to increase their exposure, a critical source of credit is commercial banks. Regardless of how poorly a firm is performing, it seldom is "motivated" to declare bankruptcy as long as liquidity is sufficient or credit is available. Therefore, we can expect that the propensity to fail will be increased during periods of relatively tight credit conditions vis-à-vis periods of easy credit.

Compounding this problem is the seemingly discriminatory policy against smaller concerns during periods of tight money. Since the great majority of failures are small firms, the so-called small business "credit rationing" effect, which is alleged to occur during tight money conditions, is potentially an important influence on the total failure experience of U.S. businesses. The hypothesized relationship between credit availability and business failures is therefore inverse. Measures which we choose to reflect credit and liquidity conditions are the nation's monetary stock, free reserves, and interest rates.

Credit conditions are affected by the combined forces of supply and demand for funds as well as the monetary policy being pursued by the Federal Reserve System. In this chapter, we attempt to observe an economic consequence of adjusting the money supply. Previously mentioned reasons for attempting to adjust the supply of money and credit concern overall economic growth goals, the containment of price inflation, and balance of payments problems. Related to the overall consequence of shifts in money supply are the costs (or gains) of increasing (decreasing) business failures. Whether or not monetary policy manifestations are associated with individual firm failures will be examined. Cumming and Saini (1981) found that the interest cost burden was statistically significant for Japan and the United Kingdom, indicating that restrictive monetary policy may be an important determinant of bankruptcy change.

The two other cited measures of money market conditions—free reserves and interest rates—are probably less consistent in their relationship to credit conditions. Both may be looked upon as transmitters of Federal Reserve action. We did examine these measures as well.

Investor Expectations

The potential failing firm is not likely to take the necessary steps of voluntary failure "declaration" if the future appears hopeful. This is logical whether the optimism is manifest internally or from forces external to the firm. One sector of external influence is the investment community's expectations which are reflected in the prices paid for financial asset ownership. The relationship between common stock prices and business failures is predicated on both empirical and theoretical grounds. Empirically, business cycle analysts had, for many years, reported that business failures and stock prices were both leading indicators of cyclical turning points. The fact that we observe these two aggregate series moving together periodically, with both indicating changes in future economic activity, is interesting but not necessarily indicative of a causal relationship. Both are likely to be related to a third factor—expected economic conditions—and therefore their mutual association is not clearly direct.

A case could be made for a more direct relationship between stock prices and failures if we consider that the definition of insolvency in bankruptcy is the situation where the firm's liabilities exceed the economic value of its assets. An accurate indicator of just how much of a fall in asset value is necessary before this insolvency situation is manifest is the market value of the equity in a firm as a percentage of its debt (MV/D). A MV/D ratio of 0.25 indicates that the company's asset values can only fall 20% before insolvency occurs. The argument here is that market values, in a fairly accurate way, reflect economic values. A drop in the growth of overall stock prices affects most firms, but it can be crucial to the existence of a marginal firm. The failure symptoms may have been present in the firm for some time, yet the decision to liquidate or reorganize in bankruptcy is rarely invoked while the firm's equity is still selling at some tangible positive value. Therefore, the drop in stock price to some negligible value is the "immediate" cause of failure. This is more likely to occur in a bear market than in more favorable stock market conditions. We utilize the MV/D measure again in the Z-score model (Chapter 3).

In order to reflect overall stock market performance, we choose the change in the Standard & Poor (S&P) index of stock prices. The major reasons for this choice are the relative comprehensiveness of this index and the availability of quarterly observations during the entire post-World War II period. Since most firms that fail are not listed corporations, the use of the S&P index is a proxy for investor expectations. Also, the S&P index is the one utilized by the National Bureau of Economic Research as one of their economic indicators.

A second type of investor expectation variable which may have some relationship with business failures is a risk premium measure. All financial instruments except risk-free assets contain an element of risk which is reflected in the yield which investors require. The difference between this yield and the risk-free rate is the risk premium, and the more risky the security, the greater the risk premium. Although we do observe a stable ordinal relationship between rates of return on various risky assets over time, this by no means implies that the yield differential is numerically stable. Indeed, we find greater fluctuations in yield in the relatively high-risk securities.

The above phenomenon is possibly reflected in the relationship between the yield on the highest grade corporate fixed-income bonds and the yield on more risky bonds. We have chosen the differential between *Moody's* Aaa and Baa bonds. During stable times, we hypothesize that this differential is relatively small, and it increases as investors become less optimistic as to the ability of some firms to fulfill their financial obligations. While the credit risk component of all *rates* is expected to rise as future conditions become less certain, the expected increase in that component rate on the more risky securities is greater. Therefore, the absolute differential should increase during, or perhaps slightly before, periods of increased uncertainty. Since we also expect to experience an increase in failure rates in these periods, the hypothesized relationship between our "risk premium" variable and the failure series is positive. We are aware that risk premiums may be associated with several of the other explanatory variables specified earlier and do not expect that all will appear together in our multivariate model.

Business Population Statistics

The time series association between the change in business failures and the change in business population statistics is both obvious and somewhat subtle. On the one hand, increased business formation can be thought of as coincident with positive profit expectations. We would expect that the failure *rate* would diminish due to fewer failures and a larger business population. The latter *coincident* association would probably preclude econometric interpretation since the dependent and independent variables would be impacted simultaneously. Still, when we observe the frequency distribution of failures with respect to the age of the firm, aggregate data show quite clearly that over one-half of all failures occur within

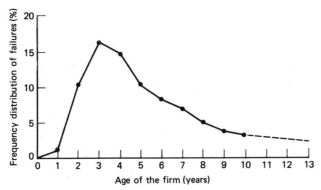

Chart 2-2   Frequency Distribution of Failures versus Age of the Firm.

a firm's first five years and almost one-third within three years. The young firm is usually a marginal operation and is one type of vulnerable entity which we are concerned with in this study. See the discussion in Chapter 1 on age of failed firms.

On closer inspection, we find that there is a relative distribution of failures versus age of the firm which is quite interesting (Chart 2-2). It takes some time for a firm actually to fail, and so failures of firms in their *initial year* are relatively infrequent (1% of all failing firms go out of business in their first year). The second year, however, shows a marked increase in failure propensity to 10.5% and the third year the rate is 16%. We observe a rather flat but high propensity to fail until the firm's seventh year, and then the frequency tails off. As one would expect, at some point the older the firm the less likely it is to fail since it has an established position. In our econometric examination to follow, we will include the change in new business formation as one of our potentially important explanatory variables, but the lagged relationship between it and the change in failure rate will not be coincident at its beginning point. That is, we postulate that new business formation leads business failures by a substantial amount of time. As we postulated in Chapter 1, the relatively large net business formation rate in 1976 through 1979 may have contributed to the rise in failures from 1980 into 1982.

Price Level Changes

In recent years, the nation's most disturbing economic problem has been the rate of inflation. Despite the debilitating overall effects of consistent and sizable price level increases, a case can be made for their "positive" short-term impact upon a firm's propensity to survive; that is, increases in prices, especially unanticipated increases, tend to be inversely correlated with failure rates.

Poorly managed companies may be kept afloat for a longer period of time during unanticipated price increases since these firms tend to be highly leveraged and are able to repay their debts with "cheaper" money. This so-called net monetary debtor-creditor theory (Alchian-Kessel, 1955) could have accounted for lower failure rates, for example, in the late 1970s and it might continue, *ceteris paribus*, as long as lenders settle for interest charges which eventually prove to be lower than the rate of inflation. (There are indications that interest rates in early 1980, e.g., prime rates over 20%, were adjusting for recent past underestimates.)

It can also be argued that inflation helps marginal companies by reducing competitiveness and protecting inefficiency. Price level increases are more easily passed through to the consumer during rising price level periods and perhaps can aid the firm selling inferior goods. Reported profits of all firms appear more attractive due to "inventory earnings" and depreciation rates are unrealistically low—hence higher earnings. To the extent that lending institutions assess these earnings in their credit analysis, the chances of a favorable extension of credit is perhaps greater.

ECONOMETRIC STRUCTURE OF THE MODEL

Aggregate influences on the business failure rate will be analyzed within first difference, quarterly, regression models with emphasis on the distributed lag properties of a number of explanatory variables. The specified structure of the model will combine both first degree and second degree polynomials (Almon, 1965) of the form

$$Y_t = \alpha + \beta \, (W_0 \Delta X_t + W_1 \Delta X_{t-1} + W_2 \Delta X_{t-2} \cdots W_n \Delta X_{t-n}) + \epsilon_t$$

for a set of independent variables X, assuming that:

$$W_i = C_0 + C_1 i + C_2 i^2; \; i = 0, 1, 2, 3, \ldots n$$

where

Y_t = change in the business failure rate (BFR) in period t,

X_1 = percentage change in real GNP (RLGNP),

X_2 = percentage change in the money supply (M_2),

X_3 = percentage change in the Standard & Poor index (S&P), and

X_4 = percentage change in new business formation (NEWINC).

We use percentage changes for our independent variables to adjust for scale effects over time.

Before examining our estimated results, we should discuss the nature of the model's structure. We do expect that our specified explanatory variables will have a significant coincident association with the business failure rate, but there is likely to be greater information inherent in cumulative or distributed lag structure. Firms usually fail after a number of internal and external pressures build up and finally the fragile entity bursts.

While a geometric lag, that is, a declining set of lagged weights, is quite useful, it is limited in its range of potential uses. The more general polynomial distributed lag structure assumes that the lagged weights can be specified by a continuous function. The polynomial function can be approximated by evaluating the function at discrete points in time. We might assume, for example, that $W_i = C_0 + C_1 i + C_2 i^2$ (second degree) for RLGNP and that $i = 0, 1, 2, 3, 4, 5$ (six quarters of observations starting from period zero and going to five quarters prior to the failure rate observation quarter) with $W_i = 0$ for both i less than 0 (future RLGNP) and "greater" than 5 (more remote than $t - 5$). The choice of the number of lag periods depends essentially on the nature of the problem specified, so that rules of thumb are not available. It is quite common to vary the degree of polynomial and the length of the lag where no precise theory exists. In our case, we first estimate second degree polynomial equations for each independent variable specification (univariate analysis) and observe the structure, amount, and significance of the various lagged periods parameters.

EMPIRICAL RESULTS

Univariate Structure

We start by estimating the univariate BFR relationships for four prime independent variables of the form

$$Y_t = \sum_{i=0}^{n-1} W(i) \, X_{j,t-1}$$

where

$\dot{Y}_t = \Delta\text{BFR in } t,$

$X_j = \Delta \text{ independent variable } j,$

$i = \text{quarterly designation},$

$n = 7$, and

w = weight.

We utilized a second degree polynomial in each case although higher degrees allow greater flexibility in structure of the lag pattern. The results are illustrated in Table 2-1.

As expected, we find a negative correlation among each of the first three variables RLGNP, M_2, and S&P and the business failure rate. The parameters conform to the second degree form and the significance level for the parameters of $t(0) \rightarrow t - 3$ is for the most part at the 0.05 level (or better) and in only one case at the 0.10 level. In each case, except the M_2 variable, the significance level is highest in the coincident period t_0 and slowly falls until the fourth lag ($t - 3$); thereafter the weights are insignificant and/or show changes in sign. The M_2 variable's significance level actually increases in $t - 1$, $t - 2$, and $t - 3$, indicating that the change in money supply is probably a leading indicator of the change in business failure rates.

The NEWINC variable also performed as expected, but the results and interpretation are quite different from the other three measures. We do find a significant negative correlation in quarters $t(0)$ and $t - 1$, but this could be explained simply by the impact of the change in new incorporations on the number of firms covered by D&B: hence, everything held equal, the failure rate will fall as the number of firms increase in any one period. We also find that the sign change in NEWINC in period $t - 4$ is followed by highly significant *t-values in periods* $t - 5$ and $t - 6$, indicating that the more distant lagged positive association between BFR and NEWINC could be due to the failure concept explored earlier. In fact, we find the expected positive correlation continuing for many more quarters after $t - 6$.

Overshooting

We observe that after several quarters of the expected correlation between RLGNP, M_2, and S&P and the business failure rate, the sign changes and the opposite correlation manifests. While this type of overshooting will be helpful in specifying our multivariate lagged structure, it is difficult to explain the relationship conceptually. However, since the proper interpretation of lagged weights is to sum them, it seems reasonable that at some point the signs will change. We already explained why NEWINC in prior periods can be expected to affect failure rates in current periods and, as noted above, we observe this "positive" effect continuing well beyond $t - 6$. We will exploit this finding in our multivariate specification.

Table 2-1 Quarterly Distributed Lag Parameters—Failure Rate Model: 1951–1978 (Univariate Models); Dependent Variable = Δ Failure Rate (t_0).

Independent Variable	R^2	F-test	D-W	Distributed Lag Parameters[2]						
				t_0	t_{-1}	t_{-2}	t_{-3}	t_{-4}	t_{-5}	t_{-6}
% Δ Real GNP	0.096	5.59	2.22	-0.123 (-2.53)	-0.190 (-2.43)	-0.201 (-2.25)	-0.155 (-1.81)	-0.052 (-.067)	0.106 (1.13)	0.321 (2.13)
% Δ M_2	0.093	5.40	2.19	-0.162 (-2.95)	-0.259 (-3.03)	-0.289 (-3.16)	-0.254 (-3.28)	-0.153 (-2.53)	0.015 (0.16)	0.248 (1.36)
% Δ S&P	0.085	4.85	2.08	-0.029 (-2.80)	-0.044 (-2.68)	-0.046 (-2.45)	-0.035 (-1.93)	-0.011 (-0.64)	0.027 (1.39)	0.078 (1.57)
% Δ NEWINC	0.110	6.50	2.15	-0.028 (-2.15)	-0.041 (-1.94)	-0.040 (-1.59)	-0.024 (-0.95)	0.007 (0.32)	0.053 (2.30)	0.114 (2.44)

[a] t-statistics in parentheses.

Note: All series are seasonably adjusted with the exception of the Standard & Poor Index. Data sources for quarterly GNP, S&P, and money supply are respectively: *National Income and Product Accounts of the United States and Survey of Current Business* (U.S. Department of Commerce); Standard & Poor Trade and Securities *Statistics*; and the *Federal Reserve Bulletin*. The latter source presents the most recent revised series of money supply data and reflects adjustments for Eurodollar transactions. recent benchmarks, and seasonal factors. Quarterly failure rate and number of enterprises data are available in *Dun's Statistic Review* until 1957 and in *Dun's Review* and the *Failure Record* thereafter.

Table 2-2 Distributed Lag Structure—Inflationary Effects on Failure Rates (Various Sample Periods); Dependent Variable = Δ Failure Rate (t_0), Independent Variable = Δ GNPDFL.

Sample Period	R^2	F-test	$D\text{-}W$	t_0	t_{-1}	t_{-2}	t_{-3}	t_{-4}	t_{-5}
1950–1971	0.016	0.87	2.04	0.119 (0.80)	0.157 (0.75)	0.110 (0.62)	-0.011 (-0.12)	-2.17 (-1.27)	-5.04 (-1.11)
1950–1960	0.003	0.05	1.69	-0.087 (0.22)	0.148 (0.25)	0.183 (0.27)	0.192 (0.31)	0.175 (0.29)	0.132 (0.15)
1961–1970	0.059	1.16	2.46	-0.417 (-0.62)	-0.514 (-0.55)	-0.289 (0.36)	0.257 (0.67)	1.125 (1.30)	2.314 (1.05)
1971–1979	0.125	2.06	2.44	0.298 (1.98)	0.421 (1.94)	0.368 (1.82)	0.140 (1.04)	-0.263 (-1.39)	-0.842 (-1.90)

The explanatory power (R^2) of our individual variables are all in the
0.09-0.11 range with significant (at the 0.01 level) F-ratios. The Durbin-
Watson test does not indicate serial correlation. We find that the change in
business failures is negatively correlated with percentage changes in overall activity (RLGNP), money supply (M_2), and the general stock market
behavior (S&P) and positively related (with a year's lag) to changes in the
new business incorporation rate (NEWINC).

Variables not included

We found that the RLGNP variable had a slightly higher negative correlation with the business failure rate than did corporate profits. This was a
bit surprising since conditions which lead to changes in corporate profits
are also related to business failure. Other aggregate variables not utilized
but on which we ran tests on both a univariate and a multivariate basis
were the unemployment rate (business conditions), Federal Reserve discount rate, free reserves, the prime rate (interest rates and credit conditions), and the difference between the corporate AAA and BBB rates
(market risk premium). All of the not-included variables displayed the
expected signs but did not add explanatory power when added to the
multivariate model or substituted for similar indicators.

We experienced some problems when we attempted to measure the
impact of changes in the inflation rate (GNP price deflator) on changes in
the business failure rate over the period 1950–1979. Not surprisingly, we
do not observe any significant or meaningful association over most of the
sample period since the first 20 years plus are distinguished by relatively
stable price levels. We do, however, observe a highly significant (in terms
of R^2) correlation in the most recent years, 1971–1979 (2nd quarter) as the
economy has changed to a more unstable and accelerating inflationary
period. This is indicated in Table 2-2, which shows the univariate results
for GNPDFL for various subsample periods as well as the entire period.

Note that, although the entire and the most recent period's distributed
lag structure are the familiar second degree form with some overshooting
(sign changing from positive to negative), the period 1961–1970 shows the
reverse situation. Since the model's temporal nature is not consistent, we
do not include here the price level change variable in our multivariate
results for the entire sample period. One should not, however, ignore the
potential of this variable to be a meaningful one in the future.

Multivariate Results

The combined model for explaining aggregate failure rate experience in
the United States, 1951 to 1978, is illustrated in Table 2-3 and is of the form

$$BFR_t = a_0 + a_1 \% \Delta \text{S\&P}_{t-1} + \sum_{i=0}^{3} W(i) \% \Delta \text{RLGNP}_{t-i}$$

$$+ \sum_{i=0}^{3} W(i) \% \Delta M_{2_{t-l}} + \sum_{i=3}^{10} W(i) \% \Delta \text{NEWINC}_{t-i}.$$

The Business failure rate (BFR), therefore, is a function of the percentage of change in real GNP, M_2, S&P, and new incorporations. The first two variables are specified in a four-quarter distributed lag structure with the starting point in the coincident period with Δ BFR. The NEWINC variable's starting point is, however, $t - 3$, and the number of lagged quarters is eight since a more sustained impact on failure rates is observed. All distributed lag forms assume that the lag weights outside the interval are zero. In addition. one other variable (S&P)$_t$ is specified. A simple one-period lag proved slightly more significant than a distributed lag form for the S&P variable in the multivariate run.

The overall results (Table 2-3) are quite encouraging, with the expected cumulative sign for all parameters, significant coefficients for many of the parameters of each distributed-lag variable, and relatively good explanatory power. The $R^2 = 0.26$ is fairly good in view of the nature of the aggregation problem, that is, cumulating a series of microeconomic failure events to get an aggregate figure for the economy.

In order to assess the expected impact of these macroeconomic changes on business failure rates, one would cumulate the various lag parameters' products with their appropriate variables. In this way, one could, for example, estimate the effects of diminished GNP activity, reductions in credit availability, and changes in stock prices on the propensity of firms to fail. If, for instance, we expect real GNP to fall by 2% per quarter for the next four quarters, money supply to drop by 4% per quarter, and stock prices to remain fairly constant, than one could trace out the cumulative effects in business failure rates.

In fact, we have done this with some consensus estimates of GNP, S&P, and $M2$ behavior for 1980 combined with actual 1979 and 1978 statistics, and our overall estimate was for the business failure rate to rise to approximately 36–40 per 10,000 firms from the 1979 level of 28 per 10,000 (an increase of at least 25%). Translated into the number of business bankruptcies filings, we expected a record number of filings in 1980 and 1981 (*Business Week,* March 25, 1980, pp. 104–108). In fact, filings did break all records in both 1980 (36,411) and 1981 (over 47,000). In the case of the failure rate, the 1980 figure was 42 (slightly above our estimate).

Table 2-3 Business Failure Rate Model (1951–1978): Quarterly Distributed Lag Specification (Multivariate Model); Dependent Variable = Δ Failure Rate (t_0).[a]

Independent Variable	t_0^b	t_{-1}	t_{-2}	t_{-3}	t_{-4}	t_{-5}	t_{-6}	t_{-7}	t_{-8}	t_{-9}	t_{-10}
Constant	0.506 (0.70)										
% Δ S&P		−0.099 (−2.19)									
% Δ Real GNP	−0.114 (−1.07)	−0.131 (−1.09)	−0.050 (−0.68)	0.128 (0.52)							
% Δ M2	−0.226 (−1.85)	−0.283 (−1.88)	−0.168 (−1.81)	0.116 (0.43)							
% Δ NEWINC				0.020 (1.77)	0.036 (1.88)	0.048 (2.01)	0.055 (2.18)	0.058 (2.39)	0.058 (2.55)	0.053 (2.26)	0.043 (1.44)

[a]t-statistic in parentheses.

Note: Test results in equation: Adj. R^2 = 26; F-Test = 4.85; D-W = 2.31; N = 112.

SUMMARY AND IMPLICATIONS

The purpose of this analysis is to examine the influences of aggregate economic conditions on the business failure rate experience. The period 1951 through 1978 was chosen, and a set of explanatory variables reflecting various macroeconomic pressures was examined within a first difference, distributed lag regression structure. Findings indicate that a firm's propensity to fail is heightened due to the cumulative effects of reduced (1) real economic growth, (2) stock market performance, (3) money supply growth, and (4) business formation. The latter variable was found to have a more remote but rather important and lengthy lagged association with the failure rate.

The implications of these findings relate both to macroeconomic conditions and to the marginal firm itself. Although we do not advocate that the expected impact on business failures should be the prime consideration when deciding on the nation's fiscal and monetary policies, we should still be cognizant of the effects on the marginal enterprise.

On the micro side, if a firm finds its very existence in a tenuous state and the aggregate economic conditions indicate increased failure pressures, then drastic preventive measures should be implemented—if possible and if deemed desirable. For instance, the alternative to eventual failure and perhaps liquidation may be to seek a merger with a sound company, or perhaps the firm should declare bankruptcy and attempt to reorganize. These decisions, if made early enough, may salvage the economic value of the firm's assets if the problems are temporary and not chronic. Of course, if the value of the firm as a going concern is less than its liquidation value, then early liquidation in the face of expected continued micro and macro pressures would be expedient.

The results indicate the potential to combine selected aggregate economic variables with the unique microeconomic characteristics of specific firms in order to explain and predict individual business failures more efficiently. It should be made clear, however, that statistical models for classifying and predicting individual firm business failures cannot directly utilize macroeconomic measures as additional explanatory variables. This is due to the traditional paired sample approach whereby nonbankrupt firms are matched, usually by industry and *year*, to bankrupt firms (see Chapters 3 and 4). Therefore, the values of macroeconomic variables will be identical in both groups and no discriminatory power will be achieved. Where macroeconomic *expectations* could be extremely important is in the choice of appropriate prior probabilities of failure. This level is useful in adjusting the optimum cutoff score for micro bankruptcy prediction models. We will explore this subject in Chapter 4.

3 Predicting Corporate Bankruptcy: The Z-Score Model

BACKGROUND

We have shown that aggregate economic conditions, exogenous to the individual firm, may contribute to its eventual failure. It should be made clear, however, that in almost all cases the fundamental business failure problems lie within the firm itself. The purposes of this chapter are two-fold. First, those unique characteristics of business failures are examined in order to specify and quantify the variables which are effective indicators and predictors of corporate bankruptcy. By doing so, we hope to highlight the analytic as well as the practical value inherent in the use of financial ratios. Specifically, a set of financial and economic ratios will be investigated in a bankruptcy prediction context wherein a multiple discriminant statistical methodology is employed. Through this exercise, we will explore not only the quantifiable characteristics of potential bankrupts but also the utility of a much maligned technique of financial analysis: ratio analysis. Although the model that we will discuss, known as Z-score, was developed in the late 1960s, for the first time we will extend our tests and findings to include application to firms not traded publicly.

Academicians seem to be moving toward the elimination of ratio analysis as an analytical technique in assessing the performance of the business enterprise. Theorists downgrade arbitrary rules of thumb (such as company ratio comparisons) widely used by practitioners. Since attacks on the relevance of ratio analysis emanate from many esteemed members of the scholarly world, does this mean that ratio analysis is limited to the world of "nuts and bolts"? Or has the significance of such an approach been unattractively garbed and therefore unfairly handicapped? Can we bridge the gap, rather than sever the link, between traditional ratio analysis and the more rigorous statistical techniques which have become popular among academicians in recent years? Along with our primary interest, corporate bankruptcy, we also will be concerned with an assessment of ratio analysis as an analytical technique.

I made much the same argument concerning ratio analysis almost 15 years ago, and although the conceptual basis of ratios is still an issue of some controversy, the analytic understanding of ratios as a tool of financial analysis has progressed mainly through frequent debate in the literature. Of course, ratios are as popular as ever as a pragmatic tool. Their use, however, is far more sophisticated in the 1980s than it was a decade or two ago.

First, a brief review of the development of traditional ratio analysis as a technique for investigating corporate performance is presented. Following this review, criticism of the traditional utility of ratios is discussed and a statistical technique called multiple discriminant analysis (MDA) is introduced. The emphasis will be on the compatibility of ratio analysis and this sophisticated statistical technique. It will be shown that they can be an extremely efficient predictor of corporate bankruptcy. After the various techniques are explained, we will focus on a discriminant model whereby an initial sample of 66 manufacturing firms is utilized to establish a criterion which discriminates between companies in two mutually exclusive groups: bankrupt and nonbankrupt firms. We examine the model's predicitive ability on several completely different holdout samples of companies and illustrate how the technique can be utilized without the continual use of a computer. Finally, we will extend and modify the basic model to the privately held firm in a manner which is scientifically and pragmatically acceptable.

It should be pointed out that the basic research for much of the material in this chapter was performed in 1966 and 1967 and that several subsequent studies have commented upon the Z-score model and its effectiveness. Indeed, this author has developed a "second generation" model (Zeta—see the discussion in the following chapter) and an even more recent attempt (A-score). In this new volume, we continue to present the "old" Z-score model since it is still used on a fairly widespread basis amongst practitioners and is an analysis that instructors and students find useful for pedagogic reasons.

TRADITIONAL RATIO ANALYSIS

The detection of company operating and financial difficulties is a subject which has been particularly amenable to analysis with financial ratios.

Prior to the development of quantitative measures of company performance, agencies were established to supply a qualitative type of information assessing the credit-worthiness of particular merchants. (For instance, the forerunner of the well-known Dun & Bradstreet, Inc. was organized in 1849 in Cincinnati, Ohio, in order to provide independent credit investigations.) Formal aggregate studies concerned with portents of business failure were evident in the 1930s. A study of that time, Smith and Winakor (1935), and several later ones concluded that failing firms exhibit significantly different ratio measurements than continuing entities (Merwin, 1942). In addition, Hickman (1965) was concerned with ratios of large asset-size corporations that experienced difficulties in meeting their fixed indebtedness obligations.

One of the classic works in the area of ratio analysis and bankruptcy classification was performed by Beaver (1967). In a real sense, his univariate analysis of a number of bankruptcy predictors set the stage for the multivariate attempts, by this author and others, which followed. Beaver found that a number of indicators could discriminate between matched samples of failed and nonfailed firms for as long as five years prior to failure. He questioned the use of multivariate analysis, although a discussant, Neter (1967), recommended attempting this procedure. The Z-score model did just that. A subsequent study by Deakin (1972) utilized the same 14 variables that Beaver analyzed, but he applied them within a series of multivariate discriminant models.

The aforementioned studies imply a definite potential of ratios as predictors of bankruptcy. In general, ratios measuring profitability, liquidity, and solvency prevailed as the most significant indicators. The order of their importance is not clear since almost every study cited a different ratio as being the most effective indication of impending problems.

Although these works established certain important generalizations regarding the performance and trends of particular measurements, the adaptation of the results for assessing bankruptcy potential of firms, both theoretically and practically, is questionable. In almost every case, the methodology was essentially univariate in nature and emphasis was placed on individual signals of impending problems. Ratio analysis presented in this fashion is susceptible to faulty interpretation and is potentially confusing. For instance, a firm with a poor profitability and/or solvency record may be regarded as a potential bankrupt. However, because of its above average liquidity, the situation may not be considered serious. The potential ambiguity as to the relative performance of several firms is clearly evident. The crux of the shortcomings inherent in any univariate analysis lies therein. An appropriate extension of the previously cited studies, therefore, is to build upon their findings and to combine several measures into a meaningful predictive model. In so doing, the highlights of ratio analysis as an analytical technique will be emphasized rather than downgraded. The questions are which ratios are most important in detecting bankruptcy potential, what weights should be attached to those selected ratios, and how should the weights be objectively established.

DISCRIMINANT ANALYSIS

After careful consideration of the nature of the problem and of the purpose of this analysis, we chose multiple discriminant analysis (MDA) as the appropriate statistical technique. Although not as popular as regression analysis, MDA has been utilized in a variety of disciplines since its first application in the 1930s (Fisher, 1935). During those earlier years, MDA was used mainly in the biological and behavioral sciences. In recent years, this technique has become increasingly popular in the practical business world as well as in academia. A recent book (Altman *et al.* 1981) discusses discriminant analysis in depth and reviews several financial application areas.

MDA is a statistical technique used to classify an observation into one of several *a priori* groupings dependent upon the observation's individual characteristics. It is used primarily to classify and/or make predictions in problems where the dependent variable appears in qualitative form, for example, male or female, bankrupt or nonbankrupt. Therefore, the first step is to establish explicit group classifications. The number of original groups can be two or more. Some analysts refer to discriminant analysis as "multiple" only when the number of groups exceeds two. We prefer that the multiple concept refer to the multivariate nature of the analysis.

After the groups are established, data are collected for the objects in the groups; MDA in its most simple form attempts to derive a linear combination of these characteristics which "best" discriminates between the groups. If a particular object, for instance, a corporation, has characteristics (financial ratios) which can be quantified for all of the companies in the analysis, the MDA determines a set of discriminant coefficients. When these coefficients are applied to the actual ratios, a basis for classification into one of the mutually exclusive groupings exists. The MDA technique has the advantage of considering an entire profile of characteristics common to the relevant firms, as well as the interaction of these properties. A univariate study, on the other hand, can only consider the measurements used for group assignments one at a time.

Another advantage of MDA is the reduction of the analyst's space dimensionality, that is, from the number of different independent variables to G-1 dimension(s), where G equals the number of original *a priori* groups. This analysis is concerned with two groups, consisting of bankrupt and nonbankrupt firms. Therefore, the analysis is transformed into its simplest form: one dimension. The discriminant function of the form $Z = V_1 X_1 + V_2 X_2 + \ldots + V_n X_n$ transforms the individual variable values to a single discriminant score, or Z value, which is then used to classify the object where

$V_1, V_2, \ldots, V_n$ = discriminant coefficients, and
$X_1, X_2, \ldots, X_n$ = independent variables.

The MDA computes the discriminant coefficients, V_j while the independent variables X_j are the actual values, and $j = 1, 2, \ldots, n$.

When utilizing a comprehensive list of financial ratios in assessing a firm's bankruptcy potential, there is reason to believe that some of the measurements will have a high degree of correlation or collinearity with each other. While this aspect is not serious in discriminant analysis, it usually motivates careful selection of the predictive variables (ratios). It also has the advantage of potentially yielding a model with a relatively small number of selected measurements which convey a great deal of information. This information might very well indicate differences among groups, but whether or not these differences are significant and meaningful is a more important aspect of the analysis.

Perhaps the primary advantage of MDA in dealing with classification problems is the potential of analyzing the entire variable profile of the object simultaneously rather than sequentially examining its individual characteristics. Just as linear and integer programming have improved upon traditional techniques in capital budgeting, the MDA approach to traditional ratio analysis has the potential to reformulate the problem correctly. Specifically, combinations of ratios can be analyzed together in order to remove possible ambiguities and misclassifications observed in earlier traditional ratio studies.

The Z-score model is a linear analysis in that five measures are objectively weighted and summed up to arrive at an overall score that then becomes the basis for classification of firms into one of the *a priori* groupings. As an example, Fig 3-1 shows a two-variable analysis where measures of profitability and liquidity are plotted for a sample of healthy (x) and sick (o) firms. The discriminant model selects the appropriate weights which will separate as far as possible the average values of each group while at the same time minimizing the statistical distance of each observa-

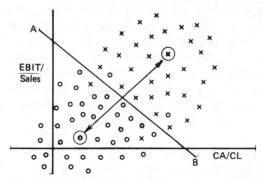

Fig. 3-1 Linear Discriminant Analysis: An Example. (o = bankrupt firms; x = nonbankrupt firms. Group means are circled.)

tion (the individual x's and o's) and its own group mean. Each observation is then "projected" on the line (AB) which best discriminates between the two groups.

For a technical explanation of discriminant analysis in general, see W. Cooley and P. Lohnes, *Multivariate Procedures for the Behavioral Sciences* (New York: John Wiley, 1962); R. Eisenbeis and R. Avery, *Discriminant Analysis and Classification Procedures: Theory and Applications* (Lexington, Mass: D.C. Heath, 1972). For the application of classification techniques to business, banking, and finance, see Edward I. Altman, R. Avery, R. Eisenbeis, and J. Sinkey, *Application of Classification Techniques in Business, Banking and Finance* (Greenwich, Conn.: JAI Press, 1981).

DEVELOPMENT OF THE Z-SCORE MODEL

Sample Selection

The initial sample is composed of 66 corporations with 33 firms in each of the two groups. The bankrupt group (Group 1) are manufacturers that filed a bankruptcy petition under Chapter X of the national bankruptcy act from 1946 through 1965. A 20-year period is not the best choice since average ratios do shift over time. Ideally, we would prefer to examine a list of ratios in time period t in order to make predictions about other firms in the following period $(t+1)$. Unfortunately, it was not possible to do this because of data limitations. (For discussions of the predictability problem, see Joy and Tollefson (1975) and Altman and Eisenbeis (1978). The mean asset size of these firms is $6.4 million, with a range of between $0.7

million and \$25.9 million. Recognizing that this group is not completely homogeneous (due to industry and size differences), we attempted to make a careful selection of nonbankrupt firms. Group 2 consists of a paired sample of manufacturing firms chosen on a stratified random basis. The firms are stratified by industry and by size, with the asset size range restricted to between \$1 and \$25 million. The mean asset size of the firms in Group 2 (\$9.6 million) was slightly greater than that of Group 1, but matching exact asset size of the two groups seemed unnecessary. Firms in Group 2 were still in existence in 1966. Also, the data collected are from the same years as those compiled for the bankrupt firms. For the initial sample test, the data are derived from financial statements dated one annual reporting period prior to bankruptcy. The data were derived from *Moody's Industrial Manuals* and selected annual reports. The average lead time of the financial statements was approximately seven and one-half months.

An important issue is to determine the asset-size group to be sampled. The decision to eliminate both the small firms (under \$1 million in total assets) and the very large companies from the initial sample essentially is due to the asset range of the firms in Group 1. In addition, the incidence of bankruptcy in the large-asset-size firm was quite rare prior to 1966. (As we have illustrated in Chapter 1, however, the large firm is no longer invulnerable to financial distress.) The absence of comprehensive data negated the representation of small firms. A frequent argument is that financial ratios, by their very nature, have the effect of deflating statistics by size, and that therefore a good deal of the size effect is eliminated. The Z-score model, discussed below, appears to be sufficiently robust to accommodate large firms.

Variable Selection

After the initial groups are defined and firms selected, balance sheet and income statement data are collected. Because of the large number of variables found to be significant indicators of corporate problems in past studies, a list of 22 potentially helpful variables (ratios) is complied for evaluation. The variables are classified into five standard ratio categories, including liquidity, profitability, leverage, solvency, and activity. The ratios are chosen on the basis of their popularity in the literature and their potential relevancy to the study, and there are a few "new" ratios in this analysis. The Beaver study (1967) concluded that the cash flow to debt ratio was the best single ratio predictor. This ratio was not considered here because of the lack of consistent and precise depreciation data. The results obtained, however, are superior to the results Beaver attained with his single best ratio.

From the original list of 22 variables, five are selected as doing the best overall job together in the prediction of corporate bankruptcy. We utilized the Cooley-Lohnes (1962) computer program in this model. This profile did not contain all of the most significant variables measured independently. This would not necessarily improve upon the univariate, traditional analysis described earlier. The contribution of the entire profile is evaluated and, since this process is essentially iterative, there is no claim regarding the optimality of the resulting discriminant function. The function, however, does the best job among the alternatives which include numerous computer runs analyzing different ratio profiles.

In order to arrive at a final profile of variables, the following procedures are utilized: (1) observation of the statistical significance of various alternative functions including determination of the relative contributions of each independent variable; (2) evaluation of intercorrelations among the relevant variables; (3) observation of the predictive accuracy of the various profiles; and (4) judgment of the analyst.

The final discriminant function is as follows:

$$Z = 0.012X_1 + 0.014X_2 + 0.033X_3 + 0.006X_4 + 0.999X_5$$

where

X_1 = working capital/total assets,
X_2 = retained earnings/total assets,
X_3 = earnings before interest and taxes/total assets,
X_4 = market value equity/book value of total liabilities,
X_5 = sales/total assets, and
Z = overall index.

X_1, **Working Capital/Total Assets (WC/TA).**   The working capital/total assets ratio, frequently found in studies of corporate problems, is a measure of the net liquid assets of the firm relative to the total capitalization. Working capital is defined as the difference between current assets and current liabilities. Liquidity and size characteristics are explicitly considered. Ordinarily, a firm experiencing consistent operating losses will have shrinking current assets in relation to total assets. Of the three liquidity ratios evaluated, this one proved to be the most valuable. Inclusion of this variable is consistent with the Merwin (1942) study which rated the net working capital to total asset ratio as the best indicator of ultimate discontinuance. Two other liquidity ratios tested were the current ratio and the quick ratio.

X_2, **Retained Earnings/Total Assets (RE/TA).** Retained earnings is the account which reports the total amount of reinvested earnings and/or losses of a firm over its entire life. The account is also referred to as earned surplus. It should be noted that the retained earnings account is subject to manipulation via corporate quasi-reorganizations and stock dividend declarations. While these occurrences are not evident in this study, it is conceivable that a bias would be created by a substantial reorganization or stock dividend and appropriate readjustments should be made to the accounts. This measure of cumulative profitability over time was cited earlier as one of the "new" ratios. The age of a firm is implicitly considered in this ratio. For example, a relatively young firm will probably show a low RE/TA ratio because it has not had time to build up its cumulative profits. Therefore, it may be argued that the young firm is somewhat discriminated against in this analysis, and its chance of being classified as bankrupt is relatively higher than that of another, older firm, *ceteris paribus*. But, this is precisely the situation in the real world. The incidence of failure is much higher in a firm's earlier years. In 1980, approximately 54% of all firms that failed did so in the first five years of their existence (see material in Chapter 1).

X_3, **Earnings before Interest and Taxes/Total Assets (EBIT/TA).** This ratio is a measure of the true productivity of the firm's assets, abstracting from any tax or leverage factors. Since a firm's ultimate existence is based on the earning power of its assets, this ratio appears to be particularly appropriate for studies dealing with corporate failure. Furthermore, insolvency in a bankrupt sense occurs when the total liabilities exceed a fair valuation of the firm's assets with value determined by the earning power of the assets.

X_4, **Market Value of Equity/Book Value of Total Liabilities (MVE/ TL).** Equity is measured by the combined market value of all shares of stock, preferred and common, while liabilities include both current and long term. The measure shows how much the firm's assets can decline in value (measured by market value of equity plus debt) before the liabilities exceed the assets and the firm becomes insolvent. For example, a company with a market value of its equity of $1,000 and debt of $500 could experience a two-thirds drop in asset value before insolvency. However, the same firm with $250 in equity will be insolvent if assets drop only one-third in value. This ratio adds a market value dimension which other failure studies did not consider. The reciprocal of X_4 is the familiar debt/ equity ratio often used as a measure of financial leverage. X_4 is a slightly modified version of one of the variables used effectively by Fisher (1959) in a study of corporate bond interest rate differentials. It also appears to be a more effective predictor of bankruptcy than a similar, more commonly used ratio: net worth/total debt (book values). At a later point, we will substitute the book value of net worth for the market value in order to derive a discriminant function for privately held firms.

X_5, Sales/Total Assets (S/TA).   The capital-turnover ratio is a standard financial ratio illustrating the sales generating ability of the firm's assets. It is one measure of management's capacity in dealing with competitive conditions. This final ratio is quite important because, as indicated below, it is the least significant ratio on an individual basis. In fact, based on the statistical significance measure, it would not have appeared at all. However, because of its unique relationship to other variables in the model, the sales/total assets ratio ranks second in its contribution to the overall discriminating ability of the model. Still, there is a wide variation among industries in asset turnover, and we will specify an alternative model, without X_5, at a later point.

A Clarification

The reader is cautioned to utilize the model in the appropriate manner. Due to the original computer format arrangement, variables X_1 through X_4 must be calculated as absolute percentage values. For instance, the firm whose net working capital to total assets (X_1) is 10% should be included as 10.0% and not 0.10. Only variable X_5 (sales to total assets) should be expressed in a different manner; that is, a S/TA ratio of 200% should be included as 2.0. The practical analyst may have been concerned by the extremely high relative discriminant coefficient of X_5. This seeming irregularity is due to the format of the different variables. Table 3-1 illustrates the proper specification and form for each of the five independent variables.

Over the years many individuals have found that a more convenient specification of the model is of the form

$$Z = 1.2X_1 + 1.4X_2 + 3.3X_3 + 0.6X_4 + 1.0X_5.$$

Using this formula, one inserts the more commonly written percentage, for example, 0.10 for 10%, for the first four variables (X_1-X_4) and rounds the last coefficient off to equal 1.0 (from 0.99). The last variable continues to be written in terms of *number of times*. The scores for individual firms and related group classification and cutoff scores remain identical. We merely point this out and note that we have utilized this format in some recent work, for example, Altman and LaFleur (1981).

Table 3-1   Variable Means and Test of Significance.

Variable	Bankrupt Group mean[a]	Nonbankrupt Group Mean[a]	F Ratio[b]
X_1	− 6.1%	41.4%	32.60[c]
X_2	−62.6%	35.5%	58.86[c]
X_3	−31.8%	15.4%	26.56[c]
X_4	40.1%	247.7%	33.26[c]
X_5	1.5X	1.9X	2.84

[a] $n = 33$.
[b] $F_{1.60} (0.001) = 12.00$; $F_{1.60} (0.01) = 7.00$; $F_{1.60} (0.05) = 4.00$.
[c] Significant at the 0.001 level.

Variable Tests

To test the individual discriminating ability of the variables, an F-test is performed. This test relates the difference between the average values of the ratios in each group to the variability (or spread) of values of the ratios within each group. Variable means measured at one financial statement prior to bankruptcy and the resulting F-statistics are presented in Table 3-1.

Variables X_1 through X_4 are all significant at the 0.001 level, indicating extremely significant difference in these variables among groups. Variable X_5 does not show a significant difference among groups and the reason for its inclusion in the variable profile is not apparent as yet. On a strictly univariate level, all of the ratios indicate higher values for the nonbankrupt firms. Also all of the discriminant coefficients display positive signs, which is what one would expect. Therefore, the greater a firm's bankruptcy potential, the lower its discriminant score.

One useful technique in arriving at the final variable profile is to determine the relative contribution of each variable to the total discriminating power of the function. One relevant statistic is observed as a scaled vector. Since the actual variable measurement units are not all comparable to each other, simple observation of the discriminant coefficients is misleading. The adjusted coefficients shown in Table 3-2 enable us to evaluate each variable's contribution on a relative basis. In the next chapter, we will explore additional measures of individual variable importance.

The scaled vectors indicate that the large contributors to group separation of the discriminant function are X_3, X_5, and X_4, respectively. The profitability ratio contributes the most, which is not surprising if one considers that the incidence of bankruptcy in a firm that is earning a profit is

Table 3-2   Relative Contribution of the Variables.

Variable	Scaled Vector	Ranking
X_1	3.29	5
X_2	6.04	4
X_3	9.89	1
X_4	7.42	3
X_5	8.41	2

almost nil. What is surprising, however, is the second highest contribution of X_5 (sales/total assets). Recall that this ratio was insignificant on a univariate basis; the multivariate context is responsible for illuminating the importance of X_5. A probable reason for this unexpected result is the high negative correlation (-0.78) we observe between X_3 and X_5 in the bankrupt group. The negative correlation is also evident in subsequent bankrupt group samples. See Cochran (1964) and Cooley and Lohnes (1962) for a discussion of how a seemingly insignificant variable can contribute a great deal in a multivariable context.

In an evaluation of the discriminant function, Cochran (1964) concluded that most correlations among variables were positive and that, by and large, negative correlations are more helpful than positive correlations in adding new information to the function. The logic behind the high negative correlation in the bankrupt group is that as firms suffer losses and deteriorate toward failure, their assets are not replaced as much as they were in healthier times. Also, the cumulative losses have further reduced the asset size through debits to retained earnings. The asset size reduction apparently dominates any sales movements.

It is clear that four of the five variables display significant differences between groups, but the importance of MDA is its ability to separate groups using multivariate measures. A test to determine the overall discriminating power of the model is the F-value which is the ratio of the sums-of-squares between-groups to the within-groups sums-of-squares. When this ratio is maximized, it has the effect of spreading the means (centroids) of the groups apart and, simultaneously, reducing dispersion of the individual points (firm Z-values) about their respective group means. Logically, this test (commonly called the F-test) is appropriate because the objective of the MDA is to identify and utilize those variables which best discriminate between groups and which are most similar within groups.

The group means of the original two-group sample are:

$$\text{Group } 1 = -0.29 \qquad F = 20.7$$
$$\text{Group } 2 = +5.02 \qquad F_{5.60}\,(0.01) = 3.84$$

The significance test therefore rejects the null hypothesis that the observations come from the same population.

Once the values of the discriminant coefficients are estimated, it is possible to calculate discriminant scores for each observation in the sample, or any firm, and to assign the observations to one of the groups based on this score. The essence of the procedure is to compare the profile of an individual firm with that of the alternative groupings. The comparisons are measured by a chi-square value and assignments are made based upon the relative proximity of the firms' score to the various group centroids.

EMPIRICAL RESULTS

At the outset, it might be helpful to illustrate the format for presenting the results. In the multigroup case, results are shown in a classification chart or accuracy matrix. Table 3-3 shows how the chart is set up.

The actual group membership is equivalent to the *a priori* groupings, and the model attempts to classify these firms correctly. At this stage, the model is basically explanatory. When new companies are classified, the nature of the model is still basically one of classification unless the firms are assessed in periods after the model was built. In this case, we begin the prediction phase.

The H's stand for correct classifications (hits) and the M's stand for misclassifications (misses). M_1 represents a Type I error and M_2 a Type II error. The sum of the diagonal elements equals the total correct "hits," and when it is divided into the total number of firms classified (66 in the case of the initial sample), it yields the measure of success of the MDA in classifying firms, that is, the percent of firms correctly classified.

Table 3-3   Classification Results Format.

	Predicted Group Membership	
Actual Group Membership	Bankrupt	Nonbankrupt
Bankrupt	H	M_1
Nonbankrupt	M_2	H

Table 3-4   Classification Results, Original Sample.

	Number Correct	Percent Correct	Percent Error	n	Actual	Predicted Group 1	Predicted Group 2
					Group 1	31	2
					Group 2	1	32
Type I	31	94	6	33			
Type II	32	97	3	33			
Total	63	95	5	66			

Initial Sample (Group 1)

The initial sample of 33 firms in each of the two groups is examined using data compiled one financial statement prior to bankruptcy. Since the discriminant coefficients and the group distributions are derived from this sample, a high degree of successful classification is expected. This should occur because the firms are classified using a discriminant function which, in fact, is based upon the individual measurements of these same firms. The classification matrix for the original sample is shown in Table 3-4.

The model is extremely accurate in classifying 95% of the total sample correctly. The Type I error proved to be only 6% while the Type II error was even better at 3%. The results, therefore, are encouraging, but the obvious upward bias should be kept in mind, and further validation techniques are appropriate.

Results Two Statements prior to Bankruptcy

The second test observes the discriminating ability of the model for firms using data compiled two statements prior to bankruptcy. The two-year period is an exaggeration since the average lead time for the correctly classified firms is approximately 20 months, with two firms having a 13-month lead. The results are shown in Table 3-5. The reduction in accuracy is understandable because impending bankruptcy is more remote and the indications are less clear. Nevertheless, 72% correct assignment is evidence that bankruptcy can be predicted two years prior to the event. The Type II error is slightly larger (6% vs. 3%) in this test, but still it is extremely accurate. Further tests will be applied below to determine the accuracy of predicting bankruptcy as much as five years prior to the actual event.

Table 3-5 Classification Results, Two Statements prior to Bankruptcy.

	Number Correct	Percent Correct	Percent Error	n	Actual	Predicted Group 1 (Bankrupt)	Group 2 (Nonbankrupt)
					Group 1	23	9
					Group 2	2	31
Type I	23	72	28	32			
Type II	31	94	6	33			
Total	54	83	17	65			

Potential Bias and Validation Techniques

When the firms used to determine the discriminant coefficients are reclassified, the resulting accuracy is biased upward by (1) sampling errors in the original sample; and (2) search bias. The latter bias is inherent in the process of reducing the original set of variables (22) to the best variable profile (five). The possibility of bias due to intensive searching is inherent in any empirical study. While a subset of variables is effective in the initial sample, there is no guarantee that it will be effective for the population in general.

The importance of secondary sample testing cannot be overemphasized, and it appears appropriate to apply these measures at this stage. A method suggested by Frank *et. al.* (1965) for testing the extent of the aforementioned search bias was applied to the initial sample. The essence of this test is to estimate parameters for the model using only a subset of the original sample, and then to classify the remainder of the sample based on the parameters established. A simple *t*-test is then applied to test the significance of the results. Five different replications of the suggested method of choosing subsets (16 firms) of the original sample are tested, with results listed in Table 3-6. (The five replications include: (1) random sampling; (2) choosing every other firm starting with firm number one; (3) starting with firm number two; (4) choosing firms 1 through 16; and (5) choosing firms 17 through 32.)

The test results reject the hypothesis that there is no difference between the groups and substantiate that the model does, in fact, possess discriminating power on observations other than those used to establish the parameters of the model. Therefore, any search bias does not appear significant.

Table 3-6 Accuracy of Classifying a Secondary Sample.

Replication	Percent of Correct Classifications	Value of $t^{a\,b}$
1	91.2	4.8[a]
2	91.2	4.8[a]
3	97.0	5.5[a]
4	97.0	4.5[a]
5	91.2	4.8[a]
Average	93.5	5.1[a]

[a]Significant at the 0.001 level.

[b]$t = (\text{proportion correct} - 0.5) \div \sqrt{0.5(1.0 - 0.5)/n}$.

Note: Total number of observations per replication (n) = 34.

Secondary Sample of Bankrupt Firms

In order to test the model rigorously for both bankrupt and nonbankrupt firms, two new samples are introduced. The first contains a new sample of 25 bankrupt firms whose asset size range is similar to that of the initial bankrupt group. On the basis of the parameters established in the discriminant model to classify firms in this secondary sample, the predictive accuracy for this sample as of one statement prior to bankruptcy is described in Table 3-7.

The results here are surprising in that one would not usually expect a secondary sample's results to be superior to the initial discriminant sample (96% vs. 94%). Two possible reasons are that the upward bias normally present in the initial sample tests is not manifested in this investigation and/or that the model, as stated before, is not optimal.

Table 3-7 Classification Results, Secondary Sample of Bankrupt Firms.

	Bankrupt Group (Actual)			Predicted	
	Number Correct	Percent Correct	Percent Error	Bankrupt	Nonbankrupt
				24	1
				n	
Type I (Total)	24	96	4	25	

Secondary Sample of Nonbankrupt Firms. Up to this point, the sample companies were chosen either by their bankruptcy status (Group 1) or by their similarity to Group 1 in all aspects except their economic well-being. But what of the many firms which suffer temporary profitability difficulties, but in actuality do not become bankrupt? A bankruptcy classification of a firm from this group is an example of a Type II error. An exceptionally rigorous test of the discriminant model's effectiveness would be to search out a large sample of firms that have encountered earnings problems and then to observe the Z-score's classification results.

In order to perform the above test, a sample of 66 firms is selected on the basis of net income (deficit) reports in the years 1958 and 1961, with 33 from each year. Over 65% of these firms had suffered two or three years of negative profits in the previous three years. The firms are selected regardless of their asset size, with the only two criteria being that they were manufacturing firms which suffered losses in the year 1958 or 1961. (They were taken at random from all firms listed in *Standard & Poor's Stock Guide,* January 1959, 1962, that reported negative earnings.) The two base years are chosen due to their relatively poor economic performances in terms of GNP growth. The companies are then evaluated by the discriminant model to determine their bankruptcy potential.

The results, illustrated in Table 3-8, show that 14 of the 66 firms are classified as bankrupt, with the remaining 52 correctly classified. Therefore, the discriminant model correctly classified 79% of the sample firms. This percentage is all the more impressive when one considers that these firms constitute a secondary sample of admittedly below-average performance. The t-test for the significance of the result is $t = 4.8$; significant at the 0.001 level.

Another interesting facet of this test is the relationship of these "temporarily" sick firms' Z-scores and the "zone of ignorance." The

Table 3-8 Classification Results, Secondary Sample of Nonbankrupt Firms.

	Nonbankrupt Group (Actual)			Predicted	
	Number Correct	Percent Correct	Percent Error	Bankrupt	Nonbankrupt
				14	52
				n	
Type II (Total)	52	79	21	66	

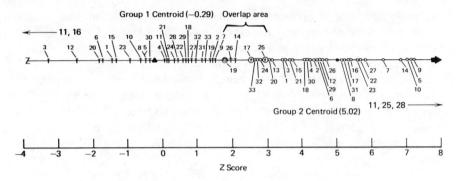

Key:

    † = Discriminate Points (Group 1 - Bankrupt Firms)   n = 33.

    o = Discriminate Points (Group 2 - Nonbankrupt Firms) n = 33.

    ⊕ = Misclassified Firms (Group 1) = 2   one year prior.

    ⊚ = Misclassified Firms (Group 2) = 1

Fig. 3-2 Individual Firm Discriminant Scores and Group Centroids, One Year prior to Bankruptcy ($Z = 0.012\ X_1 + 0.014\ X_2 + 0.033\ X_3 + 0.006\ X_4 + 0.999\ X_5$).

zone of ignorance is that range of Z-scores (see Figure 3-2) where misclassification can be observed. Fig. 3-2 illustrates the individual firm Z-scores (initial sample) and the group centroids. These points are plotted in one dimensional space and, therefore, are easily visualized.

Of the 14 misclassified firms in this secondary sample, 10 have Z-scores between 1.81 and 2.67, which indicates that although they are classified as bankrupt, the prediction of their bankruptcy is not as definite as it is for the vast majority in the initial sample of bankrupt firms. In fact, just under one-third of the 66 firms in this last sample have Z-scores within the entire overlap area, which emphasizes that the selection process is successful in choosing firms which showed signs (profitability) of deterioration.

Long-Range Accuracy. The previous results give important evidence of the reliability of the conclusions derived from the initial sample of firms. An appropriate extension, therefore, would be to examine the firms to determine the overall effectiveness of the discriminant model for a longer period of time prior to bankruptcy. Several studies, for example Beaver and Merwin, indicated that their analyses showed firms exhibiting failure tendencies as much as five years prior to the actual failure. Little is mentioned, however, of the true significance of these earlier results. Is it

Table 3-9   Five-Year Predictive Accuracy of the MDA Model (Initial Sample).

Year prior to Bankruptcy	Hits	Misses	Percent Correct
1st $n = 33$	31	2	95
2nd $n = 32$	23	9	72
3rd $n = 29$	14	15	48
4th $n = 28$	8	20	29
5th $n = 25$	9	16	36

enough to show that a firm's position is deteriorating or is it more important to examine when in the life of a firm its eventual failure becomes an acute possibility? Thus far, we have seen that bankruptcy can be predicted accurately for two years prior to failure. What about the more remote years?

To answer this question, data are gathered for the 33 original firms from the third, fourth, and fifth years prior to bankruptcy. The reduced sample is due to the fact that several of the firms were in existence for less than five years. One would expect on an *a priori* basis that, as the lead time increases, the relative predictive ability of any model would decrease. This was true in the univariate studies cited earlier, and it is also quite true for the multiple discriminant model. Table 3-9 summarizes the predictive accuracy for the total five-year period.

It is obvious that the accuracy of the model falls off consistently with the one exception between the fourth and fifth years, when the results are the opposite of what one would expect. The most logical reason for this occurrence is that after the second year, the Z-score model becomes unreliable in its predictive ability, and also that the change from year to year has little or no meaning. We will shortly see, however, that more recent models (e.g. ZETA® in Chapter 4) have demonstrated high accuracy over a longer period of time. We will also test the Z-score model for samples of bankrupt firms during the period 1969 through 1975 (Chapter 4) and 1970 through 1979 (Chapter 7).

IMPLICATIONS

Based on the above results, it is suggested that the Z-score model is an accurate forecaster of failure up to two years prior to bankruptcy and that the accuracy diminishes substantially as the lead time increases. In order

Table 3-10 Average Ratios of Bankrupt Group prior to Failure—Original Sample.

Ratio	Fifth Year		Fourth Year		Third Year		Second Year		First Year	
	Ratio	Change[a]	Ratio	Change[a]	Ratio	Change[a]	Ratio	Change[a]	Ratio	Change[a]
Working capital/total assets (%) (X_1)	19.5		23.2	+ 3.6	17.6	− 5.6	1.6	−16.0[b]	(6.1)	− 7.7
Retained earnings/total assets (%) (X_2)	4.0		(0.8)	− 4.8	(7.0)	− 6.2	(30.1)	−23.1	(62.6)	−32.5[b]
EBIT/total assets (%) (X_3)	7.2		4.0	− 3.2	(5.8)	− 9.8	(20.7)	−14.9[b]	(31.8)	−11.1
Market value equity/total debt liabilities (%) (X_4)	180.0		147.6	−32.4	143.2	− 4.4	74.2	69.0[b]	40.1	34.1
Sales/total assets (%) (X_5)	200.0		200.0	0.0	166.0	−34.0[b]	150.0	−16.0	150.0	0.0
Current ratio (%)	180.0		187.0	+ 7.0	162.0	−25.0	131.0	−31.0[b]	133.0	+ 2.0
Years of negative profits	0.8		0.9	+ 0.1	1.2	+ 0.3	2.0	+ 0.8[b]	2.5	+ 0.5
Total debt/total assets (%)	54.2		60.9	+ 6.7	61.2	+ 0.3	77.0	+15.8	96.4	+19.4[b]
Net worth/total debt (%)	123.2		75.2	−28.0	112.6	+17.4	70.5	−42.1[b]	49.4	−21.1

[a] Change from previous year.
[b] Largest yearly change in the ratio.

to investigate the possible reasons underlying these findings, the trend in the five predictive variables is traced on a univariate basis for five years preceding bankruptcy. The ratios of four other important but less significant ratios are also listed in Table 3-10.

The two most important conclusions of this trend analysis are (1) that all of the observed ratios show a deteriorating trend as bankruptcy approaches, and (2) that the most serious change in the majority of these ratios occurred between the third and the second years prior to bankruptcy. The degree of seriousness is measured by the yearly change in the ratio values. The latter observation is extremely significant as it provides evidence consistent with conclusions derived from the discriminant model. Therefore, the important information inherent in the individual ratio measurement trends takes on deserved significance only when integrated with the more analytical discriminant analysis findings.

ESTABLISHING A PRACTICAL CUTOFF POINT

The use of a multiple discriminant model for predicting bankruptcy has displayed several advantages. But bankers, credit managers, executives, accountants, and investors will typically not have access to discriminant computer procedures. Therefore, it will be necessary to attempt to extend our model for more general application. The procedure described below may be utilized to select a cutoff point which enables predictions without computer support.

By observing those firms which have been misclassified by the discriminant model in the initial sample, it is concluded that all firms having a Z-score greater than 2.99 clearly fall into the nonbankrupt sector, while

Table 3-11   Firm Whose Z-Score Falls within Gray Area.

Firm Number Nonbankrupt	Z-score	Firm Number Bankrupt
2019[a]	1.81	
	1.98	1026
	2.10	1014
	2.67	1017[a]
2033	2.68	
2032	2.78	
	2.99	1025[a]

[a]Misclassified by the MDA model; for example, firm 19 in Group 2.

Table 3-12   Number of Misclassifications Using Various Z-Score Criteria.

Range of Z	Number Misclassified	Firms
1.81–1.98	5	2019, 1026, 1014, 1017, 1025
1.98–2.10	4	2019, 1014, 1017, 1025
2.10–2.67	3	2019, 1017, 1025
2.67–2.68	2	2019, 1025
2.68–2.78	3	2019, 2033, 1025
2.78–2.99	4	2019, 2033, 2032, 1025

those firms having a Z below 1.81 are all bankrupt. The area between 1.81 and 2.99 will be defined as the zone of ignorance or gray area because of the susceptibility to error classification (see Figure 3-2). Since errors are observed in this range of values, we will be uncertain about a new firm whose Z-value falls within the zone of ignorance. Hence, it is desirable to establish a guideline for classifying firms in this area.

The process begins by identifying sample observations which fall within the overlapping range. These appear as in Table 3-11. The first digit of the firm number identifies the group, with the last two digits locating the firm within the group. Next, the range of values of Z that results in the minimum number of misclassifications is found. In the analysis, Z's between (but not including) the indicated values produce the misclassifications shown in Table 3-12. The best critical value conveniently falls between 2.67 and 2.68, and therefore 2.675, the midpoint of the interval, is chosen as the Z-value that discriminates best between the bankrupt and nonbankrupt firms.

Many persons and institutions choose to utilize the upper and lower boundaries of the zone of ignorance for unambiguous guidance and are simply cautious about firms whose score falls in between. Therefore, the 1.81 and 2.99 scores are the classification criteria that have given most confidence to users of the Z-score model.

ADAPTATION FOR PRIVATE FIRMS' APPLICATION

Perhaps the most frequent inquiry that I have received from those interested in using the Z-score model is, "What should we do to apply the model to firms in the private sector?" Credit analysts, private placement dealers, accounting auditors, and firms themselves are concerned that the original model is only applicable to publicly traded entities (since X_4 re-

Table 3-13 Revised Z'-Score Model Format: Private Firm Application.

Variable	Mean Bankrupt	Mean Nonbankrupt	Univariate F	Stepwise Order	Percent of Discriminatory Power (Scaled Vector)
$X_1 = \dfrac{\text{working capital}}{\text{total assets}}$	−0.061	0.414	32.6	5	0.067
$X_2 = \dfrac{\text{retained earnings}}{\text{total assets}}$	−0.626	0.353	58.8	1	0.121
$X_3 = \dfrac{\text{EBIT}}{\text{total assets}}$	−0.318	0.153	26.6	4	0.318
$X_4 = \dfrac{\text{N.W. (book value)}}{\text{total liabilities}}$	0.494	2.684	25.8	2	0.203
$X_5 = \dfrac{\text{sales}}{\text{total assets}}$	1.503	1.939	2.8	3	0.291

Note: Multivariate $F = 20.33$; $F\,(5,60) = 7.30$ (0.01 level).

$Z' = 0.717(X_1) + 0.847(X_2) + 3.107(X_3) + 0.420(X_4) + 0.998(X_5)$.

quires stock price data). And, to be perfectly correct, the Z-score model *is* a publicly traded firm model and *ad hoc* adjustments are not scientifically valid. For example, the most obvious modification is to substitute the book value of equity for the market value and then calculate V_4X_4. Prior to this writing, analysts had little choice but to do this procedure since valid alternatives were not available.

A revised Z-Score model

Rather than simply to use a proxy variable and insert it into an existing model to calculate Z-scores, I advocate a complete reestimation of the model substituting the book value of equity for the market value in X_4. One expects that all of the coefficients will change (not only the new variable's parameter) and that the classification criterion and related cut-off scores would also change. That is exactly what happens.

Table 3-13 lists the results of our new Z'-score model with a new X_4 variable. The equation now looks different than the earlier model; note, for instance, the coefficients for X_1 (0.717 vs. 1.210) and for X_2 (0.847 vs. 1.410), and so on. The actual variable that was modified, X_4, showed a coefficient change to 0.420 from 0.600; that is, it now has less of an impact on the Z-score. X_3 and X_5 coefficients were virtually unchanged. The univariate F-test for the book value of X_4 (25.8) is lower than the 33.3 level for the market value and the scaled vector results show that the revised book value measure is still the third most important contributor.

Table 3-14 lists the classification accuracy, group means, and revised cutoff scores for the Z'-score model. The Type I accuracy is only slightly

Table 3-14   Revised Z'-Score Model: Classification Results, Group Means, and Cutoff Boundaries.

Actual	Classified		
	Bankrupt	Nonbankrupt	Total
Bankrupt	30	3	33
	(90.9%)	(9.1%)	
Nonbankrupt	1	32	33
	(3.0%)	(97.0%)	

Note: Bankrupt group mean = 0.15; nonbankrupt group mean = 4.14.
$Z' < 1.23$ = Zone I (no errors in bankruptcy classification); $Z' > 2.90$ = Zone II (no errors in nonbankruptcy classification); gray area = 1.23 to 2.90.

Table 3-15 Revised Z''-Score Model—Four Variables; Univariate and Multivariate Tests.

Variable	Mean Bankrupt	Mean Nonbankrupt	Univariate F	Stepwise Order	Percent of Discriminatory Power (Scaled Vector)
$X_1 = \dfrac{\text{working capital}}{\text{total assets}}$	-0.061	0.414	32.6	4	0.267
$X_2 = \dfrac{\text{retained earnings}}{\text{total assets}}$	-0.626	0.353	58.8	1	0.205
$X_3 = \dfrac{\text{EBIT}}{\text{total assets}}$	-0.318	0.153	26.6	3	0.304
$X_4 = \dfrac{\text{N.W. (book value)}}{\text{total liabilities}}$	0.494	2.684	25.8	2	0.224

Note: Multivariate $F = 19.01$; $F_{4,61} = 7.00$ (0.01 level).

$Z'' = 6.56(X_1) + 3.26(X_2) + 6.72(X_3) + 1.05(X_4)$.

less impressive than the model utilizing market value of equity (91% vs. 94%) but the Type II accuracy is identical (97%). Note that the non-bankrupt group's mean Z'-score is lower than that of the original model (4.14 vs. 5.02). Therefore, the distribution of scores is now tighter with larger group overlap. The gray area (or ignorance zone) is wider, however, since the lower boundary is now 1.23 as opposed to 1.81 for the original Z-score model. All of this indicates that the revised model is probably less reliable than the original, but only slightly less. Due to lack of a private firm data base, we have not tested this model on secondary sample bankrupt and nonbankrupt entities. We await tests by practitioners on this relevant alternative.

A Further Revision—Eliminating Sales/Assets (The Z''-Score Model)

Our final computer run analyzed the characteristics and accuracy of a model without X_5—sales/total assets. We do this in order to minimize the potential industry effect which is more likely to take place when such an industry-sensitive variable as asset turnover is included. The book value of equity was used for X_4 in this case.

Note (Tables 3-15 and 3-16) that the classification results are identical to the revised five-variable model (Z'score). Of course, all of the coefficients for variables X_1 to X_4 are changed as are the group means and cutoff scores. This particular model is also useful within an industry where the type of financing of assets differs greatly among firms and important adjustments, like lease capitalization, are not made. Further tests of this model are needed on a broad cross-section of bankrupt and nonbankrupt firms.

Table 3-16   Four-Variable Z''-Score Model: Classification Results, Group Means, and Boundary Scores.

Estimated	Actual		
	Bankrupt	Nonbankrupt	Total
Bankrupt	30	3	33
	(90.9%)	(9.1%)	
Nonbankrupt	1	32	33
	(3.0%)	(97.0%)	

Note: Bankrupt group mean = −4.06; nonbankrupt group mean = +7.70. $Z'' < 1.10$ = Zone I (no errors in bankruptcy classification); $Z'' > 2.60$ = Zone II (no errors in nonbankruptcy classification); gray area = 1.10 to 2.60.

CONCLUDING REMARKS

The purpose of this chapter has been to examine the characteristics of a sample of bankrupt manufacturing companies. The analysis was extended to several years prior to the actual bankruptcy date in order to determine the bankruptcy classification merits of a multiple discriminant statistical model. At the same time, we are seeking to assess the analytical quality of financial ratio analysis; several of these ratio types were the primary ingredients of the model. The results of our analysis showed impressive evidence that bankruptcy can be predicted as much as two reporting periods prior to the event and that the correct classifications were evident for samples of firms as well as for the original groups of companies.

Whether or not such a general bankruptcy model is practically suitable for all manufacturing firms is debatable. The model did not scrutinize very large or very small entities, the latter classification comprising by far the largest number of business failures. Also, the period covered was quite long (almost two decades) and the analysis included only manufacturing firms. Ideally, we would like to develop a bankruptcy prediction model utilizing a homogeneous group of bankrupt companies and data as near to the present as possible. For instance, if we are interested in a particular industry grouping, or perhaps a group of related industries, we should first gather data from healthy and failing firms in these groupings for the last couple of years. In this manner, the results are more closely representative of the type of firm and of the business environment. Unfortunately, this is not an easy task due the lack of data in a particular sector. The analyst interested in practical utilization of the Z-score model is therefore advised to be careful.

The practical and theoretical applications of bankruptcy prediction models are many and varied. We will explore a number of these application areas in subsequent chapters. These include banking and credit analysis (Chapter 5), assessment of an individual firm's strengths and weaknesses and ways to manage a financial turnaround (Chapter 6), accounting and legal extensions (Chapters 7 and 8), and investor implications (Chapters 9 and 10).

4 ZETA® Analysis and Other Attempts to Classify and Predict Business Failures

INTRODUCTION

Following the early models of Beaver (1967) and our own Z-score model (1968, Chapter 3), numerous studies have attempted to improve upon and extend the bankruptcy classification problem. The financial and business environment has changed a good deal since the earlier models, and the bankruptcy subject is now of prime interest to researchers and practitioners alike. Indeed, there are now several services supplying statistics on business risk and failure which are subscribed to by many types of financial institutions. The purpose of this chapter is to explore, in detail, one of these models, ZETA (Altman, Haldeman, and Narayanan, 1977), which theorists and practitioners have found attractive. We also review a number of other models developed in the United States over the past decade. Most of the models are also annotated in Exhibit 3 of the appendix to this chapter. For a description of models developed outside the United States, see Chapter 12. Finally, we will discuss a recent study by Scott (1981) which compares many of these empirical studies, both to one another and to theoretical issues.

Since the ZETA model was developed jointly with a private financial firm, and the results are now being marketed by *ZETA Services, Inc.* (Mountainside, New Jersey), we cannot publish the coefficients of the model. This means, of course, that one cannot easily test the model, as one can test the Z-score model.

THE ZETA STUDY

Purposes of the ZETA Study

Despite the fact that the "old" Z-score approach had gained a great deal of respectability and popularity (both in the literature and among practitioners), there were at least five reasons for our expectation that a new model could improve upon past structures.

1.   There had been a dramatic change in the size, and perhaps the financial profile, of the businesses failing in recent years, with consequent greater visibility and concern from financial institutions, regulatory agencies, and the public at large. Most of the past studies used relatively small firms in their samples with the exception of Altman's (1973) railroad study and several commercial bank studies, for example, Sinkey (1975), Korobow and Stuhr (1975), and Martin (1978). Any new model should be as relevant as possible to the population to which it will eventually be applied. The ZETA study utilizes a bankrupt firm sample where the average adjusted asset size two annual reporting periods prior to failure was approximately $100 million. No firm had less than $20 million in assets. This is in contrast to the Z-score model where the *largest firm* had assets of less than $25 million.

2.   A new model should be as current as possible with respect to the temporal nature of the data. With the exception of three (out of 53) firms, every bankrupt firm in our new sample failed in the prior seven years (1969–1975). The entire sample of both bankrupt and nonbankrupt firms is listed in Exhibit 1 of the appendix to this chapter.

3.   Past failure models concentrated either on the broad classification of manufacturers or on specific industries. We feel that with the appropriate analytical adjustments, retailing companies, a particularly vulnerable group of firms (prior to 1977 and even more so in late 1970s and early 1980s) could be analysed on an equivalent basis with manufacturers.

4.   An important feature of this study is that the data and footnotes to financial statements have been scrupulously analyzed to include the most recent changes in financial reporting standards and accepted accounting practices. Indeed, in at least one instance (lease capitalization), a change which was implemented a few years after the ZETA study was completed was applied. The purpose of these operations was to make the model relevant not only to past failures, but also to the data that will appear in the future. The predictive as well as the classification accuracy of the ZETA model is implicit in our efforts. The major modifications are discussed in the next section.

5. A new model would enable us to test and assess several of the recent advances and still controversial aspects of discriminant analysis. Recent articles in the literature indicated that this statistical technique is being utilized with increasing frequency but not without controversy. For a discussion of applications of discriminant analysis, particularly with respect to failure prediction, see Altman, Avery, Eisenbeis, and Sinkey (1981).

Principal findings

We conclude that the ZETA model for bankruptcy classification appears to be quite accurate for up to five years prior to failure, with successful classification of well over 90% of our sample one year prior and 70% accuracy up to five years. We also observe that the inclusion of retailing firms in the same model as manufacturers does not seem to affect our results negatively.

We also find that the ZETA model outperforms alternative bankruptcy classification strategies in terms of expected cost criteria, utilizing prior probabilities and explicit cost of error estimates. Scott [1981] finds that the ZETA model ranks first among empirical bankruptcy studies in terms of accuracy and similarity to conceptual specifications of distress analysis. In our investigation we were surprised to observe that, despite the statistical properties of the data which indicate that a quadratic structure is appropriate, the linear structure of the same model outperforms the quadratic in tests of model reliability. This was especially evident regarding the long-term accuracy of the model.

SAMPLE, DATA CHARACTERISTICS, AND STATISTICAL METHODOLOGY

Sample Characteristics

Our two samples of firms consist of 53 bankrupt firms and a matched sample of 58 nonbankrupt entities. The latter are matched to the failed group by industry and year of the data. Table 4-1 lists the bankrupt firms by type, size, and year of bankruptcy petition. Note that our sample is divided almost equally into manufacturers and retailer groups and that 94% (50 of 53) of the firms failed during the period 1969 to 1975. As mentioned earlier, the average asset size of our failed group is almost $100 million, indicative of the increasing size of failures. The bankrupt firms represent publicly held industrial failures which had at least $20 million in

Table 4-1   Sample Characteristics.

	Bankrupt	Nonbankrupt	Number of Firms	Year of Bankruptcy
Number of firms	53	58		
Type of firm				
Manufacturer	29	32		
Retailer	24	26		
Average size (tangible assets)	$96 million	$167 million		
			9	1975
			9	1974
			14	1973
			3	1972
			5	1971
			5	1970
			5	1969
			1	1967
			2	1962
			53	Total

assets, with no known fraud involved and where sufficient data were available. Five nonbankruptcy-petition companies were included; one firm received substantial government support, in one case there was a forced merger, and in three cases the banks took over the business (see Exhibit 1, Appendix to Chapter 4).

Variables Analyzed

A number of financial ratios and other measures have been found in other studies to be helpful in providing statistical evidence of impending failures. We have assembled data to calculate these variables and in addition have included several 'new' measures that were thought to be potentially helpful. The 27 variables are listed in Exhibit 2 of the appendix to this chapter along with certain relevant statistics which will be discussed shortly. Note that in a few cases, for instance 7 and 9, tangible assets and interest coverage, the variables are expressed in logarithmic form in order to reduce outlier possibilities and to adhere to statistical assumptions.

Reporting Adjustments

We have adjusted the basic data of our sample to consider explicitly several of the most recent and, in our opinion, the most important accounting modifications. These adjustments include the following:

1. *Capitalization of leases.* Without doubt, the most important and pervasive adjustment made was to capitalize all noncancellable operating and finance leases. The resulting capitalized lease amount was added to the firms' assets and liabilities, and we have also imputed an interest cost to the 'new' liability. The procedure involved preparation of schedules of current and expected lease payment obligations from information found in footnotes to the financial statements. The discount rate used to capitalize leases was the average interest rate for new issue, high-grade corporate bonds in the year being analyzed plus a risk premium of 10% of the interest rate. For example, if a firm had lease payments of $100,000 a year for the next 10 years and the current interest rate was 7.3%, the capitalized lease equals $671,000. Symbolically,

$$CL = \sum_{t=1}^{N} \frac{L_t}{(1 + r + 0.1r)^t}$$

where

CL = capitalized lease,

L_t = lease payment in period t,

r = average interest rate for new issue high grade corporate bonds, and

N = the number of years of leasehold rights and obligations.

An amount equal to the interest rate used in the capitalization process times the capitalized lease amount is added to interest costs.

2. *Reserves.* If the firm's reserves were of a contingency nature, they were included in equity and income was adjusted for the net change in the reserve for the year. If the reserve was related to the valuation of certain assets, it was netted against those assets.

3. *Minority interests and other liabilities on the balance sheet.* These items were netted against other assets. This allows for a truer comparison of earnings with the assets generating the earnings.

4. *Captive finance companies and other nonconsolidated subsidiaries.* These were consolidated with the parent company accounts as well as the information would allow. The pooling of interest method was used.

5. *Goodwill and intangibles.* These were deducted from assets and equity because of the difficulty in assigning economic value to them.

6. *Capitalized research and development costs, capitalized interest, and certain other deferred charges.* These costs were expensed rather than capitalized in order to improve comparability and give a better picture of actual funds flows.

Statistical Methodology

Bankruptcy classification is again attempted through the use of the multivariate statistical technique known as discriminant analysis. In this chapter, the results using both linear and quadratic structures are analyzed.

The test for assessing whether a linear or quadratic structure is appropriate—sometimes referred to as the H_1 test (derived from Box, 1949)—will provide the proper guidance when analyzing a particular sample's classification characteristics. This test and the actual quadratic algorithm are incorporated into a computer program known as MULDIS, developed by Eisenbeis and Avery (1972). We have utilized a revised version of their original program. Essentially, if it is assessed that the variance–covariance matrices of the G groups are statistically identical, then the linear format which pools all observations is appropriate. If, however, the dispersion matrices are not identical, then the quadratic structure will provide the more efficient model (for the original sample of firms) since each group's characteristics can be assessed independently as well as between groups. Efficiency will result in more significant multivariate measures of group differences and greater classification accuracy of that particular sample. What had not been assessed up to this point is the relative efficiency of linear as opposed to quadratic structures when the sample data are not the same as those used to construct the model, that is, holdout or secondary samples. We will analyze this point shortly.

EMPIRICAL RESULTS

The Seven-Variable Model

After an iterative process of reducing the number of variables, we selected a seven-variable model which not only classified our test sample well, but also proved the most reliable in various validation procedures. That is, we could not significantly improve upon our result by adding more variables, and no model with fewer variables performed as well.

X_1, **return on assets,** is measured by the earnings before interest and taxes/total assets, variable 1 in Exhibit 2 of the appendix to this chapter. This variable has proven to be extremely helpful in assessing firm performance in several past multivariate studies.

X_2, **stability of earnings,** is measured by a normalized measure of the standard error of estimate around a 10-year trend in X_1 (variable 24). Business risk is often expressed in terms of earnings fluctuations, and this measure proved to be particularly effective.

X_3, **debt service** (variable 9), is measured by the familiar interest coverage ratio, that is, earnings before interest and taxes/total interest payments (including that amount imputed from the capitalized lease liability). We have transposed this measure by taking the log 10 in order to improve its normality and homoscedasticity.

X_4, **cumulative profitability,** is measured by the firm's retained earnings (balance sheet)/total assets (variable 19). This ratio, which imputes such factors as the age of the firm and dividend policy as well as its profitability record over time, was found to be quite helpful in past studies. As our results will show, this cumulative profitability measure is unquestionably the most important variable—measured univariately and multivariately (Table 4-2 below).

X_5, **liquidity,** is measured by the familiar current ratio (variable 16). Despite previous findings that the current ratio was not as effective in identifying failures as some other liquidity measures, we find it slightly more informative than others, such as the working capital/total assets ratio.

X_6, **capitalization,** is measured by common equity/total capital (variable 22). In both the numerator and the denominator the common equity is measured by a five-year average of the total market value rather than book value. The denominator also includes preferred stock at liquidating value, long-term debt, and capitalized leases. We have utilized a five-year average to smooth out possible severe but temporary market fluctuations and to add a trend component (along with X_2 above) to the study.

X_7, **size,** is measured by the firm's total tangible assets. This variable is adjusted for recent financial reporting changes. The capitalization of leasehold rights has added to the average asset size of both the bankrupt (by 23%) and nonbankrupt groups (by 17%). We have also transformed the size variable by a logarithmic transformation to help normalize the distribution of the variable due to outlier observations.

Relative Importance of Discriminant Variables

The procedure of reducing a variable set to an acceptable number is closely related to that of determining the relative importance within a given variable set. Several of the prescribed procedures for attaining the 'best' set of variables, stepwise analysis, for example, can also be used as a criterion for ranking importance. Unfortunately, there is no one best method for establishing a relative ranking of variable importance. Hence, we have assessed this characteristic by analyzing the ranks suggested by

Table 4-2 Influence of Each Variable in the ZETA Model, in Order of Importance.

Variable	Variable Number	Forward Stepwise Discriminant Analysis	Backward Stepwise Discriminant Analysis	Scaled Vector Test (Relative Contribution)	Separation of Means Test (Relative Contribution)	Conditional Deletion Test	Univariate F-Statistic
Overall profitability	1	7	7	7 (5%)	5	7	2
Stability of earnings	2	2	2	2 (20%)	2	2	4
Debt service	3	6	6	6 (6%)	7	6	6
Cumulative profitability	4	1	1	1 (25%)	1	1	1
Liquidity	5	5	5	5 (11%)	4	5	3
Capitalization	6	3	3	3 (18%)	3	3	5
Asset size	7	4	4	4 (15%)	5	4	7

six different tests (Table 4-2). In several studies that I have analyzed, the rankings across these tests are not consistent and the researcher is left with a somewhat ambiguous answer. This was definitely not the case in this study.

As noted in Table 4-2, regardless of which test statistic is observed, the most important variable is the cumulative profitability ratio, X_4. These tests include: (1) forward stepwise, (2) backward stepwise, (3) scaled vector (multiplication of the discriminant coefficient by the appropriate variance–covariance matrix item), (4) separation of means test [suggested by Mosteller and Wallace (1963) and supported by Joy and Tollefson (1975)], (5) the conditional deletion test which measures the additional contribution of the variable to the multivariate F-test given that the other variables have already been included [supported by Altman and Eisenbeis (1978)], and (6) the univariate F-test.

Linear versus Quadratic Analysis

The H_1 test of the original sample characteristics clearly rejects the hypothesis that the group dispersion matrices are equal. Therefore, the linear structure classification rule (excluding error costs),

$$X'\Sigma^{-1}(U_1 - U_2) - \tfrac{1}{2}(U_1 + U_2)'\Sigma^{-1}(U_1 - U_2) \geq \ln P,$$

is not appropriate, and the quadratic structure is suggested. The classification rule is: assign a firm to one group for example, nonbankrupt,

$$X'(\Sigma_1^{-1} - \Sigma_2^{-1})X - 2(U_1'\Sigma_1^{-1} + U_2'\Sigma_2^{-1})X + U_1'\Sigma_1^{-1}U_1 - U_2'\Sigma_2^{-1}U_2$$
$$\geq \ln|\Sigma_2^{-1} \cdot \Sigma_1^{-1}| - 2\ln P$$

where X = variable vector, U_1, U_2 = mean vectors of groups 1 and 2, Σ_1, Σ_2 = dispersion matrices of Groups 1 and 2, and P = prior probability of an observation being drawn from one group divided by the prior probability of it being drawn from the other group.

Essentially these equations are cutoff scores for classification in a two-group analysis. I will introduce costs of errors into the actual cutoff score when we assume unequal priors and unequal costs.

As I will show in the next section, the quadratic and linear models yield essentially equal overall accuracy results for the original sample classifications, but the holdout sample tests indicate a clear superiority for the linear framework. This creates a dilemma, and we have chosen to concentrate on the linear test, because of (1) the possible high sensitivity to individual sample observations of the quadratic parameters (that is, we observe 35 different parameters in the quadratic model compared with only seven in the linear case, not including the intercept), and (2) the fact that all of the relative tests of importance, discussed above, are based on the linear model.

Classification Accuracy—Original and Holdout Samples

Table 4-3 presents classification accuracy of the original sample based on data from one year prior to bankruptcy. Lachenbruch (1967) validation tests suggest an almost unbiased validation test of original sample results by means of a type of jackknife approach (one isolated observation at a time). The individual observation's classification accuracy is then cumulated over the entire sample. The "holdout" sample results of years 2 through 5 are also presented. The latter results are analyzed for both the linear and quadratic structures of the seven-variable model.

The linear model's accuracy, based on one-year-prior data, is 96.2% for the bankrupt group and 89.7% for the nonbankrupt group (Table 4-3). The upward bias in these results appears to be slight, since the Lachenbruch results are only 3% less for the failed group and identical for the nonfailed group. As expected, the failed group's classification accuracy is lower as the data become more remote from bankruptcy, but still quite high. In fact, we observe 70% accuracy as far back as five years prior to failure. This compares very favorably to the results recorded by Altman (1968), where the accuracy dropped precipitously after two years prior. For a comparison of these two studies, see Table 4-4.

Alternative temporal-type bankruptcy modeling strategies would include either completely separate models in each of the years (five) of

Table 4-3   Overall Classification Accuracy (in Percentages).

Years prior to bankruptcy	Bankrupt Firms		Nonbankrupt Firms		Total	
	Linear	Quadratic	Linear	Quadratic	Linear	Quadratic
1 Original sample	96.2	94.3	89.7	91.4	92.8	92.8
1 (Lachenbruch validation test)	(92.5)	(85.0)	(89.7)	(87.9)	(91.0)	(86.5)
2 Holdout	84.9	77.4	93.1	91.9	89.0	84.7
3 Holdout	74.5	62.7	91.4	92.1	83.5	78.9
4 Holdout	68.1	57.4	89.5	87.8	79.8	74.0
5 Holdout	69.8	46.5	82.1	87.5	76.8	69.7

Table 4-4 Comparative Classification Accuracy between the ZETA Model and Various Forms of a Prior Bankruptcy Model (in Percentages).

Years prior to Bankruptcy (1)	ZETA Model		Altman's 1968 Model[a]		1968 Model, ZETA Sample		1968 Variables, ZETA Parameters	
	Bankrupt (2)	Nonbankrupt (3)	Bankrupt (4)	Nonbankrupt (5)	Bankrupt (6)	Nonbankrupt (7)	Bankrupt (8)	Nonbankrupt (9)
1	96.2	89.7	93.9	97.0	86.8	82.4	92.5	84.5
2	84.9	93.1	71.9	93.9	83.0	89.3	83.0	86.2
3	74.5	91.4	48.3	n.a.	70.6	91.4	72.7	89.7
4	68.1	89.5	28.6	n.a.	61.7	86.0	57.5	83.0
5	69.8	82.1	36.0	n.a.	55.8	86.2	44.2	82.1

[a]Source: Altman (1968).

analysis or the same variables for each of the five years. In the latter strategy, the parameters would change to reflect the differences in data as bankruptcy becomes more remote. This was first presented by Deakin (1972) using Beaver's (1967) 14 variables. We think this latter approach is of some interest, but for application purposes the analyst is left somewhat confused as to which model to apply to new data. We did, however, experiment with this approach, and we found that the year 1 model was, overall (five years combined), more accurate than the other years' alternative models. Of course, each individual year's model was the most accurate in reclassifying that particular year's observations.

An interesting result was obtained by comparing the quadratic structure's results with that of the linear (Table 4-3). The total sample's classification accuracy is identical for the two structures in period 1, with the linear showing a slight edge in the bankrupt group and the quadratic in the nonbankrupt group. The most important differences, however, are in the validation and holdout tests of the bankrupt group. Here, the linear model is clearly superior, with the quadratic misclassifying over 50% of the future bankrupts five years prior. The Lachenbruch validation test also shows a large difference (over 7% favoring the linear model). Subsequent analysis will report only the linear results.

COMPARISON WITH THE 1968 Z-SCORE MODEL

The 1968 model has received a good deal of exposure in leading finance texts; for example, Weston and Brigham (1981), Van Horne (1981), and Brigham (1982); in nonacademic publications, such as *Dun's Review* (1975), *Boardroom Reports* (1975), *The New York Times,* Metz (1976), and also in immediate Johnson (1970) and delayed Joy and Tollefson (1975), Moyer (1976), and Moriarity (1980) criticism. To some extent, it has become a standard of comparison for subsequent bankruptcy classification studies. We compare the ZETA model with the earlier (1968) model in several ways. First, we compare the five-year accuracy of each model using the particular sample of firms of each study. These results are reported in columns 2 through 5 of Table 4-4. Note that the newer ZETA model is far more accurate in bankruptcy classification in Years 2 through 5 with the initial year's accuracy about equal. The older model showed slightly more accurate nonbankruptcy classification in the two years when direct comparison is possible.

Second, we have utilized the 1968 model's five variables and parameters, calculated the five variables for the new sample of firms, arrived at each of these firms' Z-scores and classified them as bankrupt if $Z \leq 2.675$ (the 1968 model's cutoff score) and as nonbankrupt if $Z > 2.675$. The observed accuracy of applying the new sample to the old model is illustrated in columns 6 and 7 of Table 4-4. In every year (with the exception of Year 5, nonbankrupts) the ZETA model dominates the 1968 model applied to the ZETA sample, especially in Years 1 and 5.

This type of test is more akin to an assessment of the 'predictive' accuracy of the 'old' model than to the "classification" and "validation" accuracy involved with observations from the same periods as that of the model's sample. The bankrupt sample's predictive accuracy (column 6, Table 4-4) is higher for the ZETA sample than we found in a prior study (Altman and McGough, 1974); 86.8% and 83.0% for Years 1 and 2 respectively versus 82.0% and 58.0% in that 1974 study.

Finally, we selected the five variables utilized in the 1968 model and calculated the parameters based on the 111-firm ZETA sample. Columns 8 and 9 list the five-year classification accuracy of the new sample based

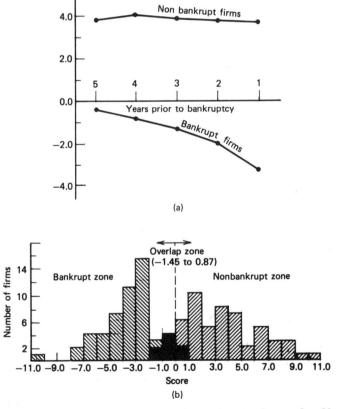

Fig. 4-1 (a) Mean ZETA Score. (b) Distribution of ZETA Scores One Year prior to Bankruptcy.

on the old variables, with Year 1 as the standard and Years 2 through 5 as "holdouts." Once again the ZETA model dominates in every year, but notice that the new seven-variable model is, in some years, only slightly more accurate than the 'old' five-variable model when the data is comparable, that is, adjusted for more meaningful evaluation.

DISTRIBUTION OF ZETA

Fig. 4-1(a) illustrates the mean ZETA score for the two groups from five years prior to bankruptcy to one year prior. While the average ZETA for bankrupts diminishes as bankruptcy approaches, the standard deviation for each period remains fairly stable: 2.7, 2.5, 2.5, 2.7, and 3.0 for Years 1 through 5. The nonbankrupt group's variances are also quite stable, although slightly higher, averaging 3.0. Fig. 4-1(b) shows the actual ZETA distribution for the 111 firms. Note that the overlap area (the interval of ZETA where errors in classification are observed) is relatively small: from −1.45 to +0.87. As expected, the overlap range widens (except in Year 5) as the time prior to bankruptcy is more remote.

THE ZETA RISK EVALUATION STATISTICAL SERVICE

The conceptual and empirical findings from the Zeta analysis was packaged into a statistical service and has been available to practitioners, on a subscription basis, since 1977 (ZETA Services, Inc., Mountainside, N.J.). Since that time, over three dozen institutions, primarily financial institutions, have subscribed to the service. This is tangible evidence that the model has had a degree of acceptance in practical circles as well as a scholarly journal. The service covers over 2,400 firms listed on the *Compustat* primary, secondary, and tertiary tapes and provides up to a 10-year history for each firm. Subscribers may analyze all or a portion of this population depending upon their needs.

SOME SAMPLE ZETA REPORTS

Figs. 4-2 and 4-3 reproduce a portion of the ZETA reports for two firms. One, Commonwealth Oil and Refining Co., showed a deteriorating ZETA score since 1971 and a negative ZETA for the first time as of the end of 1975. The firm filed for bankruptcy in March 1978; hence the ZETA model classified Commonwealth as a high-risk, potential failure over two

CUSIP: 20320110

S&P'S RATING: CCC

COMMONWEALTH OIL REFNG INC

(CWO)

SIC CODE: 2911

MOODY'S RATING: CAA

FISCAL YEAR END	ZETA		ADJUSTED PER SHARE DATA				UNFUNDED PENSION LIABILITIES AS A % OF NET ASSETS
	WEIGHTED SCORE	RELATIVE PERCENTILE	EARNINGS	DIVIDENDS	HIGH PRICE	LOW PRICE	
CHAPTER XI MARCH 3, 1978							
12/76	−2.57	9	−2.24	0.0	11.75	6.75	0
12/75	−1.72	13	−1.75	0.0	12.63	5.25	0
12/74	0.26	26	0.60	0.0	14.88	5.00	0
12/73	0.63	26	2.38	0.0	14.42	6.01	0
12/72	1.12	29	0.07	0.0	16.94	7.33	0
12/71	4.25	58	1.00	0.39	16.83	10.77	0
12/70	3.37	49	1.25	0.52	20.72	11.76	0
12/69	4.10	55	1.49	0.52	25.14	14.68	0
12/68	*******	**	1.18	0.52	26.33	15.97	0
12/67	*******	**	1.15	0.52	25.57	16.51	0

Fig. 4-2 Portion of ZETA Report for Commonwealth Oil Refining, Inc.

Commonwealth Oil filed a Chapter XI bankruptcy petition on March 3, 1978. Commonwealth's ZETA® score became negative as of its December, 1975 financial statements, once again signalling the company's highly risky situation. Equally important warning signals were the yearly drops in the ZETA® score between 1971 and 1974. Each change raised questions about the fundamentals of this company.

CUSIP: 11009710

S&P'S RATING: AA

BRISTOL MYERS CO

(BMY)

SIC CODE: 2844

				MOODY'S RATING: AAA UPGRADED FROM AA IN DECEMBER, 1977

FISCAL YEAR END	ZETA		ADJUSTED PER SHARE DATA				UNFUNDED PENSION LIABILITIES AS A % OF NET ASSETS
	WEIGHTED SCORE	RELATIVE PERCENTILE	EARNINGS	DIVIDENDS	HIGH PRICE	LOW PRICE	
12/78	11.74	97	3.08	1.22	40.38	28.00	0
12/77	11.26	96	2.72	1.10	35.88	28.75	0
12/76	11.08	96	2.45	0.90	41.88	30.63	0
12/75	11.15	97	2.22	0.82	36.88	23.25	0
12/74	10.99	96	1.88	0.76	28.19	15.31	0
12/73	10.54	95	1.58	0.81	35.88	21.75	0
12/72	10.36	95	1.30	0.60	36.63	27.94	***
12/71	10.03	94	1.22	0.60	35.19	28.00	***
12/70	8.96	89	1.21	0.60	37.63	23.75	***
12/69	7.88	86	1.11	0.60	37.50	27.00	***

AVERAGE ZETA SCORE FOR:

AA	AAA
7.5	9.0

Average ZETA® scores for Moody's Aaa and Aa industrials are about 9.0 and 7.5 respectively. Bristol Myers' ZETA® score has been at or above the Aaa average since 1970 but it was only in December 1977 that Moody's upgraded this company's bonds to the highest rating. ZETA® indicated a reduction in financial risk nearly seven years before it was recognized by the rating agency.

Fig. 4-3 Portion of ZETA Report for Bristol Myers Co.

years prior to its eventual demise. Bristol Myers (Fig. 4-3), on the other hand, displayed a very strong financial ZETA profile throughout the 1970s. Its risk profile actually improved to a level similar to the highest fixed income security rating given by *Moody's* (Aaa) as early as 1971. *Moody's* did raise Bristol Myers' rating in December 1977. See the discussion in Chapter 9 on ZETA and bond ratings.

APPLICATION AREAS

The above examples indicate at least two application areas that practitioners have found useful: credit risk analysis for lending decisions and bond analysis. Other areas include portfolio management, dividend and price change analysis, audit risk, legal analyses, and several additional ones not mentioned here. We will devote several subsequent chapters to these application areas. At this point, however, we simply want to highlight the fact that academic models for risk analysis can be adapted for practical purposes and adopted by a variety of practitioners. Indeed, the "old" Z-score model has been utilized by a wide variety of institutions and individuals.

ZETA SCORES AND FUNDAMENTAL BETAS

In addition to solvency risk services, a well-known service marketed by Barr Rosenberg Associates (California) emphasizes a firm's risk characteristic through a statistic known as a fundamental Beta. Much like the popular security return Beta measuring systematic (market-related) risk, a fundamental Beta is a relative measure of an individual firm's risk characteristics.

The ZETA model is far more straightforward and is intuitively appealing to practitioners since the variables are understood and used by market professionals on an ongoing basis. We have found that the correlation (negative) between Zeta and the fundamental Beta of a company is extremely high. In a recent study, we observed that the ZETA and Beta correlation was well over -0.80 for a sample of 100 companies. In addition, ZETA has a very highly negative correlation (-0.86) with the *Value Line Investment Survey's* financial strength score. The latter is a well-known index of individual firm risk. We intend to expand these sample tests over time, but preliminary results imply that the greater a firm's fundamental risk qualities, the lower the ZETA.

Table 4-5 Companies Which Have Failed Since ZETA Was Developed (1977–1982).

Company Name	Date Bankrupt	Final Statement Date	Final Statement Date	Final Statement Date −1	Final Statement Date −2	Final Statement Date −3	Final Statement Date −4	Number of Months with Negative Score prior to Failure
					ZETA Scores			
AM International	4/14/82	7/81	−4.60	−0.18	0.35	1.01	0.32	20
Acme Hamilton Mfg.	2/28/78	10/76	−5.54	−4.40	−4.25	−4.00	−4.12	124
Advent	3/17/81	3/80	−6.10	−4.22	−1.41			36
Alan Wood Steel	6/10/77	12/76	−4.92	−3.18	−0.31	−0.84	−1.33	89
Allied Artists	4/5/79	3/78	−7.07	−8.18	−7.14	−2.29	−1.40	120
Allied Supermarkets	11/6/78	6/78	−6.11	−5.28	−4.59	−2.92	−2.41	88
Apeco Corp.	10/19/77	11/76	−8.29	−1.53	−2.16	0.94	4.67	35
Arctic Enterprises	2/17/81	3/80	−4.12	−2.06	−0.78	0.26	0.54	35
Auto Train Corp.	9/80	12/79	−9.30	−8.42	−5.76			33
Barclay Inds. Inc.	6/81(?)	7/80	−10.47	−4.80	−3.78	−2.83	−0.17	59
Bobbie Brooks	1/17/82	4/81	−1.98	−1.69	−0.29	−0.97	−3.03	103
Braniff Airlines	5/13/82	12/80	−3.40	−2.18	1.21	1.02	0.63	28
B. Brody Seating	2/4/80	8/79	−4.87	−3.02	−1.15	−0.41	−1.32	53
Capehart Corp.	2/16/79	3/78	−11.34	−6.54				24
Commonwealth Oil	3/3/78	12/76	−2.57	−1.72	0.26	0.63	1.12	26
Cooper Jarrett	12/28/81	12/80	−8.56	−6.93	−5.18	−4.04	−3.98	120
Eagle Clothes	11/1/77	12/75	−2.89	−2.38	−2.30	−1.83	−1.18	70
Ernst, E. C.	12/4/78	3/78	−4.49	0.78	2.00	1.81	2.04	8
FDI Inc.	12/1/78	4/77	−5.75	−5.93	−5.06	−0.58	−0.45	79
Filigree Foods	4/2/76	7/74	−3.89	−3.97	−3.80	−4.87	−5.62	68
First Hartford	2/23/81	4/79	−10.00	−7.30	−7.67	−5.45	−5.42	123
Food Fair Inc.	10/3/78	7/77	−0.61	−0.68	−1.01	0.52	0.62	38

Frigitemps	3/24/78	12/76	−1.65	−1.08				27
GRT Corp.	7/14/79	3/78	−3.46	−1.62	−2.92			39
Garcia Corp.	8/8/78	7/77	−4.69	−2.49	0.61			24
Garland Corp.	4/29/80	10/79	−1.85	−0.61	−0.04	2.54	0.70	30
General Recreation	12/21/78	12/77	−14.41	−6.79	−4.39	−0.67		48
Goldblatt Bros.	6/16/81	1/80	−2.35	−1.71	−0.59	0.36	0.46	41
Good, L. S. & Co.	5/27/80	1/79	−2.75	−2.17	−1.63	−1.37	−1.31	64
Inforex	10/79	12/78	−3.69	−4.22	−3.66	−4.43		46
Itel	1/19/81	12/79	−6.62	−1.79	−1.88	−1.15	−1.68	85
Keydata Corp.	11/31/80	7/80	−15.79	−9.55	−8.44	−7.25	−7.17	64
Lionel	2/82	12/80	−1.61	−1.91	−2.19	−1.23	−1.70	121
Lynnwear Corp.	2/81	11/79	−5.46	−2.05	−2.10	−1.80	−0.94	98
Mansfield Tire	10/79	12/78	−8.20	−1.09	1.31	0.90	0.84	22
Mays, J. W. Inc.	1/26/82	7/81	−2.03	−1.04	−0.44	−0.40	−0.74	78
McLouth Steel	12/8/81	12/80	−2.17	0.32	0.34	−0.45	2.29	11
Metropolitan Greetings	1/18/79	12/77	−5.94	−3.89	−3.63	−2.45		49
Morton Shoe Cos.	1/1/82(?)	6/81	−5.05	−2.72	−1.32	−2.05	−2.26	137
National Shoes	12/12/80	1/79	−2.56	−1.05	−0.41			46
Neisner Bros. Inc.	12/77	1/77	−2.84	−3.02	−1.81	−0.98	−1.07	58
Nelly Don Inc.	11/29/78	11/77	−16.73	−7.11	−4.28	−3.40	−1.70	72
Novo Corp.	9/78	12/76	−5.03	−4.66	−3.36	−3.07	−3.23	128
Pacific Far East	1/2/78	12/76	−3.52	−3.95	−4.28	−4.74	−2.41	72
Pathcom	11/30/81	12/80	−29.56					11
Penn Dixie Inds.	4/7/80	12/78	−2.88	−3.54	−1.71	−1.28	0.15	51
Piedmont Inds.	2/22/79	5/78	−1.90	−1.38				21
Red Ball Express (Telecom Score)	4/26/82	12/80	−2.75	−0.58	−0.62	−0.78	−2.46	94
Richton International	3/18/80	4/79	0.15	1.08	0.49	0.25	−0.59	0^a
Sambo's Restaurants	11/82	12/80	−3.51	−4.28	−0.54	1.10	1.32	35
Saxon Inds.	4/15/82	12/80	0.27	−0.06	0.14	−0.34	−0.50	0^a
Seatrain Lines	2/11/81	6/80	−2.41	−2.69	−2.58	−2.77	−3.27	115

(Continued)

145

Table 4-5 (Continued)

Company Name	Date Bankrupt	Final Statement Date	ZETA Scores					Number of Months with Negative Score prior to Failure
			Final Statement Date	Final Statement Date −1	Final Statement Date −2	Final Statement Date −3	Final Statement Date −4	
Shulman Trans. Ent.	8/21/78	12/77	−7.31	−4.29	−2.58			32
Sitkin Smlt & Ref.	3/13/78	6/77	−4.07	−3.12	−1.24	−1.52	−0.17	68
Solomon, Sam Inc.	8/29/80	1/79	−2.03	−2.09				31
Stelber Industries	3/10/76	6/73	−5.97	−2.40	−2.21	−2.93	−3.94	80
Stevcoknit Inc.	11/81	1/81	−2.47	−2.45	−0.07	0.01	0.70	34
Tenna Corp.	6/25/81	1/79	−0.70	−1.52	1.87	2.21	3.36	41
United Merch & Mfg.	7/12/77	6/76	−0.38	0.24	1.72	3.23	3.04	12
Universal Cont'r	3/22/78	11/76	−5.03	−5.32	−4.02	−2.96	−2.26	111
West Chem Prods.	2/29/79	11/78	−0.31	0.35	5.70	5.98	5.44	3[a]
White Motor Corp.	9/4/80	12/79	−1.41	−1.95	−1.80	−1.85	−2.39	116
Wickes Cos.	4/25/82	1/81	−0.92	0.39	0.48	0.77	0.91	15
Wilson Freight Co.	7/80	12/79	−3.87					7
Average Score			−5.04	−2.93	−1.81	−1.10	−0.84	
Number of firms correctly classified			61	56	45	35	31	
Number of firms incorrectly classified			3	6	13	17	18	
Total number of firms			64	62	58	52	49	
Percent correct			95	90	78	67	63	
Percent incorrect			5	10	22	33	37	
Average number of months of lead time								57

Source: ZETA Services, Inc., Mountainside, N.J. Chart compiled by R. Haldeman for conference in *Bankruptcy*, "Reorganization Under Chapter 11: Investor/Lender Viewpoint," New York, May 14, 1982.

[a] Error if less than four months of lead time.

PERFORMANCE OF ZETA (PREDICTIVE TESTS)

Table 4-5 lists 64 companies which filed for bankruptcy since the ZETA model was developed. The model appears to have retained its high accuracy with 61 of 64 (95%) firms accurately predicted (5% error) one statement prior. The accuracy remains high as time increases prior to failure with the five-year rate at 63% accurate. These rates are quite similar to the accuracy reported on the original sample. Note also that the average ZETA score decreases as bankruptcy approaches, for instance, -5.04, one statement prior. The last column of Table 4-5 lists the number of consecutive months that the ZETA score was negative. The average for the 64 firms was 57 months with the median approximately the same.

OTHER BANKRUPTCY MODELS

In the prior chapter we reviewed some of the earliest failure classification studies of the 1930s and 1940s. The first modern analysis to distress prediction was performed by Beaver (1967). We now review his work, and that of others, in depth.*

BEAVER (1967)

Definition of Failure and Sample Selection

Beaver defined failure as the inability of a firm to pay its financial obligations as they mature. His sample of firms "failed" during the years 1954 to 1964. He classified the failed firms according to industry and asset size. He found that the 79 failed firms represented 38 different industries and the average firm had approximately $6 million in assets (based upon the most recent balance sheet prior to failure). The asset size range was $0.6 million to $45 million.

    Beaver selected a sample of nonfailed firms using a paired sample (by industry and asset size) method. The purpose of this technique was to control for factors that otherwise might mask the relationship between financial ratios and failure. He argued that these two factors should be

---

*This review material is derived in part from Altman, *et al.*, (1981), Chapter VII (1981). Special mention goes to J. Sinkey for his work on these reviews.

controlled because across industries the same numerical value of a ratio may imply a different probability of failure and, given identical ratios, the smaller of two firms may have a higher probability of failure. This methodology has been replicated in several failure studies to date.

One of the shortcomings of a paired sample, which Beaver was careful to point out, is that the controlled variables may be important predictors of failure yet remain undetected because their predictive power is masked by the paired sample technique. If a nonpaired sample is employed, the predictive power of all relevant variables can be determined. For example, we found earlier in the ZETA analysis that size was an important factor, yet many studies (including our own original Z-score model) are stratified by size.

For each of the five years prior to failure, Beaver computed 30 ratios. The ratios were selected on the basis of three criteria: (1) popularity in the literature, (2) performance in previous studies, and (3) definition of the ratio in terms of a "cashflow" concept. On the basis of lowest percentage prediction error (in dichotomous classification tests) for each group over the five-year period, Beaver selected the following six variables as "best": (1) cash flow to total debt, (2) net income to total assets, (3) current plus long-term liabilities to total assets, (4) working capital to total assets, (5) current ratio, and (6) no-credit interval.

Beaver's Empirical Findings

Beaver conducted three major empirical experiments: (1) comparison of mean values, (2) dichotomous classification tests, and (3) analysis of likelihood ratios. He referred to the comparison of mean values as a profile analysis to indicate that it described the general relationships between failed and nonfailed firms. He found the anticipated differences in the mean values for each of the six ratios in all five years before failure. In addition, the average failed firm showed substantial deterioration as the year of failure approached. In contrast, the performance of the average nonfailed firm was relatively constant with only small deviations from trend.

Beaver's classification test involved a dichotomous prediction or binomial response (i.e., failure or nonfailure). To make the predictions, Beaver arranged each of the 30 ratios (for both failed and nonfailed firms) in ascending order. Next, he visually inspected each pair of arrays to find the cutoff point that minimized the percentage of incorrect predictions. For example, using the profitability ratio (i.e., net income per dollar of total assets) and a cutoff point of 0.02, he found that, one year before failure, 88% of the firms were classified correctly. Beaver used the percentage of observations misclassified as a crude index of a ratio's predictive ability.

Beaver concluded that the cash flow/total debt ratio was the overall best predictor. However, its Type I error increased substantially as the number of years before failure increased. For example, the Type I error was 22% one year prior to failure and 47% four years prior to failure. In contrast, the Type II error was fairly low and stable, ranging between 3 and 8%.

In most predictions of this type, Type I errors are more costly than Type II errors, and therefore a truly minimized misclassification rate should incorporate these differing costs. We will explore the error cost question in the next chapter. Beaver treated the costs of misclassification as being symmetrical and employed an *a priori* probability of failure of .5. In other words, a loss function incorporating the product of the ratios of *a priori* probabilities and costs of misclassification is equal to one.

Likelihood ratios are useful for examining the overlap, skewness, and normality of the ratio distributions. For example, one year before failure, the profitability distributions of the failed and nonfailed firms showed relatively little overlap between the groups. Regarding skewness, the profitability distributions of the failed firms were skewed to the left in each of the years before failure and the skewness increased as the year of failure approached. For the nonfailed firms, the skewness was in the opposite direction (i.e., to the right) and much less pronounced. Beaver found rather pronounced skewness in most of the distributions analyzed, suggesting they were not normally distributed. To test directly for normality, Beaver used cumulative density functions. On the basis of these tests, he concluded that the six ratios were not normally distributed. Because most multivariate techniques assume normality, Beaver concluded that multivariate failure prediction models are suspect if they use similar data.

Major Conclusions, Qualifications, and Suggestions for Future Research

Beaver claimed that his most important contribution was to suggest a framework for the evaluation of accounting data, not merely for failure prediction, but for any purpose. His major finding was that financial ratios, or more generally, accounting data, have the ability to predict failure for at least five years before failure. However, he felt that there were important qualifications regarding the use of ratio analysis for failure prediction. First, not all ratios predict with the same degree of accuracy. Second, ratios have greater success predicting nonfailure than failure. Third, for decision-making purposes, financial ratios should be complemented by frequency distributions and likelihood ratios.

BLUM

Purpose

The purpose of Blum's 1974 work was to develop a failing company model (FCM) to aid the antitrust division of the Justice Department in assessing the probability of business failure. The failing company doctrine [*International Shoe* v. *FTC*, 280 U.S. 291 (1930)] is one of the few acceptable defenses to a merger prosecution. According to the "doctrine," the defense applies when one of two merging companies is failing and the distressed company has not received an offer to merge from a company with which a merger would be legal. One of the difficulties in applying the doctrine is determining the point at which a company is considered "failing." The legal jargon loosely defines failing as a "grave probability of failure." Blum's purpose was to quantify this probability by analyzing the financial and market data of failed firms. We will comment more fully on the Failing Company Doctrine in Chapter 8 of this book.

Definition of Failure and Sample

Blum's definition of failure was based upon the criteria of the International Shoe decision. According to this case, one of the following three events constitutes failure: (1) inability to pay debts as they come due; (2) entrance into a bankruptcy proceeding; or (3) an explicit agreement with creditors to reduce debts.

His sample consisted of 115 firms that failed from 1954 to 1968 with a minimum of $1 million in liabilities at the time of failure. Acquired firms with less than $1 million in liabilities usually are not challenged as antitrust violations. The failed firms were paired with 115 nonfailed firms on the basis of industry, size, and fiscal year.

Selection of Variables and Empirical Results

Unlike most authors of discriminant analysis studies, Blum did not search through a large set of variables to arrive at his FCM. Instead, he postulated, like Beaver (1966), a general framework for variable selection based upon the concept of a business firm as a reservoir of financial resources with the probability of failure expressed in terms of expected cash flows. Blum's FCM was constructed with three common factors underlying the cash flow framework: liquidity, profitability, and variability. He selected 12 variables to measure these cash flow parameters.

Interpreting Blum's empirical findings is somewhat difficult because of the different number of results presented. For example, regarding the classification results for one year prior, six sets of results corresponding to the number of years used for calculating the variability elements (ranging from three to eight years) are presented. He hypothesized that the ranges with periods of four, five, and six years will be more reliable for predictive purposes.

Blum's validation tests are constructed by splitting the samples in half, using one-half to compute a discriminant function and the other as a validation sample for classification purposes. The overall accuracy rates for the four-year, five-year, and six-year ranges are quite similar, on average, 94%, 80%, and 70% for one, two, and three years prior, respectively. In addition, except for the first year prior, the Type I and Type II errors have relatively stable and realistic values across the three ranges.

Critique

Motivated by the failing company doctrine, Blum's research is theoretically sound and technically competent for a 1969 MDA study. A modernized version would require the covariance matrices to be tested for equality and alternative ranking procedures to be considered for determining a "consensus" ranking. Blum, like others, criticized the Z-score (Chapter 3) model for "searching" to establish the model. Yet, in his suggestions for future research, Blum proposed that alternative ratios be considered. How does a researcher determine which theoretically justified variables are the important ones? "He or she searches." (Sinkey in Altman, et al., 1981, p. 280.)

DEAKIN

Purpose

The purpose of Deakin's 1972 study was to propose an alternative business failure model to the ones developed by either Beaver or Altman. In a subsequent study, Deakin (1977) used his 1972 model as modified by Libby (1975) to assess the impact, frequency, and nature of bankruptcy misclassification.

Deakin's 1972 Framework

Deakin liked Beaver's empirical results for their predictive accuracy and Altman's multivariate approach because of its intuitive appeal. His plan was to capture the best of both of these studies by employing the 14 ratios Beaver used and to search for the linear combination of these ratios with greatest predictive accuracy. He analyzed 32 firms that failed between 1964 and 1970. Each failed firm was matched with a nonfailed firm on the basis of industry classification, asset size, and year of financial data.

Using the 14 ratios from Beaver's (1967) study, Deakin replicated Beaver's dichotomous classification tests. Deakin's and Beaver's classification results using the cash-flow-to-total-debt ratio are quite similar. However, for the first three years prior to failure, Beaver found that the ratio of net income to total assets had the same overall accuracy as the cash-flow-to-total-debt ratio. In contrast, except for the third year prior when the ratio of total debt to total assets was the most accurate predictor (78%), Deakin's results favored the cash-flow-to-total-debt ratio.

To gain some operational insight into what is happening in these firms as they approach failure, consider the components of the cash-flow-to-total-debt ratio. Cash flow is defined as net income plus depreciation, depletion, and amortization; total debt is total liabilities plus preferred stock. (I strongly advocate including capitalized leases and all short-term debt in any leverage or coverage measure. This was probably less important in the 1960s, and the necessary data are not easily available.) Both data sets reveal a similar pattern with respect to cash flow and net income. As failure approaches, negative net income seriously impairs the average failed firm's cash flow. The failed firms analyzed by Deakin show highly volatile movements in total debt compared to the monotonic upward trend observed by Beaver. The nonfailed firms in both samples have relatively stable movements in cash flow, net income, and total debt.

Using discriminant analysis, Deakin hoped to improve upon the univariate classification results by linearly combining the 14 variables for each of the five years prior to failure. The discriminant function was not derived using Deakin's paired samples. Instead, the 32 failed firms were combined with a random sample of 32 nonfailed firms, drawn from *Moody's Industrial Manual* for the years 1962–1966. Given the potential interrelatedness of the data, it is somewhat surprising that the pooled variance--covariance matrices were nonsingular and that Deakin was able to derive linear combinations for each 14-variable set. The *F*-statistics indicated that the mean vectors were significantly different in each of the five years prior to failure. Deakin classified the original sample of 64 firms and a holdout sample consisting of 11 failed firms and 23 nonfailed firms selected at random from *Moody's Industrial Manual*.

Deakin's total misclassification rates on the original sample for the first three years prior were all less than 5%. These descriptive classifications indicated that the two groups are quite distinct; that is, there is little group overlap. In the fourth and fifth years prior, however, the groups were less distinct and the error rates, according to Deakin, "probably were too high for decision-making purposes." The holdout results indicated the presence of some sample bias, as expected. The most interesting result was the substantial deterioration in the error rates for the first year prior, a result that Deakin contended "cannot be explained by the presence of any unusual events peculiar to the sample used." (Deakin, 1972:176)

Deakin's 14-variable set produced his most accurate classification results. When he tried to reduce the number of variables the classification error increased substantially. He concluded that discriminant analysis can be used to predict business failures "as far as three years in advance with a fairly high accuracy." Given the relatively small size of his samples, he suggested that further testing is required before a conclusive judgment about his model can be rendered.

Critique

We are not convinced by Deakin's results which emphasize accuracies based on specific models built for each year prior to failure. How are these models to be applied? Is each firm tested separately on each model. And what happens if a firm scores well in some years and less well in others, for instance, appearing healthy based on Year 1 data, showing a high failure probability in Years 2 and 3, and again appearing relatively healthy in Year 4?

LIBBY

Purpose

Libby's study was designed to determine whether accounting ratios provide useful information to loan officers trying to predict business failures. Using a subset of Deakin's 14-variable set, commercial bank loan officers were asked to analyze the ratios and then to predict either "failure" or "nonfailure." The usefulness of the information was judged on the basis of the accuracy of the loan officers' predictions. Libby's sample consisted of 60 of the 64 firms from Deakin's sample; 30 failed firms and 30 non-failed firms drawn at random were used. Next, the 14 ratios are computed for one of the three years prior to failure (chosen at random), to result in an equal number of firms for each of the three years before failure (10 failed and 10 nonfailed).

Dimensionality Reduction and Classification Results

Using principal components analysis, Libby identified five independent sources of variation within the 14-variable set. The reduced set classifications, comparing favorably with the entire 14-variable set, correctly reclassified 51 of the 60 firms based upon the derivation sample and 43 of 60 using a "double, cross-validation" sample. The classifications using all 14 variables were slightly better for the derivation sample but slightly worse for the holdout sample. Given these results and the greater manageability of the five-variable set for his test purposes, Libby used the reduced set for his experiment.

The Loan Officers and The Experiment

Forty-three commercial loan officers participated in Libby's experiment. Each loan officer was given 70 ratio data sets of five ratios each. To set the *a priori* probabilities, they were told that one-half of the firms experienced failure within three years of the statement date. The loan officers were instructed to work independently and to complete the cases within one week. They were told that a correct prediction was worth one point and that an incorrect prediction cost one point.

Libby found that the loan officers' predictive accuracy was superior to random assignment (i.e., fail–nonfail) and concluded that the ratio information was utilized correctly by the loan officers. On the basis of other tests, Libby concluded that (1) there was no significant difference between the mean predictive accuracy of the small and the large bank representatives; (2) there were no significant correlations between predictive accuracy and loan officer characteristics, such as age and experience; (3) there were no differences in short-term, test–retest reliability between user subgroups; and (4) there was a relatively uniform interpretation of the accounting data across bankers.

Critique

Libby concluded that his reduced set of accounting ratios permits bankers with diverse backgrounds to make accurate predictions of business failures. While I find his experiment interesting and useful (indeed, several similar studies have subsequently been performed), I am concerned about the fact that the loan officers were told beforehand that one-half of the firms being analyzed failed. This type of information is, of course, not available to analysts. Indeed, Casey (1980) found that loan officers who were not informed about failure frequencies could only correctly predict 27% of a sample of bankrupt firms. Nonbankrupt accuracy was much better, however.

DEAKIN (1977)

Purpose

Building upon Libby's factor analysis contribution, Deakin extended his 1972 analysis to a 1977 study. The purpose of the extension was twofold: (1) to provide an indication of the frequency and nature of misclassification of nonfailing companies, and (2) to compare auditors' opinions with the model's predictive ability.

Deakin's failed group consisted of 63 firms: the 32 companies from his 1972 study and 31 firms (from a 1974 study by Altman and McGough) that failed in 1970 and 1971. The nonfailed group consisted of 80 firms randomly selected from *Moody's Industrial Manual* and matched only by year of data. Data two years prior to failure was employed, and for each of the 143 firms, the five-ratio set derived by Libby is computed.

Classification Results

Deakin's linear and quadratic classification results using the Lachenbruch holdout technique were 94.4% and 83.9% respectively. The Type I and Type II errors were very different between the linear and quadratic equations; hence, Deakin adopted the following fail–nonfail decision rule for his validation tests: (1) classify as failing if both the linear and quadratic functions classify as failing; (2) classify as nonfailing if both the linear and quadratic functions classify as nonfailing; and (3) investigate further if the functions produce conflicting results. Deakin contends that this eclectic rule tends to minimize the overall misclassification rate, if the "investigate further" group is excluded.

Deakin's validation test for the five-variable model was applied to 1980 firms on the *Compustat 1800* file for fiscal year 1971. The linear and quadratic models agreed that 290 firms (16.29%) had characteristics that were more similar to those of the failed group than those of the nonfailed group. The corresponding figure for the nonfailed group was 1317 firms (73.99%). 173 (9.72%) were assigned to the "investigate further" category.

To determine the accuracy of these predictions, Deakin scrutinized the financial performances of the 290 firms predicted to fail and 100 of the 1,317 firms predicted not to fail. However, he did not follow up on any of the firms in the "investigate further" group. This is unfortunate because such analysis might have been useful in assessing the predictability of linear versus quadratic discriminant analysis.

Deakin's follow-up analysis was for the three-and-one-half-year period from 1972 until June 30, 1975. Interpreting his findings critically depends upon the definition of failure employed. Because Deakin's model was developed with failure defined as bankruptcy, liquidation, or reorganization, this would appear to be the appropriate criterion for judging the predictive accuracy of the model. On this basis, only 18 (6.2%) of the 290 predicted failures were accurately classified. If the seven mergers that occurred were arranged under distressed conditions (Deakin does not indicate whether they were), the number of failures correctly identified is 25 (8.6%). Regarding the firms predicted not to fail, none of the 100 sample firms failed.

Using a weaker definition of distress to include dividend cuts or omissions as well, Deakin's model correctly identified 224 firms (77.2%) as failures. However, based upon the sample of 100 predicted nonfailures, 35 firms that eventually had stress (15 cut or omitted dividends while 20 had major disposal of assets) were not identified as failures, a 35% error rate.

As an alternative test of his model, Deakin analyzed 47 companies that went bankrupt from 1972 to 1974. The purpose of the test was to assess the model's accuracy with respect to a holdout sample of "hard-core" failures. Two years prior to failure, the five-variable model correctly identified 39 of the failures, misclassified one firm, and identified seven companies as in need of further investigation.

EDMISTER (1972)

Purpose and Sample

Edmister's purpose was to develop and test a number of methods of analyzing financial ratios to predict the failure of small businesses. A small business was defined as one with a loan from the Small Business Administration (SBA). The firms employed were borrowers and guarantee recipients from the SBA for the period 1954 to 1969. Loss borrowers were designated as failures and nonloss borrowers were considered to be nonfailures. Under the stipulation that three consecutive annual financial statements be available from the period prior to the date when the loan was granted, the sample included 42 loss borrowers; when only one statement was required, the number increased to 562 firms with a like number of nonloss borrowers.

Selection of Variables and Methodology

Edmister analyzed 19 financial ratios, including most of those found to be important in previous failure prediction studies. His methodological framework focused upon testing four hypotheses: (1) a ratio's level as a predictor of small business failure; (2) the three-year trend of a ratio as a predictor of small business failure; (3) the three-year average of a ratio as a predictor of small business failure; and (4) the combination of the industry relative trend and the industry level for each ratio as a predictor of small business failure.

Edmister employed a zero–one regression technique. The relationship between discriminant and regression coefficients is a proportional one in the two-group case. Edmister chose to use zero–one regression because he believed that the regression computer programs were somewhat better developed. He was intent upon limiting multicollinearity in his regression equation. Accordingly, he employed an arbitrary stepwise procedure in which a variable was not permitted to enter the regression equation if its simple correlation coefficient with an included variable was greater than 0.31. A major shortcoming with this approach is that important explanatory power may be excluded from the regression equation because of the arbitrary correlation coefficient cutoff point.

Rather than have the independent variables enter in their raw ratio form, he transformed each ratio into qualitative, zero–one variables based upon arbitrary cutoff points. For example, if the ratio of annual funds flow (defined as net profit before taxes plus depreciation) to current liabilities was less than 0.05, the ratio was assigned a value of one; otherwise it was assigned a value of zero. Such a transformation, however, reduces information, in our opinion, and should be avoided. Edmister's rationale for the transformations was (1) to prevent extreme values from unduly affecting estimated parameters, and (2) to permit level and trend variables to be combined into a single dichotomous variable.

Regression Results

Edmister developed a seven-variable, zero–one linear regression equation:

$$Z = 0.951 - 0.423X_1 - 0.293X_2 - 0.482X_3 + 0.277X_4$$
$$\quad\quad\quad (4.24)\quad\quad (2.82)\quad\quad (4.51)\quad\quad (2.61)$$

$$\quad - 0.452X_5 - 0.352X_6 - 0.924X_7$$
$$\quad\quad (2.60)\quad\quad (1.68)\quad\quad (7.11)$$

with $R^2 = 0.74$, $F = 14.02$, and $N = 84$. (Figures in parentheses are t-statistics.) The variables are:

Z, the zero–one dependent variable. It equals one for nonfailure (non-loss borrower) and zero failure (loss borrower).

X_1, the ratio of annual funds flow to current liabilities. It equals one if the ratio is less than 0.05, zero otherwise.

X_2, the ratio of equity to sales. It equals one if the ratio is less than .07, zero otherwise.

X_3, the ratio of net working capital to sales divided by the corresponding RMA average ratios. It equals one if the ratio is less than -0.02, zero otherwise.

X_4, the ratio of current liabilities to equity divided by the corresponding RMA average ratio. It equals one if less than 0.48, zero otherwise.

X_5, the ratio of inventory to sales divided by the corresponding RMA industry ratio. It equals one if the ratio has shown an upward trend, zero otherwise.

X_6, the quick ratio divided by the trend in RMA quick ratio. It equals one if trend is downward *and* level just prior to the loan and is less than 0.34, zero otherwise.

X_7, the quick ratio divided by RMA quick ratio. It equals one if the ratio has shown an upward trend, zero otherwise.

The classification results all have an overall accuracy of at least 90%. For example, using $Z \geqslant 0.530$ to determine nonfailure and $Z < 0.530$ for failure, all of the failed firms and 86% of the nonfailed firms were classified correctly for an overall accuracy rate of 93%.

The actual Z-score cutoff point is a product of the minimized loss function, which depends upon the population priors, Type I and Type II errors, and costs of misclassification. See our discussion of these factors in the following chapter. Edmister argued that because many lenders do not know the costs of misclassification, a practical alternative for setting up Z-score decision rules is a "black-gray-white" method. "Gray" refers to firms subject to classification error, the Z-score's (Chapter 3) zone of ignorance. White refers to the unambiguous nonloss borrowers and black to the unambiguous loss borrowers. Edmister's method called for accepting the white, rejecting the black, and further investigating the gray.

Conclusions and Critique

Edmister concluded that the predictive power of ratio analysis depends upon both the choice of analytical method and the selection of ratios. Two of the methods he found useful are: (1) dividing a ratio by its respective industry average, and (2) classifying ratios by quartiles. In addition, Edmister stated that no single ratio predicts as well as a small group; independent predictors are superior to nonindependent predictors; and some ratios that are insignificant by themselves add important information when combined with other variables. However, unlike Altman, Beaver, and Blum, who found that one financial statement is sufficient for accurate classification, Edmister concluded that three consecutive statements are required for effective analysis of small businesses.

The large number of small business failures and recent interest in assisting small businesses indicate a need for identifying the financial characteristics of distressed small businesses. Although Edmister's classification results are quite good, they may be due in part at least to his data transformations (e.g., converting ratios into zero–one variables). However, since the financial ratios for small businesses usually are dispersed widely, it is difficult to obtain a meaningful data set without some sort of adjustment. To the best of our knowledge, this model is not being used by the SBA or any other lending institution, but we invite the reader to consider it.

ELAM

Purpose and Sample

Elam's purpose was to determine if capitalization of (nonpurchase) leases enhanced the accuracy of a failure prediction model. Given the significant increase in leasing as a means of financing, especially over the last decade, the effect of lease data on the predictive ability of financial ratios was a timely and important issue. It is even more so today as many leases now (since 1980) must be capitalized on the balance sheet for reporting purposes. I estimate that lease capitalization adds almost 20% to the average U.S. industrial company's assets.

Elam compiled a sample of firms that failed from 1966 to 1972. At least one financial statement prior to failure was required, with reporting of lease information in the footnotes of the financial statements. Elam was left with 48 failed firms. Each bankrupt firm was matched with a non-bankrupt firm according to (1) fiscal year, (2) Standard Industry Classification, (3) net sales in the fifth year prior to bankruptcy within the industry class, and (4) reporting of uncapitalized long-term leases.

Long-Term Lease Data, Conversions, and Capitalization

Lease information was obtained from footnotes to the sample firm's original financial statements. Given the annual lease payments and lease life, Elam capitalized the future lease commitments for each firm using an interest rate of 6%. We utilized a slightly different approach in the Zeta analysis with the interest rate permitted to fluctuate over time depending

Table 4-6   The Ratio of Capitalized Leases to Total Assets.

	Number of Years to Bankruptcy				
Firms	1	2	3	4	5
Bankrupt	0.197	0.173	0.200	0.311	0.269
Nonbankrupt	0.154	0.167	0.090	0.080	0.082

Source: R. Elam (1975), p. 31.

on actual interest rates. The value of the capitalized leases and the ratio of capitalized leases to total assets (excluding leases) for Elam's bankrupt and nonbankrupt groups are presented in Table 4-6.

Five years prior to failure, the average bankrupt firm was leasing quite heavily. The lease indebtedness increases over the next year and then declines, remaining fairly constant over the last three years prior to bankruptcy. In contrast, the average nonbankrupt firm gets into leasing much more gradually and not to the extent of the average bankrupt firm. We found similar results in the ZETA study.

Major Hypothesis and Findings

Elam's null hypothesis was that inclusion of lease data does not improve the accuracy of a failure prediction model. The alternative hypothesis is that the accuracy is improved. Single and multivariable models were tested.

Based upon either single ratio or multiple ratio tests, Elam found that the addition of capitalized lease data did *not* significantly improve the overall classification accuracies of the models tested. Moreover, in some cases the classifications were less accurate when lease data were included. In actuality, Elam did not test the alternative hypothesis, that the revised ratios actually resulted in poorer accuracy.

Critique

Elam's stated purpose was to analyze an effect (lease capitalization) on predictive power. He did not attempt to reduce the number of variables below 25. Accordingly, it is possible that potential predictive power is deliberately masked by the large number of variables. For example, Edmister concluded that "when ratios are added without consideration of independence to an analysis with ratios already included, the real predictive power of the analysis does not increase" (Edmister, 1972:1490). Thus, when lease data are added to 10 of the 25 ratios, their potential contribution may be obscured by the overabundant and redundant information already contained in the model.

In my own published critique (Altman, 1976) of Elam's work, I commented upon several illogical aspects of the study. First and foremost, regardless of whether or not lease capitalization improves classification accuracy, the fact that firms in the future will be capitalizing leases makes that adjustment absolutely necessary for any model which will be applied. To be fair to Elam, prediction was not the primary purpose of his model. Second, Elam's results are unconvincing since we only need to know one *fact* to determine if lease adjusted data should yield "different" results; that is, improved or unimproved accuracy. If one population of firms, for instance, bankrupt firms, leases significantly more than the other population, then we would expect the lease adjusted ratios to deteriorate for the bankrupt firms as assets, liabilities, and profits change. This is the case with Elam's and our own ZETA sample. Indeed, the differential is greatest in Years 3 through 5 (Table 4-5), and we would expect accuracies to differ more so in those years. But Elam does not report the expected findings. We can only conclude that his model was insensitive to the expected effects.

WILCOX

Purpose

Wilcox's research focused upon applications of the gambler's ruin model to business risk. The purpose of his 1971 article was to develop a theoretical model to explain Beaver's results better and to generate hypotheses leading to potentially better predictors of failure. Wilcox was critical of Beaver, Altman, et al., because he claimed that the studies lacked a conceptual framework. Consequently, scarce bankruptcy information was statistically "used up" by searching procedures. His plan was to develop a useful generalization or model first and then to test it.

Wilcox adapted the classic gambler's ruin problem (Feller, 1968) to measuring business risk and focused upon net liquidation value (NLV) and the factors that cause it to fluctuate. NLV is simply a dollar level determined by liquidity inflow and outflow rates. For a given period, Wilcox defined the inflow rate as net income minus dividends and the outflow rate as the increase in the book value of assets minus the increase in the liquidation value of those assets. Using the familiar bathtub analogy, NLV is the water level in a tub with both its spigot and drain open. When the inflow rate exceeds the outflow rate, NLV increases; when the opposite occurs, NLV decreases. Combining the inflow and outflow variables, Wilcox referred to this net flow as the "adjusted cash flow," the period-to-period change in NLV, excluding stock issues, accounting changes, and other noncontinuing processes.

Alternatively, Wilcox defined NLV as asset liquidation value less total liabilities. For test purposes, Wilcox (1976) used the following weights to determine liquidation values:

Cash and cash equivalents	1.00
Other current assets	0.70
Long-term assets	0.45+

The plus sign on the weight for long-term assets indicates an adjustment for inflation using the GNP deflator for the past four years (e.g., in 1975 the adjustment factor is 0.30 and the weight 0.75).

The main concern of the model was with predicting when NLV will be negative, which often portends bankruptcy. Assuming a "stable process," Wilcox postulated that the probability of NLV being reduced to zero (interpreted as bankruptcy or ultimate failure) is a function of (1) the current NLV or current wealth, (2) the average adjusted cash flow, and (3) the variability of the adjusted cash flow, measured by its variance, σ^2. To summarize,

$$P_r \text{ (NLV} < O) = f(\overset{+}{\text{NLV}}, \overset{+}{\mu}, \overset{-}{\sigma^2}).$$

Other things being equal, the smaller the NLV, the smaller the adjusted cash flow, and the larger the variation of the adjusted cash flow, the greater the chance of failure (P_r). To determine how much NLV and average adjusted cash flow are needed for a given degree of safety, Wilcox (1976) introduced a concept called the "size of bet" (S). He interprets S as the adjusted cash flow at risk each year or as the simplest probabilistic process underlying the NLV cash flows.

In terms of the gambler's ruin model, NLV = NS (where N is the number of states away from failure and S is the size of bet) = $\mu^2 + \sigma^2$. As an approximation, Wilcox measured S^2 as the average of the squared annual changes in NLV. The firm was viewed, at time t, as being in state N with wealth of NLV = NS. In period $t + 1$, the firm (the gambler) moves either to state $N - 1$ with wealth of (NLV − S) or to state $N + 1$ with wealth of (NLV + S). In period $t + 2$, the firm moves from its *new* initial state to a new state with a change in wealth of either + S or − S depending upon whether it "wins" or "loses." If the probability of winning is denoted by

P and the probability of losing by Q (with $P + Q = 1$), the probability of failure (or ruin) is

$$P_r(F) = (Q/P)^n.$$

If $P \leq, Q$ then failure or ruin is inevitable.

A firm's average winnings per period, μ, is equal to $S\,(P - Q)$. Defining μ/S as X, the ratio Q/P is equal to $(1 - X)/(1 + X)$. Thus,

$$P_r(F) = \left(\frac{1-X}{1-X}^N\right) \cong 1 - 2XN.$$

While Wilcox conceded that the gambler's ruin model (in this business failure context) is an extreme oversimplification, he argued that the parameters X and N are fundamental indicators of relative financial risk, especially if they are based upon five years of adjusted cash flows.

Definition of Failure, Sample Firms, and Empirical Results

Wilcox's (1973) definition of failure was a Chapter X or XI bankruptcy petition. A sample of 52 firms that failed between 1955 and 1971 was selected. Each failed firm is matched with a nonfailed firm on the basis of (1) industry group (five years prior); (2) size (within 20% of total assets, five years prior); and (3) availability of data for the same years as the failed firm up to nine years prior.

The data items collected were:

1 Net income (including special or extraordinary)
2 Cash dividends
3 Stock issued (in merger or acquisition)
4 Cash plus marketable securities
5 Current assets
6 Total assets
7 Total liabilities (including reserves)

Using these data, NLV, μ and σ^2 were calculated for each firm, with μ and σ^2 based upon five observations. Then, $X(=\mu/S)$ and N were calculated.

Wilcox's 1976 empirical tests updated his 1973 experiment. His original classifications (1973) were based upon a paired test of the formula $[(1 - X)/(1 + X)]N$, with a complicated set of tie-breaking rules when either X

or N was negative for both firms. Wilcox's (1976) updated results were based upon a linear gambler's ruin score defined by $10X + N$, which indicated a firm's distance from the best diagonal line in $X N$ space.

Wilcox contended that his gambler's ruin approach compared "very favorably" with Beaver's and Altman's models, especially since (1) his model did not represent the result of statistical searching; (2) his model was tested over a long time period, during which inflation had altered typical financial ratios; and (3) his model was derived from a conceptual framework with implications for the managerial process.

Remedial Attention and Conclusions

Within the context of the gambler's ruin model, Wilcox focused upon three means for reducing the risk of ruin: (1) increase NLV directly, (2) increase μ, and/or (3) reduce S. NLV can be increased directly via one-time changes such as mergers, acquisitions, and stock issues. Increasing the average adjusted cash flow requires increasing the inflow rate and/or reducing the outflow rate. Significant changes in cash flow usually cannot be made overnight, although disinvestment of unprofitable ventures is an exception. Some of the important factors in determining cash flow are effective capital budgeting, controlled growth, careful profit planning and analysis, and effective overall planning. The size of bet S is governed by the variability of liquidity flows, which is influenced by such factors as dividend policy, earnings and investment stability, and the covariation between investments and profits.

Wilcox concluded that the most bankruptcies can be avoided. However, such prevention requires more than the superficial attempts to reduce risk that have characterized most bankruptcies over the past three decades.

Critique

Although Wilcox's earlier works specified a functional form of ultimate ruin, he found the probability of failure was not empirically meaningful since over half of his sample's data violated the theory's assumptions and the results were disappointing. Wilcox (1976) abandoned the functional form structure and built a prediction model based upon the variables that his earlier model suggested. The classification accuracy was impressive, but it is difficult to assess its reliability since a holdout sample was not used. In addition, many firms had bankruptcy probabilities which were at the extremes of the distribution, that is, near zero or near 100%, and the model did not appear to be sensitive to firm performance away from the extremes. Also, no adjustments are made for recent accounting changes.

Wilcox claims that his model is sufficiently general to be applied across many industries, including hospitals and other service firms. The gambler's ruin model is now being marketed by Advantage Financial Systems, Inc. (AFS), Cambridge, Mass.

Santomero and Vinso (1977) provided an additional application of the gambler's ruin model using commercial bank data. No real tests of their model are provided although they do estimate the probability of ruin for each bank at a future point in time and search for the time when this probability will be at a maximum. Their results show bank median and individual bank bankruptcy probabilities of an extremely low percentage, indicating that the banking system is quite safe and stable. These results seem to be unrealistically low. Vinso (1979) uses a version of the gambler's ruin model to estimate industrial default probabilities but presents no convincing tests of the model.

AN OVERALL EVALUATION—SCOTT

Scott (1981) compared several of the leading empirical models discussed above, that is, Beaver (1967), Altman (1968), Deakin (1972), Wilcox (1971, 1976), and Altman *et al.* (1977), in terms of their observed accuracies and of their coherence to Scott's own conceptual bankruptcy framework. Scott's model includes assumptions about firms with (1) imperfect access and (2) perfect access to external capital markets. He concluded that "though the models are not based on explicit theory their success suggests the existence of a strong underlying regularity" (p. 324). While he found it hard to determine which model discriminated best, due to different data and different procedures, he felt that the best multidimensional models outperformed the best single variable models; although not every multidimensional model behaved in this way.

Scott concluded that

Of the multidimensional models, the ZETA model is perhaps most convincing. It has high discriminatory power, is reasonably parsimonious, and includes accounting and stock market data as well as earnings and debt variables. Further it is being used in practice by over thirty financial institutions. As a result, although it is unlikely to represent the perfect prediction model, it will be used as a benchmark for judging the plausibility of the theories discussed in the following sections (pp. 324–325).

We certainly are pleased with Scott's conclusions but caution the reader as to the use of these models. At best, the models for bankruptcy classification and prediction are helpful tools and guides for action and for channeling resources. We will pursue applications of these models to a number of managerial and analytical areas in the following five chapters.

APPENDIX TO CHAPTER 4

Exhibit 1 Sample Failed Firms and Year of Failure.

Company	Year of Failure
American Beef Packers (M)	1975
American Book—Stratford Press (M)	1973
Ancorp National Service (R)	1973
Arlans Department Stores (R)	1973
Atlas Sewing Centers (R)	1962
Beck Industries (R)	1970
Bishop Industries (M)	1970
Bohack Stores (R)	1975
Botany Industries (R)	1971
Bowmar Instruments (M)[e,r]	1974
Coit International (R)	1975
Commodore Corp. (M)	1974
Daylin (R)	1975
Diversa (M)	1969
Dolly Madison Ind. (M)	1970
Douglas Aircraft (M)*	1967
Dynamics Corp. (M)	1972
Ecological Science (M)	1970
Electrospace (M)[r]	1973
Esgro Corp. (M)	1973
Farrington Mfg. (M)	1969
Federals Corp. (R)	1973
Fishman, M. H. (R)	1974
Giant Stores (R)	1973
Grant, W. T. (R)	1975
Gray Mfg. (M)	1975
Grayson Robinson Stores (R)	1962
Hartfield-Zody's (R)	1974
Harvard Industries (M)	1972
Hoe, R. (M)	1969
Horn & Hardart Baking (R)	1971
Interstate Dept. Stores (R)	1974
Kenton Corp. (R)	1974

(Continued)

Exhibit 1 (Continued)

Company	Year of Failure
Ling-Tempco-Vought (M)*	1971
Lockheed Aircraft (M)*	1971
Mangel Stores (R)	1975
Meister Brau (M)	1971
Memorex Corp. (M)*	1973
Miller Wohl (R)	1973
Mohawk Data Sciences (M)*	1975
National Bellas Hess (R)	1974
National Video (M)	1969
Omega–Alpha (M)	1973
Parkview-General (R)	1973
Penn Fruit (R)	1975
Photon (M)^e	1972
Potter Instruments (M)	1975
Roberts Co. (M)	1969
Scottex (M)	1973
Sequoyah Industries (M)	1973
Simon Stores (R)	1970
Unishops (R)	1973
Westgate California (M)	1974

Note: (M) indicates manufacturer; (R) indicates retailer; * indicates the firm remained a non-bankrupt only due to extraordinary external support.

Exhibit 2 Listing of All Variables, Group Means, and _F_-Tests Based on One Period prior to Bankruptcy Data[a].

Variable		Population means		Univariate
Number	Name	Failed	Nonfailed	_F_-Test
(1)	EBIT/TA	−0.00555	0.11176	54.3
(2)	NATC/TC	−0.02977	0.0742	36.6
(3)	Sales/TA	1.312	1.620	3.3
(4)	Sales/TC	2.107	2.160	0.0
(5)	EBIT/Sales	0.00209	0.07709	30.2
(6)	NATC/Sales	−0.01535	0.04002	33.1
(7)	Log tang. assets	1.985	2.222	5.5
(8)	Interest coverage	−0.5995	5.341	26.1
(9)	Log no. (8) & 15	0.9625	1.162	26.1
(10)	Fixed charge coverage	0.2992	2.1839	15.7
(11)	Earnings/debt	−0.0792	0.1806	32.8
(12)	Earnings/5 yr. mats	−0.1491	0.6976	8.8
(13)	Cash flow/fixed charges	0.1513	2.9512	20.9
(14)	Cash flow/TD	−0.0173	0.3136	31.4
(15)	WC/LTD	0.3532	2.4433	6.0
(16)	Current ratio	1.5757	2.6040	38.2
(17)	WC/total assets	0.1498	0.3086	40.6
(18)	WC/cash expenses	0.1640	0.2467	5.2
(19)	Ret. earn./total assets	−0.00066	0.2935	114.6
(20)	Book equity/TC	0.202	0.526	64.5
(21)	MV equity/TC	0.3423	0.6022	32.1
(22)	5 yr. MV equity/TC	0.4063	0.6210	31.0
(23)	MV equity/total liabilities	0.6113	1.8449	11.6
(24)	Standard error of estimate of EBIT/TA (norm)	1.687	5.784	33.8
(25)	EBIT drop	−3.227	3.179	9.9
(26)	Margin drop	−0.217	0.179	15.6
(27)	Capital lease/total assets	0.251	0.178	4.2
(28)	Sales/fixed assets	3.172	4.179	3.5

[a]EBIT = earnings before interest and taxes; NATC = net available for total capital; TA = total tangible assets; LTD = long-term debt; MV = market value; TC = total capital; TD = total debt; WC = working capital.

Exhibit 3 Summary of Major Studies Using Statistical Classification Techniques for Predicting the Failure of Nonfinancial Firms.*

Purpose and Sample Characteristics	Statistical Method and Important Variables	Contribution and Critique
1. *W. Beaver (1967).* To test the usefulness of ratio analysis in the context of failure prediction. Analyzes 79 firms that "failed" from 1954 to 1964 and a paired sample of nonfailed firms. Matching characteristics: industry classification code and asset size	Does *not* use a multivariable approach. Empirical tests focus upon comparison of means, dichotomous classification tests, and analysis of likelihood ratios. Of 30 ratios tested, cash flow to total debt is key variable	One of the first and most extensive failure-prediction studies. Concludes that accounting data (i.e., financial ratios) can predict failure at least 5 years in advance. Cautions against using ratio analysis indiscriminately because different ratios have different predictive abilities and because it is easier to predict nonfailure than failure. Major shortcomings: definition of failure and lack of multiple-variable analysis
2. *E. Altman (1968).* To assess the quality of ratio analysis as an analytical technique using the prediction of corporate bankruptcy as an example. Thirty-three failed manufacturing firms from the period 1946 to 1965 and a paired sample of nonfailed firms are analyzed. Pairings made on the basis of industry and asset size	Uses multiple discriminant analysis to analyze 22 variables. Develops a five-variable *linear* model consisting of (1) working capital/total assets, (2) retained earnings/total assets, (3) earnings before interest and taxes/total assets, (4) market value of equity/book value of total debt, (5) sales/total assets	Reconfirms usefulness of ratio analysis and demonstrates importance of multiple-variable analysis. To date, most widely referenced failure-prediction model. Shortcomings: model doesn't have predictive ability beyond 2 years prior to failure; doesn't develop a theoretical framework for failure prediction; fails to avoid several potential MDA pitfalls

3. *E. Deakin (1972)*. To develop an alternative to the Beaver and Altman models. Analyzes 32 firms that fail between 1964 and 1970 and a paired sample of nonfailed firms matched by industry classification, asset size, and year of data

Uses *linear* multiple discriminant analysis and 14 of Beaver's ratios to find combination of variables with greatest predictive accuracy. Ratio of cash flow-to-total debt is an important variable

Model predicts failure as far as 3 years in advance with fairly high accuracy. Only minor extension of Beaver and Altman. Shortcomings: small-sample problems; doesn't attempt to find a subset of 14-variable set; pitfalls in application of MDA not avoided

4. *R. Edmister (1972)*. To test the usefulness of financial ratio analysis for predicting *small* business failure. Works with two different samples of loss and nonloss SBA borrowers. Each sample contains an equal number of loss and nonloss cases (42 and 562). The large sample only has data for 1 year prior to loss (failure); the small sample has 3 years of data

Uses stepwise, zero–one, linear, multiple regression analysis. Nineteen ratios are tested and a 7-variable regression equation developed. The independent variables (regressors) are transformed to dichotomous zero–one variables

First failure-prediction model for small businesses. Finds that at least three consecutive financial statements are required for accurate discrimination between loss and nonloss borrowers. Shortcomings: transformation of independent variables to zero–one form gives up information and is arbitrary; selection of "less than .31" as the correlation–coefficient cutoff point for an included regression variable (in the stepwise procedure of the regression) may exclude important variables and also is arbitrary

5. *M. Blum (1974)*. To aid in assessing the probability of business failure, where failure is defined in accordance with the meaning the courts have given to it in the context of antitrust defense (i.e., The Failing Company Doctrine). Paired sample of 115 failed firms (1954 to 1968) and 115 nonfailed firms. Matching characteristics: industry, sales, employees, and fiscal year

Uses *linear* multiple discriminant analysis. A 12-variable model with emphasis upon liquidity, profitability, and variability is developed. One year before, failure model is 93–95 percent accurate, 80 percent two years before, and 70 percent thereafter up to 5 years before

Application of MDA using accounting and financial market data to Failing Company Doctrine. Stresses the importance of a failure-prediction model to have theoretical justification and sound validation procedures. Shortcoming: doesn't test for equality of group dispersion matrices

(Continued)

171

Exhibit 3 (Continued)

Purpose and Sample Characteristics	Statistical Method and Important Variables	Contribution and Critique
6. *R. Libby (1975)*. To jointly evaluate (1) the predictive power of ratio information and (2) the ability of loan officers to evaluate ratio information in a failure-prediction framework. Employs Deakin's (1972) sample	Uses principle-components analysis to identify five independent sources of variation in the Beaver–Deakin 14-variable set and MDA to test classification accuracy. The five dimensions are labeled (1) profitability, (2) activity, (3) liquidity, (4) asset balance, and (5) cash position. The 5-variable set is only slightly less accurate than the 14-variable set	Illustrates the usefulness of principal-components analysis in reducing the dimensionality of a data set and shows that accounting ratios enable bankers to make highly accurate and reliable predictions of business failures
7. *R. Elam (1975)*. To determine if capitalization of nonpurchase leases enables financial-statement users to predict bankruptcy more accurately than without such an adjustment. Analyzes 48 bankrupt firms (1966–1972) with reported lease information and a matched sample of nonbankrupt firms. Matching characteristics; data year, industry, sales, and reported leases	Uses MDA to test a set of 28 ratios. Single-ratio and multiratio predictions are made. Models with lease data are not more accurate than ones without lease data	First researcher to incorporate and test the effect of lease data on the accuracy of bankruptcy predictions. Rejects hypothesis that lease data enhances ability to predict bankruptcy. Shortcomings: doesn't attempt to find "best" model, simply tests 25-variable model; several misconceptions about theory and application of MDA. Altman (1976) concludes that the effect of leasing on failure prediction is not yet resolved

8. J. Wilcox (1976). To show how to usefully quantify the risk of financial failure through the gambler's ruin approach. Uses matched samples of 52 bankrupt firms and 52 nonbankrupt firms from Wilcox (1973)	Uses gambler's-ruin model to discriminate between bankrupt and nonbankrupt firms. Important variables are net liquidation value, average adjusted cash flow, and the concept of "size of bet." Model's accuracy is comparable to other failure-prediction studies	Develops a strong conceptual framework with implications for the management process and prevention of bankruptcy. Seems to be overly concerned about "evils" of statistical searching. Extreme probability estimates
9. E. Deakin (1977). To assess the impact, frequency, and nature of bankruptcy *misclassification* using his 1972 model as modified by Libby (1975). A sample of 63 bankrupt firms (1966–1971) and a *nonmatched* sample of 80 nonfailing companies are analyzed. Data are from the period 1964 to 1969	Uses both linear and quadratic MDA. The five ratios from Libby (1975) are: (1) net income/total assets, (2) current assets/total assets, (3) cash/total assets, (4) current assets/current liabilities, and (5) sales/current assets	Focuses upon the concepts of *failing* and *nonfailing* rather than *failed* and *nonfailed* to emphasize that a company may enter the failing state and still avoid the failed state. Adopts a unique classification rule based upon both linear and quadratic equations. Compares model's predictions with auditors' opinions. Shortcomings: doesn't attempt to measure costs of misclassification; overly concerned about size of the Type-II error; to reduce costs of the Type-I error, the firms in the "investigate-further" group could be classified as failing
10. E. Altman, R. Haldeman, and P. Narayanan (1977). To construct, analyze and test a new bankruptcy classification model that explicitly considers recent developments with respect to business failures. A sample of 53 bankrupt firms (1969—1975) and a matched sample of nonbankrupt firms are analyzed	Both linear and quadratic classification equations are employed. The "ZETA" model is a seven-variable one consisting of (1) return of assets, (2) stability of earnings, (3) debt service, (4) cumulative profitability, (5) liquidity, (6) capitalization, and (7) size. ZETA model outperforms Altman's 1968 model	Most sophisticated and up-to-date MDA model of corporate bankruptcy. Employs linear and quadratic equations; tests for model efficiency; explicitly considers cost of misclassification and *a priori* probabilities; among others.

Reproduced from Altman *et al.* (1981), Appendix to Chapter 7, pp. 303–306.

5 Fine-Tuning Failure Classification Models: A Commercial Bank Lender's Perspective

INTRODUCTION

In Chapters 3 and 4, we explored in depth two models for failure classification and prediction. These models were of a generalized nature and did not give consideration to the particular user of the results. I realize that while they may indeed be helpful for a variety of individuals and institutions, they also can be modified to better suit the specific characteristics of the firms being analyzed and the utility functions of those individuals using the models.

The two primary types of modifications possible are estimates about (1) the *prior probabilities of group membership* of the firms comprising the portfolio of firms being assessed, and (2) the *costs of the various errors* that can be made in the model classification process. These factors have been known for many years but have rarely been formally introduced into model classification criteria, primarily because the necessary inputs were difficult to estimate accurately. Also, most discriminant computer programs have options only for the prior probability input. The purpose of inserting accurate estimates for priors and costs is to adjust the cutoff score of the model with the objective of increasing its efficiency, that is, reducing the costs of misclassification.

Due to the difficulties mentioned above (which will be further elaborated upon), most analysts have simply accepted the "default" option available in discriminant computer packaged programs, assuming that the costs of the Type I and Type II errors are equal and also that the prior probabilities of being classified bankrupt or not are equal. We will show that this results in a cutoff score of zero. As in the ZETA analysis model, firms with scores above zero are classified as continuing entities and those with scores below zero are classified as potential bankrupts.

In probability terms, a firm with a zero score has a 50% probability of being classified as either bankrupt or not. (The cutoff score was not zero in the Z-score model since that model did *not* include a constant term.) We will attempt to investigate these inputs and measure them empirically so as to fine-tune our cutoff score.

OPTIMUM CUTOFF SCORE DETERMINATION

Despite the fact that statisticians have specified an optimal cutoff score formulation under certain assumptions (e.g., linear discriminant models with common group covariance matrices and multinormal populations), no one to my knowledge has attempted to measure the relevant inputs to the formulation, as specified by Anderson [1962],

$$CS = \ln \frac{q_1 \cdot C_1}{q_2 \cdot C_2} \ .$$

where

CS = optimal cutoff score,
q_1, q_2 = prior probability that an observation will be classified as bankrupt (q_1) or nonbankrupt (q_2),
C_1 = cost of misclassifying a bankrupt entity, and
C_2 = cost of misclassifying a nonbankrupt entity.

Note that if the assumption of multinormality and common dispersion matrices is violated, the cutoff score derived may not be optimal.

One of the primary purposes of this chapter's analysis, originally discussed in Altman *et al.* (1977) and Altman (1980), is to estimate the *costs* of misclassifying a firm as either bankrupt or not. When dealing with costs, one needs to specify exactly who the user is and what costs are relevant. We have selected the commercial bank as the institution for which costs will be estimated. Commercial credit scoring is an obvious use of bankruptcy models as banks have much of the relevant data necessary for our analysis. Indeed, many banks have tested and are now using either the Z-score or ZETA models in the loan assessment and loan review function. Prior probabilities will be estimated based on overall population failure propensities since we have not, for this purpose, worked with individual banks and their own portfolios of loans.

An important by-product of our bank analysis will be a comprehensive assessment of the loan chargeoff and "bad loan" recovery experience of U.S. commercial banks. I will specify what I believe to be a more comprehensive and meaningful statistic than what is traditionally reported by banks and their trade associations for intra- and interbank comparisons of bank effectiveness in "collecting" on their bad loans.

Before we measure the so-called costs of misclassification, it will be helpful to examine a stylized representation of the bank lending process. This will, I believe, enhance our understanding of the lending process as an integrated set of decisions and events and present background material for our unique specification of bankruptcy misclassification costs. The commercial bank loan analog to bankruptcy or not is loan default versus successful repayment of interest and principal.

THE COMMERCIAL LENDING PROCESS

The commercial lending process, although relatively straightforward, has rarely been studied in its entirety. Cohen, Gilmore, and Singer (1966) did attempt a general analysis of the process, concentrating on the successful repayment situation. Chart 5-1 represents my conceptualization of the lending process. The events involving decisions by commercial banks are represented by squares while the circled items are customer applicant-related. I have also noted several types of specific analyses performed by bankers in order to reach their decisions. The lending process essentially involves four steps: (1) application for a loan; (2) credit evaluation; (3) loan review; and (4) repayment performance. If the repayment experience is unsuccessful, chargeoff and workout procedures ensue; if successful, a loan renewal application is often forthcoming.

The loan request is manifested by a perceived need to add to firms' external debt financing. Financial requirements are forecasted based on a variety of methods including capital expenditure plans, *pro forma*, and flow-of-funds analyses. Formal credit analysis follows the receipt of the application. Again, forecasting and other traditional techniques are utilized, including ratio and industry analyses. The essence of good credit analysis is to determine repayment probabilities. Combined with whatever qualitative factors are considered, the objective is to provide the basis for the lending decision and for the pricing and structuring of the loan agreement.

Another type of analytical credit tool increasingly used by banks is

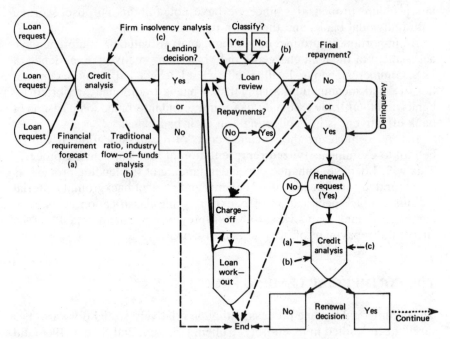

Chart 5-1 Commercial Lending Process.

firm insolvency analysis, which seeks to quantify the likelihood of continued company existence. These techniques are relevant to loan review as
well. When quantitative credit scoring techniques are used to evaluate
new loan requests, most systems consider the historical repayment experience of the bank on similar loans in the past. What is not usually considered is the cost of making errors in lending decisions. This cost is a function of the repayment and recovery experience, and this experience, in
turn, can assist in refining the process for determination of optimal cutoff
score criteria in the accept/reject decision.

After the initial lending decision is made, the process either ends with a
rejection or continues with the structuring of the loan. Interest and principal repayments follow as the loan is paid off. At some point, all banks
perform a review of the existing loan portfolio. This review relies on
many of the same procedures applied to the initial loan with the exception
of financial requirement forecasts. In fact, credit scoring approaches advocated by many such as Abate (1979), Orgler (1970, 1975), Edmister
(1971), Altman (1970), Bates (1973), and Dietrich and Kaplan (1982) are
essentially loan review procedures since the inputs are based upon the
existing portfolio. If a loan is showing serious signs of difficulty, banks

may choose to "classify" the account. The decision to classify is usually an internal one but often is encouraged by external bank examiners. Classification implies a close and continuous analysis and an action program to keep the loan from being charged off.

When intermediate repayments are missed, or the final repayment is not received, the bank may decide that all or part of the loan is not collectible and a decision is made to charge off that amount. The decision to charge off is evident if the firm formally defaults and petitions the courts for bankruptcy. A common practice by banks is to attempt to "set-off" existing credit balances in the customer's account against the outstanding loan amount. Bank setoffs occur when information about a client's likely bankruptcy reaches the bank and all existing balances are assumed by the bank as partial repayment of the loan. The setoff is possible prior to a formal bankruptcy petition since the "automatic stay" (Chapter 1) provision prevents setoffs after bankruptcy. Banks can appeal, however, for receipt of "adequate protection" based on their secured claims, even after the automatic stay goes into effect.

The remainder of the loan is then turned over to a special team of workout personnel who try to recover as much as possible. When these efforts are exhausted, the lending process is ended. On the other hand, assuming successful repayment of the loan throughout, or delinquencies that are eventually cleared up, the customer will decide whether to submit a new request. The lending process, illustrated in Chart 5-1, is not necessarily followed by all banks, but most of the steps are common to the process.

AN EARLY SPECIFICATION

This chapter expands upon the Altman *et al.* (1977) cost analysis with a more comprehensive discussion and empirical exploration of the cost of making a loan to a firm which eventually defaults on its obligation: the C_1 cost. C_1 was specified as that proportion of the charged off loan that was not recovered in subsequent periods, that is,

$$C_1 = 1 - \frac{\text{LLR}}{\text{COA}}$$

where

  LLR = loan loss recovered, and
  COA = charged off amount.

We will explore, at a later point, a major adjustment to this specification—particularly in the numerator of this equation. We recognize, however, that the net amount recovered should be adjusted downward to consider such nonreported costs as the foregone interest revenues on the "tied up" funds, the bank officer opportunity cost of his time spent on workout operations, and the legal chargeoff and workout expenses. The latter will most likely be passed along to the debtor, as per most loan agreements, but there is no assurance that there will ever be direct compensation for these expenses. The very nature of these costs makes them extremely difficult to measure and input into our empirical analysis, unless a particular bank compiles these data. The resulting C_1 loss percentage will therefore be understated and our recovery measure should be coded simply as a recovery proxy.

Our initial attempt (Altman *et al.*, 1977) at quantifying this C_1 cost involved a small sample of 33 regional banks and 25 large city banks which returned questionnaires for the period 1971 through 1975, with the results indicating that the average gross C_1 loss ranged from about 77% for the regional banks to 83% for the major banks, when the recoveries and chargeoffs were measured contemporaneously. The banks' performances appeared to be better when chargeoffs lagged recoveries by one year, with the major banks experiencing a 72% loss and small banks a 69% loss. We estimated, for computation purposes, that the C_1 was 70% for commercial banks.

ADDITIONAL EMPIRICAL TESTS

Since the previously reported results were based on relatively small numbers of commercial banks, we attempted to extend the analysis to as large a number of banks as possible. Working with New York Federal Reserve Bank data, I estimated recovery rates on loan losses for the seven-year period from 1969 through 1976, involving data from the entire population of member banks (over 5,000 banks). We calculated the arithmetic average and median results of the ratio [loan losses recovered/loan losses] for banks stratified by asset size. Selected asset size ranges are illustrated in Table 5-1. Data stratified by geographic location are available but not reported here. Asset size groupings ranged from $0-million to $10-million banks up to banks with assets over $6 billion.

In any one year for any bank, the recovery/loss ratio can be extremely high, with estimates ranging up to 40 or 50 times. For this reason, the average ratio is expected to be quite high relative to the median, and in most asset size categories we find this to be true. For instance, the aver-

Table 5-1 Average Recovery Ratio (Recoveries/Losses); All member banks nationwide stratified by assets.

Asset size ($ millions)	1969	1970	1971	1972	1973	1974	1975	1976	8-Yr. Average
$0 to $10									
Average recovery ratio	0.507	0.473	0.582	0.723	0.685	0.576	0.606	0.563	0.577
Standard deviation	1.105	0.918	1.214	1.925	1.640	1.933	1.396	1.618	1.443
Number of banks	1626	1523	1278	1077	884	864	795	744	1098
Median	0.286	0.264	0.333	0.340	0.294	0.250	0.265	0.222	—
Maximum	22.000	18.000	24.000	29.000	20.000	43.000	20.000	33.000	—
$20 to $50									
Average recovery ratio	0.565	0.416	0.520	0.657	0.622	0.475	0.581	0.669	0.569
Standard deviation	1.180	0.686	1.380	2.032	2.258	0.952	2.042	3.092	1.945
Number of banks	1075	1145	1241	1359	1492	1598	1715	1758	1423
Median	0.333	0.268	0.322	0.360	0.314	0.276	0.302	0.328	—
Maximum	22.000	9.333	43.000	57.000	56.000	19.333	50.000	98.000	—
$1,000 to $3,000									
Average recovery ratio	0.299	0.180	0.230	0.317	0.290	0.197	0.182	0.203	0.233
Standard deviation	0.178	0.118	0.137	0.193	0.176	0.150	0.141	0.146	0.163
Number of banks	41	49	54	58	67	73	73	70	61
Median	0.268	0.146	0.199	0.294	0.254	0.162	0.130	0.171	—
Maximum	0.882	0.521	0.674	0.945	0.990	0.997	0.875	0.778	—
$500 to $1,000									
Average recovery ratio	0.335	0.215	0.351	0.288	0.348	0.228	0.219	0.231	0.274
Standard deviation	0.311	0.202	0.918	0.234	0.289	0.194	0.203	0.137	0.386

(Continued)

Table 5-1 (Continued)

Asset size ($ millions)	1969	1970	1971	1972	1973	1974	1975	1976	8-Yr. Average
Number of banks	51	69	76	84	81	83	83	91	77
Median	0.270	0.150	0.203	0.246	0.272	0.187	0.172	0.204	—
Maximum	2.068	1.313	8.089	1.776	1.824	1.130	1.292	0.546	—
$6,000 to $99,999									
Average recovery ratio	0.308	0.125	0.145	0.221	0.268	0.141	0.076	0.127	0.169
Standard deviation	0.142	0.090	0.074	0.089	0.270	0.068	0.050	0.114	0.146
Number of banks	9	10	11	13	15	16	16	20	14
Median	0.324	0.096	0.125	0.211	0.177	0.136	0.059	0.097	—
Maximum	0.482	0.325	0.285	0.438	1.162	0.273	0.214	0.554	—
Total all banks									
Average recovery ratio	0.522	0.457	0.543	0.696	0.598	0.492	0.549	0.588	0.556
Standard deviation	1.226	1.036	1.227	4.036	1.832	1.421	2.303	2.466	2.160
Number of banks	4792	4893	4889	4950	5022	5160	5218	5252	5022
Median	0.304	0.265	0.317	0.341	0.304	0.255	0.267	0.283	0.292
Maximum	36.000	30.000	43.000	—	60.000	43.000	—	98.000	—

age recovery ratio for banks up to $10 million in assets in 1976 was 56%, while the median was 22%.

The median recovery ratio for all banks (5,252) studied in 1976 was 28.3%. The data reported cover all loans including both commercial and consumer. The annual, median recovery ratio for all banks ranged from 25.5% in 1975 to 34.1% in 1972. If we simply average the seven-year median recovery ratios, we find that the experience for all banks was 29.2%. If we take the complement of this result [this is similar to the way we calculated the cost (C_1) of making a bad loan], we find the result is a 70.8% loss—almost identical to the average result for the two prior samples when the data were measured with a one-year lag.

Bank Size and Recovery Experience

One final note is the relationship between bank size and loan loss recovery experience. The recovery experience appears to peak in the $10-million to $20-million asset range with an eight-year average median recovery ratio of 32.8%. The ratio drops consistently as the asset size of banks increases beyond $20 million (Chart 5-2). It is interesting to note that the

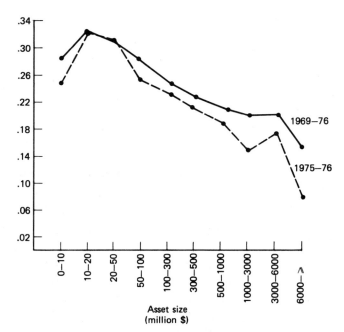

Chart 5-2 Median Recovery (Loan Loss Recoveries/Losses) by Bank Asset Size, 1969–1976 (Coincident Losses and Recoveries).

year-to-year instability of the median recovery ratio is greater in the banks of larger assets, probably because of the relatively small number of banks in those classes.

Why larger banks seem to recover less on charged off loans than do their smaller counterparts is difficult to know. The initial results were, frankly, a bit surprising. Even within specific asset size classes, the chargeoff policy can vary tremendously. Some banks "ride" with a problem loan longer while others write off loans at an early indication of trouble. On the other hand, the individual bank's policy with respect to "reducing their exposure" when problems emerge also could explain differential recovery experience. Since larger banks typically make larger loans and often are part of a lending consortium, it may be more difficult to extricate an individual bank once the loan is clearly in default.

In the next section we will explore, for a large sample of individual *loans,* not only the post-chargeoff experience of banks, but the prior-to-chargeoff events as well. I believe that what happens before a loan is formally written off dictates to some extent what happens afterward. These results will also clear up the "mysterious" finding that large banks recover less than smaller banks.

Loan Loss Recovery Analysis

The prior analysis concentrated upon recovering proceeds from charged off loans. This is the traditional banking industry procedure of examining what occurs after the bank has essentially given up on the account. In our opinion, this procedure is too narrow in its scope. It ignores an important variable in the lending process: what happens in the period immediately prior to chargeoff. The term "recovery" should be broadened to include the bank's efforts to reduce its exposure or to collect prior to the actual chargeoff date.

The point that I am trying to make is perhaps best explained by an example. If a loan of $100 is outstanding and just prior to chargeoff the bank collects $20 (perhaps from a loan setoff), the chargeoff amount will be $80. If subsequent to chargeoff another $20 is recovered, then the traditional method of accounting will indicate a 25% ($20/$80) recovery rate or a 75% loss rate. This was our method in prior analysis. In reality, however, the bank has collected $40 ($20 + $20) on an "original" balance of $100, or a $40 "recovery" rate (60% loss rate). The purpose of this section is to specify explicitly a revised method for calculating the loss rate and then to examine empirically recent bank performance.

The expanded version of our Type I error cost (cost of making a bad loan) is of the form

$$C_1 = \text{LLR} = 1 - \frac{a + b}{\text{LB}_t}$$

where

LLR $=$ rate of loss on loans,
a $=$ amount collected prior to chargeoff,
b $=$ amount recovered after chargeoff, and
LB_t $=$ loan balance at some point t prior to chargeoff.

The amount collected prior to chargeoff is given by the difference between the prior loan balance (LB) and the amount of chargeoff (COA). It remains to define the relevant point in time prior to chargeoff. Admittedly, this is an arbitrary date which should reflect a sufficient period of time to reduce the bank's exposure, but not so long as to bear little relation to the customer's operating situation and funds requirements during the period that problems existed. We have chosen a period of 12 months prior to chargeoff as our benchmark. Probably, something less than 12 months would have been satisfactory, but since we utilized questionnaire responses to analyze individual loan experience, a round number (one year) was chosen for simplicity.

Individual Loan Empirical Results

We have utilized large data bases for assessing recovery experience at the bank level, but unfortunately data bases of individual loans do not exist. We had no choice but to attempt our investigation on a loan-by-loan basis, sending out a short questionnaire to bank representatives in the New York, Southeastern, and Northern California regions of the United States. In all, we sent out over 500 questionnaires, and we received 55 responses of which 49 were usable. Each bank was asked to select up to three charged off loans for each of the years 1975, 1976, and 1977, and to provide us with (1) the loan balance 12 months prior to chargeoff, (2) the balance charged off, and (3) the amount recovered after chargeoff. We recognize that there may be a selection bias since we left the choice of the bad loan up to the reporting bank. In all, we received usable data on 377 loans.

The bank asset size distribution is fairly normal, with the $100- to $300-million size range represented most heavily. Almost one-quarter of the sample are small banks with assets below $100 million and a similar proportion of large banks with assets over $1 billion.

The loan size is most heavily represented by small loans of under $10,000 (one-third of sample), but about one-quarter were over $100,000 and 4.2% over $1 million. Therefore, our results reflect a broad spectrum of bank sizes and loan amounts.

We will examine the following statistics for our sample of 377 loans:

1   $(LB_{12} - COA)/LB_{12}$
2   Recovered amount after CO/LB_{12}
3   Total "recovery" rate = (1) + (2)
4   Traditional recovery rate = recovered amount after CO/COA

The results are illustrated in Table 5-2, with columns (b) − (e) equivalent to 1–4 above.

The average percentage collected before chargeoff ($LB_{12} = COA)/LB_{12}$ was 16.5%. The average can be measured in two ways. We can simply sum up each bank's ratio and divide the total by $N=377$. This was the 16.5% rate noted above. Alternatively, we can calculate the average by summing the amounts of each variable for the entire sample. Interestingly enough, 18 loans (4.7%) actually had chargeoff amounts greater than the 12-month prior balance, which indicates either that significant accrued interest was added to the charged off total, and/or that the bank actually increased the funds available during that period. More than likely, the accrued interest exceeded the reduction in loan balance in a majority of those 18 cases. In addition, 178 loans had identical balances 12 months prior to CO and at the chargeoff date. Therefore, the median prior-to-chargeoff collection rate was 0%. Since outliers (on the high side) are not possible when dealing with individual loans, we will examine the average experience as well as the median.

The average (ratio method) ex-post-chargeoff recovery rate relative to LB_{12} (statistic 2) was 21.1%. Adding the first two statistics (16.5% + 21.1%) we arrive at the average total "recovery" rate of 37.6% (statistic 3). The median percentage for this statistic was 24%. The results indicate that if we measure recovery performance of banks on bad loans and include ex-ante as well as ex-post-chargeoff experience, the average recovery rate is 37.6%. Or, we can say that the loss rate (Type I error) on defaulted loans is slightly over 62%. This compares favorably (for banks) with our previous finding that the Type I error rate for commercial banks is approximately 70%. Banks appear to be more efficient in this function than prior estimates indicated. Note that the banking industry also calculates the recovery statistic in the manner which results in the "lower recovery" experience.

Table 5-2 Collection and Recovery Experience on Sample of Charged Off Loans, 1975–1977.

1975	(a) Loan Size	(b) LB_{12}–COA/LB_{12} (Percentage)	(c) Recovery/LB_{12} (Percent)	(d) Total $(b) + (c)$ (Percent)	(e) Recovery/ COA (Percent)
Mean[a]	$233,730	16.7	22.7	39.4	29.3
Mean[b]	—	37.0	13.0	50.0	20.7
Median	28,500	0.0	7.5	30.0	9.5
Correlation with loan size	1.000	0.256	−0.103	0.100	−0.008
1976					
Mean[a]	$180,000	18.8	21.2	40.0	25.1
Mean[b]	—	44.2	16.3	60.5	29.3
Median	26,200	0.0	2.0	23.0	2.0
Correlation with loan size	1.000	0.299	−0.050	0.181	−0.013
1977					
Mean[a]	$141,000	13.9	19.5	33.4	22.7
Mean[b]	—	33.1	5.9	39.0	8.8
Median	25,800	0.0	1.0	21.0	3.5
Correlation with loan size	1.000	0.244	−0.142	0.049	−0.141
1975–1977					
Mean[a]	$185,200	16.5	21.1	37.6	25.7
Mean[b]	—	38.4	12.3	50.7	20.0
Median	26,200	0.0	3.0	24.0	4.0
Correlation with loan size	1.000	0.263	−0.089	0.114	−0.027

[a] Average of the ratios for the N banks.
[b] Average of the summation of each component for the N banks.

OPTIMAL CUTOFF SCORE ANALYSIS—EMPIRICAL ESTIMATES

As noted earlier, the important inputs for cutoff score determination are the prior probabilities of group membership and the costs of misclassification errors. The specification of loan misclassification costs involves making a loan to a firm which eventually defaults on its obligation (C_1) or not making a loan to a firm which would have repaid successfully (C_2). The priors stand for the bankers' ex-ante assessment that a loan will default or not, before examining the characteristics of the particular loan applicant.

The reason for the differential between the results of the two averaging methods (Table 5-2) is that the correlation between the loan balance 12 months prior and the ex-ante collection experience was +0.263 for the 377 loans. Therefore, it appears that some reduction in risk exposure and/or loan setoff is more likely as loan size increases. On the other hand, the correlation between loan size and recovery after chargeoff was −0.089, indicating that a smaller proportion of larger loans are recovered. This result is perfectly consistent with our previous results on recovery experience with larger banks versus smaller banks (Table 5-1 and Chart 5-2). Table 5-3 indicates the various average recovery statistics by loan size. We observe that the collection and recovery experience before and after chargeoff is fairly uniform for loans up to $100,000 and thereafter changes consistently as the size increases. This is the case regardless of how the average is calculated.

Table 5-3   Average Collection and Recovery Experience by Loan Size, Charged Off Loans Sample.

Loan Size ($ Thousands)	N	Average of Ratios			Average Based on Summation		
		Col-lection	Re-covery	Collection and Recovery	Col-lection	Re-covery	Collection and Recovery
0–10	128	8.9%	23.5%	32.4%	7.2%	27.6%	34.8%
10–50	105	12.3	23.2	35.5	12.5	21.6	34.1
50–100	49	11.7	22.8	34.5	12.0	21.5	33.5
100–200	35	24.1	20.7	44.8	25.9	18.1	44.0
200–1000	44	37.8	11.4	49.2	42.3	12.7	55.0
>1000	16	45.3	10.7	56.0	42.6	9.8	52.4
Total	377						

We can return for a moment to our earlier question concerning recovery performance and bank size. We now observe, by implication, that large banks (actually banks granting larger loans) do considerably better than smaller banks when the *total recovery experience* is observed. This is what we would expect, although the reasons are not perfectly clear. A larger, more impersonal bank is probably more likely to reduce its risk exposure *prior* to writing off the loan whereas the smaller bank will "carry" its small customer for a longer period of time. When a loan is finally charged off, there will be less available for recovery when the collection experience prior to chargeoff has been more successful. There are probably other valid reasons as well.

Type II Error Cost

The cost of not making a loan to a prospective "successful" repayment customer is based on an opportunity cost concept. The bank foregoes the return on the rejected loan but can invest the relevant funds elsewhere. The formulation, therefore, is:

$$C_2 = r - i$$

where

r = effective foregone rate of return on the "rejected" loan, and

i = effective opportunity cost for the bank.

Various relevant abstractions are not considered here, such as the loss of the customer's interest payments on *future* loan agreements, not to mention any returns for other services provided by the bank. In mathematical words, the total opportunity cost is the integral of the interest rate differential over the lifetime horizon of the bank or the firm, whichever is shorter, discounted back to the present on a continuous basis. Assuming $r - i > 0$, we could approximate this loss as a perpetuity of $r - i$ discounted at the bank's cost of capital.

At one end of the limit, $r - i$ equals zero. This will manifest when the bank's opportunity cost implies another loan at the same interest rate, that is, at the same risk, and which is assumed to repay successfully. Note that if r equals i, $C_2 = 0$, and the optimal cutoff score will equal positive infinity, and all loans will be rejected. Realistically speaking, however, a loan applicant is rejected due to its high risk characteristics and an alternative loan, *at the same risk,* will also be rejected. Therefore, the alternative use for the funds implies a loan where the perceived risk is lower. Hence, $r - i$ will be positive but conceivably quite low.

At the other extreme, the bank's minimum opportunity cost is to invest at the risk-free rate, that is, government securities of the same maturity as the loan. The interest rate differential will be higher under this assumption; probably in the 3-to-5% range. The $r - i$ differential will vary over time and is particularly sensitive to demand and supply conditions for loanable funds.

As an approximation, we specify that $C_2 = 2\%$, hence the C_1/C_2 ratio is approximately 31 times (0.62/0.02). Recall that C_1 was estimated at 0.62.

Prior Probabilities of Group Membership

Most discriminant studies assume either that the prior probabilities of group membership are equal or that they equal the relative size of the groups being examined empirically. Since most bankruptcy studies have utilized approximately equal sample sizes in the two groups, the priors were also equal. Deakin (1977) was an exception.

I recognize that the probability that a U.S. corporation will fail is significantly lower than 50%. Yet, it is difficult to know the exact propensity, even if we were considering a particular population of loan applicants known to a specific bank. As we observed in Chapter 1, Dun & Bradstreet's recent failure data indicate that between 0.5 and 1% of those firms covered actually fail in *any given year*. It is not correct, in my opinion, however, to utilize a single calendar year as the criterion, and failure propensities should be assessed over several years with the minimum being the life of the loan. Even this is probably an underestimate of the relevant horizon since a bank/customer relationship is continuous, especially for lines of credit or revolving credit arrangements. In addition, there are many definitions of failure that are critical to the bank, such as the need to renegotiate loan agreements and certainly the accrual of unpaid interest.

In the final analysis, I do not know the exact bankruptcy prior probability to use, but I am confident that the estimate should be based on a multiyear horizon and that this prior has been increasing in recent years. The probability of failure group membership is probably in the 1-to-5% range for all U.S. corporations. The complement of this percentage is the prior probability of nonbankruptcy. For calculation purposes we have selected that $q_1 = 0.02$ and $q_2 = 0.98$.

Calculation of the Optimal Cutoff Score

Using the estimates derived above, we have:

$$CS = \ln \frac{q_1 c_1}{q_2 c_2}$$

and

$$CS = \ln \frac{0.02 \times 0.62}{0.98 \times 0.02}$$

$$CS = -0.458.$$

We observe that the optimum cutoff score falls from the zero cutoff we utilized in our previous ZETA (Chapter 4) discussion to -0.45. The change in the cutoff score will result in more loan applicants being accepted now that the cutoff or hurdle score is lower. In actuality, the ZETA result using this new score has two additional Type I errors (from two to four errors out of 53, or an error rate of 7.6% vs. 3.8%), while the Type II error was reduced from 10.3% to 7.0%. The total error rate and number of errors are unchanged.

It does not appear that the classification results of the model were affected very much by our efforts to insert realistic estimates for the priors and costs. This was primarily due to neutralizing influences of the two ratios; that is, the ratio of C_1/C_2 was high, and the ratio of q_1/q_2 was low. In the original ZETA study, (Altman *et al.*, 1977) we did simulate various priors and costs and the resulting cutoff scores and error rates.

Adjustments to the Cutoff Score and Practical Applications

In addition to the utilization of prior probabilities of group membership and cost estimates of classification errors for comparative model efficiency assessment, these inputs could prove valuable for practical application purposes. For instance, the bank lending officer or loan review analyst may wish to be able to adjust the critical cutoff score logically to consider his own estimates of group priors and error costs and/or to reflect current economic conditions in his environment. One could imagine the cutoff score falling (thereby lowering the acceptance criterion) as business conditions improve and the banker's prior probability of bankruptcy estimate falls from, say, 0.02 to 0.015. Or, a rise in cutoff scores could result from a change (rise) in the estimate of the Type I error cost vis-à-vis the Type II error cost. The latter condition possibly will occur for different decision-makers. For instance, the cost to a portfolio manager of not selling a security destined for failure is likely to be extremely high relative to his cost of not investing in a stock (which does not fail) due to its relatively low ZETA. The portfolio manager may indeed want to raise the cutoff or threshhold level to reduce the possibility of intangible (a lawsuit) as well as tangible (lower prices) costs involved with holding a failed company's stock.

Another example of a practical application of cutoff score adjustment is the case of an accounting auditor. He might wish to use the model to decide whether a going concern qualified opinion should be applied. His expected cost for doing so is likely to be quite high (loss of client) relative to the expected cost of a stockholder lawsuit. This might lead to a fairly low cutoff score. On the other hand, the environment may be such that the lawsuit's expected cost is prohibitive. We will return to applications in the accounting industry in Chapter 7.

ARE FAILURE MODELS BEING USED?

The answer to this relevant question is a documented *yes*! This author is familiar with at least one dozen commercial banks which are using some form of a failure-default classification model in their lending function, and at least another dozen that are using them in some other area—primarily security and portfolio analysis. Another increasingly popular use for such models is to apply a credit risk assessment, that is, a type of bond rating, to private placements of corporate debt. Users for this purpose are the corporate finance and investment banking divisions of banks as well as the lenders—primarily insurance companies.

Although banks are using the old Z-score and ZETA models, their usage is not usually in the original lending function. More than likely, banks use such models for special situations and for loan review (see Chart 5-1 above). A loan review committee may be interested in evaluating a loan in its early stage, but most field lending officers are not likely to use it in their recommendations to lending committees. This is probably due to concern that the computerized model might be a threat to the lending officer's position and function and that nothing could replace the "hands-on" experience of a competent loan officer. I have no quarrel with the position that the lending officer's function is crucial. What would seem appropriate, however, is to add an unambiguous and appropriately developed bankruptcy model to the tools already available to lending officers and review committees.

This suggestion is not only mine. Recently, a banker, Bettinger (1981), made a similar recommendation and cited some work that he did on his own. He finds that while "bankruptcy prediction models can be a useful tool in reducing bank loan losses . . . most banks are not using such models as part of their analysis procedure." Bettinger modified the Z-score model (Chapter 3) by substituting the book value of equity/debt ratio for the market value compilation. (He did not have access to the model which is described at the end of Chapter 3 whereby the initial model is recompiled using the book value figure.) His revised model was applied to a very small sample (six) of defaulted bank loan companies. He found that for the six firms, the revised Z-score model "predicted" the failure accurately four years prior in two cases and three years in advance in the remaining four cases. He observed 100% accuracy for a control sample of six nonbankrupts. Bettinger concludes that such a model could help commercial bankers as a "useful supplement to the overall credit analysis procedure."

LENDING OFFICER JUDGMENTS VERSUS MODEL PREDICTIONS

My prior comments implied that loan officers should not consider their evaluations of the repayment likelihood of customers as opposed to those indications of failure models as a type of challenge. Still, it is useful to observe if such models can be of some assistance to banks. Several studies [e.g., Libby (1975) and Casey (1980)] have looked at lending officer evaluations of financial statements as those belonging to either healthy firms or future bankrupts. While the results of these behavioral studies are not all consistent with each other, I conclude that there is substantial information content in business failure models which combines a great deal of financial information into a single score to present an unambiguous assessment of failure propensity.

In Chapter 4, we reviewed the work of Libby (1975), who tried to assess whether accounting information, particularly a reduced set of just five financial ratios taken from Deakin's (1972) original set of 14, could provide useful information on business failure prediction. He found that loan officers could predict failure and nonfailure with a great deal of accuracy and that the ratios permit bankers with diverse backgrounds to make these accurate predictions. The controversial part of Libby's experiment was that the bankers knew beforehand that half of the sample of firms would fail within three years.

Casey (1980) extended Libby's work and attempted to parallel more closely the loan officer's usual decision-making environment. That is, Casey did *not* indicate what percentage of his 30-firm sample actually went bankrupt. He did include a debt/equity measure in addition to Libby's five variables, and he utilized three years of data as opposed to Libby's one year. Casey sent out a questionnaire to bank loan officers asking them to analyze the 30 subject firms and to indicate which ones were likely to go bankrupt within three years. His response rate was excellent (82%). Average overall accuracy was 17 out of 30 (57%) with only four of the 15 bankrupt firms correctly classified. Casey attributes this low accuracy rate (relative to Libby and to all other models reviewed earlier) to the lack of knowledge about failure frequency of the sample. In addition, Casey, unlike Libby, did not find that a "composite" judge prediction model outperformed the average subject.

CONCLUSION

In this chapter we have concentrated upon the commercial banking industry. This was convenient for at least two purposes. First, it illustrates an empirical methodology that can be used to fine-tune failure prediction cutoff score determination. Second, credit analysis in general and bank commercial credit scoring in particular are obvious and important application areas for solvency models. In the following five chapters, we will explore several other applications.

6 Bankruptcy Models: A Catalyst for Constructive Change— Managing a Financial Turnaround

INTRODUCTION—PRESCRIPTIVE ACTION FOR CRISIS SITUATIONS

Over the last dozen years or so, I have frequently been asked by managers and analysts the very difficult question, "Now that your model has classified the entity as having a high probability of failure, what should be done to avoid this dismal fate?" Not being an operating manager or financial "magician" myself, I had to throw up my hands and reluctantly reply, "Get yourself some new management or specialists in crisis management," or, even less satisfying, "That is your problem!" Needless to say, these answers were not accepted with applause, nor did the response capture the spirit of a true "early warning system." Such a system usually connotes prescribed rehabilitative action when the warnings are in other areas, such as medicine or military science. Unfortunately, management science applications of early warning systems are essentially unique to the entity, and it is difficult to generalize rehabilitative prescriptions.

My attitude toward this important and inevitable outgrowth of bankruptcy prediction has changed. One recent incident has taught me a valuable lesson, one which is, I believe, transferable to other crisis situations. The lesson emanated not from a conceptual, academic analysis of the problem but from the application of the Z-score model (Chapter 3) to a real world problem by a remarkably perceptive chief operating officer.

Let me set forth the case of the GTI Corp., a manufacturer of parts, subsystems, and processing equipment for the computer, automotive, and electronic industries. GTI Corp. is listed on the American Stock Exchange, and its chief executive officer for the last seven years has been James LaFleur.

ACTIVE VERSUS PASSIVE USE OF FINANCIAL MODELS*

Statistically verified predictive models have long been used in the study of business. Generally, these models are developed by scientists and tested by "observers" who do not interact with or influence the measurements of the model. Consequently, the models, when valid, have predicted events with satisfactory accuracy, and business analysts regard them with a reasonable degree of confidence.

This "passive" use of predictive models, for credit analysis, investor analysis, and so on, overlooks the possibility of using them actively. In the "active" use of a predictive model, the role of the observer is shifted to that of a "participant." For example, a manager may use a predictive model that relates to business affairs of a company by deliberately attempting to influence the model's measurements. The manager, acting as a participant rather than as an observer, makes decisions suggested by the parameters of the model in order to "control" its prediction.

In the specific case we will discuss, the Z-score bankruptcy predictor Model was used *actively* to manage the financial turnaround of a company, GTI Corp., that was on the verge of bankruptcy. Michael Ball has written about GTI Corp. in the context of small business management ("Z Factor: Rescue by the Numbers," *Inc. Magazine,* December 1980). C. Hofer has written about turnaround situations in general ("Turnaround Strategies," *The Journal of Business Strategy,* Summer, 1980).

A series of management decisions were made over a period of five years to foil the model's prediction of bankruptcy. These decisions, many of which were specifically motivated by considering their effect on the financial ratios in the model, led directly to the recovery of the company and the establishment of a firm financial base.

The success in the active use of this specific model suggests that it may be worthwhile to consider the "active approach" to the use of other appropriate predictive models.

As noted earlier, what I did not indicate in my earlier work was what

*Much of the material in this section is derived from, E. Altman and J. LaFleur, "Managing A Return to Financial Health," *Journal of Business Strategy,* Summer, 1981.

management could do with the results of the model once the indication was that a firm was headed toward bankruptcy; in other words, that its overall financial profile was consistent with that of other firms whch had gone bankrupt in the past. It took GTI Corp., and specifically the management strategy formulated and implemented by Jim LaFleur, to turn the model "inside out" and show its ability to help shape business strategy to avert bankruptcy.

WHAT THE Z-SCORE TOLD GTI

When Jim LaFleur took charge of the company, GTI had experienced the following changes during the first six months of 1975:

Working capital decreased by $6 million

Retained earnings decreased by $2 million

A $2-million loss incurred

Net worth decreased from $6.207 million to $4.370 million

Market value of equity decreased by 50%

Sales decreased by 50%

Noticing an article in *Boardroom Reports* about the Z-score, LaFleur saw the potential application of the bankruptcy predictor to the problem at hand. As we discussed in Chapter 3, the Z-score model is:

"Z" Factor Components Definitions

Factor	Definition	Weighting Factor
X_1	$\dfrac{\text{working capital}}{\text{total assets}}$	1.200
X_2	$\dfrac{\text{retained earnings}}{\text{total assets}}$	1.400
X_3	$\dfrac{\text{earnings before interest expense and taxes}}{\text{total assets}}$	3.300
X_4	$\dfrac{\text{market value of equity}}{\text{book value of liabilities}}$	0.600
X_5	$\dfrac{\text{sales}}{\text{total assets}}$	0.999

Plugging in the preliminary numbers for the five ratios, LaFleur put the Z-score predictor to work for GTI: the resulting Z-score was 0.7. At that level, the predictor forecasts almost certain bankruptcy. When more accurate numbers were inserted into the Z-score formula, it fell even lower, to 0.38, about half the earlier calculation. The prognosis was grave.

A TOOL FOR RECOVERY

Despite its portent of doom, the Z-score was also seen as a management tool for recovery. Clearly, the predictor's five financial ratios were the key to the Z-score movement, either up or down. While the previous management had inadvertently followed a strategy which had decreased the ratios and caused the Z-score to fall, GTI's new management decided to reverse the plunge by deliberate management action to increase the ratios.

Inherent in the Z-score predictor was the message that *underutilized assets* could be a major contributor to the deterioration of a company's financial condition. Such deterioration had taken place at GTI over several years. The company's total assets had grown out of proportion to other financial factors. I have found this to be the case of many business failures, particularly larger ones.

By using retrospective analysis, LaFleur concluded that the Z-score could have predicted GTI's turn toward financial distress. For example, historical data showed that GTI's Z-score started to dive precipitously two years earlier, in 1973. The retrospective Z-score slide became even steeper in 1974, as GTI dropped at year-end to $0.19 in earnings per share. Thus, GTI's Z-score had been falling for several years, as shown in Chart 6-2, even during periods when the company's profits were rising. That was further proof of the predictor's validity and suggested its ability to help set strategy to guide the company's recovery.

THE EFFECTS OF GROWTH FEVER

For more than two years previously, as a member of the board of directors, LaFleur had cautioned against what appeared to be overaggressive policies of debt and expansion by GTI's operating management. The warnings, unfortunately, had little effect.

Along with most of the industry, GTI had succumbed through the 1960s to a highly competitive growth fever. During those years, many managers focused almost entirely on their P&L statements. They were willing to borrow what was necessary to increase sales and profits. With stock values rising, they expected to obtain very favorable equity funding in the future to pay off the accumulated debt. That strategy served well until economic downturns of 1969 and 1972. Then, with profits falling, many companies had trouble servicing the debt that had looked so easy to handle a few years earlier. But GTI, like many others, continued pursuing the same strategy, despite changed economic conditions. That worked for a while.

But early in 1975, GTI started losing money. Before that profit slide could be stopped, GTI's 1975 net loss accumulated to over $2.6 million on sales of $12 million, a loss of $1.27 per share.

TAKING QUICK ACTION

Then, during the month of May, a member of the audit committee discovered information indicating that the figures for the first quarter of 1975 were reported incorrectly. As the evidence developed during the ensuing audit meetings, it was obvious that the company's problems were serious. GTI's auditing firm began a thorough reexamination of the company's first-quarter activities. The auditors quickly confirmed that there was, indeed, a material discrepancy in the figures and set to work revising first-quarter figures.

A chairman of the audit committee, LaFleur contacted the SEC, disclosing the discrepancy and promising to define and correct it. He also asked the American Stock Exchange to halt trading of the company's stock. By finding the reporting errors quickly, GTI had the stock back in trading in less than ten days. No delisting of the stock ever occurred, and the company even received compliments from some observers on its rapid self-policing action.

At that point, GTI's board of directors chose a new executive team, asking LaFleur to become part of management and take over as chairman and chief executive officer. Having observed GTI going into debt to finance its operations over several prior years, even with record sales and profits on paper, LaFleur was determined to find the underlying problems. It didn't take long.

Inventory, out of control, revealed itself as a major contributor to the company's ballooning assets. In many instances, returned goods had been set aside and not properly accounted for. Adding to that difficulty, work-in-process was grossly out of proportion to sales. Again, these symptoms seem to be common amongst crisis corporations.

GENESIS OF STRATEGY

From this new evidence of excess assets, a recovery strategy began to emerge. It was to find ways to decrease GTI's total assets without seriously reducing the other factors in the numerators of the Z-score's X ratios: working capital, retained earnings, earnings before interest and taxes, market value of equity, and sales. GTI started looking for assets that were not being employed effectively—that is, not earning money. When identified, such assets were sold and the proceeds used to reduce the company's debt. The effect was a decrease in the denominators of all five X ratios simultaneously. It is not enough simply to sell assets—the proceeds must be utilized as soon as possible. GTI's Z-score rose accordingly.

Having evolved the strategy, LaFleur began to implement the action to eliminate GTI's excess assets. Excess inventory was sold as quickly as possible, even at scrap value in some cases.

While the bankruptcy predictor was originally designed for an observer's analysis of a company's condition, GTI used it as an aid to managing company affairs. The predictor actually became an element of active strategy to avoid GTI's impending bankruptcy.

Stopping the Cash Bleed

In quick order, GTI's cash bleed was stanched. The staffs at two unprofitable West Coast plants were sliced to a skeleton crew within ten days, and the corporate staff at headquarters was pared from 32 to six. A year earlier, with company profits at $1.5 million, the corporate staff expense had been over $1 million! All capital programs were frozen. Only the most

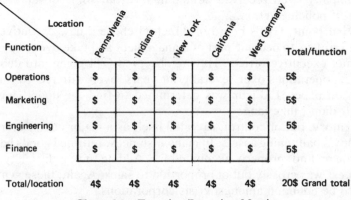

Chart 6-1   Function/Location Matrix.

critical production needs, repair, and maintenance were authorized. GTI asked its creditors for additional short-term credit, then pushed strenuously ahead on its collections. Inventories were placed under strict control. Taking effect, these measures got cash and expenses under control and improved debt service capability.

Reducing costs further took more analysis. A management function/ location matrix, a "job-versus-cost" grid, was constructed for each of GTI's plants. The grid showed each executive's job, what work he performed, and how much that job cost the company. When overlaps or duplications were found, jobs were consolidated. The grid is illustrated in Chart 6-1. Where the revenues from different locations did not cover the identifiable costs, it was clear that a problem existed.

Finding Lost Profits—Employee Assistance

Employees were also involved in the turnaround. A simple questionnaire was handed out to the 250 employees of GTI's largest plant in Saegertown, Pennsylvania, asking their opinions on why the plant was no longer profitable. The implied question, of course, was about the underutilized assets that had depressed GTI's Z-score. The employees knew what was wrong. They were specific about how to improve the use of their machines. Many of the suggestions were implemented, and productivity improved. Eventually, however, this plant was sold and product lines moved elsewhere.

Several weeks later, similar questions were asked at GTI's plant in Hadley, Pennsylvania. The employee responses resulted in changing the plant's organization from functional to product line, another move that more effectively employed the company's assets. Because they participated in the changes, the plant's employees really worked to make the reorganization succeed. After a few weeks, the plant began to return to profitability. In fact, profitable product lines were moved from Saegertown to Hadley.

Those profits were the forerunner of profits that would be produced in other parts of the company as time went on. The Z-score, while it did not jump as a result of those profits, did begin to react. By mid-1976, after slanting down for three years, the Z-score bottomed out and started up. GTI began turning the corner.

Selling Off a Product Line

Though cost reduction and increased profits had eased the problems, GTI needed stronger recovery actions. The function/location matrix analysis was extended to include products and was used to rate product profitability throughout the company. Plans were made to eliminate the losers and

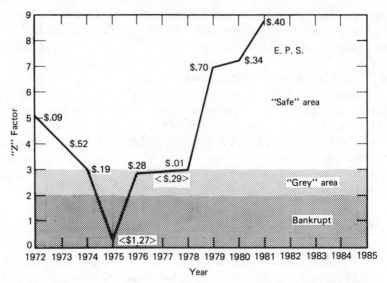

Chart 6-2 *Z*-Score Bankruptcy Predictor as Applied to GTI Corp.

strengthen the winners. As a result, late in 1976, GTI sold one of its major underutilized assets. GTI's crystal base product line had appeared fairly strong, but the product matrix analysis presented a different view. Crystal bases were not complementary to GTI's other products, and though the line had been marginally profitable in the past, demand for its products was likely to decrease. The line also appeared to need a great deal of capital to be competitive in the future.

The cash generated by the sale of the crystal base product line was used to reduce debt. The consequent simultaneous decrease of both total assets and debt produced a dramatic effect. The *Z*-score leaped from under 1.0 to 2.95. In one transaction, GTI zoomed almost all the way into the *Z*-score predictor's safe zone.

Although to outside observers the company did not appear to turn around for another year and a half, LaFleur felt the firm was on the road to recovery with the sale of the crystal base product line. The company had come from almost certain bankruptcy to the stage where it could begin contemplating new products. In less than 18 months, the *Z*-score had climbed from 0.38, in the near-death bankrupt zone, almost all the way to the *Z*-score's safe zone (see Chart 6-2).

With heightened confidence in the model, GTI started working to put the *Z*-score firmly in the safe zone. Since the company's improving stability and profitability were corroborating the *Z*-score approach, GTI's headquarters staff began figuring how a proposed new product or financial transaction would affect the rising Z-score. Further, GTI extended the product evaluation matrix from simple profit and loss to multiyear projections of return on assets. This involved taking a hard look at projected working capital and capital expenditure requirements, product by product. This analysis established what costs would be if the company attempted to expand within its current markets.

Progress in Operations

While doing this planning, GTI continued to make progress on the operations side, finishing 1976 with $0.28 earnings per share and an increasing Z-score as well. In 1977, earnings sagged to $0.01 per share; but with an improving overall financial condition, GTI's Z-score continued gradually to rise. The company even bought out a competitor's glass seal product line with notes secured by the acquired assets—with negligible adverse impact on the Z-score.

Then in 1978, GTI boosted its Z-score again by shutting down an entire division, which made ceramic capacitors, and selling its assets. That transaction, again based on the strategy of selling underutilized assets to pay off debt, occurred later than it should have. This was a case of emotion interfering with a rational, proven strategy. LaFleur had been swayed toward saving this technically interesting product line, though the Z-score strategy consistently suggested disposal. Though delayed, the difficult disposal decision was made.

As a result of the closing of the capacitor division and the sale of its assets, GTI's 1978 bottom line sustained a $0.29 per share loss, but the Z-score increased automatically as the company paid off more debt. As anticipated, operating profits continued to gain throughout the year, paving the way for a strong 1979. Once again, the asset-reduction strategy had worked.

INTO THE SAFE ZONE

Since then, GTI's Z-score has continued climbing, rising through the Z-score's safe zone, as 1979 pretax profits reached $1.9 million and $0.70 per share on sales of $21 million. From a balance sheet viewpoint, GTI's strategy, in five years, had decreased the debt to equity ratio from 128% to 30%, and increased stockholder's equity from $3.5 million to $4.7 million. The debt to equity (market equity) improved even more in 1981, to just under 10%! See Table 6-1 which compares results in 1975, 1979, and

Table 6-1   Getting GTI into the Safe Zone.

	1975	1979	1981
Comparative Balance Sheet ($ Millions)			
Current assets	5.1	5.3	8.1
Total assets	9.6	8.3	13.0
Current liabilities	3.7	2.5	3.4
Total liabilities	6.1	3.6	4.4
Equity	3.5	4.7	8.6
Total liabilities and equity	9.6	8.3	13.0
Comparative Income Statement ($ Millions)			
Net sales	12	21	19
Cost of goods sold	11	15	13
Gross profit	1	6	6
SG&A	(3.5)	(4.1)	4
Other expenses	(.5)	-0-	-0-
Profit (loss) before taxes	(3.0)	1.9	1.6
Miscellaneous Financial Factors ($ Millions)			
Working capital	1.4	2.8	4.7
Market value of equity	1	15[a]	10.6
Debt/equity (market value)	128%	30%	9.5%
Current ratio	1.38	2.10	2.40
Acid ratio	0.78	1.29	1.50

[a]1980 high.

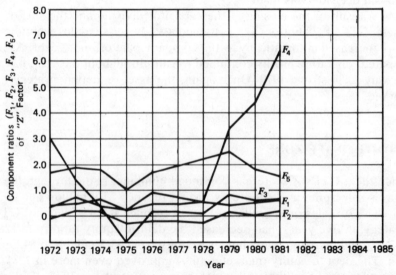

Chart 6-3   Components of Z-Score Bankruptcy Predictor as Applied to GTI Corp.

1981 (the latest data available). The dramatic improvement can also be seen in Chart 6-3 which shows how each of the Z-score's five components trended since 1972.

GTI is today a financially sound company pursuing new avenues to controlled growth. In major part, that success came about from implementing a financial strategy suggested by the Z-score bankruptcy predictor model.

During 1980 and 1981, GTI further consolidated its financial position and increased stockholders' equity. The company continued its policy of conservative financial management augmented by close attention to the Z-score in business decision making.

That spirit was reflected in August of 1980, when the company entered into an agreement with an R&D limited partnership to research and develop several new projects for the partnership for $925,000. Further, to raise return on investment and to provide more funds for new growth in electronics, GTI disposed of a metal and plastics product line in early 1981. In July of 1981, GTI negotiated a 10-year loan for $1.0 million at a fixed 16% to provide increased working capital.

Moreover, as a result of careful financial planning and continued profitability, GTI has attained positive flow in the net interest of its investment and loan portfolio. Essentially, the company now has internalized "control" of the Z-score, because it has sufficient funds available to pay off debt. In terms of the model, the firm can actively impact and control the financial ratio X_4 or the relation between its equity value and outstanding debt. GTI's Z-score zoomed to 7.0 in 1979 and continued to rise to 8.8 as of year-end 1981 mainly as a result of improvement in X_4. This rise is all the more impressive in view of the recessionary period in the early 1980s, including a drop in earnings in 1980.

CONCLUSION TO THE GTI STORY

We believe that certain predictive models offer opportunities to be used as management tools. Supporting that view, GTI's employment of the Z-score bankruptcy predictor has been described as a specific illustration of how an ordinarily passive model can be used actively with substantial success.

With emphasis made on prudent selection and use, managers are encouraged to search out and review predictive models that relate to their company's activities. Improved business strategies could well result. It is quite conceivable that a large number of firms presently in a distressed situation can learn from and perhaps be put on the road to recovery by the strategies used by GTI Corp.

7 Accounting Implications of Failure Prediction Models

INTRODUCTION

Most of the recent literature and discussion in the public accounting sector concerned with failing firms has centered around the qualified opinion as to whether a firm is or is not a "going concern" and the responsibilities of auditors to identify and report potential solvency problems. Solvency analysis is certainly relevant to the going concern concept, but it is related to other aspects of auditing. This chapter will explore going concern issues, and, in addition, it will discuss constructive potentialities inherent in the professional association between an accounting firm and its clients.

An accurate and reliable failure classification model would appear to be an important and persuasive analytical tool for an auditor when discussing problems with clients and recommending effective changes in policies and procedures. Despite an auditor's expertise and familiarity with a client's business, it is felt that the existing auditor-client relationship lacks some degree of objectivity. In essence, the auditor may be "too close" to the situation or lack the influence necessary to effect positive change even if problems are deemed to be likely. If, however, the well-informed but subjective assessment of a company's strengths and weaknesses is complemented by a warning from an objective model, management might very well be persuaded to effect change, before, it is hoped, it becomes necessary to "force" change in top management. Changes and guidelines mentioned in the dramatic story of the financial turnaround by GTI Corp. [see Chapter 6] illustrate how an external influence can bring about meaningful change in cooperation with informed management.

I will address again the going concern qualification issue [see Altman and McGough (1974) for an early analysis in this area] from several viewpoints. Some recent empirical work analyzing the efficacy of failure prediction models in assisting audit teams is presented in conjunction with a discussion of the relative costs of audit, going concern qualification errors. Throughout, I will discuss the controversy over the responsibilities of auditors in this sensitive area.

The going concern qualified opinion has been under constant review by the accounting industry. In a recent (April 1982) meeting of the Auditing Standards Board, a vote of ten for, three against, and two abstentions sanctioned the publication of a new exposure draft to be issued in June 1982. This exposure draft will recommend the elimination of "subject to" qualified opinions and require adequate disclosure in footnotes as to the nature of contingencies which could have led to "subject to" opinions in the past. Hence, "clean" opinions would be consistent with an imminently failing situation as long as adequate disclosure is made. Such disclosure when a question arises as to an entity's continued existence has been advocated by the accounting industry for many years, most recently in the Statement on Auditing Standards (SAS) No. 34, Paragraph 10 (March 1981).

Industry analysts expect the SEC's accounting staff to dispute this new exposure draft idea and continue to hold that there is valid public benefit derived from the information content of qualified going concern opinions. It is not clear how the majority of accounting practitioners will react to this new move to eliminate qualified opinions due to uncertainty over the going concern issue. Canadian accounting auditors eliminated the going concern qualification in 1981.

Failure classification models of the Z-score and ZETA (Chapters 3 and 4) type should not be used by auditors primarily as failure prediction tools to determine going concern problems. While the applicability of such models is obviously related to the auditors' opinions on this issue, the main purposes for the use of such models should be to present a more comprehensive picture of a firm's relative strengths and weaknesses and also to assess performance. In this regard, Z-scores and the component variables can be presented not only in absolute terms, but also in percentile comparisons with over 2,000 listed companies. The analyst can use these percentiles as another piece of information in his overall evaluation.

FAILURE MODELS AND GOING CONCERN QUALIFICATIONS

Financial statements quantify information concerning the financial position of an entity and the results of its operations. An auditor's report adds a qualitative dimension to that information. Within the confines of generally accepted accounting principles, it is the auditor's charge to judge the fairness of those statements. Users rely on the independent auditor to call to their attention situations that impair the fair presentation of financial statements in conformity with accepted principles.

A basic objective of financial statements is to provide information useful for making economic decisions. If the uncertainty of future events undermines the usefulness of information, the auditor has a responsibility to call that uncertainty to the attention of the reader. The most fundamental judgment by an auditor concerning the future of an enterprise is its ability to continue to operate as a going concern. Investment decisions take on a new perspective when that company is facing possible liquidation, bankruptcy, or reorganization.

An underlying assumption in the accounting process is that the reporting enterprise will continue as a going concern. *Accounting Principles Board* Statement No. 4 makes this assumption explicit where the entity is viewed as continuing in operation in absence of evidence to the contrary. Because the going concern assumption is so basic, the standard auditor's report does not make reference to it. The auditor is constantly being reminded, however, to watch for signs of financial distress. For example, the recent SAS ruling No. 34 (Section 340), March 1981, "The Auditor's Consideration When A Question Arises About An Entity's Continued Existence," attempts to specify under what conditions an auditor might be alerted with respect to contrary information (Section 340.04) and "mitigating factors" (Section 340.05,06). Carmichael (1972:94) lists problems as financial in nature (e.g., liquidity deficiency, equity and solvency deficiency, debt default, and funds shortage) and/or operational in nature (continued losses, prospective doubtful revenues, legal uncertainties affecting operations, and poor control over operations). Heath (1978) attempts to compare long-run solvency problems with short operating ones.

In cases where unresolvable uncertainties exist in such magnitude that the continued existence of the operation is uncertain, the auditor is in a quandary. The reporting standards of the accounting profession require the auditor to highlight material uncertainties and call attention to them by stating that his opinion is "subject to" the effects of the resolution of the matter. In some cases the auditor may consider the uncertainties so significant he declines to express any opinion at all (disclaimed) on the statements. Presumably the latter treatment would apply where the auditor feels there is no longer a going concern, but, since an auditor's opinion is taken seriously by the financial community, the disclaimer might itself trigger the end of the going concern.

Several important observations should be made at this point. First, the auditor's responsibility is clearly not to predict bankruptcy. Rather, the auditor is assessing the facts known to him at the time of the report in order to determine if imminent liquidation is evident. The auditor is concerned with the recoverability and classification of recorded assets and with the amounts and classifications of liabilities, rather than predicting bankruptcy *per se*.

An auditor's report that contains an exception for going concern considerations actually constitutes disclosure. In all other matters except going concern considerations, disclosure is the responsibility of the company, not the auditor. The so-called Cohen Commission Report (1978), "The Commission On Auditors' Responsibilities," concluded (p. 30):

> Thus, even the extreme uncertainty about a company's ability to continue operations can be more effectively communicated by disclosure in or adjustment of financial statements than by audit reporting requirements.

That same Cohen Commission Report realizes, however, that users of financial statements often view the qualification or nonqualification on the basis of going concern as a prediction of insolvency. My own personal experience and observation in court cases corroborate this conclusion, to some extent. For example, in *U.S.* v. *Black & Decker* (D. Md. (1976) 430 F. Supp. 729), the court ruled that McCulloch (the acquired firm in a contested merger with Black & Decker) was a "failing firm" because, among other reasons given, it was not likely that the auditors of McCulloch would be issuing a "clean" opinion as to going concern. Incidentally, this case was probably the first instance whereby a model was used to assess a firm's insolvency potential. In *F. & M. Schaefer Corp* v. *C. Schmidt & Sons*, (SDNY (1979) 597 F.2d 814), one reason given as to why Schaefer was not a failing firm was that the auditors continued to give Schaefer a clean opinion without qualification.

CAN FAILURE PREDICTION MODELS HELP?

It is clear that the auditor is not necessarily qualified for, not does he want to be in, the bankruptcy prediction business. While the accounting firm must remain alert for evidence that might negate the going concern assumption, it cannot spend time measuring this "behavioral" event for all firms at all times. Can the auditor be assisted in the oversight problem? I feel that there is an important role that a rapid, reliable business failure model can play in the overall audit risk assessment. I noted earlier how models can assist the auditor in his continuing relations with clients. In addition, such review techniques can help channel scarce resources into a more comprehensive examination of problem clients. The Cohen Commission indicated that statistical failure models might very well be considered by auditors in their overall assessment (1978:30). In subsequent analysis, I will explore some evidence of the correlation between going concern qualifications and actual bankruptcy, and I will also assess whether a failure classification model could have been useful in this context.

EMPIRICAL EVIDENCE ON GOING CONCERN OPINIONS, MODELS, AND BANKRUPTCY

Analysis of Bankrupt Companies

The bankruptcy classification model and the auditor's report have different but analogous functions. The model is developed to assess potential bankruptcy. The auditor does not attempt any such prediction. An unqualified opinion is not a guarantee that a company will continue as a going concern, and an exception because of going concern problems is not a prediction of liquidation. An opinion expressing doubts concerning a company's ability to continue as a going concern is based on the uncertainty of the fairness of presentation of the financial statements. It would be possible for financial statements based upon historical cost to be fairly presented when the company is facing bankruptcy if the carrying value of the assets of that company represents the realizable value of those assets. Still, a proven prediction technique may alert the auditor to certain problems that may be difficult to detect by traditional auditing procedures.

It is then the responsibility of the audit team to devote the necessary resources for establishing whether a going concern opinion is warranted. Alternatively, it might be felt that a financial turnaround is feasible.

I have examined a number of separate samples of bankrupt companies to assess the association between three related "events": bankruptcy, the bankruptcy classification model's score and prediction, and the auditor's opinion as to whether or not the firm is a going concern. The three samples include that which was first used by Altman and McGough (1974) for 28 bankrupt firms from 1970 through 1973 and a more recent sample of 37 bankrupt firms from 1974 through 1978, also comparing the model with auditor opinion. Finally, we assess 44 bankrupts in the period from 1978 through 1982, comparing auditor opinion and a modified Z-score measure.

Results

The original Altman-McGough test showed that the Z-score model was approximately 82% accurate in bankruptcy identification based on the last financial statement prior to failure (Tables 7-1 and 7-2). The accuracy

Table 7-1 Comparison of Z-Score Model Results to Auditor Opinions for Bankrupt Companies (1970–1973).

Company	Bankruptcy Date	Z-Score		Opinions	
		One Year-end prior	Two Year-ends prior	One Year-end prior	Two Year-ends prior
Advance Metal Products	December '72	-0.33	0.71	E[a]	E
Beck Industries	August '70	2.14	7.77	OK[b]	OK
Bishop Industries	October '70	0.84	0.74	OK	OK
Botany Industries, Inc.	April '72	2.16	2.13	E	OK
Century Geophysical	April '71	0.60	2.47	E	OK
Cle-ware Industries	February '71	1.70	2.74	E	OK
Computer Applications	October '70	1.95	2.42	OK	OK
Dolly Madison Industries	June '70	1.89	2.85	OK	OK
Electro Data Inc.	April '73	0.57	14.63	E	OK
Eon Corp.	January '73	-1.07	1.18	E	E
Escro, Inc.	March '73	2.12	2.75	E	OK
Executive House, Inc.	March '71	2.12	3.76	OK	OK
Farrington Manufacturing Co.	January '71	0.89	2.04	E	OK
Federal's, Inc.	August '72	2.36	2.47	OK	OK
Fluidic Industries, Inc.	June '73	2.81	3.15	OK	OK
GF Industries	October '70	—	2.07	—	OK
Great Markwestern Packing Co.	October '71	4.39	5.64	OK	OK
Gro-Plant Industries, Inc.	August '72	0.86	1.09	E	OK
Hoffman Products, Inc.	June '73	0.32	1.33	E	E
Information Machines	October '72	9.47	—	OK	—

Company	Date				
J. D. Jewell, Inc.	October '72	—	—	3.85	OK
Medical Analytics	March '73	2.31	OK	4.02	OK
Milo Electronics	July '70	1.75	OK	2.44	OK
National Radio Company	August '70	0.84	E	1.54	E
RAI International	February '73	2.33	OK	2.64	OK
R.E.D.M. Corp.	March '72	4.56	OK	4.78	OK
Remco Industries	January '71	3.48	OK	6.15	OK
RIC International Industries	September '70	1.31	E	7.24	OK
Roberts Company	February '70	—	—	2.07	OK
Tilco, Inc.	February '73	—	—	2.37	E
Topper Corp.	February '73	—	—	2.11	OK
Torginal Industries	March '73	—	—	0.86	E
Transogram, Inc.	February '71	1.96	OK	2.13	E
Visual Electronics	July '70	−0.98	E	3.29	OK

[a] E = exception because of going concern problems.
[b] OK = no mention of going concern problems.

213

Table 7-2 Summary of Comparison of Z-Score Model to Auditor Opinions (1970–1973).

	Z-Score		Opinions	
	One Year-end prior	Two Year-ends prior	One Year-end prior	Two Year-ends prior
Predicted bankruptcy	23	19	13	7
Unsuccessful prediction	5	14	15	26
Total companies	28	33	28	33
Total success rate	82.1%	57.6%	46.4%	21.2%

Table 7-3 Comparison of Z-Score Model Results to Auditor Opinions for Bankrupt Companies (1974–1978).

Company	Bankruptcy Date	Z-Score		Opinion	
		One Year-end prior	Two Year-ends prior	One Year-end prior	Two Year-ends prior
Acme-Hamilton Manufacturing Corp.	2/78	1.070	1.830	E	OK
Alan Wood Steel	77	1.210	1.340	E	OK
Allied Leisure Industries, Inc.	3/77	2.450	3.610	E	OK
Apeco Corp.	78	2.065	2.748	OK	OK
Bowmar Instruments	74	(1.701)	4.069	E	OK
Caribbean Leisurewear Inc.	2/78	0.984	2.300	E	OK
Commodore Corp.	8/74	(2.595)	(0.155)	E	OK
Compucorp	10/76	(0.946)	0.125	OK	OK
Downen Zieu Knits, Inc.	6/77	0.898	1.297	OK	OK
Duplan Corp.	76	1.204	1.384	OK	OK
Dynapac	6/77	5.241	4.180	E	OK
Epidyne, Inc.	1/78	4.460	4.612	OK	OK
Fields Plastic and Chemical, Inc.	7/77	(0.125)	(0.151)	E	OK
Flock Industries, Inc.	4/77	1.517	1.772	E	OK
G & R Industries	10/77	0.576	0.742	E	E
Gay Gibson	5/77	1.154	2.509	E	OK
Gladding Corp.	4/77	2.162	1.660	E	OK
Gray Manufacturing	75	1.396	2.200	OK	OK
Gruen Industries	4/77	1.473	1.159	OK	OK
Hers Apparel Industries, Inc.	5/74	3.889	3.025	OK	OK
House of Knitting	1/75	3.421	4.786	E	OK
International Video Corp.	6/77	1.272	0.440	E	OK

(Continued)

Table 7-3 (*Continued*)

Company	Bankruptcy Date	Z-Score		Opinion	
		One Year-end prior	Two Year-ends prior	One Year-end prior	Two Year-ends prior
Julyn Sportswear Inc.	11/77	3.721	2.894	OK	OK
Larson Industries	8/75	(4.297)	0.206	E	OK
Mark Systems, Inc.	8/77	(14.896)	0.347	E	OK
Nelly Don	5/78	0.229	0.830	E	OK
Omega-Alpha	75	(0.219)	0.938	E	OK
Permameer	11/76	(0.356)	(0.153)	E	E
Precision Polymers	10/76	2.352	3.140	OK	OK
Rosenau Brothers	4/75	2.901	3.476	E	E
Rupp Industries	2/76	1.762	0.900	OK	E
Sitkin Smelting & Refining	3/78	1.650	1.860	OK	OK
Stellar Industries	4/75	(0.200)	(0.810)	E	E
Supronics Corp.	10/76	1.141	1.560	OK	OK
Tennessee Forging Steel Corp.	12/77	(0.052)	2.644	E	OK
United Merchants and Manufacturers	77	2.220	1.830	OK	OK
Universal Container Corp.	3/78	2.829	2.615	OK	OK

Table 7-4   Summary of Comparison of Z-Score Models to Auditor Opinions (1974–1978).

	Z-Score		Opinions	
	One Year-end prior	Two Year-ends prior	One Year-end prior	Two Year-ends prior
Predicted bankruptcy	30	27	22	5
Unsuccessful prediction	7	10	15	32
Total companies	37	37	37	37
Total success rate	81.1%	73.0%	59.5%	13.5%

Table 7-5 Corporate Bankruptcies: Scores and Auditor Opinions (1978–1982).

Company	Auditor	Bankruptcy Filing Date	Modified Z-Scores		Auditor Opinions	
			One Year prior	Two Years prior	One Year prior	Two Years prior
Advent Corp.	Arthur Andersen	3/81	-0.49	-0.78	E	E
Allied Artists	Price Waterhouse	4/79	-0.82	-1.26	OK	OK
Allied Supermarkets	Deloitte Haskins & Sells	11/78	-0.83	-0.74	OK	OK
Arctic Enterprises	Arthur Andersen	2/81	-0.83	-0.05	OK	OK
Barclay Enterprises	Touche Ross	6/81	-0.99	-0.21	E	OK
Bobbie Brooks	Peat Marwick Mitchell & Co.	1/82	-0.29	-0.05	OK	OK
Capehart	Laventhol & Horwath	2/79	-0.56	-0.98	OK	E
City Stores	Touche Ross/Ernst & Ernst	7/79	-0.31	-0.35	OK	OK
Commonwealth Oil Refining	Deloitte Haskins & Sells	7/79	-1.20	-0.83	E	E
Cooper-Jarrett, Inc.	Peat Marwick Mitchell & Co.	12/81	-1.22	-0.97	E	E
E.C. Ernst	Richard Eisner	12/78	-0.81	0.44	OK	OK
Garcia Corp.	Ernst & Ernst	8/78	-1.02	-0.58	E	OK
General Recreation	Arthur Andersen	12/78	-2.41	-1.25	E	OK
Goldblatt Bros.	Arthur Andersen	6/81	-0.54	0.21	OK	OK
GRT Corp.	Price Waterhouse/Ernst & Ernst	7/79	-0.66	-0.25	OK	OK
Inforex, Inc.	Arthur Andersen	10/79	0.24	-0.06	OK	OK
Interlee (FDI)	Arthur Young & Co.	12/78	-0.32	-0.31	OK	OK
Lafayette Radio Electronics	Touche Ross	1/80	-0.77	-0.44	E	OK
Lionel Corp.	Price Waterhouse	2/82	-0.19	0.28	OK	OK
Lynnwear Corp.	Brout & Co.	2/81	-0.59	-0.06	OK	OK
Mansfield Tire and Rubber	Arthur Young & Co.	10/79	-0.90	-0.24	E	E

Company	Auditor	Date				
Mays Department Stores	Arthur Andersen	1/82	1.18	1.07	OK	OK
McLouth Steel	Ernst & Whinney	12/81	−0.49	0.06	OK	OK
Metropolitan Greeting Cards	Touche Ross/J.K. Lasser	1/79	−0.95	−0.30	E	OK
Murphy Pacific Marine						
Salvage Company	Timothy Kip Firm	5/79	−0.49	0.21	OK	OK
National Shoes	Peat, Marwick, Mitchell & Co.	12/80	−0.16	−0.15	OK	OK
North American Development Corp.	Arthur Young & Co.	N.A.	−2.58	−2.30	OK	OK
Orange Blossom Products	Levine, Cohn et al./Haskins & Sells	6/79	−2.46	−2.19	E	OK
Pantry Pride	Laventhol & Horwath	10/78	−0.12	−0.15	OK	OK
Pathcom Inc.	Ernst & Ernst	1/78	−0.98	−0.70	E	OK
Penn Dixie Industries	Coopers & Lybrand	4/80	−0.70	0.19	E	OK
Piedmont Industries	Ernst & Ernst/S.P. Leidesdorf	2/79	−0.29	−0.22	OK	OK
Reinell Industries	Price Waterhouse	1/79	−1.43	−1.18	E	E
Richton International	Arthur Andersen	3/80	−0.08	0.62	E	E
Sambo's Restaurants Inc.	Touche Ross	6/81	0.11	−0.35	E	OK
Sam Solomon	Arthur Young & Co.	5/81	−0.27	−0.20	E	N.A.
Shulman Transport Enterprises	Rouche Ross	8/78	−1.11	−0.97	N.A.	OK
Stevecoknit, Inc.	Arthur Andersen	11/81	−0.36	0.10	OK	E
Swift Industries	Coopers & Lybrand	N.A.	−1.86	−1.08	OK	E
Tenna	Ernst & Whinney	12/79	−0.27	−0.67	OK	E
The Upson Co.	Price Waterhouse	6/80	−0.44	−0.27	OK	OK
West Chemical Products	Ernst & Ernst	1/79	−0.12	1.05	E	OK
White Motors	Ernst & Whinney	9/80	−0.24	−0.35	OK	OK
Wilson Freight	Ernst & Whinney	7/80	−0.92	−0.55	OK	OK

Summary of Results

Number of Correct Bankruptcy Indications			41	34	17	9
Number of Observations			44	44	43	43
Percentage Accuracy			93%	76%	40%	21%

219

drops to 57.6% in Year 2 prior. The auditors were qualifying (E = exception) based on going concern considerations in 46.4% and 21.2% for Years 1 and 2 respectively. While the model obviously was far more accurate, I was a bit surprised that in as much as 46% of the cases, the statements were being qualified. Obviously, the model could have been extremely useful in a number of those cases where the auditors, based on their normal risk analysis assessment, did not deem the situation serious enough to qualify their reports. This seems to have been the case in almost 40% of the bankruptcies. The 82% accuracy rate (18% error) is also a type of holdout prediction test on the original Z-score model.

The second sample of 37 bankruptcies (Tables 7-3, 7-4) indicates a similar result with a Z-score accuracy rate of 81.1%, one statement prior, and an improved 73.0% two statements prior. The auditor going concern opinion frequency was 59.5% one statement prior and 13.5% two statements prior.

The final sample includes 44 of the most recent bankrupt companies, and this time a variation on Z-score was utilized. With this model, a negative score indicates a greater than 50% probability of being classified as bankrupt. The classification accuracy was 93% and 76% compared to auditor opinion accuracy of 40% and 21% (Table 7-5). The auditor's opinion was somewhat less accurate than in previous results. If we combine the three samples' results (109 observations), we find that the failure models predict with 86.2% accuracy (one statement prior). On the other hand, auditors were qualifying the bankrupt firms' statements 48.1% of the time (Table 7-6).

The costs to auditors of giving a going concern opinion when failure does not occur is possibly quite high, and most observers that I have

Table 7-6 Summary of Bankruptcy Classification Accuracy: Model and Auditor Opinions (1970–1982).

Sample Number	Observations	Bankruptcy Classification by Model		Going Concern Classification	
		Year 1	Year 2	Year 1	Year 2
1 (1970–1971)	28	23	19	13	7
2 (1972–1978)	37	30	27	22	5
3 (1979–1982)	44	41	34	17	9
Total	109	94	80	52	21
Percent accurate		86.2%	73.4%	48.1%	19.3%

talked with do not believe that the frequency of going concern opinions is very high. We will explore this issue below.

We conclude that bankruptcy classification models would have been an effective adjunct to the normal audit risk analysis of accounting auditors in spotting likely failures prior to the event of bankruptcy. Indeed, if corrective action could have prevented the failure, the audit team might have "denied" me bankruptcy observations. I will now discuss auditor attitudes toward going concern qualifications and the perceived costs of auditor "errors."

AUDITOR ATTITUDES ON GOING CONCERN QUALIFICATIONS

As pointed out by Kida (1980), comparison between model accuracy and auditors' qualified opinions may not be unbiased since the opinion given may be confounded by extraneous factors. For example, although an auditor may feel that the firm is a likely bankruptcy candidate, a qualified opinion may not be given due to the perceived consequences of qualifying. I will discuss several of these consequences when we address the subject of costs of errors related to going concern opinions.

Kida examines the interaction between qualification decisions and attitudes. The latter are determined by perceived outcomes of qualifying or not. First, audit partner abilities to spot firm problems based on financial ratios were determined and compared to the accuracy of a mathematical model. The partners (27) were asked to assess how many of the 40 manufacturing firms under consideration were likely to experience one or more of the following: (1) receivership, (2) reorganization, (3) default on interest payments, (4) its third consecutive year of substantial losses (5) significant deficits, or (6) liquidation of its assets. They were not told how many of the 40 firms actually suffered these problems (in reality, half of the 40 did). The auditors were asked to rate each firm on a six-point scale as to the likelihood of its continuing and then were asked whether or not, given their belief about the firm's going concern status, they would issue a(n) unqualified, qualified, or disclaimed opinion. Since the firm names were not given, the results were not influenced by the subjects' knowledge of the various firms.

Using a five-variable discriminant model, similar to my Z-score model, 85% of the problem and 95% of the no-problem firms (90% overall) were correctly classified based on a holdout (jackknife) test. The average number of correct decisions made by the auditors was 33.2 out of 40. Kida concluded that the use of ratios enabled the auditors to achieve excellent accuracy, remarkably close to that of the discriminant model. It is interesting to note that these findings, at least in terms of the usefulness of ratios, were quite different from those reported by Moriarity (1979) in his study of multidimensional graphics (faces) versus ratios as bankruptcy predictors. Moriarity found that simple "faces" were more effective bankrupt/nonbankrupt indicators than the ratios when tested on students and auditors.

Finally, Kida compared those instances when a problem was identified by the auditor with the frequency of mention of a going concern problem. On the average, problems were indicated for 17.5 out of 40 firms, but only in 13.2 out of 40 cases was a qualified or disclaimed opinion rendered. One auditor thought that as many as 22 firms had problems, but he only qualified six, and another did not qualify one although he recognized 14 problems. Kida concludes that this discrepancy between recognition and action was caused by subject attitudes and contributes to the discrepancy between actual problems and qualifications that were found by Altman and McGough (1974) and those found in this chapter (see Tables 7-4 and 7-6).

Kida's finding that a positive association exists between auditors' qualifying decisions and attitudes seems plausible. At the same time, it is difficult to adjust the discrepancy between audit opinion and model efficiency since both attitudes and risk of firms are changing over time. It appears that auditors in recent years are more likely to qualify or disclaim than they were 10 years ago, because of the increased pressure from within and without their profession to take a greater interest and responsibility to detect firm distress. The best testimony to that is the existence of the aforementioned SAS 34 on "The Auditor's Consideration When a Question Arises About an Entity's Continued Existence" (1981). Further, I feel that laboratory tests similar to ones conducted by Kida probably overestimate the bankruptcy prediction accuracy of auditors and also their going concern opinion frequency relative to reality. How great is this discrepancy, I do not know.

THE COSTS OF AUDITOR GOING CONCERN "ERRORS"

An important consideration in determining the appropriate courses of action to take when considering a going concern opinion is to examine the costs involved. We will define the types of error as follows:

	Audit Opinion Classification	
Actual Results	Going Concern Exception	No Exception
Bankrupt	Correct	Type 1 error
Not bankrupt	Type 2 error	Correct

Type I Errors

A Type 1 error occurs when a liquidation or reorganization occurs and the auditor did not qualify the opinion. The frequency of Type 1 errors was reported earlier: for a large sample of bankrupt firms, going concern exception opinions are observed in 48% of the cases, hence a 52% Type 1 error.

This Type 1 error occurs very frequently. Of course, part of the reason is that the audit report is not intended to be a prediction of bankruptcy. Nevertheless, the frequency of Type 1 errors is quite high (although not as high as I had initially expected).

The primary costs of a Type 1 error include the following:

Company management may not be as aware of the seriousness of the situation as when an audit exception is given. Perhaps better awareness by management would motivate corrective action earlier; a financial turnaround might yet be managed. However, this possibility is probably not large as long as existing management remains. According to the *Business Failure Record* statistics compiled by Dun & Bradstreet in 1980, 93% of all bankruptcies occur because of management problems including inexperience and incompetence, and it is questionable whether existing management can be motivated early enough to avoid failure. In theory, however, this is a distinct potential advantage of an audit risk early warning system.

The investors of the company may not have sufficient warning of the imminent liquidation in order to adjust the security prices accordingly. This is really a problem of disclosure, and the empirical evidence indicates that an analysis using certain financial ratios is a better indicator of imminent liquidation than auditors' reports. If this is the case, the theory of efficient capital markets would indicate that all the information has already been digested and reflected in security prices. We have some evidence, however, that this is not the case.

The costs to the audit firm include embarrassment and the possibility of lawsuits. The main issue in lawsuits is most likely to be inadequate disclosure that leads to losses by investors and creditors. Recently there have been a number of lawsuits of this type—most settled out of court.

The Self-Fulfilling Prophecy Argument

The observation has often been made that a failure prediction model, if popular enough, can become a self-fulfilling prophecy. The implication here is that the company would have continued as a going concern but for the model. While this might be so in an isolated case, I sincerely do not think that many companies fail due to a model's prediction. Most companies fail on their own, without the help of any person or model.

The self-fulfilling prophecy argument can be extended to the going concern opinion, as well. Assuming that the opinion conveys information which is considered seriously (by creditors, investors, suppliers, and customers) but is erroneous, then there is a potential expensive *cost* to the qualification. This problem was recognized by the Cohen Commission (1978:30):

> Creditors often regard a "subject to" qualification as a separate reason for not granting a loan, a reason in addition to the circumstances creating the uncertainty that caused the qualification. This frequently puts the auditor in the position of, in effect, deciding whether a company is able to obtain the funds it needs to continue operating. Thus, the auditor's qualification tends to be a self-fulfilling prophecy: The auditor's expression of uncertainty about the company's ability to continue may contribute to making it a certainty.

It is not clear where to insert the self-fulfilling prophecy notion in our discussion of the cost of errors. For one thing, we cannot be sure if an error has taken place since the firm quite likely will fail regardless of the auditor's opinion. To the extent this is not the case and the exception opinion precipitates the failure, we discuss it below. In 1974, Altman and McGough followed seven companies whose auditors were no longer expressing doubts about going concern problems. Four of those firms took some corrective action (e.g., disposed of unprofitable operations), and two had increased revenues.

SUBSEQUENT STATUS OF COMPANIES RECEIVING GOING CONCERN OPINIONS

Shindledecker (1980) and I have updated this information by examining companies with opinions modified for going concern problems from 1972 through 1978. Utilizing the AICPA's National Automated Accounting Research System (NAARS), we obtained a listing of companies whose auditors had given qualified opinions for going concern problems. Then we obtained various lists of bankruptcies and we compared the two lists. Neither the NAARS data base nor the lists of bankruptcies were a complete source, so our data are subject to error. It is useful, however, for comparative purposes and gives further evidence of the probable magnitude of Type 2 errors. The results of that study are reported in Table 7-7. In 75% of the cases, the firm receiving a going concern qualification did not go bankrupt.

Table 7-7 Subsequent Status of Going Concern Opinions (1972–1978).

Status by End of 1979	Audit Report with Going Concern Exception in 1972–1978		Companies Who Changed Auditors	
	Number	Percentage	Number	Percentage
Companies entered bankruptcy (No error)	53	25%	5	9%
Companies did not enter bankruptcy (Type 2 error)	160	75%	7	4%
Total	213	100%	12	6%

Type 2 errors are defined as those situations in which the auditor gives a going concern exception but the company survives. Altman and McGough (1974) listed 21 companies whose auditors either disclaimed or qualified their opinions in 1970 or 1971. The results of that study are reported in Table 7-8. Note that in the 1974 study, 29% entered bankruptcy compared to 25% for the later (Table 7-7) study. Of course, the possibility remains that companies may file for bankruptcy in the future. It is therefore likely that the Type 2 error will decrease somewhat from the preliminary 75% estimate. The auditor's Type 2 error appears to be more frequent than the Type 1 error.

The primary costs associated with a Type 2 error are as follows:

A potentially significant cost of this type of error is the self-fulfilling prophecy idea discussed above; that is, a company's demise is actually caused by the receipt of a going concern opinion. It occurs here to the extent that the auditor's exception may erroneously contribute to the liquidation of a good company. The economy, the employees, the management, and the consumers would possibly suffer for the loss of the company, particularly if the product was a competitive and valuable one.

A cost to the auditor is the potential loss of a client. In this connection, we recorded the frequency of auditor turnover for companies that had received going concern exceptions. Of the 213 companies, only 12 changed auditors, a relatively small percentage (5.6%).

It is also interesting to note that change in auditors occurred twice as often in companies that actually entered bankruptcy as in those that did not. Of course, auditor turnover could have occurred for many reasons other than the going concern problems, and if the change in auditors resulted in an elimination of the going concern exception, the company would not have been included in the NAARS list for later years (i.e., the change in auditors would not be evident in the data).

Table 7-8   Subsequent Status of Companies Receiving Going-Concern Opinions (1970–1971).

	Audit Report with Going Concern Exception in 1970 or 1971	
Status by 1974	Number	Percentage
Entered bankruptcy	6	29%
Still had going concern problems according to the auditor's report	8	38%
Auditor no longer giving a going concern exception	7	33%
Total	21	100%

SOME OBSERVATIONS AND CONCLUSIONS

Perhaps the main benefit obtained by requiring auditors to modify their opinions for going concern problems is disclosure. The disclosure is intended to provide information regarding the recoverability and classification of liabilities. Disclosure is not intended to predict bankruptcy. The question then is what is the best way to communicate uncertainties about a company's ability to continue operation.

The Cohen Commission's answer is to provide the information by disclosure or adjustment to the financial statements rather than by audit reporting requirements. The commission does not, however, state exactly how this can be done. The commission's conclusion is possibly based on the contention that the costs seem to exceed the benefits of auditors' disclosing going concern problems, particularly in light of the "accuracy" of those opinions when compared to actual bankruptcies. This comparison is not really fair in an absolute sense since auditors' opinions are not intended to be predictions of bankruptcy. The comparison, however, does shed valuable light on the costs involved in "erroneous" going concern opinions.

The Cohen Commission may not be the only group that believes going concern problems are a matter for financial statement disclosure rather than audit reporting disclosure. It is difficult to know, at this point, how the Securities and Exchange Commission will view the problem. In *Accounting Series Release No. 115*, the SEC said that a going concern qualification regarding a company's ability to attain profitable operations and/ or successfully obtain additional capital indicates serious doubts as to whether the preparation of financial statements on the going concern basis is warranted. The SEC's opinion is that if the business will not continue and the proceeds of the present offering will simply be used to pay existing creditors, then the offering may be deceptive, and no amount of change of the accountant's opinion would appear to solve the underlying problem. Still, the SEC opposed abandonment of the going concern opinion in 1980, and many feel they will oppose it again in 1982.

The accounting profession is not in perfect agreement as to auditor responsibilities to detect and disclose financial distress situations. The most recent declaration on this matter is from the recent SAS (1981) on auditor considerations and the continued existence of entities. The auditor's explicit responsibility is recognized as being alert, and several guidelines are mentioned, including the adverse trend of key financial ratios. While this SAS does not go as far as to advocate the use of failure prediction models, the implication that the industry's thinking is consistent with this tool is clearly evident—at least to this, admittedly biased, observer.

Once the distress situation is identified, however, the dilemma still exists as to whether to qualify or not. As long as auditor responsibilities acknowledge client advice on strengths and weaknesses, it is my strong opinion that auditors should explore modern analytical methods to assess the performance of firms and to help direct their efforts for more in-depth investigation. If going concern opinions remain a part of the auditor function, then such models can be useful in this context as well.

8 Legal Implications of Bankruptcy Classification

The potential role in the law for models of bankruptcy and failing companies classification is increasing as models become more developed and, more importantly, as they become more well known and credible. As Blum (in Altman and Sametz, 1977) has described in his excellent commentary, the potential for application of such a role is primarily found in regard to (1) assistance in the making of a legal decision, and (2) determination of whether a post-decision process was reasonable. Blum's arguments will be reviewed, and we will then present some of our recent work on the efficacy of failure classification models in legal settings.

THE NATURE OF MODELS

One can ask whether probabilistic models, such as those of business failure, can have proper roles in the eyes of the law. Resolution of this question requires a brief analysis of the nature of models.

Models are reasonable representations of reality, which are handier to work with than reality itself. A model of business failure is, to the extent that it relies upon accounting and other financial data, a model of symptoms of failure, not actual causes of failure. There is no connection between cause and effect. Rather, there is a correlation, or association, between past data patterns for companies that failed and companies that did not fail, and this association is only as good as (1) the theoretical underpinning of the model, (2) the validity of the statistical test of the model, and (3) the reasonableness of extrapolation to the future from the past time period upon which the model is grounded, that is, model reliability.

The necessity for an adequate validation procedure must be emphasized, particularly with reference to the use of powerful statistical techniques such as discriminant analysis. An adequate validation procedure requires application of the model to completely fresh data, from which the model was not derived, which is called the validation sample. The accuracy of the model based on the validation sample represents a reasonable basis for extrapolation to the future, given that the future is not expected to be reasonably different from the past period tested. The accuracy of the model computed with regard to the primary sample, which is the sample used to estimate the model parameters in the first place, is not a reasonable basis for extrapolation. For instance, if the predictive accuracy of the primary sample is 98% and that of the validation sample is 75%, only the 75% figure serves as a valid basis for extrapolation.

Once validated, it is necessary to fit a model of business failure into a decision procedure. A mere specification of the probability of failure of a business, such as 95%, is insufficient for the making of a decision. The probability of failure, whether 95%, higher, or lower, must be sufficiently grave and imminent as to allow the user of the forecast to act on it, by invoking the failing company doctrine, for instance (discussed below). The questions of gravity and imminence can only be resolved by consideration of the relative penalties for erroneous decision, as will be pointed out in the discussion of the regulatory and prosecutorial applications of models. With these qualifications in mind, the process of applying models of business failure in a legal context is reasonable.

AID IN MAKING DECISIONS: THE FAILING COMPANY DOCTRINE

Models of business failure can be helpful in deciding whether a business firm is sufficiently weak economically that it should be allowed to complete a business combination otherwise offensive to antitrust laws or to laws governing regulated industries. This determination is usually made in accordance with the rationale of the failing company doctrine, although upon occasion the doctrine is not invoked by name. The failing company doctrine provides that two companies can complete an otherwise illegal business combination if, but for the business combination, one of the two companies would fail and there is no other good-faith "purchaser" for the failing company (*International Shoe* v. *FTC,* 280 U.S. 291 (1930)). We will return to this subject at a later point.

There are numerous settings in which a model of business failure may aid a decision or assist analysts. Regulated industry decisions made by the administrative agency concerned, for example, the Civil Aeronautics Board, and decisions made usually in regard to nonregulated industries by the governmental arms charged specifically with policing antitrust laws, the Antitrust Division of the Justice Department and the Federal Trade

Commission, could utilize a model's results. For simplicity, the former setting will be referred to here as regulatory and the latter as prosecutorial.

In addition, investors and financiers could be vitally concerned with the likelihood that a company will eventually be considered a failing firm or not. Arbitragers in merger investment decisions would need to consider the failing status of a firm if an antitrust violation were raised in a tender offer.

An understanding of the principal distinction between the regulatory and prosecutorial decision settings is a good clue to how a model of business failure can fit into a legal (or other) decision process. A regulatory agency is usually charged with the dual responsibility of ensuring adequate service to the public by the regulated industry without contributing unduly to monopolistic conditions, while a prosecutorial agency is usually concerned only with minimizing antitrust violations. As a result, the decision process of a regulatory agency is likely to weigh more heavily the penalty for having wrongly predicted a failed firm as not failing (Type I error) than would a prosecutorial agency. In other words, a regulatory agency is more likely than a prosecutorial agency to approve a merger that may better serve the public in the near term.

Conversely, a regulatory agency is likely to weigh more lightly the penalty for having wrongly predicted a nonfailed firm to fail (Type II error) than would a prosecutorial agency. Therefore, a regulatory agency is more likely than a prosecutorial agency to approve a possibly unnecessary merger because the public would still be served by the combined resources of both merging parties. Here, the regulatory agency's erroneous prediction of failure would be less undesirable from its viewpoint than the same error by a prosecutorial agency.

According to Blum (1977), the U.S. Supreme Court has recognized this distinction. In *United States* v. *Philadelphia National Bank,* 374 U.S. 321 (1963), the Supreme Court indicated that the failing company doctrine would be applied more liberally to potentially failing banks than it would in general for commercial and industrial situations. This distinction has also been recognized by Congress in legislation that protects mergers of financially weak newspapers from antitrust prosecution. [Newspaper Preservation Act, 15 U.S.C., 1804–04 (1970)].

Regulatory Applications

A frequent example in the regulatory area where models of business failure could be useful is the allowance of mergers of weak banks with stronger banks, under the auspices of the Federal Reserve Board (for bank holding companies) or the Comptroller of the Currency (for national banks). In March 1976, the Federal Reserve Board reversed its ruling of November 10, 1975, and allowed Citicorp to acquire West Coast Credit Corp. for the reason that the Seattle-based consumer finance company's economic situation had deteriorated significantly. Similarly and in the same month, the Comptroller of the Currency approved the combination of the Continental Bank of Burien, Washington ($18 million in deposits) with the Puget Sound National Bank of Tacoma ($346 million in deposits and sixth largest in Washington State), and the Federal Reserve Board approved the acquisition of the Security State Bank of Pompano Beach, Florida (deposits of $4,500,000) by the Landmark Banking Corp. of Fort Lauderdale ($707,500,000 in deposits and eighth largest in Florida).

Prosecutorial Applications

Models of business failure can also be of direct aid in the prosecutorial decision process. For example, models can be consulted to determine whether an antitrust prosecution should be filed or whether a letter of clearance should be granted authorizing a business combination, based on the Hart-Scott-Rodino Antitrust Act (1976) whereby premerger clearance by the FTC on sizable mergers is possible.

For instance, the preliminary results of a model of business failure were available to certain officials of the Justice Department during the making of its initial decision not to oppose the merger of White Motor and White Consolidated. This decision became famous because on May 3, 1976, by a split board decision, the directors of White Consolidated decided not to go through with the acquisition, citing as one reason that the Justice Department had made "renewed inquiries" about the proposed transaction (*Wall Street Journal*, May 4, 1976, p. 6). Several years later, the ZETA model (Chapter 4) was clearly indicating a potential White Motor failure (ZETA = -1.95, *Business Week*, March 24, 1980, p. 107) and the firm did fail on September 4, 1980. Indeed, White Motor's ZETA score was -1.80 in 1977, making the firm a strong candidate for bankruptcy. If the Justice Department was unsure of White Motor's failure probability, the use of the ZETA model would certainly have added an objective "opinion." It is conceivable that the directors of White Consolidated might have decided to go ahead with the merger attempt despite Justice Department opposition if they were confident that White Motor's failing status could be sustained in court.

Failure prediction models were probably not used during litigation until just recently. Nevertheless, certain judicial and regulatory agency opinions have taken into consideration data similar to those used in modern models of business failure. Courts have reviewed trends in financial ratios, for example. The Federal Trade Commission did so in 1960 in regard to Pillsbury Mills' proposed acquisition of the Ballard and Ballard Co., and so did the Supreme Court in 1930 in regard to International Shoe's acquisition of the McElwain Co. (Blum, 1977, p. 123). I agree with Blum that it is not persuasive to look at the decline in a particular ratio to determine a failing condition. What must be analyzed are a particular firm's ratios in reference to similar ratios for failing and nonfailing companies; even better, one should look at a *financial profile* of a firm based on a number of measures. Then it must be determined whether the particular firm's profile or score is more like that of companies that have failed than it is like that of companies that have not failed. That is the essence of a computerized discriminant model.

May 20, 1976 was probably the first time a model of business failure was introduced in court. (See *United States* v. *Black & Decker,* DMd 430 T. Supp. 729 1976.) The occasion was Black & Decker's invocation of the failing company doctrine to excuse its allegedly anticompetitive purchase, as a potential entrant into the gasoline-powered chain saw market of McCulloch Corp. The court ruled in favor of the merger primarily based on the belief that competition would be substantially lessened. Interestingly, McCulloch (the acquired company) was ruled *not* to be a failing company due to the fact that Black & Decker was the only potential purchaser contacted. The court did acknowledge that McCulloch was beset by financial difficulties and that it likely would not have been valued as a going concern by its auditors, had it not been merged. In essence, McCulloch passed the failing firm criterion but not the good-faith-purchaser criterion. Recall that both criteria must be met in a successful failing company defense.

In a later case, *F&M Schaefer* v. *C. Schmidt & Sons,* SDNY, 597 F.2d 814 (1979), the Z-score model was introduced in a case involving the implied merger of two regional beer companies, where one of the issues was whether Schaefer was a failing company. Schaefer brought an action under the federal securities laws seeking to enjoin Schmidt's from purchasing securities from a bank holding convertible debt of Schaefer. The antitrust argument was accepted by the trial court, and affirmed on appeal, despite Schaefer's tenuous position. Since that decision, Schaefer was purchased by Stroh's Beer Co.

Assessing the Reasonableness of the Decision Itself

Models of business failure can also be used as a standard for assessing the reasonableness of investment or credit extension decisions. There are two ways in which a model can be so used. First, a model's prediction may be referred to by a court or administrative body as an aid in assessing the reasonableness of a past decision. However, a court typically brings to bear on such a decision many facts beyond those that a model of business failure takes into account. Also, if the model is based upon annual financial statements, the court may have access to more timely information from interim financial reports. Therefore, while it is possible that a court may look at a model in such a situation, it is unlikely that it will rely solely upon such a model.

However, there is a second way in which a model of business failure can play a part in a court's assessment. A litigant may raise the question as to whether or not an investor or creditor's decision was reasonable since it was not made with regard to the prediction of a particular, well-known model of business failure. Thus the question presented is whether or not as a matter of prudent procedure the lender or investor used a sound model as a screening device. Of course, such lenders or investors could contend that they customarily review many more factors than those upon which models are based. However, if it is the case that a particular investment was in a company predicted by a model to fail, and the investor or creditor gave that investment no unusual attention, it would be exposed to easy, later criticism that the investment which should have been flagged for special attention was not flagged. Here, all that is required to make the use of models of business failure widespread is the success of one such complainant in a court suit.

There are several legal contexts in which a model of business failure would be relevant to assessing the reasonableness of a past decision procedure.

Trust and Investment Funds, Particularly Index Funds. Following the ancient trust rule that a trustee must be prudent with regard to each decision, trustees cannot afford to rely upon their overall investment performance. This is the lesson of *Bank of New York* v. *Spitzer* (1974), a case in which a trustee was originally held possibly liable for the consequences of four bad investments in securities listed on the New York Stock Exchange despite the fact that the fund as a whole had a reasonable performance.

> The fact that this portfolio showed substantial overall increase in total value during the accounting period does not insulate the trustee from responsibility for imprudence with respect to individual investments for which it would otherwise be surcharged . . . To hold to the contrary would in effect be to assure fiduciary immunity in an advancing market such as marked the histo-

ry of the accounting period here involved. The record of any individual investment is not to be viewed exclusively, of course, as though it were in its own water-tight compartment, since to some extent individual investment decisions may properly be affected by considerations of the performance of the fund as an entity, as in the instance, for example, of individual security decisions based in part on considerations of diversification of the fund or of capital transactions to achieve sound tax planning for the fund as a whole. The focus of inquiry, however, is nonetheless on the individual security as such and factors relating to the entire portfolio are to be weighed only along with others in reviewing the prudence of the particular investment decisions. 35 N.Y. 2d 512, 517, 364 N.Y.S. 2d 164, 168, 323 N.E. 2d 700 (1974), followed in *In Re Will of Jacob W. Bavliss,* 80 Misc. 2d 491, 493, 363 N.Y.S. 2d 285 (1975). (" . . . Satisfactory results produced by proper investments do not serve to absolve trustees of any liability for investments that are invalidly made and result in a loss.")

I made much the same argument in Altman (1977) when commenting upon the use of the *Z*-score or ZETA models for index fund portfolio management. We will pursue this point again in the next chapter.

On appeal, the trustee, while possibly liable, was found in fact not to have made any unreasonable investment. It is also interesting to note that this case occurred in reference to a rising stock market.

Banks and Other Financial Institutions. Here it should be noted that certain banks are now using models of business failure as a screening device as part of the loan decision (and investment fund management) process. Such banks are presumably protected already, provided that the models are sound and are reasonably applied.

Securities Industry. Professionals, such as investment bankers, lawyers, and accountants, are ever eager to avoid risks and could be especially enthusiastic users of such models of business failure if one of them is involved in a lawsuit alleging, *inter alia,* that failure to consult a model was negligent. Models could be consulted by such professionals not only upon public issuance of securities, but also during compilation of annual financial statements. For example, public accountants could consult such models before deciding upon going concern qualifications, as we pointed out in Chapter 7.

Pension Funds. This application area should be treated separately, not as a subset of trust or investment funds, because of the impact of the Employee Retirement Income Security Act of 1974 as amended by the Multiemployer Pension Plan Act of 1980 (ERISA) 20 U.S.C. §1001 *et seu*

(1974). ERISA has brought more persons within the definition of fiduciary and more decisions within the rubric of investment decisions. Also, ERISA has established broad standards of cofiduciary liability and high standards of conduct, measuring investment decisions by the standard of a prudent qualified investor and not simply by the standard of a reasonable person who may not be an investment specialist. Furthermore, by mandating extensive disclosure of both investment performance and fiduciary liability to all of a plan's participants and beneficiaries, ERISA has enhanced the opportunity for a disgruntled individual to file suit.

Defensive Tactic: Routinize Use of Models

A reasonable solution for business concerned in this regard is to use models as screening devices. The success of this preventive measure depends upon the soundness of the model and the precision of its application, for example, to data similar to those upon which the model was built.

While the routine use of a model may provide persuasive and corroborating evidence of the prudence of an investment or credit extension decision procedure, one must not lose sight of the model's probabilistic character. The model will flag the need for special documentation in some, but not all, doubtful cases.

FAILING COMPANY DOCTRINE—SOME QUESTIONS AND EMPIRICAL FINDINGS

As noted earlier, there are two major requirements for the invocation of the failing company doctrine (FCD): that the company be failing, and that there be no other good-faith purchaser. Both of these requirements have been characterized by ambiguity although the merger guidelines of the Department of Justice are stated in such terms as (1) depleted resources, (2) prospects for rehabilitation remote, and (3) clear probability of failure (see Lake, 1982). Lake does present some practical suggestions on how and when to use the business failure defense. He notes that the defense is applicable for failing *divisions,* as well as firms, but this is even more difficult to apply except in "the clearest of circumstances." While I would agree that the performance of divisions is more difficult to assess than is the performance of a corporate entity, such techniques as Z-score are still applicable.

In considering the lack of any good-faith purchaser, the courts have never analyzed how much the failing firm must forego, in terms of opportunity cost, to preserve competition. One issue is, therefore, at what point does the noncompeting offerer become a "good-faith purchaser"? Should an offer of half as much as some other firm's be considered a bona fide offer?

Related to this question of whether a merger should be sanctioned by the court is the question of the tradeoff between the anticompetitive costs to society of the merger and the costs to society of a bankruptcy. One could, and indeed many have, argued that a Chrysler bankruptcy would result in tremendous costs to the American economy and the individuals involved. Altman and Goodman (1980) suggest a framework for analyzing the economic tradeoff between anticompetitive mergers and societal bankruptcy costs while White (1980) explores the societal bankruptcy costs issue in more depth.

What is a Failing Firm?

The question, "What is a failing firm?" has received a good deal of attention. Bauman (1968) notes that the court has held "that a company does not have to be actually in a state of bankruptcy to be exempt from Section 7 provisions:" and that "it is sufficient to be heading in that direction with the probability that bankruptcy will ensue." Blum (1974) notes that the courts have not been consistent in their definition of what is a failing firm. My own experience has also been that the term is problematic.

While the FCD has arisen in numerous circumstances, no case has been located where the court's decision rested solely on the fact that the subject company was failing. In fact, Bock (1969) found that the conditions under which a firm can acquire a failing company without risking challenge was steadily narrowed by the courts in the late 1960s and speculated that the merger alternative for companies that cannot survive will be problematic, especially for strong acquiring companies and for acquired companies accounting for substantial shares of concentrated markets.

There are infrequent examples of judicial concern for bankruptcy costs, although even in those cases, it was not clear whether the decision was economically motivated or not. Perhaps the prime example of a recent failing company merger sanction is one which did not get to the courts for analysis and interpretation. In 1978, Attorney General Griffin Bell permitted the merger of Ling Temco Vought and Lykes Corp. Both firms had major steel manufacturing subsidiaries (the seventh and eighth largest producers), with the Youngstown Street & Tube subsidiary of Lykes apparently on the road to failure. Overruling the Justice Department, Bell decided that, despite the potential for serious anticompetitive consequences in the steel industry, the merger would not be contested. "In justifying his action, he invoked the so-called 'failing company' defense under the antimerger law . . ." (Adams, 1978).

Table 8-1 Sample of Companies that Have Used the Failing Company Defense (Exclusive of Financial Institutions).

Name	Failing Company	Allowed	Type of Company	Year
Arden Publishing	Citizen Publishing	no	private	1940
Blatz Brewery Co.	Pabst Brewery, Inc.	no	public	1958
Brown Shoe Co.	Kinney Shoe Co.	no	public	1962
Continental Oil Co.	Malco Refineries, Inc.	no	subsidiary	1959
Crown Zellerbach	St. Helens	no	public	1961
Dean Foods	Bowman Dairy Corp.	no	private	1966
Diebold	Herring-Hall-Marvin	no	private	1958
El Paso Natural Gas	Pacific NW Pipeline	yes	public	1964
Erie Sand and Gravel	Sandisky Corp.	no	subsidiary	1961
Farm Journal, Inc.	Country Gentlemen	no	private	1956
General Dynamics	United Electric	yes	public	1974
Maryland and Virginia Milk Prod.	Richmond Dairy	yes	private	1957
Pabst Brewing Co.	Carling National Breweries	no	public	1966
Pillsbury Mills	Ballard & Ballard	no	public	1960
United Airlines	Capital Airlines	yes	public	1962
U.S. Steel	Certified Industries	no	public	1964
Von's Grocery, Inc.	Shopping Bag Food Store	no	public	1966

Recent Related Cases

Name	Failing Company	Allowed	Type of Company	Year
Lancaster Colony	Federal Glass Division[a] (Federal Paper Board)	no	public	1978
Jones & Laughlin (Ling-Temco Vought)	Youngstown Sheet & Tube (Lykes Corp.)	yes	public	1978
Schmidt's Beer[b]	Schaefer Beer	no	public	1978
White Consolidated[c]	White Motor Co.	yes	public	1976

238

[a]Was not litigated.

[b]The two firms were the contestants—no federal agencies involved.

[c]White Consolidated dropped the case but the Justice Department would not have contested.

The results of invoking the FCD are not usually so positive for the acquiring company, especially when the issue reaches the litigation phase. Table 8-1 lists 17 such cases after 1950, and in only four (23%) did the courts allow the merger to proceed. In most of these cases, anticompetitive consequences were the evident basis for decision, and rarely, if ever, did the court articulate the tradeoff in costs. The table also lists four recent instances where the FCD was invoked in a nontraditional setting. The sample listed in Table 8-1 is not meant to be comprehensive, but it does represent my best effort to find relevant cases.

It might be of interest to track these firms, especially to see what happened to those "failing" firms where the merger was disallowed or dissolved. While our search of corporate records did not always reveal definitive results, it appears that of the 10 publicly held failing firms which were divested or not allowed to merge, the following occurred: three firms or divisions were later dissolved or were liquidated (Ballard & Ballard, Certified Industries, and the Federal Glass Division of Federal Paper Board); five are still in existence in some form; in two cases we simply could not find any company records. We cannot draw any definitive conclusions from these results, but in a few cases, the court's or regulatory agency's decision probably helped to determine the unfortunate fate of the failing firm.

Conclusion

There is a potential for future use of models of business failure in certain areas of decision-making where legal issues are at stake, such as the failing company doctrine. Also investment managers, lenders, accountants, and professional advisors may find it advantageous to defend their decisions from later criticism if a well-known model of business failure had been used to aid in the decision where the model was not indicating a distress situation. This defensive usage, which is not yet prevalent, may become so quickly if a shareholder wins a derivative suit in which inattention to such a model is alleged. As a result, models of business failure as one element in the legal decision process could possibly increase in frequency and sophistication.

It may even be possible one day for the Antitrust Division, the Federal Trade Commission, and other governmental agencies to incorporate a model of business failure and a probabilistic decision rule into administrative determinations, such as issuing letters of clearance for proposed business combinations.

9 Investor Implications of Bankruptcy and Bankruptcy Models

Numerous references have been made throughout the book to the various security holders of bankrupt corporations. Indeed, one of the intriguing aspects of corporate bankruptcy is the "second chance" effect whereby the reorganization process involves a restructuring of the firm's capital contributors' claims and securities. The moratorium period and general deterioration in securities prices just before and just after formal bankruptcy declaration can provide excellent investment opportunities for the astute and persistent investor. Numerous professional publications have recently documented instances whereby investors could have made "fabulous" returns; among them *Barrons* (February 8, 1982) and *Forbes* (March 1, 1982) and have speculated on potential turnaround situations (*The New York Times,* January 10, 1982). The latter article quotes one Wall Street analyst as saying, "We think a stock will go up when a bankruptcy is announced; and in many cases these companies have become some of the best investments . . .".

The first part of this chapter is concerned with investing in the debt and equity of bankrupt companies—after the firms have entered reorganization. We will explore documentation of the investment experience in these securities, and we will also explore the effect of potential bankruptcy on expected shareholder wealth over time. We also discuss how a failure prediction model may assist index fund portfolio management. Next, we look into the market risk parameters of bankrupt companies. Finally, we present some recent findings on abnormal price behavior of a sample of firms whose financial profile indicated significant bankrupt potential but which did not go bankrupt.

The primary focus of this chapter will be on equity securities. We devote the entire next chapter to the fixed income market.

VALUATION AND INVESTING

We have explored the reorganization valuation process in Chapter 1 and its appendix and conclude that it is critical to the debtor. In addition, the value of the firm as a continuing entity is the prime determinant of the recapitalization terms for the old creditors and owners and will be the key ingredient for those investors interested in purchasing bankrupt securities. Although a majority of bankrupt firms end their existence in liquidation or are eventually evaluated as insolvent in bankruptcy (i.e., liability claims exceed the assessed value of the assets), those firms which are reorganized successfully, that is, those which emerge from reorganization as going concerns, present potentially excellent returns to the old debt holders, to the new debt or equity holder and, on less frequent occasions, to the old stockholders.

A somewhat ancient but still relevant study performed by this author (Altman, 1969) found that equity investors of bankrupt companies tended to do about as well as other equity investors if the reorganized firm lasted at least five years after its initial bankruptcy petition. The percentage of firms studied whose old equity did last five years was relatively small (32%). It is interesting to note that over 90% of the firms had reorganization plans consummated in less than five years. Although it is impossible to know for certain, it may be that the tax laws regarding operating losses had some influence on this five-year total. The majority of firms actually settled in under two years. The latter figure, however, includes a large number of firms whose stockholders suffered 100% losses. Approximately 65% (34 of 52) of all those firms which consummated reorganization plans in two years or less saw their stockholders suffer a total loss. This percentage is slightly above the 56% figure for all firms (90) in that study, but substantially greater than the 33% figure for firms whose reorganization was consummated after two years.

These statistics, and others to be presented shortly, indicate that the longer a firm remains in bankruptcy reorganization, the better the stockholder's chance for remuneration of some type. This appears to be the case because a firm's insolvency, or solvency, can usually be determined in a short time, but once solvency is established, the exact details of a fair and feasible plan often require a long period of time.

INVESTMENT STRATEGIES

The trick is to determine which firms are likely candidates for successful reorganization and then to wait a period of time after the petition date to purchase appropriate securities. I have found that the price of bankrupt firm equities falls on average 25% from one month before failure to one month after. This was measured for a sample of almost 100 securities (Altman, 1969) whereby the "bankruptcy information effect" (BIE) as measured by,

$$\text{BIE} = \frac{P_{b+1}}{P_{b-1}}$$

where

P_{b+1} = average price in the month after bankruptcy, and

P_{b-1} = average price in the month prior to bankruptcy

was 0.742. The primary price drop generally occurred in the days immediately preceding and just after bankruptcy declaration. I have not measured the abnormal price change by adjusting for risk and market movement over this short period. I am confident, however, that the fall in price cannot be explained by risk and market factors alone and that failure with probability of 1.0 does convey "new" information to the market. We will see, at a later point, that one of our bankruptcy classification models could easily signal the price fall for the vast majority of bankrupt securities and also for a sample of firms whose profile looked very much like bankrupt firms.

It should be noted that the stockholders of a bankrupt firm do poorly, as one would expect, once bankruptcy is declared (Altman, 1969). If, however, one had bought the bankrupt firm's equity just one month after bankruptcy, the return to these shareholders would have been approximately equal to that of the investor in the average listed company on the stock exchange.

Just how to spot potential successful candidates is indeed an art and is practiced by a few savvy investors on a regular basis *(Barrons,* February 8, 1982, p. 8). One of these investors (Whitman, *Wall Street Journal,* October 21, 1980, p. 6) has been quoted as looking for companies which (1) are unencumbered by significant debt, (2) are being run by honest management, (3) have a great deal of available information about their operations, and (4) have stock selling below the net value of their assets. Whitman notes that "Chapter 11 companies have those characteristics in abundance; and if this is so, the risk is not very great." He and others are interested in debt securities and possibly the equity of such companies. Indeed, one can find a successful reorganization whereby the company is doing very well while in reorganization and also upon emergence, but

Table 9-1 Investment Performance of Debtholders and Stockholders of Bankrupt Firms.

(1) Original Company and (Reorganization Filing Date)	(2) Total Liabilities ($ Millions)	(3) Security of Bankrupt Company	(4) Prebankruptcy[c] Market Value of 1 Bond or 100 Shares	(5) New Company and (Date Reorganization Complete)	(6) Securities in New Company or Cash Received in Reorganization or Liquidation for 1 Bond or 100 Shares	(7) Value[b] Based on Recent Market (Jan. 31, 1982)	(8) Present Value (at 10%) of Recent Market Price[b]
Penn Central Transportation Co., (June 1970)	$3,600	New York Central 6% bonds due 1980	$ 720	Penn Central Corp., (October 1978)	0.275 Series A and 0.164 Series B mortgage bonds + 21.98 shares B preferred + 9.91 shares common + $147	$ 3,585	$1,324
	$ 125	Common	$ 150		4 shares common	$ 132	$ 68
W.T. Grant Co., October 1975	$1,031	4¾% Sinking fund debentures due 1978	$ 360	Company is in liquidation	$ 1,000	$ 1,000	—
		4% Convertible subordinated debentures due 1990	$ 317.50		14% of face value (judge's approval February 1980 pending 90% agreement of recipients)	$ 140	$ 91
		4¾% Convertible subordinated debentures due 1966	$ 235		14% of face value (judge's approval February 1980 pending 90% agreement of recipients)	$ 140	$ 91
		Common stock	$ 338		Probably none		
Equity Funding Corp. of America, (April 1973)	$ 594	9½% Debentures due 1990	$1,098	Orion Capital Corp., (March 1976)	71.2 shares common	$ 935	$ 391
		5½% Convertible subordinated debentures due 1991	$ 800		25.5 shares common	$ 335	$ 140
		Common stock	$2,538		28.7 shares common	$ 377	$ 158

Company (petition date)	$	Securities outstanding	$	Reorganized as (date)	Distribution	$	$
Interstate Stores, Inc., (May 1974)	$ 208	4% Convertible subordinated debentures due 1992		Toys "R" Us, Inc., (April 1978)	117 shares common	$ 3,919	$1,827
		4⅜% Convertible subordinated debentures due 1981	$ 220		1 share per $10 claim	$ 3,350	$1,561
		Common stock	$ 450				
King Resources Co. (August 1971)	$ 117	5½% Convertible subordinated debentures due 1988	$ 163	Phoenix Resources Co., (January 1978)	66.7 shares common	$ 2,234	$1,041
		Common stock	$ 90		55.5 shares B common + $2.83	$ 1,585	$ 562
Bowmar Instruments Corp., (February 1975)	$ 51	No public debts		Bowmar Instruments, (April, 1977)	1 share B common + $2.13	$ 31	$ 11
		Common stock	$ 181				
Miller-Wohl Co., Inc., (September 1972)	$ 32	No public debt		Miller-Wohl Co., Inc., (November 1973)	66.7 shares common	$ 247	$ 119
		Common stock	$ 438				
United Merchants & Manufacturing, Inc., (July 1977)	$ 380	Common stock	$ 675	United Merchants & Manufacturers, Inc., (June 1978)	100 shares common	$18,534	$7,322
		9½% Sinking fund debentures due 1995	$ 890		50% of principal + accrued interest, 9½% interest on remainder to be retired 1989	$ 636	$ 406
		4½% Convertible subordinated debentures due 1990	$ 502.50		All interest and principal pursuant to original indenture	$ 280	$ 179
Unishops, Inc., (November 1973)	$ 112	Common stock	$ 538	Unishops, Inc., (April 1975)	100 shares common	$ 413	$ 264
		No public debt			66.7 shares common	$ 175	$ 78
		Common stock	$ 163				

(Continued)

245

Table 9-1 (Continued)

(1) Original Company and (Reorganization Filing Date)	(2) Total Liabilities ($ Millions)	(3) Security of Bankrupt Company	(4) Prebankruptcy[c] Market Value of 1 Bond or 100 Shares	(5) New Company and (Date Reorganization Complete)	(6) Securities in New Company or Cash Received in Reorganization or Liquidation for 1 Bond or 100 Shares	(7) Value[b] Based on Recent Market (Jan. 31, 1982)	(8) Present Value (at 10%) of Recent Market Price[b]
Neisner Bros., Inc., (December 1977)	$ 46	No public debt		Merged with Ames Department Stores, Inc., (October 1978)			
		Common stock	$ 325		25 shares Ames convertible preferred (convertible to 1.25 shares common)	$ 664	$ 442
Daylin, Inc., (February 1975)	$ 250	8.35% debentures due 1997	$ 700	Daylin, Inc., (November 1976), merged with W. R. Grace, (March 1979)	$158 + 0.121 "A" notes + 0.558 "A" debentures + 54 shares common	$ 1,056	$ 530
		5% subordinated debentures due 1989	$ 220		0.085 class "B" notes + 0.032 class "B" debentures + 290 shares common	$ 1,164[a]	$ 584[a]
		Common stock	$ 150		100 shares common—received $4.0625 a share in Grave merger	$ 406	$ 271

[a]Assumes: 0.085 class "B" note is that listed in *Bank and Quotation Record* as NT 12.625 on 9/15/96 (price = 83); 0.032 Class "B" note is that listed in *Bank and Quotation Record* as SDCV 6.50% on 11/15/96 (Price = 149).

[b]Includes interim dividend or interest payments.

[c]Investment date is assumed to be just prior to bankruptcy.

because the confirmed plan has eliminated the old shareholders there is a total writeoff to these unfortunate security holders. The old creditors become the new shareholders and, along with the investor who perhaps has waited until after emergence, reap the benefits. Such appears to be the case of the recently emerged Duplan Corp. (plan confirmed in December 1981 after a four-and-a-half-year reorganization—new name, Panex Corp.). More information on Duplan can be found in the Appendix to Chapter 1. There are other examples; see Tables 9-1 and 9-2.

Table 9-2   Stock Price Value of Recently Bankrupt Firms (1978–1980).

Company	Bankruptcy Filing Date	Stock Price		
		Near Filing	Recent	Percent of Change
Allied Artists	4/4/79	$1^3/_4$	$^1/_4$	−86
Allied Supermarkets	11/6/78	$^5/_8$	$1^1/_{16}$	70
Capehart	2/16/79	$^3/_8$	0	−100
City Stores	7/30/79	$2^1/_4$	$3^1/_2$	56
Common Oil Refining	7/23/79	$10^1/_4$	$^5/_8$	−94
EC Ernst	12/04/78	4	$1^1/_4$	−69
Inforex[a]	10/24/79	$1^7/_8$	$^1/_4$	−87
Interlee (FDI)[b]	12/04/78	$7^1/_2$	$^3/_4$	−90
Lafayette Radio Electronics[a]	1/04/80	$^7/_8$	$1^1/_{16}$	21
Mansfield Tire & Rubber	10/02/79	$^3/_4$	0	−100
National Shoes	12/12/80	$1^3/_4$	$2^1/_2$	43
Pantry Pride (Food Fair)[b]	10/03/78	$2^7/_8$	$4^1/_8$	43
Penn-Dixie Industries	4/07/80	$2^3/_8$	$1^1/_2$	−37
Piedmont Industries	2/22/79	$1^1/_4$	$^1/_4$	−80
Richton International	3/18/80	$1^1/_4$	$1^1/_2$	20
Sam Solomon	8/21/80	$3^3/_4$	$1^1/_4$	−67
Tenna	12/05/79	$1^3/_8$	0	−100
Triton Gr (Chase Man M&R Tr)[b]	2/22/79	$^7/_8$	$^7/_{16}$	−50
The Upson Co.	6/25/80	$1^1/_8$	$^1/_2$	−56
West Chemical Products	1/22/79	$4^3/_8$	$6^1/_2$	49
White Motor	9/04/80	$5^3/_8$	$^1/_4$	−95
Wilson Freight	7/23/80	2	$^1/_4$	−88

Source: Forbes, March 1, 1982, p. 134.

[a]Acquired.

[b]Former name.

Note: These firms filed for bankruptcy in the three years prior to 1981. Shares in most of them have slumped, but there are a few winners.

It should be noted that because of the recent increase in large firm bankruptcies, the number of sophisticated investors who are interested in the investment prospects of bankrupt firm securities has increased dramatically.

Table 9-1 lists a number of fairly recently bankrupt firms which have attempted to reorganize—in most cases successfully. We have indicated the prebankruptcy value (just prior to failure) of 100 common shares or one bond in column (4). We then trace the recapitalization of the firm in terms of the "old" securities when the plan was confirmed or the liquidation was arranged. Columns (7) and (8) list the market value of the exchanged securities, as of 1982, plus interim payments and their present value as of the bankruptcy date.

Of the 22 different securities noted in Table 9-1, nine have present values of the reorganized securities greater than the prebankruptcy market value. We have arbitrarily selected a 10% discount rate as a proxy for stockholder opportunity costs over the period between the bankruptcy date and January 31, 1982. The remaining 13 securities had lower, but still quite positive, present values. We conclude that indeed it is possible to make money on investments in bankrupt company securities (see Table 9-2), but in most cases the yield will be lower than shareholder opportunity costs.

INDEX FUND PORTFOLIO MANAGEMENT

It seems paradoxical to suggest that a failure prediction model for individual firms could be used effectively in conjunction with an index fund investment strategy. The latter is based on the belief that it is fruitless and costly to attempt to outperform the market on a continuous basis, and a portfolio which is made up of the securities which comprise the market is a passive, but effective, strategy. As such, there would appear to be little place for individual analysis. Yet, in my opinion, there is an important role that failure prediction can play for portfolio managers, even index fund managers.

The reason for this assertion, explained more completely in Altman (1977), is that index funds typically do not purchase *every* stock comprising the index. Instead, for example, the top 200 companies in terms of market capitalization are purchased with the rationale that a 200-stock portfolio is likely to be well diversified and the risk and return performance of such a fund closely approximates the entire index, for instance, the S&P 500. This strategy has explicitly utilized market capitalization as the screening mechanism without concern for the risk characteristics of individual stocks.

I advocate a slight modification of the above. Why not use a two-stage screening procedure? First, select the number of securities thought desirable to achieve proper diversification and to save on transaction costs for those stocks not purchased. Then, subject the subindex portfolio to a rigorous failure model, such as ZETA, in order to screen out undesirable risky stocks. Recent experience would imply that something like 20 stocks of the S&P 400 industrials would have negative ZETAS, which translates into less than 10 for the top 200. The manager would then substitute these 10 to achieve the 200-firm portfolio or simply continue with 190 stocks.

The cost of such a screen would be trivial compared to the potential savings of a court suit brought by a disgruntled owner of the fund. For example, we discuss the *Bank of New York* v. *Spitzer* case in Chapter 8, wherein a plaintiff was suing the trust for investing in a failed company despite the fact that the overall portfolio did well in an up market. Langbein and Posner (1976) present the argument that the overall portfolio's performance is the essence of evaluation and not any specific security in the fund. Yet, even they concede that a relatively low-cost failure screen could be justified to avoid annoying repercussions of a law suit.

BANKRUPTCY COSTS

In recent years, one of the more controversial debates in the theoretical literature centers on the impact of expected bankruptcy costs on optimal capital structure of corporations. A number of analysts point toward the potentially significant direct and indirect costs of bankruptcy as a deterrent for firms continually to make use of relatively low-cost debt capital. They argue that the value of a firm will increase for a time as debt is added to the capital structure, but after some point, the marginal expected costs of bankruptcy exceed the marginal tax subsidy on debt. [See Scott (1977), Kim (1978), and DeAngelo and Masulis (1980) for a theoretical discussion and Brigham (1982) for a textbook exposition of this line of reasoning.] On the other hand, theorists such as Miller (1977) and Haugen and Senbet (1978) argue that bankruptcy costs are trivial or irrelevant to capital structure decisions.

Direct bankruptcy costs are defined as those additional administrative fees and managerial opportunity costs which arise due to the bankruptcy process. Indirect costs, according to most analysts, refer to those foregone opportunities and increased credit costs which are inherent in the process. Since the indirect costs are probably impossible to measure definitively and are difficult, at best, to measure indirectly, the only empirical work to date has concentrated on the direct costs. Even here, the most

Table 9-3 Absolute and Relative Bankruptcy Costs: Retailing and Industrial Samples.

Bankrupt Company	Bankruptcy Costs, Direct (BCD) ($ Thousands)	Value of Firm (v)[a]				BCD/Value					
		t-3	t-2	t-1	t	t-5	t-4	t-3	t-2	t-1	t
Retailing											
Abercrombie & Fitch (76)	471	10.7	12.5	13.0	10.5	0.049	0.042	0.044	0.038	0.036	0.044
Ancorp National Service (75)	523	104.2	104.3	110.5	49.8	0.005	0.004	0.005	0.005	0.005	0.011
Beck Industries (70)	650	47.7	114.4	145.6	108.4	0.020	0.016	0.014	0.006	0.005	0.006
Fishman (74)	703	41.2	36.5	40.6	8.6	0.016	0.009	0.017	0.019	0.017	0.018
Food Fair (78)	n.a.	376.2	387.7	466.8	416.9	n.a.	n.a.	n.a.	n.a.	n.a.	n.a.
Grant, W.T. (75)	2,000	1393.0	1269.7	1076.0	917.0	0.002	0.001	0.002	0.002	0.003	0.003
Interstate Stores (74)	1,664	269.1	249.9	202.6	98.2	0.005	0.006	0.006	0.007	0.008	0.017
Kenton (74)	950	47.0	47.5	34.6	29.7	0.014	0.023	0.020	0.020	0.028	0.032
Mangel Stores (74)	9,019	47.5	52.3	60.0	38.6	0.155	0.206	0.190	0.173	0.151	0.234
National Bellas Hess (72)	255	42.7	41.0	45.5	40.0	0.004	0.005	0.006	0.006	0.006	0.006
Neisner Bros (77)	1,630	86.9	99.1	94.2	91.0	0.017	0.020	0.019	0.016	0.017	0.018
United Merchants & Manufacturers (77)	9,513	407.6	433.5	306.0	203.6	0.020	0.021	0.023	0.022	0.031	0.047
Average-N = 11	2,489	239.5	237.4	216.3	167.7	0.028	0.032	0.031	0.030	0.027	0.040
Median	950	67.3	101.7	102.1	70.4	0.016	0.016	0.017	0.016	0.017	0.017

Industrial

Bowmar Instruments (75)	1,950	35.7	67.3	29.2	11.3	0.278	0.170	0.055	0.029	0.067	0.173
Drew National (75)	2,278	32.5	16.5	12.7	11.1	0.135	0.099	0.070	0.138	0.179	0.205
Frier Industries (78)	297	6.3	9.0	9.1	6.9	0.028	0.046	0.047	0.033	0.033	0.043
Precision Polymers (76)	468	13.9	8.1	6.1	3.6	0.123	0.121	0.034	0.058	0.077	0.129
Universal Container (78)	500	11.7	14.7	14.8	16.0	0.029	0.042	0.043	0.034	0.039	0.031
Valley Fair (77)	541	8.4	9.5	7.4	17.7	0.160	0.133	0.147	0.192	0.089	0.064
Winston Mills (78)	335	9.1	11.2	18.8	8.2	0.024	0.041	0.037	0.030	0.038	0.041
Average ($N = 7$)		16.8	19.5	14.0	10.7	0.111	0.093	0.062	0.073	0.075	0.098
Median		11.7	11.2	12.7	11.1	0.123	0.099	0.047	0.034	0.067	0.064

[a]V = market value equity + B.V. debt + M.V. debt + capitalized leases.

widely quoted study (Warner, 1977) only measures the administrative costs which are documented. He does admit, however, that managerial lost time and other "indirect" costs are potentially significant.

Warner examined 11 bankrupt railroads. He found that the direct costs accounted for about 1% of the market value of the firm measured seven years prior to failure, and this increased to about 5% just prior failure. He found that the larger the railroad, the greater the absolute amount of direct costs but the smaller the percentage of total firm value. Firm value was found to drop by 80% from seven years prior to the bankruptcy date. The implication of Warner's study is that bankruptcy costs are trivial.

While Warner's study suffers from several constraints, his work is important as a first step to analyzing empirically the impact of bankruptcy costs. The restricted nature of his sample of firms in a regulated industry (railroads), his small sample (11 firms), the lack of consideration of all direct costs and none of the indirect costs, and the absolute rather than marginal character of his analysis lead me to conclude that the results are not convincing and more work in this area is vital.

I have begun to investigate the question on an empirical basis, attempting to measure both direct and indirect costs. The latter are measured based on lost profits for the three years prior to failure due to the increased probability of ultimate failure. The methodology is still being refined, but some results can be presented on a preliminary and very tentative basis. Table 9-3 lists two samples of firms—one in the retailing industry and the other a small sample of industrials. We find that the direct costs are in line with Warner's results; that is, they are relatively low on average as a percentage of firm value. There are some instances of relatively large direct costs, however (e.g., Mangel, Bowmar, Drew). We also find that firm value does not deteriorate nearly so much or so fast as Warner found in his railroad study, even though bankruptcy prediction models were indicating potentially serious problems in almost every case.

Our findings (Altman, 1984) are that the indirect costs (not indicated in the table) are in many cases quite large relative to the direct costs and together with the direct costs can be a significant proportion of total firm value for several years prior to failure. Since this methodology is still being refined, I can only say at this point that we essentially are looking at the *unexpected* fall in profits as bankruptcy approaches. It is difficult to isolate these unexpected losses but we are convinced that as a firm's problems become clearer to potential customers, suppliers, creditors, and owners, there is a cost to this recognition. Firms like Chrysler, International Harvester, Continental Airlines, Braniff Airlines, and World Airways are all suffering now, to some extent, from the expected bankruptcy stigma. One might argue, on the other hand, that if markets are perfect and individuals are perfectly diversified, the losses to the potential bankrupt firm will be the benefits to competitors. We are not convinced by this argument in total, although I do recognize that the Chrysler potential buyer can go to General Motors—or Toyota, for that matter!

The issue of bankruptcy costs is still open, in my opinion. One must, however, consider the costs in terms of expectations rather than absolutes. On this subject, I have applied models like Z-score or ZETA to the firms to determine bankruptcy probabilities and to adjust both the costs of bankruptcy and the tax shelter from debt payments by the relevant probabilities as well as their present values (Altman, 1984).

REORGANIZATION TIME AND TERMS—EMPIRICAL FINDINGS

As noted above, one of the important costs in the bankruptcy reorganization process is the additional administrative expense involved. These outlays relate to, among other aspects, trustee salaries, legal fees, creditor and stockholder meetings costs, and the unquantifiable cost of the productive energies foregone by some of the firms' employees. These energies are necessarily diverted in order to concentrate on the task of reorganization.

The one variable which is directly related to every cost cited above is time: time in reorganization. Obviously, the relationship between expense and time is positive. In order to estimate the average time spent in reorganization, the actual experience of 90 bankrupt firms is examined. Reorganization time is defined as that period from the month the reorganization petition is granted to the month the reorganization plan is confirmed. The breakdown of this duration for the 90 firms is shown in Table 9-4.

The average time spent in reorganization of the 90-firm sample was two and one-quarter years, with the median time being one and two-thirds years. The range of values is between two months and nine and one-half years. It is possible that the sample mean is below the population mean of all bankrupt reorganizations since bankruptcies before 1941 are not included. Several large railroad bankruptcies occurred in the 1930s, with settlement taking over 10 years. My own estimate for reorganization time for the average railroad was between seven and eight years. Warner (1977) found that the reorganization duration was over 13 years. The two-and-one-quarter-year period appears to be a realistic estimate for Chapter X and XI industrial manufacturing company bankruptcy reorganizations.

One of the objectives of the new bankruptcy act is to speed up the reorganization process under Chapter 11. This will, if realized, provide a real benefit since time can certainly be costly. Preliminary results from the recent bankruptcies on this subject are not conclusive.

Table 9-4   Bankruptcy Reorganization Time Experience.

Months	Number of Firms	Percent of Total	Cumulative Percent
0–6	9	10	10
7–12	18	20	30
13–18	14	16	46
19–24	11	12	58
25–30	9	10	68
31–36	7	8	76
37–42	5	6	82
43–48	2	2	84
49–54	4	4	88
55–60	3	3	91
> 60	8	9	100
Total	90	100	

Note: Average time in reorganization = 27 months; median time = 20 months.

BANKRUPTCY AND STOCK MARKET RISK

In Chapters 3 and 4 we analyzed the risk of firms going bankrupt by studying the characteristics of those manufacturing firms which eventually failed. One of the variables we examined contained a market value ratio, and thereby introduced a dimension which is not wholly endogenous to the particular firm. It was shown that the market adjusts to new information about potentially insolvent companies, but in general, the plight of these firms is underestimated. In fact, we found that the average price decline for the 33 bankrupt firms in our original sample was 45% lower than the S&P index over a 15-month period (the average period when the Z-score model first classified the firm into the bankrupt group). In a subsequent section, we will examine price movements for "bankrupt profile" firms. These firms, however, did not go bankrupt.

Beaver (1968) reported that the market reacts negatively to failure potential as much as five years prior to bankruptcy, while we also show that equity values decline quite noticeably as bankruptcy approaches. While these results are quite indicative of the movement of share prices prior to bankruptcy and imply that the market itself is an accurate predictor of failure, it does not exhaust the possible information that can be derived from studying stock price behavior. Westerfield (1970) has taken the analysis one step further in his assessment of the market risk component of share price behavior peculiar to bankrupt firms. More recently, Aharony, Jones, and Swary (1980) found similar results.

MARKET AND SYSTEMATIC RISK

Westerfield (1970) assessed the monthly price performance of bankrupt companies over a 10-year period prior to failure. Utilizing the basic Sharpe-Lintner market model

$$R_{it} = \alpha_i + \beta_i R_{mt} + e_{it}$$

where

R_{it} = return on asset i in period t,

R_{mt} = return on market portfolio m in period t,

α_i = constant parameter whose expected value is such that the expected value of e_{it} is zero,

β_i = parameter (Beta coefficient) unique to asset i and called a measure of systematic or nondiversifiable risk, and

e_{it} = random variable representing the error term,

he concluded that there were market reassessments of the solvency position of failed firms nearly six years before bankruptcy but that failure itself is not expected by the market until very close (during the last year) to the failure date.

The above market model was also utilized to assess the relationship between the systematic risk measure (β) and the rate of failure. The hypothesis is that firms whose common equity exhibits high systematic risk with market movements (high Betas) experience a higher rate of failure than those assessed as low risk (low Betas). Essentially, the Beta coefficient's efficacy as a failure indicator is examined. This was done in the following manner. First, the period July 1926 to June 1954 was broken into four seven-year periods, July 1926–June 1933, July 1933–June 1940, and so on, and Beta coefficients were estimated for all firms with continuous price and dividend data during each sample period.

For each sample period, the risk estimates were broken into deciles, and the 90% decile, the highest 10%, and the lowest decile were segregated for further analysis. For the first sample period, 41 firms had systematic risk measures above 1.616 and qualified as the most risky securities. Of these 41 firms, "sixteen failed, five merged, one was a war casualty, and two had miscellaneous capital changes. In contrast only two of the low-risk firms failed while eight merged." Table 9-5 illustrates the results from Westerfield's study covering the four sample periods. In every sample period, the number of delisted firms in the high-risk category far exceeds the number in the low-risk category. Can we expect a linear or

Table 9-5 Market Risk and Failure.

Causes of Delisting	High Beta Firms				Low Beta Firms			
	7/26-6/33	7/33-6/40	7/40-6/48	7/48-6/54	7/26-6/33	7/33-6/40	7/40-6/48	7/48-6/54
1. Merger	5	16	28	30	8	8	16	10
2. Bankruptcy	16	10	11	4	2	2	3	5
3. Reclassification	1					3	1	
4. War Casualty		1	2			1		
5. Other	2	5	7	5	3	1	1	6
Total delist	24	32	48	39	13	15	21	21
No change	17	28	25	48	28	45	52	66
Total Firms	41	60	73	87	41	60	73	87
Beta of F 0.90	1.616	1.581	1.606	1.565				
Beta of F 0.10					0.498	0.436	0.500	0.473

Source: R. Westerfield, ''The Assessment of Market Risk and Corporate Failure'' (Wharton School of Finance, August 1970).

near linear relationship between failure and risk measures broken down by fractile statistics? My intuitive feeling is that we cannot because of the expected random failure experience among firms making up the middle fractiles and perhaps extending all the way to the extreme fractiles.

Westerfield concludes that high-risk firms do experience failure at greater rates than low-risk companies. Also, he observes that the propensity to merge is greater in the high-risk category. Perhaps, corporate managers of high-risk firms do seek out mergers to a greater degree than managers of low-risk firms do. An alternate theory is that high-risk firms experience severe stock price declines which make them more attractive to aggressive firms seeking sick companies for various motives. He also found that security delisting occurred more frequently for these same high-risk companies.

IMPLICATIONS

All of the prior mentioned studies, regardless of the time period and duration analyzed, conclude that bankruptcy risk and market price behavior are intimately related. The market appears to be somewhat able to adjust for increasing signs of corporate insolvency, but the fact that we observe the most serious declines in the last year prior to bankruptcy means that the ultimate failure reality is not fully discounted and the market as a predictor is therefore something less than perfect. This is certainly understandable, especially when you consider that many firms with high bankruptcy risk characteristics never go bankrupt and in these cases, the market was acting rationally and digesting information efficiently. The final section of this chapter examines just these firms.

STOCK MARKET RESPONSE TO FIRM DETERIORATION

In studying the use of accounting information, most studies, for instance, Ball and Brown (1968) and Gonedes (1974), are based on the presumption that the market is efficient with respect to this information. Results have indicated that all information from the annual report is incorporated in stock prices before and/or upon the publication of the accounting numbers. In other words, if the information content of the data is not an instance of inside information, (Jaffe, 1974), then abnormal price adjustments should not be expected after the data are announced.

Altman and Brenner (1981) focused on the information effect of newly reported data, but the information is filtered through the Z-score model to "create new information." We concentrate on a group of extremely poorly performing companies, where the new information indicates a change in status from that of a going concern to one of potential bankruptcy; that is, the firms possess characteristics similar to those of other firms that have gone bankrupt. We are mainly concerned with the stock market's speed of response to this new information.

The test is a joint test of market efficiency and the multivariate model as providing new signals of firm deterioration (i.e., the model provides new pessimistic information not directly observable). A finding that *ex post* residual behavior is not significantly different from zero is consistent with market efficiency and the model not providing new information; that is, the new information was digested before or upon publication of the annual report. However, if we find excess negative returns indicating that the information provided by the model is new, and that these returns are slow in their manifestation, then we may have evidence that the market has not efficiently digested the information when it was first available.

METHODOLOGY

Altman and Brenner (1981) follow the "residual" methodology first outlined in Fama, Fisher, Jensen, and Roll (1969). We first use the two-factor market model which is consistent with the two-parameter capital asset pricing model and which has been utilized quite frequently in the most recent relevant empirical studies:

$$\tilde{R}_{jt} = \tilde{\gamma}_{0t} + \tilde{\gamma}_{1t}\beta_{jt} + \tilde{e}_{jt} \tag{1}$$

where

$\tilde{R}_{jt}$ is the rate of return on security j in period t,

β_{jt} is the systematic risk of security j in period t,

$\tilde{e}_{jt}$ is an error term specific to company j,

and $\tilde{\gamma}_{0t}$ and $\tilde{\gamma}_{1t}$ are market factors that relate $\tilde{R}_{jt}$ and β_{jt}.

The rate of return on security j is affected by the market factors $\tilde{\gamma}_{0t}$ and $\tilde{\gamma}_{1t}$ and by the two specific factors β_{jt} and $\tilde{e}_{jt}$.

Since $\tilde{\gamma}_{0t}$, $\tilde{\gamma}_{1t}$, and β_{jt} are not directly observable, we use estimates of these variables. The estimates $\hat{\gamma}_{0t}$ and $\hat{\gamma}_{1t}$ are obtained from a study by Fama and MacBeth (1973).

Using $\hat{\gamma}_{0t}$, $\hat{\gamma}_{1t}$, and $\hat{\beta}_{jt}$, we can now calculate the residual rate of return $\hat{e}_{jt}$. The operational equation is

$$\hat{e}_{jt} = R_{jt} - (\hat{\gamma}_{0t} + \hat{\gamma}_{1t}\hat{\beta}_{jt}). \tag{2}$$

After netting out the common effects of the market factors, e_{jt} is our estimate of the effect of new information on a specific company, j, at time t. In order to study the company-specific effects in a statistically meaningful way, we average e_{jt} for a sample of companies at different points in time and obtain the statistic

$$\overline{e}_t = \frac{1}{n} \sum_{j=1}^{n} \hat{e}_{jt}, \; j = 1, \ldots, n \tag{3}$$

where t is the month relative to month 0. Month 0 is defined as the month in which the new information is obtained. A useful and popular statistic for testing the EMH is the so-called "cumulative average residual" (CAR) which accumulates the average residual $\overline{e}_t$ over time. The CAR is computed as

$$E_T = \sum_{t=1}^{T} \overline{e}_t. \tag{4}$$

An alternative measure, reported here, is the "abnormal performance index" (API) computed as

$$\text{API}_T = \frac{1}{n} \sum_{j=1}^{n} \prod_{t=1}^{T} (1 + \hat{e}_{jt}). \tag{4a}$$

Sample Data

The Annual *Compustat* Tape (ACT) was used to select our sample of companies that did poorly and had, according to the bankruptcy model, a serious chance to fail. All manufacturing companies listed on the ACT in the four years 1960, 1961, 1962 and 1963 with a December fiscal year were examined and those with $Z < 2.675$ in a particular year but $Z > 2.675$ in the prior year were chosen for our study. Recall that $Z > 2.675$ indicates a healthy company and $Z < 2.675$ indicates a sick company. The change in status (as manifested by a change in Z value) is considered here as new information. For companies with $Z < 2.675$, month 0 is March of the respective year. From the companies listed on the ACT, we obtained a sample of 105 from 1960 through 1963. Due to the unavailability of price data for some firms, our final sample consists of 92 companies; 40 in 1960, 9 in 1961, 28 in 1962, and 15 in 1963. These include 10 companies listed on the New York Stock Exchange (NYSE), 71 on the American Stock Exchange (ASE), and 11 over the counter (OTC).

Compustat Bias

A bias arises from the fact that the ACT did not contain any firms which went bankrupt in prior years. This means that we cannot select "future" bankrupts and that our selected companies are in fact all Type II errors, that is, companies that the model predicted would go bankrupt but did not. It has been shown earlier that bankrupt companies continue to experience market adjusted rates of return which are extremely negative right up to the bankruptcy date. This evidence indicates an upward bias in the expected residuals from a sample immune from bankruptcy and will work against a hypothesis of expected negative residual behavior. We cannot estimate the extent of this bias explicitly, but a large number of publicly traded firms which actually went bankrupt could have an impact on our results in an important manner, that is, they could have a dramatic negative effect on observed rates of return. Finally, the likelihood of failure for firms listed on *Compustat* is presumably lower than for the entire population of publicly traded firms.

Empirical Results—Altman and Brenner (1981)

We assumed that all annual reports are available by March 31 of each year, a full three months after the year-end. Actually, we have 20 postevent months since we gathered price data for two years after the year-end date.

Systematic risk (β) was estimated using the single-factor market model. For each company we required a minimum of 24 monthly observations before the publication (March 31) of the annual report and ran the following regression:

$$R_{jt} = \alpha_j + \beta_j R_{mt} + e_{jt} \tag{5}$$

for each of the 92 companies in our sample. The average $\hat{\beta}$ for all 92 companies using all available returns is $\bar{\hat{\beta}} = 1.48$, which is significantly larger than 1.

Table 9-6 $\overline{\hat{\beta}}$ before and after Change in Z-Score.

Group	$\overline{\hat{\beta}}_B$	$\overline{\hat{\beta}}_A$	$\Delta\overline{\hat{\beta}}$	N
1960	1.38	1.30	−0.08	40
1961	1.42	1.24	−0.18	9
1962	1.62	1.06	−0.59	28
1963	1.44	1.58	+0.14	15
Total	1.48	1.27	−0.21	92

The average ($\hat{\beta}$) for the groups in each of the four years and the total sample are given in Table 9-6. It is interesting to note that the grand average is not dominated by the 1960 group. None of the group averages is significantly different from 1.48.

Using a time series regression to estimate β assumes either that β is constant or that the changes, if there are changes, are random and not correlated with changes in other parameters of the company. If, however, changes in β are related to changes in company parameters (e.g., a change in capital structure), then using the regression estimate of β may bias the results of EMH tests. The direction of bias will depend on the way β has changed. If the companies in our sample experienced an increase in β but we use the regression estimate based on the period before the change has occurred, then the residuals that we use for testing the EMH will be biased upward (assuming $\bar{R}_m > 0$). In other words, a cumulative average residual (CAR) that slopes upward may just reflect the effect of this bias and have no implication for market inefficiency.

In Table 9-6, we present two sets of $\overline{\hat{\beta}}$. The first, denoted $\hat{\beta}_B$, is based on data just prior to the date of bankruptcy prediction, while the second, denoted $\hat{\beta}_A$, is based on data after the prediction date. We find that the overall $\overline{\hat{\beta}}$ decreases substantially from 1.48 to 1.27. The drop in $\overline{\hat{\beta}}$ may be a result of changes in some market-related parameters of these companies or a result of a regression tendency toward the mean.

Table 9-7 CAR and API for Selected Months Using the "γ_0" Model and Post-Event β.

Month	CAR($\hat{\beta}_A$)	API($\hat{\beta}_A$)
5	−0.041	0.947
10	−0.054	0.930
12	−0.096	0.899
18	−0.135	0.882

Table 9-8   Significance Tests[a] for Alternative Selected Months.

Month	t(CAR)	t(API)
5	-2.23	-2.12
10	-2.60	-1.98
12	-3.37	-2.41
18	-3.65	-2.08

[a]$t = 1.96$, significant at 0.05 level.

The Residuals' Statistics, CAR and API, Using the γ_0 Model

To test the ex-post reaction of stock prices, we computed the residuals from the so-called "γ_0" model, given by (2), using the pre-event and post-event $\hat{\beta}$'s. March 31st of each year (1961–64) was chosen as the starting point (month 0). Table 9-7 presents the CAR, $(\bar{E}_T)$ defined in (4), and the API, defined in (4a), for four alternative months.

The CAR, based on the post-event $\hat{\beta}$, shows a decline of 9.6% after one year and, -13.5% after one and one-half years. The API measure provides similar results (about -10% after one year) where most of the decline occurs within the first year. These results are puzzling, to say the least. A decline of about 10% excess return in one year seems too large to be explained away by transaction costs.

To complete the analysis of these results, we have subjected the residuals to tests of significance presented in Table 9-8. The t-values for the selected months should not be taken as independent evidence (they are dependent by construction) but rather as alternative statistics depending on the measure used (CAR or API) and the length of the period (5, 10, 12, 18). For example, the CAR of -9.6% in one year has a t-value of -3.37 and thus is significantly different from zero at the 1% level.

These results are perplexing and contradictory to much evidence concerning market efficiency. We, therefore, subjected the study to further tests based on different, though related, models.

Tests Using R_f as a Second Factor and Tests Based on the Single-Factor Market Model

The previous tests have assumed that the "γ_0" market model is the correct specification of the process generating ex-post returns. However, it has not been demonstrated that the "γ_0" model is superior to other specifications. To see whether the results obtained are sensitive to model specification, we next present results from a model that uses the risk-free rate, R_f, as a second factor and also results based on the single-factor model.

Table 9-9   CAR and *t* Values for Selected Months Using the "R_f" Model and the Single-Factor Market Model.

Month	CAR(R_f)	$t(R_f)$	CAR(α,β)	$t(\alpha,\beta)$
5	−0.050	−2.46	−0.019	−0.56
10	−0.061	−2.65	−0.000	−0.02
12	−0.097	−3.46	−0.024	−1.07
18	−0.099	−3.26	0.009	0.03

A Two-Parameter Market Model with R_f.   The following version of the two-parameter market model

$$\tilde{R}_{jt} = R_{ft} + (\tilde{R}_{mt} - R_{ft})\beta_{jt} + \tilde{e}_{jt} \tag{6}$$

where R_{ft} = risk-free rate of return in period t, is utilized to examine residual behavior. In table 9-9 we present the CARs based on equation (6) and their t-values. The general downward trend, and the statistical significance that was observed when we used the CARs from equation (1) is also observed when we use the "R_f" model, although the decline in the CAR after 18 months is about 3.6% smaller than with the previous model.

Results from the Single-Factor Market Model.   Table 9-9 also presents CARs and t-values based on the single-factor model described by equation (5). Contrary to the results obtained from the γ_0" and "R_f" models, the results here show no negative trend and the CARs are not significantly different from zero. The differences between the two two-factor models and the single-factor market model stem from the differences in the intercept terms. While R_f and γ_0 are market factors common to all companies and vary from month to month in the ex-post period, α is pertinent to a specific company and is invariant based on post-event period measurement. The results, thus, appear to be quite sensitive to the model employed.

SOME CONCLUSIONS

Altman and Brenner conclude that the results are rather ambiguous; they differ from model to model and from one test to another. Based on two two-factor market model results, it appears that the market's realization of a firm's deterioration, as reflected by subsequent excess negative returns, persists for at least twelve months. Even if we are hesitant in accepting the significance tests, we should still be concerned with the consistent decline. However, when we employed the single-factor model, the results were consistent with other studies on market efficiency; that is, the information is not new or, when it is new, the market reacts instantaneously. It should be remembered that tests of market efficiency are weak tests in the sense that we are simultaneously testing several hypotheses; that the signals provided by the multivariate model are new information, that the market reacts instantaneously, and that the market model used to test market efficiency is correctly specified. Thus, it may very well be that the observed results are a product not of market inefficiency but rather of model misspecification.

This chapter has pursued the intriguing subject of investor implications of corporate bankruptcy. Judging by the relatively large number of academic and journalistic articles on this subject, particularly in 1980 through 1982, we can expect that investor fascination with studying and devising strategies for abnormal returns in bankrupt company securities will continue.

10 Bankruptcy Prediction, Bond Ratings, and Fixed Income Investment Strategies

INTRODUCTION

One of the intriguing aspects of bankruptcy classification is the comparison between models of risk assessment, like Z-score and ZETA, and conventional risk measurement. The latter is most commonly represented by bond quality ratings given to publicly traded securities by such agencies as Standard & Poor, Moody's, Fitch, and most recently by Duff and Phelps. An additional risk measure available to the public is the *Value Line Investment Survey*'s stability measure.

We have examined the relationship between one of our bankruptcy measures (ZETA—Chapter 4) and several of the conventional ratings and have found, for the most part, a striking resemblance. For example, Table 10-1 lists the average ZETA score for both *Moody's* and *Standard & Poor*'s rating classes for the years 1978 to 1981. Note that, as expected, the better the rating the higher the average ZETA score. In fact, we observe that the average ZETA score varies approximately two points between adjacent bond ratings (with some exceptions). Perhaps the claim by bond rating agencies that they try to have equal intervals between ratings has some validity. Kaplan and Urwitz (1979) utilized a logit model to explain bond ratings precisely because they theorized that other classification techniques could not account for the different implicit intervals between ratings. Their accuracy was just mediocre, however, in explaining ratings (e.g., about 60%), and I have found this to be the case for most bond rating replication studies. See our discussion of bond ratings and computer models in Altman *et al.* (1981).

Table 10-1   Average ZETA Scores by Rating Agency and by Rating Category.

| | Senior Debt Bond Rating—ZETA Scores | | | |
	1978	1979	1980	1981
I *Moody's*				
Aaa	9.16	9.34	9.80	9.87
Aa	7.49	7.56	7.48	7.61
A	5.28	5.23	5.62	5.60
Baa	2.93	3.08	3.44	3.43
Ba	1.06	0.89	0.87	1.00
B	−2.56	−1.80	−0.24	−0.69
Caa	−5.50	−5.45	−6.08	−23.69
Ca (convertible)	−5.30	−4.33	−5.13	−4.21
II *Standard & Poor's*				
AAA	9.33	9.49	10.00	10.03
AA	7.30	7.32	7.48	7.58
A	5.29	5.30	5.62	5.65
BBB	3.31	3.51	3.75	3.61
BB	1.73	1.20	1.03	1.38
B	−1.60	−1.42	−0.52	−0.79
CCC	−5.35	−4.29	−2.45	−2.59

Spivack (1982) has found a remarkably high (over 85%) correlation between ZETA scores and the *Value Line Investment Survey* financial strength scores as published since 1965. This is further proof of the validity of ZETA as a measure of risk. Of course, bond raters claim that their assessments are qualitatively as well as quantitatively determined and it is not likely that a computer model could perfectly replicate their ratings. While this is probably true, I advocate using a model like ZETA as a type of periodic screen to pick up material discrepancies between ZETA and existing bond ratings in order better to focus the efforts of analysts and bond raters. In fact, I have argued (*Bond Week,* March 15, 1982, p. 8) that a good analyst actually becomes more valuable when his efforts are directed in a timely and reliable way to those securities where a change in risk has possibly just recently occurred.

UNITED MERCHANTS AND MANUFACTURERS

One sometimes hears the statement that models like ZETA really do not provide new information but simply substantiate "what everyone knows already." This is not always correct, as demonstrated by the United Merchants and Manufacturers (UMM) bankruptcy in July 1977. UMM was a manufacturer of textiles, a retailer (Robert Hall Stores), and a factor prior to its demise and successful reorganization in 1977-1978. Fig. 10-1 illustrates the ZETA analysis for UMM between 1967 and 1976 (note that this was prepared in December, 1976).

The ZETA score is indicated in the vertical rectangle near the top left. Note that UMM's score was a respectable 4.08 in June 1969 when it was in the 56th percentile of over 2,000 firms covered by ZETA. The score began to fall thereafter until it approached zero in June 1975, and it actually dropped into the negative range one year later. At that point, UMM had a significant bankruptcy classification probability. Thirteen months later, UMM filed for protection under Chapter XI! What is so startling about this case is that the two primary rating agencies were categorizing the outstanding debentures of UMM as triple B as late as April 1977. Recall that ZETA was indicating a distressed and deteriorating situation as early as 25 months prior and certainly at 13 months prior. Of course, the UMM example is a dramatic and carefully selected one, but it does highlight the potential of using ZETA or Z-score for bond analysis.

It should be noted that UMM is a classic case of a rapid and successful bankruptcy reorganization. In just 11 months subsequent to the bankruptcy date, the firm emerged as a smaller but viable one. As shown in Chapter 9, a purchaser of UMM's debentures just after the bankruptcy would have done very well indeed; the price increased from around $40 per bond to almost par in one year! The key, as pointed out earlier, is to find temporarily insolvent firms which have a significant proportion of positive earnings from healthy assets.

THE STEEL INDUSTRY (1977–PRESENT)

A further dramatization of ZETA's use for bankruptcy prediction and bond investment strategy is indicated by analysis within a specific industry. I have chosen the steel industry, and Table 10-2 lists the ZETA scores and bond ratings for that industry's firms as of June 1977.

In 1977, there were six firms with negative ZETA scores. Subsequent to that analysis, three companies (Alan Wood, Sitkin, and Penn Dixie) have gone bankrupt. A fourth major steel company that went bankrupt since 1977 is McLouth Steel (1981) which had a low but still healthy score (2.2) in 1977. Its score continued to deteriorate, however, until it was −2.12 in 1980, one year prior to failure. The ZETA model appears to have been quite accurate in forecasting failures in the steel industry in the late 1970s and early 1980s.

UNITED MERCHANTS & MFRS INC

(UMM)

SIC CODE: 2200

MOODY'S RATING: Baa

S&P's RATING: BBB

FISCAL YEAR END	ZETA WEIGHTED SCORE	ZETA RELATIVE PERCENTILE	ADJUSTED PER SHARE DATA EARNINGS	ADJUSTED PER SHARE DATA DIVIDENDS	ADJUSTED PER SHARE DATA HIGH PRICE	ADJUSTED PER SHARE DATA LOW PRICE	UNFUNDED PENSION LIABILITIES AS A % OF NET ASSETS
6/76	-0.38	15	-3.36	0.80	10.88	10.38	7
6/75	0.24	25	-3.12	1.25	15.50	10.88	6
6/74	1.72	36	5.18	1.35	21.00	12.00	5
6/73	3.23	48	3.31	1.30	24.38	16.63	4
6/72	3.04	47	2.50	1.30	30.38	21.25	0
6/71	3.43	50	2.71	1.30	32.00	26.63	0
6/70	3.93	53	2.81	1.30	29.88	17.00	0
6/69	4.08	56	3.92	1.22	37.50	26.13	0
6/68	*******	**	3.56	1.20	41.00	26.63	0
6/67	*******	**	2.56	1.20	29.88	22.00	0

MODEL VARIABLES — HISTORICAL ANALYSIS

FISCAL YEAR END	OVERALL PROFITABILITY		SIZE		DEBT SERVICE		LIQUIDITY		CUMULATIVE PROFITABILITY		MARKET CAPITALIZATION		EARNINGS STABILITY	
	INDEX	%-ILE	INDEX	%-ILE	INDEX	%-ILE	INDEX	%-ILE	INDEX	%-ILE	INDEX	%-ILE	INDEX	%-ILE
6/76	2	11	8	88	3	10	2	17	2	22	0	6	3	47
6/75	2	7	8	89	3	6	2	26	3	30	1	6	4	50
6/74	4	26	8	90	4	16	2	26	3	35	1	5	6	68
6/73	3	20	8	90	4	15	2	25	3	35	2	4	9	87
6/72	3	21	8	90	4	16	3	31	4	39	3	7	8	81
6/71	3	26	8	90	4	19	3	40	4	41	3	7	8	82
6/70	4	18	7	90	4	10	3	32	4	42	4	11	9	86
6/69	4	27	7	90	4	12	3	32	4	46	4	14	8	84
6/68	4	24	7	90	4	12	2	21	**	**	5	20	8	79
6/67	4	18	7	91	4	7	2	24	**	**	5	14	7	73

NOTES: IN 1971 THE INVENTORY VALUATION METHOD WAS SWITCHED FROM FIRST IN, FIRST OUT TO AVERAGE COST.

Source: ZETA Services, Inc., Mountainside, N.J., (Prepared 12/4/76).

Fig. 10-1 ZETA Analysis for UMM between 1967 and 1976

Table 10-2   ZETA Scores and Bond Ratings for Companies Engaged in the Production of Steel.*

Company Name	Bond Rating		ZETA
	Standard & Poor's	Moody's	
Ampco-Pittsburgh Corp.			9.44
Lukens Steel Co.			8.22
Carpenter Technology Corp.			7.63
Harsco Corp.	A	A	6.75
Bliss & Laughlin Industries Corp.	BB	Ba	6.15
Copperweld Corp.	A	A	5.79
Bethlehem Steel Corp.	AA	Aa	5.56
Inland Steel Corp.	AA	Aa	5.44
United States Steel Corp.	AA	Aa	4.94
Interlake Inc.	BBB	A	4.53
Republic Steel Corp.	A	A	4.38
Valley Industries, Inc.			4.30
Armco Steel Corp.	A	A	4.02
National Steel Corp.	AA	Aa	3.89
Kaiser Steel Corp.			3.31
McLough Steel Corp.			2.29[d]
Allegheny Ludlum Industries, Inc.	BBB	A	2.19
Lykes Corp.	B	B	0.70
NVF Co.	B	B	0.15
Wheeling Pittsburgh Steel Corp.		—	−0.10
Welded Tube Co. of America	B		−1.04
Penn Dixie Industries, Inc.	B	B	−1.28[a]
Sitkin Smlt & Refining, Inc.			−3.12[c]
Tubos De Acero De Mexico S A			−4.75
Alan Wood Steel Co.			−4.92[b]

[a]Bankrupt 1980.
[b]Bankrupt 1978.
[c]Bankrupt 1978.
[d]Bankrupt 1981. 1980 score = −2.12.
*Prepared 12/76.

Table 10-2 also indicates, in my opinion, different and rather interesting bond strategies. It would appear that the potential for both intrarating "swaps" and interrating comparisons is clearly manifest. For example, both Harsco Corp. and Allegheny Ludlum Industries were rated A by *Moody's* and sold at approximately the same yield. ZETA indicates that Harsco is far less risky, and one could achieve a satisfactory yield from that firm's debt with lower risk than from Allegheny. A similar argument, but not as striking, could be made for Copperweld as a healthy A-rated steel company.

Alternatively, Harsco would appear to be a better holding than several bonds rated AA by *Standard & Poor's* and *Moody's* where the yields on such securities as National Steel and U.S. Steel's debt were obviously lower than Harsco's. Is it possible to get higher yields at equal or lower risk? ZETA scores seem to indicate this possibility.

The analysis of comparable bond ratings and ZETA is not restricted to the steel industry, nor is it advised that every discrepancy between ZETA

Table 10-3 Junk Bonds: Bonds with BB or Lower Rating and 1978 ZETA Scores above A-Rating Average.[a]

First Name	Rating 1978 S&P's/ Moody's	Rating 1981 S&P's/ Moody's	ZETA 1978	ZETA 1981
Fischbach & Moore, Inc.	BB/Ba	BB/Ba	5.39	5.36
Riegel Textile	BB/Ba	BB/Ba	6.02	5.85
Papercraft Corp.	BB/Ba	BB/Ba	9.41	5.02
Bliss & Laughlin	BB/Ba	BB/Ba	5.48	7.08
General Tire & Rubber	BB/Ba	BB/Ba	6.39	4.11
Economics Lab, Inc.	BB/Baa	BBB/Baa	8.14	8.19
Eckerd Jack Corp.	BB/Baa	BB/Baa	6.67	8.21
Texas Eastern	BB/Ba	A/A	5.77	4.72
Delta Airlines	BB/Ba	BBB/Ba	5.40	5.65
Tyler Corp.	BB+/NR	BB+/NR	8.17	8.58
Apache Corp.	B/NR	NR	6.11	4.83
Rustcraft Greeting	BB/Ba	NR	6.77	—
Duro Test	NR/Ba	NR/Ba	8.93	9.18

[a]Average A = rated bond ZETA score = 5.60, NR = Not rated.

Note: Total number of bonds = 11; number of ratings increased = 3; number of ratings unchanged = 8; number of ZETA increases = 6; number of ZETA decreases = 6.

and ratings should be invested in (or disinvested). All that we are advocating is a careful analysis of situations which are detected by a computerized, fixed-income screening device.

JUNK BOND ANALYSIS

Another application of ZETA-type analysis is in the "junk" bond arena. An investor who is interested in such high-yield debt securities is usually also concerned with default risk. ZETA might assist in this analysis by identifying low-default-risk bonds. We have listed in Table 10-4 those junk bonds rated BB or lower in 1978 with a ZETA score greater than the industry average and also higher than the average A-rated ZETA (5.60) score (see Table 10-1). Presumably, a ZETA equal to or greater than an equivalent A-rated company has low default risk.

Of the 11 bonds with these characteristics in 1978, three had their ratings *increased* by at least one of the major agencies. The remaining eight bonds did not experience a rating change. The implication is that a normally risky investment in low rated junk bonds can be made less risky if the risk characteristics of those securities are similar to those of higher rated debt. Now, there are many other factors that one needs to consider, for instance, the underlying equity security, but ZETA would appear to be a potentially useful tool. In 1982, there are at least 11 junk bonds with "safe" (A-rated) ZETA scores.

11 Developing Failure Prediction Models for Nonindustrial Sectors

INTRODUCTION

The bankruptcy prediction models developed in Chapters 3 and 4 were of a more general industrial type. We realize that the relative heterogeneity of industrial firms, both manufacturers and retailers, constrains the model as to its expected accuracy for firms whose affiliation differs from that of the "average" industrial company. We saw this most clearly when applying the Z-score model in industries where the sales/assets ratio varies widely. The ideal would be to construct individual models for specific industries. A large, representative sample of bankrupt firms is necessary to construct a model, and since most specific industries have not experienced sufficient numbers of failures, the models developed for industrial firms have cut across many sectors. There are, however, a number of *nonindustrial* sectors which have the required number of failures, that is, 15 to 20 at a minimum, and modeling attempts are feasible.

The purpose of this chapter is to report on efforts by this author to develop and test models in the railroad, savings and loan, and broker-dealer sectors and also to summarize efforts by others in the commercial bank and credit union sectors. In all cases, the technique used to build these models was discriminant analysis, or variations on this technique. We will discuss models which utilize both linear and quadratic analyses as well as multigroup structures. It should be noted that the financial sector has witnessed dramatic changes in the late 1970s and early 1980s. As such, the models discussed below may not be directly applicable in the future since they were built from 1970 to 1977. Still, the results are relevant to the analysis of firms in such sectors and should assist researchers and practitioners in their efforts to assess firm performance.

RAILROAD BANKRUPTCY PREDICTION

Background and Purpose

More than any other industry in the business history of the United States, railroads have continually experienced operating and financial problems. One wonders how this industry with such enormous "public-interest" qualities, which has been the beneficiary of governmental subsidies and has been supervised by the ICC since 1887, could continue to be plagued by failures without some decisive measures taken to reduce or mitigate them. It has been estimated by Vance (1971) that the number of railroad receiverships, bankruptcies, and liquidations during the period 1876 to 1970 exceeded 1,100! While that number has abated in the last decade, there are now less than 50 Type I railroads (revenues over $5 million) remaining in the U.S. At the very least, one would expect that some diagnostic work would have been undertaken to predict failure as a means of forestalling or mitigating bankruptcies and their consequences.

Railroad bankruptcies have enormous consequences to the public besides the obvious costs to corporate suppliers, creditors, and stockholders. The social costs are related to reduced services, higher rates, and government subsidies and/or loan guarantees. These costs may necessitate higher taxes and shift the burden of failure among economic units in ways that no cost-benefit analysis could justify. And this unfortunate state of affairs appears to be continuing.

The large number of railroad failures has evolved due to a chain of unfavorable circumstances and poor management on a microeconomic level and also due to the regulatory nature of the industry. Because of the numerous legislative moves to regulate the transportation industry, from the Interstate Commerce Act (1887) to the Department of Transportation Act (1966), we now have an example of government regulated cartelization which has been characterized by an inability to adjust to change and, at times, by grossly inefficient management. Rather than review the history of railroad "progress" in the United States, it will serve the purpose of our discussion to summarize the major problem areas.

The major reasons for the railroad industry's dismal performance are: (1) its inability to meet competitive conditions due to an inflexible pricing and cost structure; (2) its acute susceptibility to large net income losses during periods of economic stress due to a fixed asset and liability structure which is heavily leveraged; (3) its excess capacity; (4) the acute labor and manpower rigidities; and (5) a shortage of innovative management. Many of these problems are the by-products of government regulation and industry rigidities. These have produced an industry pricing structure dictated, in part, by political and noneconomic terms rather than comparative advantage considerations.

The railroad industry is a classic illustration of the magnification effect caused by high operating and financial leverage structures. The leverage concept affirms that during periods of economic downturns, those firms which are more heavily leveraged will experience greater swings in returns on equity (possibly to negative levels) and be more vulnerable to failure than low-fixed-cost firms. Combine this situation with recurring liquidity problems common to railroads and the reasons for the high incidence of railroad bankruptcies become clear. In addition, the industry appears to be quite vulnerable to general economic declines and credit crunches, such that the induced effect of the business cycle on railroads is sizable.

Railroads are quite vulnerable to business cycle fluctuations, but the asset and capital structures do not reflect this high-risk situation. We observe that for those roads which went bankrupt, the percentage of total capital contributed by creditors, one annual statement prior to bankruptcy, averaged 91.2 %, while the industry average was approximately 50%. This implies a chronic rather than an episodic industry problem. The high-risk situation, in the light of historically low returns on invested capital, provides valid grounds for criticism of the industry's overall managerial efficiency.

The purpose of the ensuing discussion is to build, test, and monitor a railroad bankruptcy classification-prediction model. We built this model in 1971 and 1972, and although the nature of the industry has changed somewhat—that is, there has been some deregulation—we feel that the results are still valid in the early 1980s. The model was tested on the original sample of firms, on the entire railroad population as of year-end 1970 and monitored as to the performance of U.S. railroads from 1973 to 1982. The results seem to indicate that the model has retained its reliability. For a full description of the data and the model's results, see Altman (1973).

Reorganization Duration

A major consequence of filing under Section 77 of the bankruptcy act was the time it took to restructure the firm effectively in order to resume normal operations. In addition, there is always the chance that reorganization efforts will prove fruitless and that a liquidation or a "forced" merger will ensue. In those cases, all or most of the reorganization expenses will prove useless, not to mention the delay in receiving the liquidation or merger value of the railroad's assets. At the time of the enactment of

Section 77 in 1933, advocates of the new procedures claimed it would shorten the reorganization period and thus lower its costs. In addition, the old "friendly" receiver would be replaced by an unbiased trustee. Furthermore, it would lead to sounder and more permanent financial structures, thereby lowering the probability of future railroad bankruptcies.

The first proclamation—that reorganization time would be reduced, and so the consequent costs—has been clearly shown to be.invalid. The ICC, in its expressed desire to be perfectly fair and thorough, probably has been one of the prime contributors, along with the federal courts, to lengthy and drawn out proceedings.

Due to the complexities of Section 77 bankruptcy proceedings, they are significantly longer than reorganization proceedings for manufacturing firms. We examined a total of 36 Section 77 bankruptcy reorganizations during the period from 1938 to 1970. The mean bankruptcy reorganization period was seven years and seven months with the medium period being seven years and two months. This is significantly greater than the pre-1933 duration and also compares quite unfavorably with an average two years, three months for manufacturing companies in bankruptcy (Altman, 1969). Warner (1977) found that his sample of 11 large railroad bankruptcies consumed, on average, over 13 years in reorganization.

Admittedly, there should be some tradeoff between the positive effects of reaching a fair and equitable solution and the desire to reduce the time and costs of the bankruptcy process. In our opinion, the lengthy delays are not necessarily to the benefit of anyone (except perhaps the legal profession and expert witnesses) and add to the "direct" costs of bankruptcy. (See discussion in Chapter 9.)

Railroad Industry Advantages

One particularly fortunate ingredient of a multiple discriminant or even univariate railroad bankruptcy analysis is that we now have a project where the comparative analysis can be concentrated within a relatively homogeneous group of sample firms. The railroad industry study, therefore, provides an ideal framework from which we can apply a proven technique to an even more specific problem area. We will match results drawn from a group of bankrupt railroads with (1) average industry measures drawn from the same time periods as the prior-to-bankruptcy financial ratios and (2) a random sample of nonbankrupt railroads. The beauty of this homogeneous type of analysis is that we can be confident that any new firm tested in the model will have similar characteristics that were present in the group of firms used to construct the model.

Due to ICC reporting requirements, accounting data, both present and past, are for the most part available and quite comprehensive. Although these ICC requirements have changed from time to time, the comprehensiveness of the data has remained at a high level and continuity of accounting reporting has only been moderately difficult to interpret. In addition to the individual firm reporting standards, the ICC provides aggregate annual statistics for the entire railroad carrier industry which is published along with firm data in *Moody's Transportation Manual,* on an annual basis.

Model Development

A group of 21 railroads that went bankrupt between the years 1939 and 1970 was compiled and scrutinized. Balance sheet and income statement data were then gathered for one statement and two statements prior to actual bankruptcy. *Moody's* also publishes comprehensive industry data on an annual basis, and the next step was to gather financial statistics for the industry as a whole for the same years that we have bankruptcy data. Industry ratios and measures of performance are derived from aggregated totals for the various balance sheet and income statement accounts. These aggregates include all of the railroads in the industry for a particular year. The measures encompass three overall groupings of financial indicators: (1) liquidity measures; (2) profitability and efficiency measures; and (3) solvency and leverage measures. We chose industry averages primarily because individual firms might have been insolvent, though still alive.

Empirical results

We calculated averages for the 14 ratios listed in Table 11-1 for the bankrupt group sample of 21 firms based on data drawn from one statement and from two statements prior to bankruptcy. Industry averages were calculated from the same periods. For example, the sample of bankrupt firms includes three firms who declared bankruptcy in 1970, and therefore data were collected as of the end of 1969 and 1968 for each firm. Likewise, industry average ratios are calculated by giving proportional weighting to the 1969 and 1968 years (three out of 21). Since the bankrupt groups' petitions covered a relatively long span of time, the proportional weighting helps to remove any bias due to trend movements in the variable values.

The ratio results conform with our *a priori* expectations and indicate that a multivariate prediction model is a viable possibility. The bankrupt group's ratios show significantly worse measures (*F*-ratios significant at the 0.01 level) than the industry averages (with three exceptions) for both one and two statements prior to failure. In addition, the bankrupt averages all show deterioration as a failure approaches.

Table 11-1 Bankrupt Firms and Railroad Industry Ratios.

Ratio Name and Number[a]	One Statement prior to Bankruptcy			Two Statements prior to Bankruptcy		
	Average for Bankrupt Group	Average for Industry	F-Ratio[b]	Average for Bankrupt Group	Average for Industry	F-Ratio[b]
I Liquidity						
(1) NCA/TA	−11.0%	2.8%	10.4	−7.3%	2.9%	8.8
(2) NCA/OR	−42.0%	5.7	7.7	−36.6	6.8	6.2
II Profitability and Efficiency						
(3) EBIT/TA	−3.0%	5.0%	10.3	−2.0%	5.0%	9.9
(4) OR/TTP	24.8	31.8	5.7	25.2	31.4	4.1
(5) OR/NTP	30.5	41.5	0.2[a]	32.0	40.9	0.4[c]
(6) Operating ratio	87.4	75.4	15.5	85.3	75.1	18.9
(7) TE/OR	44.3	37.2	30.9	45.4	37.1	44.9
(8) EAIT/OR	−15.0	6.4	56.2	−11.0	6.1	75.5
(9) MAIN/TTP	7.3	8.7	0.3[a]	7.3	8.7	0.5[c]
(10) Growth rate in OR	1.6	3.9	0.9[a]	2.7	3.7	0.2[c]
III Solvency and Leverage						
(11) ES/TA	−31.8%	18.6%	22.4	−27.3%	18.1%	17.3
(12) TD/TA	91.2	50.5	13.8	88.2	50.7	10.9
(13) Charges earned	−0.6X	2.3X	54.1	−0.5X	2.2X	59.4
(14) Cash flow/fixed charges	−0.5X	2.3X	65.8	−0.4X	2.2X	74.5

[a]Due to space limitations these ratios appear in abbreviated form. For their full definition please refer to Altman (1973).
[b]This ratio measures the significance of the mean values between the two groups.
[c]Not significant on a univariate basis.

Variable Profile Analysis. From the original list of 14 variables, listed in Table 11-1, the discriminant profile of variables which is selected as providing an accurate railroad bankruptcy prediction model is

$$Z = f(X_{14}, X_7, X_{11}, X_{10}, X_8, X_6, X_3) \qquad (1)$$

where

X_{14} = cash flow/fixed charges,
X_7 = transportation expenses/operating revenues,
X_{11} = earned surplus/total assets,
X_{10} = three-year growth rate in operating revenues,
X_8 = earnings after taxes/operating revenues,
X_6 = operating expenses/operating revenues, and
X_3 = earnings before interest and taxes/total assets.

The ordering of these seven variables is derived from the discriminant computer program which selects variables in the order of their contributory importance. The process, a stepwise discriminant analysis, first chooses the variable with the greatest F-value [in this case X_{14} with an $F = 65.8$ (see Table 11-1)] and then includes other variables such that the resulting multivariate F-ratio is maximized for that number of degrees of freedom. The multivariate F-ratio is a test to determine the overall discriminating power of the model.

The specific parametric discriminant model selected is:

$$Z = 0.2003(X_{14}) - 0.2070(X_7) + 0.0059(X_{11}) - 0.0647(X_{10})$$
$$+ 0.1040(X_8) + 0.0885(X_6) + 0.0688(X_3). \qquad (2)$$

The group means of the two-group railroad sample are (1) bankrupt railroads = 3.640, and (2) industrial averages = + 0.299, with the F-ratio for this seven-variable profile equal to 20.1 (significant at the 0.01 level). This test rejects the null hypothesis that the observations come from the same population.

Note that in equation (2) the sign of the coefficient for X_6 is positive and therefore not what one would expect. This is due to the high direct correlation with X_7 which has the expected negative sign. When one combines the two coefficients [+0.0885(X_6) and −0.2070(X_7)] the result is very close to the coefficient of X_7 in a variable profile which excludes X_6. We chose the seven-variable model because of its slightly more accurate discrimination results. The six-variable function is

$$Z = 0.2539(X_{14}) - 0.1442(X_7) + 0.0071(X_{11}) - 0.0632(X_{10})$$
$$+ 0.0359(X_8) + 0.0434(X_3)$$

with $F = 20.2$.

Discrimination Results.   With the estimation of the discriminant coefficient values, it is possible to calculate discriminant values (Z-scores) for each observation in the sample and to classify them into one of the two initial groups. The essence is to compare the profile of an individual railroad with that of the alternative group profiles and to assign it to the group it most closely resembles.

The empirical classification results of the original two-group sample at one statement prior to bankruptcy are extremely accurate. Only one bankrupt firm was misclassified as healthy while every industrial average observation was correctly classified. This means that the Type I error was just 4.76% and the Type II error was zero.

In the calculation of Z-scores for each observation, it is important to note that the first variable (X_{14}) is expressed as number of times, for example, 2.0, while the other six variables are all expressed in "absolute" percent form. For example, X_{10} for a firm may be 35% and is expressed as 35.0.

We arbitrarily choose a Z-score of -1.465 as the cutoff point between classification into the two groups. This point is simply the midpoint between the lowest industry score and the highest correctly classified bankrupt railroad score. In total, the discriminant function classified the original sample 97.62% accurately (41 out of 42).

Two Statement Prior Results.   The accuracy of the original sample is matched by the data from two statements prior to bankruptcy petition. Using the original sample coefficients [equation (1)] we take the ratio values of the bankrupt railroads two statements prior and sum the seven products to arrive at the Z-scores. Again with the -1.465 cutoff score, only one railroad is misclassified.

An Alternative Modeling Strategy.   Earlier we mentioned reasons for selecting industry aggregate data to compare with that of the bankrupt railroad sample. We should note the possibility of a statistical bias which may result from this approach. In particular, we may observe significantly different values for the actual ratios, and more than likely the distribution of ratio values within the group will be less dispersed if we utilize industry data for various years than if we employ another sampling technique using individual firms representing the nonbankrupt sample. Since tightness of dispersion within groups is a positive attribute for good discrimination between groups, we expect better discrimination than if the dispersion within the nonbankrupt group were more dispersed.

With the above considerations in mind, we construct a second model with individual firms comprising the nonbankrupt group. For every bankrupt railroad observed in the year of the bankruptcy petition, we randomly select a nonbankrupt railroad from the nation's Class I railroads of that year. The selected firms must have remained solvent in a bankruptcy sense for at least five years after the year they were selected. From this new sample of healthy railroads we calculate values for the seven variables discussed above.

The mean values and standard deviations of each variable are displayed in Table 11-2. Note that the average values for the nonbankrupts are extremely similar to those of the industry aggregates. In fact, at least five of the seven variables have virtually the same mean values.

As expected, we find that in all cases the standard deviation within the industry aggregates sample is less than the comparable figure for the individual firm nonbankrupt group. This is due to the relatively small changes from year to year in the industry figures.

The resulting discrimination power, based on the new model shown in equation (3), is lower, but only slightly so, than the model utilizing industry data. The F-value for the entire profile equals 13.0 compared to 20.1 for the industry model, but is still significant at the 0.01 level. Note also that the group mean Z-score values are closer together in this new model,

$$Z = 0.0033(X_{14}) - 0.1211(X_7) + 0.0038(X_{11}) - 0.0510(X_{10})$$
$$+ 0.0697(X_8) + 0.0468(X_6) + 0.0499(X_3) \qquad (3)$$

also indicating potentially greater overlap between values of firms in the two groups.

	Z-Score, Nonbankrupt Group Mean	Z-Score, Bankrupt Group Mean
Industry Sample	$+0.299$	-3.640
Firm sample	-0.164	-2.695

Table 11-2   Group Means and Standard Deviations[a] Comparison.

Variable	Nonbankrupt Firm Group	Industry Aggregates Group	Bankrupt Group
EBIT/TA (X_3)	5.31 %	5.03	$-$ 3.02
	(3.99)	(2.0)	(11.3)
Operating ratio (X_6)	74.10 %	75.43	87.42
	(13.5)	(5.0)	(13.0)
TE/OR (X_7)	34.29 %	37.22	44.54
	(5.9)	(3.2)	(5.1)
EAIT/OR (X_8)	5.40 %	6.35	-14.96
	(7.9)	(3.8)	(12.5)
Growth rate OR (X_{10})	3.85 %	3.92	1.59
	(10.0)	(7.8)	(8.3)
ES/TA (X_{11})	25.43 %	18.57	-31.82
	(25.5)	(10.9)	(37.5)
Cash flow/fixed	6.88 X	2.33	$-$ 0.47
charges (X_{14})	(12.1)	(1.3)	(0.9)

[a]Standard deviations in parentheses.

Potential Bias and Validation Tests.   The empirical results reported above are indeed impressive, yet we know that they are biased upward. The bias is due, in general terms, to the fact that the same observations which are used to construct the model are also the ones classified by the model.

A method suggested by Frank *et al.* (1965) for testing the afore-mentioned biases is applied to the initial sample. The essence of this test is to estimate parameters using a subset of each of the two original groups and to test the significance of these results (called the analysis sample test); then to classify the remainder of the sample based on the parameters established (called the validation sample test). A simple *t*-test is applied to the results to test their significance.

Five different replications of this test are performed with the analysis sample each time, with 11 firms in each group, $n = 22$. The validation test sample comprises the remaining 10 observations in each replication, $n = 20$. The same variables that appear in equation (1) are present in each of these tests. The test results, illustrated in Table 11-3, reject the hypothesis that there is no difference between groups (both analysis and validation tests) and substantiates that the model does possess significant discriminating power on observations other than those used to establish the parameters of the model. Therefore, any search and sample bias does not appear to be significant.

Table 11-3   Validation Sample Tests.

	Analysis Sample		Validation Sample	
Replication	Percent of Correct Classifications	t-Value	Percent of Correct Classifications	t-Value
1	100.0	4.67[a]	85.0	3.13[a]
2	95.5	4.24[a]	95.0	4.02[a]
3	95.5	4.24[a]	90.0	3.57[a]
4	100.0	4.67[a]	80.0	2.68[b]
5	100.0	4.67[a]	65.0	1.34[c]
Average	98.2		83.0	
Observations	(22)		(20)	

[a]Significant at 0.01.
[b]Significant at 0.025.
[c]Significant at 0.25.

Random Selection Test

Thus far, we have shown that the railroad prediction model is extremely accurate in classifying firms in the original sample, both for the entire sample and for various subsets. Another type of test is now performed in order to assess the validity of the model on a completely new group of railroads, each randomly selected.

A group of 50 railroads is chosen based on a stratified, random basis. Each sample observation is derived by first randomly selecting a year between 1946 and 1969. For each year, an observation is then selected from the list of Class I railroads compiled by *Moody's* in that year.

In the 50-railroad sample, only six observations had a Z-score below the cutoff point, -1.465. Of the six railroads classified as potential bankrupts, two actually went bankrupt in years subsequent to our test, one discontinued all railroad operations, and two others were subsequently merged into larger railroad systems, both of which have actually gone bankrupt!

One road is owned by a foreign (Canadian) railway system. In essence, the railroad bankruptcy prediction model, when tested on this new secondary sample, had at most one or two errors of the Type II variety and was correct in predicting bankruptcy for roads as much as six years prior to bankruptcy.

It is difficult to estimate the Type I error in this randomly selected railroad sample. After a careful investigation of the 50 railroads' histories,

Table 11-4   Z-Scores of Class I Railroads, 1970 and Subsequent Status.

RR#	Company Name	Z-Score	Bankrupt (B-Year) Continuing (C) Status (1981)
RR01	Akron, Canton & Youngstown Railroad	1.785	C
RR02	Alabama Great Southern Railroad	1.256	C
RR03	Ann Arbor Railroad	-4.384^b	B (10/73)
RR04	Atchison, Topeka & Sante Fe Railway	1.887	C
RR05	Baltimore & Ohio Railroad	-0.896	C
RR06	Bangor & Aroostock Railroad	2.749	C
RR07	Bessemer & Lake Erie Railroad	11.935	C
RR08	Boston & Main Corp.^{a}	-5.420^b	B (3/70)
RR09	Burlington Northern Inc.	-0.262	C
RR10	Central of Georgia Railway	1.583	C (acquired)
RR11	Central Railroad Co. of New Jersey^a	-7.490^b	B (Conrail 1976)
RR12	Chesapeake & Ohio Railway	0.550	C
RR13	Chicago & Eastern Illinois Railroad	1.726	C (merged)
RR14	Chicago & North Western Railway System	-1.669^b	C
RR15	Chicago, Milwaukee, St. Paul & Pacific Railroad	-1.930^b	B (12/77)
RR16	Chicago, Rock Island & Pacific Railroad	-3.824^b	B (3/75)
RR17	Cincinnati, New Orleans & Texas Pacific Railway	2.593	C
RR18	Colorado & Southern Railway Co.	0.325	C (acquired)
RR19	Delaware & Hudson Railway Co.	-0.612	C
RR20	Denver & Rio Grande Western Railroad	2.527	C
RR21	Detroit & Toledo Shore Line Railroad	1.380	C
RR22	Detroit, Toledo & Ironton Railroad	0.415	C
RR23	Duluth, Missabe & Iron Range Railway	21.588	C
RR24	Erie-Lackawanna Railway Co.^{c}	-3.329^b	B (6/72) Conrail
RR25	Florida East Coast Railway	2.013	C
RR26	Fort Worth & Denver Railway	-3.877^b	C (acquired)
RR27	Georgia Southern & Florida Railway	1.288	C
RR28	Grand Trunk Western Railroad	-12.950^b	C (acquired)
RR29	Gulf, Mobile & Ohio Railroad	0.882	C (merged)
RR30	Illinois Central Railroad	0.791	C
RR31	Illinois Terminal Railroad	-1.432	C
RR32	Kansas City Southern Railway	0.693	C
RR33	Lehigh Valley Railroad^a	-5.841^b	B (7/70)
RR34	Louisville & Nashville Railroad	0.457	C (acquired)
RR35	Maine Central Railroad	0.004	C
RR36	Missouri-Kansas-Texas Railroad	-2.723^b	C

RR#	Company Name	Z-Score	Bankrupt (B-Year) Continuing (C) Status (1981)
RR37	Missouri Pacific Railroad	−0.002	C
RR38	Monon Railroad	0.035	C (acquired)
RR39	Norfolk & Western Railway	0.459	C
RR40	Norfork & Southern Railway	1.151	C (merged)
RR41	Penn Central Transportation Co.[a]	−5.501[b]	B (6/70) Conrail
RR42	Pittsburgh & Lake Erie Railroad	1.256	C
RR43	Reading Co.	−2.571[b]	B (6/71) Conrail
RR44	Richmond, Fredericksburgh & Potomac Railroad	4.539	C
RR45	St. Louis-San Francisco Railway	−0.492	C
RR46	St. Louis-Southwestern Railway	12.245	C
RR47	Seaboard Coast Line Railroad	0.231	C
RR48	Soo Line Railroad	−0.241	C
RR49	Southern Pacific Transportation Co.	−0.283	C
RR50	Southern Railway	1.119	C
RR51	Texas & Pacific Railroad	−0.366	C
RR52	Toledo, Peoria & Western Railroad	0.933	C
RR53	Union Pacific Railroad	2.897	C
RR54	Western Maryland Railway	0.931	C (acquired)
RR55	Western Pacific Railroad	−3.467[b]	C (merged)

[a] In bankruptcy in 1970.
[b] Classified as bankrupt.
[c] Bankrupt subsequent to 1970.

we did not find one obvious short-term error (that of predicting non-bankruptcy in a near-term failure case). Some interesting patterns do emerge, however, especially with railroads which have recently been cited as potential bankrupts. (These 1970 "potentials" are examined in the next section.) In conclusion, it appears that the railroad discriminant model is valid for secondary samples as well as the original one.

1970 Class I Railroad Results, Outlook, and Follow-Up Analysis

As a final test for our railroad bankruptcy prediction model, we examined the Class I railroads as of December 31, 1970, and determined that 55 of them could be tested by the discriminant model. We then gathered data from their 1970 financial statements and calculated Z-scores for each (listed in Table 11-4). Of the 55 roads tested, 41 had Z-scores above −1.465 and

Table 11-5 Railroads Classified as Bankrupt in 1975–1980.

Rank	Railroad	Number of Times Classified	Mean Z-Value	Comments
1.	Grand Trunk Western	4	-2.149	
2.	Akron, Canton & Youngstown	3	-2.243	
3.	Boston & Maine Corp.	4	-2.083	
4.	Missouri-Kansas-Texas	4	-1.819	
5.	Illinois Terminal	3	-1.723	
6.	Delaware & Hudson	2	-1.644	
7.	Chicago & North Western	3	-1.556	
8.	Illinois Central Gulf	3	-1.423	
9.	Western Pacific	3	-1.227	to merge with Union Pacific
10.	Louisville & Nashville	2	-1.247	
11.	Missouri Pacific	3	-1.064	to merge with Union Pacific
12.	Detroit Toledo & Ironton	2	-1.166	acquired by GTW 6/80
13.	Fort Worth & Denver	2	-0.987	
14.	St. Louis Southwestern	1	-0.564	
15.	Pittsburgh & Lake Erie	1	-0.193	
16.	Western Maryland	1	-1.021	
17.	Southern Pacific	1	-0.616	

Source: S. Bragg, ''The Railroad Bankruptcy Model in the 1975–1980 Period'' (NYU, 1981).

were classified as "healthy" railroads. The remaining 14 roads had scores below this level and are listed. Five other railroads had scores between -0.3 and -1.465, and therefore fall within the zone where classification appears to have the highest probability of error.

The 14 roads classified as bankruptcy candidates in 1970 include nine (03, 08, 11, 15, 16, 24, 33, 41, and 43) which were already in bankruptcy (four) or subsequently failed (five). There were zero Type I errors and only up to three or four Type II errors. This indicates not only that the model had a high degree of classification accuracy but also that its *predictive* content was excellent.

Model Update

Finally, we assessed the bankrupt potential of those railroads still in existence in the period from 1975 through 1980 and found that 17 (Table 11-5) had Z-scores below the -1.465 cutoff score in at least one year. The average Z-score is listed for the six-year period. It will be interesting to watch the progress of these railroads.

SAVINGS AND LOAN ASSOCIATION ASSESSMENT

S&L's: A Crisis Industry

Perhaps the most embattled industry in the U.S. in recent years has been the nation's savings and loan associations and their sister institutions, the mutual savings banks. In 1981, 24 federal savings institutions were assisted by the two major federal insurance agencies; 22 were in the S&L industry (Table 11-6). Assistance usually implies a supervisory merger arrangement between a healthy savings institution and the failing one. The acquiring institution is afforded some compensation package from the Federal Deposit Insurance Corp. (FDIC) or the Federal Savings & Loan Corp. (FSLIC). A basic element in the insurer's responsibility is to stabilize the industry and maintain public confidence by protecting depositors. It is essential, therefore, to detect signs of problems as early as possible so that preventive measures can be taken. Techniques to detect such problems have obvious benefits to society.

In the following sections, we will present the results of our efforts to construct an accurate, reliable early warning system for identifying serious problem savings & loan associations (originally reported in Altman, 1977). For the first time, we will include all of the details of the model, including model coefficients. Since the model was built based on data from the 1960s and early 1970s and since it has not been tested during the

Table 11-6 Failing Savings Institutions Assisted by Federal Insurance Agencies in 1981.

I Savings Bank Mergers Arranged by the Federal Deposit Insurance Corporation

Merged Bank	Total Assets ($ Millions)	Acquiring Bank	Total Assets ($ Millions)	Date
Greenwich Savings Bank, N.Y.	$2,500	Metropolitan Savings Bank, N.Y.	$2,200	Nov. 4
Central Savings Bank, N.Y.	910	Harlem Savings Bank, N.Y.	843	Dec. 4

II Savings and Loan Mergers Arranged by the Federal Savings and Loan Insurance Corporation

Merged Savings & Loan	Total Assets ($ Millions)	Acquiring Institution	Total Assets ($ Millions)	Date
Home Savings Association, Minn.	$ 683	First Federal Mutual, N.C.	$ 785	Jan. 18
Security Federal. N.C.	16	Asheville Savings and Loan, Ill.	170	Feb. 9
Franklin Savings. Ill.	93	Avondale Savings and Loan, Ill.	195	Feb. 10
Guardian Savings and Loan, N.Y.	122	Anchor Savings Bank, N.Y.	1,900	April 30
Arctic First Federal, Alaska	41	First Federal Mutual, Alaska	212	May 9

New York and Suburban, N.Y.	511	Anchor Savings Bank, N.Y.	2,000	June 1
Financial Security of Elk Grove, Ill.	61	Land of Lincoln, Ill.	409	June 1
Community Federal, Wash., D.C.	23	Independence Savings and Loan, Wash., D.C.	56	July 1
First Federal Savings and Loan, N.C.	62	Raleigh Savings and Loan, N.C.	250	July 1
First Financial, Tex.	6	South Texas Savings and Loan, Tex.	122	July 10
County Federal, Md.	145	Metropolitan Savings and Loan, Md.	259	Aug. 10
Franklin Society Federal, N.Y.	1,000	First Federal Savings and Loan, N.Y.	1,200	Sept. 8
West Side Savings and Loan, N.Y. & Washington Savings and Loan, Fla.	2,500 1,300	Citizens Savings and Loan, Calif.	3,000	Sept. 8
Perpetual Savings and Loan, S.D.	52	First Federal Savings and Loan, S.D.	237	Sept. 15
Lafayette Federal, Mo.	415	United Postal Savings and Loan, Mo.	292	Oct. 2
Reserve Savings and Loan, Ill.	148	Hyde Park Savings and Loan, Ill.	63	Oct. 7
First Federal Savings and Loan, Fla.	2,600	Glendale Savings and Loan, Calif.	5,100	Nov. 20

(Continued)

Table 11-6 (Continued)

Merged Savings & Loan	Total Assets ($ Millions)	Acquiring Institution	Total Assets ($ Millions)	Date
Pan American Savings and Loan, P.R.	44	First Federal Savings and Loan, P.R.	1,000	Nov. 20
Guaranty Savings and Loan, La.	32	Pelican Homestead Savings and Loan, La.	302	Nov. 30
Empire State Savings and Loan, N.Y.	266	Erie Savings Bank, N.Y.	2,400	Nov. 30
Palos Savings and Loan, Ill.	102	Hyde Park Savings and Loan, Ill.	313	Dec. 5
Boca Raton Savings and Loan, Fla.	294			
& Mohawk Savings and Loan, N.J.	88	City Federal of Elizabeth, N.J.		Dec. 10

Source: The New York Times, December 15, 1981.

most recent economic recessions, we have no evidence as to its reliable applicability for detecting problem S&L's in today's or tomorrow's environment. At the same time, we are confident that the methodological issues and empirical findings will assist both researchers and practitioners.

Group Selection

One of the unique aspects of this study is the selection of three groups of S&L's considered appropriate for the type of predictive information most useful for supervisory personnel. That is, FSLIC officials are concerned primarily with those associations which might result in a tangible contribution on the part of the insurance corporation. Despite the criticism of these groupings by Sinkey, (Altman, et al., 1981) we know that they are important to the regulators since the groups were selected with the knowledge, indeed the recommendation, of senior regulatory personnel. We will include the three groups via several pair-wise quadratic analyses and also report on results of a combined three-group analysis. The first of the three groups is the one that regulatory authorities dearly want to avoid.

Serious-Problem (SP) Associations

Originally, we observed 65 S&L's whose condition at some time during the period from 1966 to 1973 was deemed serious. These included S&L's that went into receivership; received contributions in the form of loans, purchases of assets, straight contribution, or a combination of these; and finally, those that entered into a supervisory merger which (based on expert opinion provided by senior members of the Office of Examinations and Supervision of the Federal Home Loan Bank Board) was probably the only remedy outside of direct intervention by the FSLIC. In many cases, the merger was accompanied by a contribution.

While this definition of "serious problem" is broader than the less ambiguous, more typical bankruptcy criterion, it better reflects the types of situations that the FSLIC is concerned about. In the period from 1966 to 1973, there were five S&L receiverships, 48 contributions and loans of various types, and at least 16 supervisory mergers of the type noted above. We have seen that the number of serious problem S&L's in 1981 alone totaled 22.

Temporary-Problem (TP) Associations

We then attempted to "match" as closely as possible a sample of S&L's which had fairly serious financial problems at the same time as the SP firm suffered its critical fate, but in which (that is, in the TP association's case) the problem did not result in FSLIC action.

During the years that encompass this study (1966 to 1973), the Office of Examinations and Supervision (OES) of the FHLBB has rated S&L's based on examinations made by their personnel. Although the exact numerology has changed once or twice, essentially the S&L's were rated based on approximately a dozen characteristics with a summary rating of 1 through 4, where: 1 = virtually free of adverse criticism; 2 = does not measure up to 1 in important respects but is not considered serious; 3 = one or more serious problems; 4 = major and serious problems which management appears to be unable or unwilling to correct.

Finally, a group of no-problem (NP) S&L's was again matched to the SP group as to time and SMSA location, and firms were selected at random from those S&L's rated by examiners as either 1 or 2. A final condition was that their examiner rating did not drop "below" 2 in any subsequent period.

The numbers of S&L's analyzed for the three groups were 56, 49, and 107 for the SP, TP, and NP groups, respectively. Note that the number of NP observations is larger than those of the other two groups. The selected SP and TP S&L's comprise almost the entire population in their respective groups, and we decided to sample more heavily the NP group in order to be confident of a representative sample. Since the classification algorithm involves a prior probability of group membership estimate, the actual sample size should not affect our results as long as representation is maintained.

Group Size Characteristics and Number of Groups

While we did not attempt to control our sample selection by size of the S&L's we did stratify by specific SMSA location. Admittedly, both size and location may be relevant factors in the assessment of an S&L's performance. To control by size and by specific location (i.e., a separate model for each SMSA), however, would have limited the number of observations available to work with, particularly in the TP and SP groups. We have attempted to include a locational factor in our analysis by selecting firms in the TP and NP groups from the same SMSA as the SP group. While this eliminates any intergroup bias, it does not alter the fact that particular localities may be represented to a greater or lesser extent in our sample. In the derivation of the parameters of a *quadratic* model, it makes no difference if we run the three groups in a single discriminant analysis or if we run three pairwise comparisons, that is, NP versus SP, NP versus TP, and TP versus SP. This would not be true, however, if the more common linear structure were used since all data are pooled in the latter. We have chosen to report the three two-group model results to enable more comprehensive assessment of the appropriate weightings and the construction of a composite rating for each S&L. We will also, however, indicate discrimination accuracy for the combined three-group analysis.

Data Base

The data base utilized in this chapter comprises financial statement items for five semiannual reporting periods preceding the critical date for the SP group. The period June 1966 through December 1973 inclusive was available. Still, seven different financial schedules provided raw data for the calculation of 32 financial ratios and an additional 24 trends of these ratios. When the performance prediction model concentrates on data from one reporting period preceding the critical date, we call that period 1 analysis; when it is two periods before the date, it is labeled period 2, and so on.

Analysis of the Financial Variables

Data Description and Group Mean Comparisons. We examined 32 financial ratios selected as potentially helpful contributors to our discriminant functions, the one-period and two-period trends of a number of these ratios, and the group mean comparisons of these variables. These variables are selected based on a careful analysis of the industry and discussion with regulatory personnel. The 32 ratios can be represented as a vector of point estimate variables for individual S&L's and the trends as a vector of first differences between consecutive semiannual periods (T_A trends) and one-year differences (T_B trends).

We concluded that variable 2 (net operating income/gross operating income) and its associated T_{2B} period trend measure is the most important single indicator of financial distress to be found in S&L operations. Essentially, this ratio is measuring operating efficiency through aggregate expense data. Also extremely important are the net worth/total assets, and real estate owned/total assets. Surprisingly, two measures which include scheduled items (SI)—those loans which are delinquent in repayment of worse—do not show impressive discrimination. V_8(SI/net worth) and V_9(SI/total assets) have large group mean differentials but low statistical significance due to their relatively high within-group dispersion.

The 12-Variable Discriminant Model

We now present the selected variables which comprise the performance-predictor system. The same variables encompass the three two-group models: (1) NP versus SP, (2) TP versus SP, and (3) NP versus TP. The basis for selecting the variables is derived primarily from the combined three-group analysis (presented later) since what we desire is a model that works well for the three performance prediction models. Also, since the parameters derived from the three-group analysis are identical to those derived from the various two-group tests, we are not losing information by looking at all three groups together.

After scores of runs and tests, the following 12-variable model emerged:

V_2 = net operating income/gross operating income,
V_7 = net worth/total assets,
V_{10} = real estate owned/total assets,
V_{26} = earned surplus/total assets,
V_{27} = total loans/total savings,
V_{30} = borrowed money/total savings,
V_{32} = FHLB advances/net worth,
T_{2B} = two-period trend of V_2,
T_{7B} = two-period trend of V_7,
T_{10B} = two-period trend of V_{10},
T_{25B} = two-period trend of real estate owned (SI)/total assets, and
T_{30B} = two-period trend of V_{30}.

Less than 12 variables gave lower accuracy results while increasing the number beyond 12 did not add to the correct classifications.

Of the 12 variables, two (V_2 and T_{2B} measure the profitability of the S&L. The variables V_7, V_{26}, V_{30}, V_{32}, T_{7B}, and T_{30B} all measure, in different ways, the vulnerability of S&L's to insolvency and shortage of capital. A S&L with a low net worth relative to total assets, a low cumulative earned surplus, and a tendency to rely on borrowed funds for operations is indeed a candidate for serious problem status. Also, if an S&L has an excessive amount of real estate owned—especially if it includes scheduled item (SI) real estate from bad loans—it is usually headed for trouble. Finally, a relatively high ratio of loans to savings is indicative of a high-risk operation.

Two-Group Discrimination Results: NP versus SP

Period 1. The first model is developed to discriminate between S&L's classified as no-problem (NP) and severe-problem (SP). Note that this

Table 11-7   Classification Accuracy, NP versus SP (Period 1).

Groups	Actual	Predicted	Error	Percent Accuracy[a]
NP	107	103	4	96.3
SP	56	54	2	96.4

[a]Overall accuracy = 96.35%.

model, if developed alone, would lack applicability to all S&L's since only the very healthy and the most serious-problem associations are considered. Since many S&L's fall somewhere in between, restricting classification to the extreme classes only reduces its statistical validity and practical usefulness somewhat. We will, however, combine this two-group analysis with the other two-group models to arrive at a summary classification and the latter is inclusive of virtually all S&L's.

The NP and SP groups, *a priori,* are the most different from each other of any of the basic groups, and we expect excellent classification accuracy. The results confirm our expectation. The 12-variable quadratic model classified correctly 96.35% of all observations based on data from period 1 (Table 11-7).

As in all discrimination studies, the classification accuracy is overstated since we are classifying the very same observations used to construct the discriminant function. It is therefore necessary to assess a model's accuracy based on some type of holdout-sample test. Throughout this study, we use a procedure known as the Lachenbruch (1967) test (See Chapter 4).

The cumulated result is the expected error of the test when applied to a new observation (Table 11-8). In addition, we compute 0.05 Lachenbruch confidence intervals around the expected error so that the percentage in the last column, when added or subtracted from the expected error, esti-

Table 11-8   Lachenbruch Validation Test Accuracy, NP versus SP (Period 1).

Groups	Actual	Predicted	Error	Percent Accuracy[a]	0.05 Confidence Interval
NP	107	100	7	92.0	±4.8%
SP	56	54	2	96.4	±6.7%

[a]Overall accuracy = 94.48%.

mates the magnitude of the error two standard deviations above and below the mean. Specifically, the percent interval (P_1) of experiencing an
error for the serious-problem (SP) S&L in group 1 is equal to

$$P_1 = \frac{2n_1P_{12} + Z^2 \pm \sqrt{[(2n_1P_{12} + Z^2) - 4(n_1 + Z^2)n_1P^2_{12}]}}{2(n_1 + Z^2)}.$$

where

n_1 = number of observations in group 1 (e.g., 56),

P_{12} = proportion of observations from group 1 classified into group 2
(e.g., 2/56), and

Z = percentile for the normal distribution (e.g., 1.96 for 0.05 level).

Therefore, the expected Type 1 error (predicting a healthy S&L when in
fact a serious problem develops) is 6.6% (1 − 93.4) with a two-standard-
deviation interval of 6.7%.

Periods 2-5. One of the objectives of this study is to assess the accuracy
of an early warning system for a number of semiannual periods prior to
some critical date. For all of S&L models, we will endeavor to assess the
long-term accuracy by directly measuring the 12-variable model's
accuracy for periods 1 through 3 and estimating it for 4 and 5.

Table 11-9 presents classification accuracy results for the NP-SP model
for periods 1 through 5. Note that the overall accuracy in periods 2 and 3
remains extremely high: 92.6% and 90.6% respectively. The Lachenbruch
validation tests for these two periods are also excellent at 89.3 and 86.6%
respectively. I conclude that our 12-variable model is extremely accurate
in predicting either no-problem or severe-problem situations as much as
13 to 18 months before the critical date. Periods 4 and 5 (with the A trends

**Table 11-9   Classification Accuracy, NP versus SP, With Same 12-Variable Model
(Periods 1–5).**

Period	NP	SP	Overall
1	96.3%	96.4%	96.4
2	96.1	85.1	92.6
3	94.1	83.3	90.6
4 (A trends)	92.9	75.0	87.1
5 (no trends)	92.4	81.0	88.8

and the *V*-variable models) also are excellent predictors. The final classification results for periods 4 and 5 are 87.2% and 88.8%.

Two-Group Discrimination Results: TP versus SP

The second model discriminates between firms that faced serious financial problems at a point in time but did not go out of existence or need aid from the FSLIC (the TP group) and those with severe problems which did indeed have FSLIC assistance and/or a supervisory merger (the SP group). *A priori,* discrimination between these two groups is extremely difficult because no sharp contrast is presented. At the same time, the results from this test are extremely important from a supervisory standpoint. That is, given a problem situation, is the S&L destined for failure or not?

While the classification accuracy of the TP-SP model is not, as expected, as high as that of the NP-SP model, it is still quite impressive. The classification and validation accuracy tests of the TP-SP model for period 1 are 88.6 and 80.6% overall accuracy respectively. This model contains the same 12 variables as noted earlier, only the weights are unique to the TP and SP samples. The classification results remain excellent even as we move to earlier periods. Overall accuracy drops to 81.5% in period 2, and actually increases to 84.8% in period 3. SP group accuracy does drop off faster than TP accuracy but it is still over 70% in period 3. The Lachenbruch validation test results of the TP-SP model do show a moderately high deterioration—from 80.9% in period 1 to 66.3 and 62.1% in periods 2 and 3 respectively.

Two-Group Discrimination Results: NP versus TP

Our final two-group test concerns S&L's which did not have severe problem experience and were classified by examiners as either clearly no-problem (NP), or having some temporary problem that was satisfactorily resolved (TP). This model is probably in itself the least important of the three models, but one which is necessary for completing our overall composite rating analysis. The classification results are approximately the same as those of the TP-SP model in period 1, and the validation results are even more impressive. The accuracy for periods 2 through 5 never drops below 75% and once again the period 1 model proved superior to separate weighting models in each period.

Three-Group Results: NP versus SP

Combining the three groups into a single model yields results listed in Tables 11-10, and 11-11. We see that the NP classification accuracy in

Table 11-10   Classification Accuracy: Three Groups, NP versus TP versus SP (Period 1).[a]

		Predicted Groups		
Actual Groups	Total	Group NP	Group TP	Group SP
Group NP	107	101 (94.4)	5 (4.7)	1 (0.9)
Group TP	49	12 (24.5)	33 (67.3)	4 (8.1)
Group SP	56	2 (3.6)	6 (10.7)	48 (85.7)
Overall accuracy = 85.9%				

[a]Percent accuracy in parentheses.

period 1 is 94.4% based on six misclassifications (five classified as TP and one as SP). The same accuracy was observed in the NP versus TP analysis. Further, the 85.7% SP accuracy is identical to the TP versus SP results reported earlier. The complement of these two errors, 91.9% and 75.5% respectively, are the observed accuracies for the TP group in the prior two-group models. Naturally, TP group accuracy is lowest since S&L's can be misclassified in two directions whereas NP and SP errors can only be misclassified in one direction.

Table 11-11   Validation Test Accuracy: Three Groups, NP versus TP versus SP (Period 1).[a]

		Predicted Groups		
Actual Groups	Total	Group NP	Group TP	Group SP
Group NP	107	97 (90.7)	7 (6.5)	3 (2.8)
Group TP	49	13 (26.5)	27 (55.1)	9 (18.4)
Group SP	56	2 (3.6)	8 (14.3)	46 (82.1)
Overall accuracy = 80.2%				

[a]Percent accuracy in parentheses.

Prior Probability Specification

A potentially important ingredient related to the discriminant classification rule is the assignment of appropriate *a priori* probabilities of group membership to account for the relative occurrence of different populations in the universe. Eisenbeis (1975) has discussed the possible effects of differing assumptions emphasizing that the importance of this aspect has been grossly overlooked. We discussed the prior probability question earlier in Chapter 5.

The results presented earlier assumed equal *a priori* probabilities. We realize, however, that the true priors will not be equal, although it is extremely difficult to know exactly what are the appropriate assumptions. Surely, the likelihood of being a member of the NP groups is far greater than that of belonging to either the TP or SP group, and the likelihood of being a TP is greater than that of being an SP. In order to assess the impact of assigning different *a priori* probabilities, we have run a sensitivity analysis on our 12-variable quadratic model. We alter the priors for the NP versus SP test from equal priors (0.5 NP vs. 0.5 SP) to 0.99 for NP versus 0.01 for SP. For the TP versus SP tests, the priors vary from equal to 0.90 for TP versus 0.10 for SP; and for the NP versus TP the priors vary from equal to 0.80 NP versus 0.20 TP. We feel that these extremes account for the realistic ranges of appropriate assumptions.

We find that the accuracies vary very little even as the priors change from one extreme to the other. Therefore, we conclude that the results are not sensitive, at least in this study, to the *a priori* probability assumption.

We are pleased to find this since we have not included estimates for the costs of the various types of errors. Based on discussions with S&L authorities in 1975, if we had to choose the most realistic *a priori* probabilities, something like a 0.80, 0.15, 0.05 assumption for NP, TP, and SP respectively would probably not be far from the true priors. We are not sure what would be the case in 1981, but no doubt the SP group would have a higher prior probability.

The Classification Model and Implementation

The rather large, complex model for the three-group analysis is listed in Table 11-12. Due to the linear, quadratic and variable interaction terms, the model has close to 100 terms and the results must be computerized for testing. This was done by the FHLBB personnel in 1977 and 1978 but due to the instability of one of the model's results, that is, the NP-TP relationship, supervisory personnel felt that the model was not ready for implementation on a system-wide basis. In addition, many of the key elements

Table 11-12   Discriminant Coefficients for TP-SP Model, and NP-SP Model.

Variable	Linear Terms	V2	V7	V10	V26	V27	V30	V32	T2B	T7B	T10B	T25B	T30B
TP-SP Model													
V2	1.914	-0.323											
V7	13.328	-6.444	-39.093										
V10	3.303	-5.485	-2.423	-24.284									
V26	-35.431	13.765	129.390	-12.058	-137.960								
V27	9.175	-1.627	-8.628	-2.669	33.505	-4.778							
V30	-15.139	2.666	42.667	6.147	-62.415	13.607	-17.000						
V32	0.326	-0.057	-2.535	-0.068	1.717	-0.177	1.404	-0.047					
T2B	-2.135	-1.083	-2.357	-0.315	-10.069	-2.762	-2.447	-0.004	2.605				
T7B	-62.429	5.114	34.180	-45.216	-136.400	-65.648	-96.813	1.932	-3.175	-200.550			
T10B	43.230	-16.364	64.664	-93.289	68.912	-49.949	54.196	0.638	19.613	109.320	-330.720		
T25B	-4.591	3.007	-3.785	23.601	3.013	5.175	-11.292	0.251	-4.118	8.455	54.944	-17.161	
T30B	-1.819	0.551	4.761	6.572	-8.938	1.475	-6.087	0.233	-0.759	9.356	3.735	-4.597	-1.232
NP-SP Model													
V2	-2.718	-7.286											
V7	2.109	-4.747	8.615										
V10	6.747	2.489	13.567	-163.65									
V26	-6.051	13.731	45.054	-35.818	-59.858								
V27	10.683	4.825	-1.784	-7.511	6.296	-5.957							
V30	-25.706	-7.733	22.875	27.040	-28.771	26.830	-51.066						
V32	0.744	-0.035	-2.005	-0.400	1.106	-0.632	4.601	-0.156					
T2B	-0.405	8.020	5.702	22.135	-21.096	-0.707	-2.775	0.229	-11.817				
T7B	-12.583	16.408	-109.760	126.960	98.218	18.184	1.238	-1.720	-7.672	-669.240			
T10B	9.785	3.417	-29.172	-155.840	226.300	-16.292	45.511	-3.377	-41.831	-236.390	-1546.300		
T25B	4.770	1.051	-18.271	192.660	6.344	-3.299	2.666	-0.394	-3.235	-149.260	390.320	-189.230	
T30B	0.623	4.234	6.343	0.282	-7.000	-1.802	5.046	-0.011	-6.656	4.782	-21.834	25.094	-13.886

necessary for successful implementation were not evident, especially the continuity of key personnel. See my discussion of "key elements" in the section on other financial firm early warning models at the end of this chapter.

Composite Performance Predictor Ratings

The final stage in the S&L performance predictor system is to assign an overall composite rating to each association being evaluated. This process involves a prediction of group membership utilizing each of the three two-group models discussed earlier. In doing so, the analysis covers the complete spectrum of possible designations and, in addition, enables the S&L to be even more closely evaluated. For instance, an S&L which may be classified as an SP association by the NP versus SP model might be a TP designate by the TP versus SP model. This type of S&L would be cause for concern but not as much as an S&L which was also classified as an SP by the TP versus SP model.

The possible three-model classifications are listed in Table 11-13. Note that while there are eight possible combinations, only four are realistic. We have given a final composite rating to the four realistic combinations which range from very good (VG) to very poor (VP). These qualitative composites are arbitrary but are specified to underscore the degree of seriousness of the S&L's predicated performance.

Summary and Implications of the S&L Study

The purpose of this discussion has been to construct and evaluate a performance predictor system for detecting serious problems of savings & loans associations. An integrated system of three separate two-group,

Table 11-13   Three-Model Rating Combinations and Composite Ratings.

NP versus SP	NP versus TP	TP versus SP	Composite[a]
NP	NP	TP	VG
NP	NP	SP	—
NP	TP	TP	G
NP	TP	SP	—
SP	NP	TP	—
SP	NP	SP	—
SP	TP	TP	P
SP	TP	SP	VP

[a]VG = very good, G = good, P = poor, VP = very poor, — = not realistic.

Table 11-14 Summary of Major Failure Prediction and Early Warning Studies for Financial Institutions.

Purpose and Sample Characteristics	Statistical Method and Important Variables	Contribution and Critique
I FDIC Studies		
A. *Meyer and Pifer (1970).* To develop a failure-prediction model for commercial banks. Analyzes 39 banks that failed between 1948 and 1965. Employs a paired sample based upon location, size, age, and regulatory agency.	Uses a zero–one regression model and stepwise procedures to search a 160-variable data set. A nine-variable regression model is developed. Eight of the nine variables are noncurrent ones, e.g., trends, lagged values.	One or two years before failure, the model correctly classifies about 80 percent of the sample banks. However, beyond the second year, the classifications are not better than chance. Shortcomings: narrow definition of failure, zero–one regression technique, time series or stationarity problem, and lack of predictive ability beyond two years prior to failure.
B. *Sinkey (1974–1979).* Studies have focused upon the financial characteristics of problem and failed banks; the bank-examination process; and the development of so-called early-warning systems. The ultimate purpose has been to develop screening models to identify existing or potential financial difficulties and thus aid in scheduling on-site examinations. Both paired- and random-sample techniques have been applied to examiner-determined problem banks or failed banks.	MDA has been the statistical method, either in standard or "outlier" form. In general, income–expense ratios are more important than balance-sheet ratios and two or three ratios classify about as well as seven or eight ratios.	Main contribution has been to serve as a catalyst on the early warning frontier. First research in banking to use quadratic classification technique. Shortcomings: exclusive use of MDA and ratios; and lack of a directional element in the outlier technique.

II Federal Reserve Bank of New York
Studies

A. Martin (1977). To analyze alternative types of early-warning models; to compare logit analysis with discriminant analysis; and to apply logit analysis to the case of commercial bank failure. Uses a broad definition of failure to include supervisory merger and other emergency measures. A sample of 58 Fed member failures are compared with the population of nonfailed member banks.

Uses logit analysis and MDA. Four-variable logit model consists of net income/total assets, gross charge-offs/net operating income, commercial loans/total loans, and gross capital/risk assets.

Catalogs and explains alternative early-warning models; shows relationship between logit analysis and MDA; and applies logit analysis to study of bank failures. Shortcomings: small sample size and excludes nonmember bank failures.

B. Korobow, Stuhr et al. (1974–1977). To investigate statistical techniques to assist in the supervision of banks in the Second Federal Reserve District. Sample banks restricted to "vulnerable" member banks in the Second District.

MDA and arctangent regression employed. Latest (five-variable arctangent) probability function consists of loans and leases/total sources of funds, equity capital/adjusted risk assets, operating expenses/operating revenues, gross charge-offs/net income + provision for loan losses, and commercial and industrial loans/total loans.

Along with the FDIC's research, the N.Y. Fed's efforts constitute the seminal work on statistical early-warning systems for banks. Shortcomings: small samples and use of the concept of vulnerability.

(Continued)

Table 11-14 (*Continued*)

Purpose and Sample Characteristics	Statistical Method and Important Variables	Contribution and Critique
III *Office of the Comptroller of the Currency*		
A. *National Bank Surveillance System (Haskins & Sells)*. NBSS is a device for the early detection of problem banks *and* a management tool based upon peer-group analysis of leading bank indicators. National banks with resources of $100 million to $500 million were used as a test base.	One-variable-at-a-time analysis based upon percentile rankings. Fifteen significant ratios and other variables are analyzed.	Shows that if top management wants a surveillance mechanism in a hurry and is willing to pay big dollars, an operational system can be achieved. Shortcomings: limited empirical testing and exclusive use of the outlier or peer-group approach.
IV *Board of Governors of the Federal Reserve System*		
A. *Hanweck (1977)*. To develop a simulation model for monitoring so-called problem banks *and* to develop a failure-prediction model for commercial banks. The failure study has a sample of 32 failed banks and a random sample of 177 nonfailed banks.	Uses multivariate probit analysis and develops a six-variable failure model. Ratios of net operating income to assets and loans to capital are the only significant variables.	Adds probit analysis to the MDA, arctangent, logit analysis arsenal. Attempts to implement Guttentag's suggestion regarding a simulation model for the largest banks. Shortcomings: simulation model requires real world testing whereas failure prediction model is based upon an esoteric technique that will probably prohibit its implementation.

V Other Studies (Commercial Banking)

A. *Santomero and Vinso (1977)*. To estimate the cross-section riskiness of the banking system and its sensitivity to variations in bank capital. Sample consists of 224 weekly reporting Federal Reserve banks for the period February, 1965 to January, 1974.

Use MDA to develop a problem bank screen for their safety-index distribution. The capital asset ratio and the coefficient of variation of the capital-jump size are important variables.

Sound theoretical foundation with a measure of risk that is independent of actual bank failures or examiners' ratings of bank soundness. Failure risk is defined as zero or negative net worth. Shortcomings: sample banks not representative of the population and arbitrary definition of a problem bank.

B. *Pettway (1980)*. To determine if the returns on actively traded bank equities are sensitive to increased potential for bankruptcy. Seven failed, merged, or reorganized large banks are analyzed. The control groups consists of the 24 banks that make up the Keefe Bank Stock Index.

Uses asset pricing model and standard regression model to analyze informational impact on cumulative average residuals. Methodological approach does not permit testing of alternative variables.

Shows that the market for large bank stocks exhibits characteristics of efficiency and that market information may be useful as an early warning mechanism. Shortcomings: standard criticisms of the market model apply (e.g., definition of relevant holding period, stationarity of Beta); small sample; and lack of a rigorous test for the decline of the residuals.

C. *Shick & Sherman (1980)*. To determine if significant deterioration in a bank's (examiner-determined) financial condition is reflected by a decline in the price of the bank's common stock. Analyzes 25 banks that experienced a major change in their examination rating over the period 1967 to 1976. Control group is S&P's index of banks outside NYC.

Like Pettway, uses the so-called market model. Alternative variables not tested because of the model employed.

Concludes that stock price behavior has potential as an early warning device and recommends further investigation. Shortcomings: problem group may be subject to examiners' identification error; market model problem; and test of significance of cumulative average residual may be suspect.

(Continued)

305

Table 11-14 (Continued)

Purpose and Sample Characteristics	Statistical Method and Important Variables	Contribution and Critique
D. *Pettway and Sinkey (1980)*. To develop a screening technique to identify potential bank failure using accounting and market information. Sample banks are from Pettway (1980).	See Pettway (1980) and Sinkey (1979).	Shows that both accounting and market information lead examiners' identification of problem status. Shortcomings: see previous criticisms of Pettway and Sinkey.
VI *Other Studies (Nonbanking)*		
A. *Altman and Loris (1976)*. To develop a mechanism for identifying broker-dealers that might be failure prone. Failed group consists of 40 broker-dealers placed in trusteeship during the period 1971–1973. Nonfailed group consists of 113 randomly selected nonfailed broker-dealers.	Uses quadratic MDA and develops a six-variable discriminant function. A composite variable consisting of ten elements selected by NASD personnel as indicative of problem status is the most important variable.	First MDA classification model applied to broker-dealers. Further confirmation of the usefulness of accounting data for early-warning purposes. Shortcomings: the *ad hoc* composite variable.
B. *Collins (1980)*. To compare an Altman-type model with a Meyer and Pifer-type model for 162 failed credit unions and a random sample of 162 nonfailed credit unions.	Uses a linear probability model and develops a six-variable function. Important variables are those that measure dividend rate, liquidity, loan quality, asset size, reserve strength, and loan activity.	First classification model applied to credit unions. Further confirmation of the usefulness of accounting data for the development of early-warning systems for depository institutions.

Source: E. I. Altman, *et al.* (1981), Chapter 8. See this source for a complete reference list.

quadratic discriminant models was developed, and the results were extremely impressive for predicting actual S&L performance up to three semiannual reporting periods prior to a specified critical date. To the best of my knowledge, this system was never fully implemented by the FSLIC, but I feel the results may still be of some legitimate use in the 1980s. Perhaps we need to identify new measures of S&L performance for assessment.

EARLY WARNING MODELS FOR OTHER FINANCIAL FIRMS

After manufacturing firms the type of firm which has received the most attention in the literature is the financial institution. This category includes credit unions, broker dealers, and commercial banks. There are several reasons for this, including the extremely unstable nature of the financial sector and the consequent relatively large number of recent failures. Since financial company performance has important general public interest, with several governmental insurance agencies in place to help protect that public interest, the establishment of early warning systems to help reduce the number of failures would seem logical. For example, we have seen that the Federal Home Loan Bank Board, and its ally the FSLIC, were active in promoting the study discussed earlier in this chapter. The FDIC, the Controller of the Currency, and the Federal Reserve System have commissioned studies to examine commercial bank failures. Also, the National Association of Security Dealers with the related insurance agency, The Securities Investor Protection Corporation (SIPC), have examined over-the-counter broker-dealer failures. This author has participated directly or indirectly in several of these studies.

Key Elements

With the exception of one or two of the studies reviewed in Table 11-14, we are disappointed to report that most of these efforts have not produced systems which the regulatory agencies have implemented. While perceived problems of accuracy and reliability of those "rejected" models probably have had something to do with this "regulatory inertia," I feel that political and behavioral issues have been the major reasons.

There are at least four major ingredients for successful implementation of a statistical early warning system developed at a regulatory agency:

1 An efficient and understandable system
2 Cooperation between the model developer and the key administrative personnel of the agency—especially those individuals responsible for implementing surveillance techniques

3 Support from the very top of the regulatory agency and insurance corporation

4 Continuity of key senior personnel

Usually, when a regulatory agency decides to investigate the efficiency of a system for detecting problem organizations, some individual section of the agency has the initial responsibility to develop it. This may be the economic research section, the examination and/or surveillance division, or some special deputy of the agency chairperson. The system is usually developed with assistance from outside, but this is not always the case. Unless the effort has the understanding and support from the top, however, it is doomed to failure. Needless to say, if the developed system does not test out efficiently, implementation will not be attempted. Careful education of all relevant parties about the adopted system and how it will be utilized once it is implemented is vital to its acceptance throughout the agency. Researchers that we know report that one of the most difficult aspects of establishing any sophisticated system is the "selling" of its merits and its potential to the individuals presently responsible for surveillance.

The final constraint—continuity of key personnel—is rarely considered until an individual leaves an organization. There are usually several key persons whose continued employment by the regulatory agency is critical to the implementation of the system. If the developer of the system are internal employees, they certainly are in a crucial position. Their immediate supervisor, who no doubt supported the system's development in discussion with top personnel, is also important. Finally, the head of the organization must usually be perpetuated. This could be a problem if he, and some of his key subordinates, are political appointees.

I made many of these arguments at a recent conference on financial crises which was reported in Altman and Sametz (1977). The proceedings included papers and comments by representatives of several regulatory agencies charged with protecting the public interest. In 1981, however, very few of these persons are still associated with the agencies. The political appointment process in Washington almost guarantees a large turnover of key personnel at the top of the relevant agencies. This type of behavioral instability, when combined with the economic instability so apparent in our nation's financial institutions, does not bode well for objective follow-up of past early warning efforts.

Because of the large number of early warning studies in the aforementioned financial sectors, I have extracted Joseph Sinkey's excellent appendix to this chapter "Early Warning Systems for Financial Institutions" [Chapter VIII in E. Altman, R. Avery, R. Eisenbeis, and J. Sinkey (1981)]. For more details on these studies, see that chapter or the original works. These summaries are listed in Table 11-14.

12 Business Failure Models: An International Survey

INTRODUCTION

Business failure identification and early warnings of impending financial crisis are important not only to analysts and practitioners in the United States. Indeed, countries throughout the world, even noncapitalist nations, are concerned with individual entity performance assessment. Developing countries and smaller economies, as well as the larger industrialized nations of the world, are vitally concerned with avoiding financial crises in the private and public sectors. Smaller nations are particularly vulnerable to financial panics resulting from failures of individual entities.

In the late 1960s and throughout the 1970s, numerous studies in the United States were devoted to assessing one's ability to combine publicly available data with statistical classification techniques in order to predict business failure. Studies by Beaver (1967) and Altman (1968) provided the stimulus for numerous other papers. A steady stream of failure prediction papers have appeared in the English literature, and numerous textbooks and monographs include a section or chapter on these models. [For example, see Brigham (1982), Appendix 6A.] What has gone relatively unnoticed, on an international level, is the considerable effort made to replicate and extend these models to environments outside the United States. There is no work with which we are familiar that attempts to survey these studies and to comment on their similarities and differences. The purpose of this analysis is to do just that. We survey the works by academics and practitioners in nine countries and give references to several other studies. In addition, background data on recent bankruptcy rates in several of the major countries of the world are compared with rates in the United States.

In several of the countries studied, notably Brazil, France and Canada, and most recently Australia, this author has participated directly in the construction of a failure classification model. The remaining models that we discuss were developed by other analysts. In addition to Brazil, Canada, and Australia, specific efforts in Japan, West Germany, Switzerland, Holland, England, Ireland, and France will be presented. One of the first attempts at modern statistical failure analysis was performed by Tamari (1966). We will not discuss his work here, but we point out its pioneering status.

In many cases, we can present an in-depth discussion of the models including individual variable weights. In others, we present the models in more general terms due to the lack of precise documentation. Still, we feel that this international treatment of failure prediction models is the most comprehensive effort to date. We recognize that some relevant works will possibly be overlooked in this survey and apologize for any omission.

JAPAN

Background Statistics

Despite its exceptional economic performance in the last decade, the Japanese economy, and its component firms, suffer from the same business failure realities as do the western economies. The number of business failures in recent years in Japan is at least as large as the number in the United States on a relative basis. Table 12-1 lists the number of business bankruptcies in Japan and the United States since 1965, and Table 12-2 compares the bankruptcy rate in the two countries. We can observe that the bankruptcy rates in Japan and the United States are quite similar; recently the United States had a lower rate based on GNP and population and a higher rate on a *per capita* base. Since the U.S. business bankruptcy figures include a large number of nonincorporated firms, it is also likely that this latter comparison (for corporations alone) would show the Japanese rate to be relatively higher, a fact that will surprise many observers.

In Japan, bankruptcies are concentrated in the small and medium-size firms, especially those that do not enjoy the protection of an affiliated group of companies. These groups, known as *keiretsu,* usually involve a lead commercial bank and a number of firms in diverse industries. Still, a number of larger firms listed on the first section of the Tokyo Stock Exchange have succumbed to the negative economic reality of failure. These firms, numbering close to 50 from 1963 to 1978, provide a sample sufficiently large for rigorous statistical analysis. A list of failed Japanese firms and the position of the lead bank and those that were assisted are

Table 12-1   Number of Business Bankruptcies in Japan and the United States (1965–1980).

Year	Number of Bankruptcies (Japan)[a]	Number of Bankruptcies (U.S.)[b]
1965	6,141	16,910
1966	6,187	16,430
1967	8,192	16,600
1968	10,776	16,545
1969	8,523	15,430
1970	9,765	16,197
1971	9,206	19,103
1972	7,139	18,132
1973	8,202	17,490
1974	11,681	20,747
1975	12,606	30,130
1976	15,641	35,201
1977	18,741	32,189
1978	15,875	30,528
1979	16,030	29,500
1980	17,884	36,411[c]
1981	17,610	47,414[c]

[a]Compiled by the Japanese Ministry of Finance and published by Tokyo Shoko Research, Ltd., Tokyo. Totals are on a calendar year basis.
[b]U.S. Bankruptcy Courts, Administrative Office of the President, Annual Reports. Totals are on a fiscal year (June 30) basis.
[c]*Individual* business bankruptcy filings.

provided in Table 12-3. Table 12-4 lists the causes of bankruptcies in Japan and the United States. It is interesting to note that in Japan, a significant percentage of failures are caused by other firms' problems, which illustrates the complex interactions among companies. Of course, the categories selected by two of the leading bankruptcy statistics publishers, Dun & Bradstreet and Tokyo Shoko Research Ltd., are not the same.

A number of Japanese academics have attempted to analyze the business failure classification problem. One study, Takahashi, Kurokawa, and Watase [1979], this writer knows in sufficient detail to describe. There are several other Japanese studies, perhaps eight or nine, which are relevant, but I have not seen complete translations. A summary of these studies is provided in Table 12-6. Takahashi *et al.* built upon the prior work by

Table 12-2 Relative Business Bankruptcy Rates, the United States and Japan (1976–1980).

	Bankruptcies					Population (million)			
	USA	÷	Japan	=	Ratio	USA	÷	Japan	=	Ratio
1976	35,201	÷	15,641	=	2.25	215.1	÷	113.1	=	1.90
1977	32,189	÷	18,741	=	1.72	216.8	÷	114.2	=	1.90,
1978	30,528	÷	15,875	=	1.92	217.0	÷	115.2	=	1.88
1979	29,500	÷	16,030	=	1.84	218.2	÷	116.3	=	1.88
1980	36,411	÷	17,844	=	2.04	226.5	÷	117.0	=	1.94

	Bankruptcies					Gross National Product ($U.S. billions)			
	USA	÷	Japan	=	Ratio	USA	÷	Japan	=	Ratio
1976	35,201	÷	15,641	=	2.25	1706.5	÷	565.9	=	3.01
1977	32,189	÷	18,741	=	1.72	1889.6	÷	693.5	=	2.73
1978	30,528	÷	15,875	=	1.92	2127.6	÷	974.5	=	2.18
1979	29,500	÷	16,030	=	1.84	2368.8	÷	1011.2	=	2.34
1980	36,411	÷	17,884	=	2.04	2730.6	÷	1096.0[a]	=	2.49

| | Bankruptcies | | | | Corporations | | | |
	USA	÷	Japan	= Ratio	USA	÷	Japan	= Ratio
						(million)		
1976	35,201	÷	15,641	= 2.25	2024	÷	1293	= 1.56
1977	22,189	÷	18,741	= 1.72	2241	÷	1351	= 1.66
1978	30,528	÷	15,875	= 1.92	2410	÷	1426	= 1.69
1979	29,500	÷	16,030	= 1.84	2520	÷	1494[a]	= 1.69
1980	36,411	÷	17,884	= 2.04	2605[a]	÷	1570	= 1.66

Sources: U.S. Administrative Courts, Bankruptcy Division; Statistical Abstract of the United States. *Tokyo Shoko Koshinsho; Oriental Economist,* Statistics Monthly. *Industrial Review of Japan.*

[a]Estimate.

Table 12-3 Tokyo Stock Exchange Failed Firms (1963–February 1978).[a]

Firm's Name	Lead "City" Bank's Position			Firm's Name	Lead "City" Bank's Position		
	Date of Failure	Total Loans	Shares Held		Date of Failure	Total Loans	Shares Held
Nippon Paper Mfg.	1963	n.a.	n.a.	Matsu Kogyo	1968	28.1%	2.68%
Asahi Sangyo	1963	n.a.	n.a.	Nippon Shinpu	1969	31.6%	n.a.[b]
Yamaguchi Bicycle Mfg.	1963	n.a.	n.a.	Giken Kogyo	1970	38.3%	n.a.
Nichinan Kogyo	1964	n.a.	n.a.	Shin Kogyo Kaihatsu	1970	44.8%	n.a.
Shinsei Milk Industry	1964	n.a.	n.a.	Fuji Kanko	1971	22.1%	0.85%
Fukuizumi Sake Distillery	1964	n.a.	n.a.	Sato Zoki	1971	35.0%	n.a.
Japan Special Steel	1964	n.a.	n.a.	Iwate Fuji Sangyo	1971	9.1%	n.a.
Kansai Koki	1964	n.a.	n.a.	Nagoya Seito	1971	46.9%	7.08%
Tokyo Hatsudoki	1964	n.a.	n.a.	Daiei Motion Pictures	1971	23.6%	1.25%
Shinagawa Seisakusho	1964	n.a.	n.a.	Hayakawa Tekko	1972	0.0%	n.a.
Dainichi Kikai	1965	52.1%	n.a.	Monde Shuzo	1972	4.5%	1.92%
Sanyo Tokushu Seiko	1965	22.7%	4.08%	Nihon Netsugaku	1974	14.9%	n.a.
Nihon Seni Kogyo	1965	33.2%	4.00%	Yamato Keori	1974	15.0%	3.50%
Nakasu Seisakusho	1965	24.1%	n.a.	Tokyo Tokei	1974	7.5%	2.25%

Company	Year			Company	Year		
Yokohama Zosen	1965	42.8%	n.a.	Sansei Seisakusho	1974	30.0%	0
Osaka Doboku Kogyo	1965	19.5%	n.a.	Kojin	1975	5.7%	3.40%
Matsuwoka Tool	1965	38.5%	n.a.	Yoshida Tekkosho	1975	22.4%	22.50%
Nippon Chuko	1965	26.1%	n.a.	Maruyama	1976	22.4%	6.90%
Teikoku Seitetsu	1966	7.1%	n.a.	Kaijima Mining	1976	3.4%	1.90%
Nihon Joryo Kogyo	1966	54.0%	2.50%	Nippon Ferrite	1977	20.0%	1.89%
Nitta Construction	1966	85.6%	n.a.	Nippon Shetsu Steel	1977	n.a.	n.a.
Dainihon Cellophane	1968	10.5%	n.a.	Hashiama Ship	1977	19.0%	2.77%
Bandai Kyuko Dentetsu	1968	14.0%	n.a.	Osaka Yogyo	1977	33.3%	2.90%
Art Kogyo	1968	67.7%	n.a.	Eidai	1978	23.0%	7.60%

[a]The statistics are derived from two sources: 1963–1964 are from Takahashi et al. (1979). 1965–1978 are from records of the Tokyo Stock Exchange and compiled in W. Bonds, "Business Failures and the Banks," Euromoney (July 1978, p. 122).
[b]n.a. means either that the shareholdings do not rank among the top ten or that the information is not available.

Table 12-4   Listed Categories of Business Failure Causes in the United States and Japan.

Cause	Percent of Failures (1978)
I. United States[a]	
Managerial incompetence	47.1
Lack of managerial experience	27.0
Unbalanced experience	17.9
Neglect	1.0
Fraud	0.5
Unknown	6.5
Total	100.0
II. Japan[b]	
Slowdown of sales	41.5
Irresponsible management	23.0
Directly due to other bankruptcies	11.7
Indirectly due to other bankruptcies	8.1
Undercapitalization	5.8
Bad debts	3.7
Excessive equipment investments	3.3
Other	2.9
Total	100.0

[a] *Source:*   Dun & Bradstreet, *Failure Record,* N.Y., 1980.
[b] *Source:*   *Tokyo Shoko Koshinsho,* 1980.

Altman (1968) in order to improve upon the classification accuracy of Japanese failures and nonfailures.

The Z-score model (Chapter 3) was applied to a large number of Japanese entities by the economic business publication *Nikkei-Business* (June 5, 1978). In this article, it was found that approximately 9% of the population of Japanese firms examined (90 of slightly under 1000 firms) had Z-scores below the lower bound of the Japanese cutoff score. The cutoff score was subjectively adjusted by the author of the article to account for the unique features of the Japanese environment. Essentially, the adjustments considered the difference in accounting treatment for retained earnings and for the higher fixed debt carried by firms in Japan relative to U.S. firms. The lower bound cutoff score was lowered from Altman's 1.81 to 1.0 for Japanese companies. I cannot comment on the validity of the 1.0 score but I agree that the relevant cutoff score is probably lower in

Japan, due primarily to the factors cited above and a lower average return on assets for Japanese firms.

If one would simply plug in the values for the five factors of the Z-score model for the average bankrupt firm in Japan, the resulting average bankrupt firm's score would be 0.67 compared to the average U.S. firm's score of −0.27 based on Altman's (1968) sample. But, we have noted that every firm in the original sample whose Z-score was below 1.81 failed. In this context, *Nikkei-Business'* cutoff score of 1.0 is realistic. We will explore the differences in average Z-score for a number of countries at a later point (Table 12-12).

Methodology and Results—Takahashi *et al.*

Takahashi *et al.* (1979) state that their model could be more accurate than Altman's because of (1) its simultaneous consideration of data from one, two and three years prior to failure, (2) its combination of ratios and absolute numbers from financial statements, (3) its utilization of the cash basis of accounting from financial statements as well as the accrual base, and (4) its adjustment of the data when the firm's auditors express an opinion as to the limitations of the reported results (window dressing problem).

The authors analyzed 36 pairs of failed and nonfailed manufacturing entities which were listed on the Tokyo Stock Exchange from 1962 through 1976. They conclude that models with several years of data for each firm outperformed a similar model with data from only one year prior to failure. Further, they found that absolute financial statement data contributed to the improved classification accuracy and that data from financial reports prepared external to the firm on an accrual basis were more predictive than those prepared from an "investment effect" or cash basis method. Also, adjusting the data to account for auditor opinion limitations improved the information content of the reported numbers and ratios. A holdout sample of four failed and 44 nonfailed firms was tested with the selected model. The four failed firms went bankrupt in 1977, that is, the year after the last year used in the original model.

One problem with the above model might be the use of several years of data for the same firm in order to construct a model. The authors apparently were aware of this problem but felt it was not serious. While this technique is superior, in my opinion, to the sometimes-advocated technique of utilizing several models, each based on a different year's data [e.g. Deakin (1972)], it still remains that the observations are not independent from each other. That is, while the 36 firms are independently drawn observations, the three years of data for each firm are not. We would be curious to learn just how much the model was improved over one which utilizes only 36 failed points and whether the improvement (with 108 points) justifies the bias involved.

Takahashi *et al.* analyzed 17 different model types and over 130 measures. The model that they selected as their "best" overall predictor is indicated in Table 12-5. The accuracy of this model on the original and holdout samples was simulated based on various cutoff score criteria. The Type I error was found to be quite low for the original sample (range of 0.0% to 16.7% error rates) and virtually nil on the very small four-firm holdout failed firm sample. The Type II error rates ranged greatly, from 0.0% to 52.8%, indicating the tradeoff between Type I and Type II errors as one varies the cutoff score.

The authors spend considerable effort to discuss the derivation of cutoff scores based on various assumptions of prior probabilities and cost of errors. [For a recent discussion of these estimates for banks in the United States, see Chapter 5]. In essence, Takahashi *et al.* simulate various assumptions and leave the choice of a cutoff score up to the individual user.

Ko (1982)

In addition to the models developed in Japan, Ko has also analyzed Japanese problem firms. His sample included 41 pairs of bankrupt and nonbankrupt entities from 1960 through 1980. Several accounting corrections, adjustments, and transformations, in addition to variable trends, were applied to the data set in order to reduce the biases held to be inherent in conventional Japanese reporting practices. He compared the standard linear model design against a linear model with first order interactions and also a quadratic model. He also examined a discriminant model using factor analysis for orthogonal variable transformation. On the basis of classification results, a five-variable linear independent model, without the orthogonal transformations, was selected as the best model; it yielded a 82.9% correct classification rate by Lachenbruch (1967) tests versus a 90.8% for the original sample set. It is interesting to note that the linear interaction design appeared best on the basis of group separations potential, but not for classification accuracy.

Ko found, with respect to the variables of the model, that each sign was in agreement with each variable's economic meaning and that three of the variables are similar to those in Altman's 1968 model. They are: EBIT/sales, working capital/total debts, and market equity/total debts. A fourth variable in this model is an inventory turnover change ratio. His

Table 12-5 Discriminant Function of Best Prediction Model.

	Year before Failure		
Variables	1 ($x,1$)	2 ($x,2$)	3 ($x,3$)
x_1,j = net worth to fixed assets	0.01039	0.07658	-0.01444
x_2,j = current liabilities/assets	-0.05687	0.05147	-0.03447
x_3,j = voluntary reserves plus unappropriated surplus to total assets	-0.040231	0.22167	0.13213
x_4,j = borrowed expenses (interest) to sales	1.00945	-0.72363	-0.34111
x_5,j = earned surplus	0.00814	-0.01366	0.00685
x_6,j = increase in residual value to cash sales	0.14522	-0.03596	0.00545
x_7,j = ordinary profit to total assets	-0.13034	0.07848	0.02901
x_8,j = value added (sales— variable costs)	0.00031	0.00010	-0.00007
Mahalanobis' square distance	3.13721	6.22992	
F=value (significance level)			(0.005)
nonfailed		0.06469	
Mean value failed		-0.02431	
nonfailed		0.03353	
Standard deviation failed		0.03767	

Source: Takahashi, *et al.* (1979).

Table 12-6 Summary of Bankruptcy Classification Models in Japan (1973–1981).

Author/ Researcher (Year)	Publication	Statistical Methodology	Sample Variables						Comments
			Number of Firms Bankrupt—Non-bankrupt	Type of Firms	Sample Period	Number of Variables	Number of Years	Accuracy Rate	
Nomura Securities (1973)	"Discriminant Analysis and Corporate Bankruptcy," Section 2, Chapter 2 in *Financial Constancy Clauses and Bond Ratings*, Tokyo, 1973.	linear discriminant analysis (LDA)	25–25	listed, paired sampling	1963–1972	10	1	n.a.	Propriety study; early attempt.
Toda Nagoya University (1974)	"A Comment on the Prediction of Corporate Bankruptcy in Japan," in *Internationalization of Business Management and its Problems*, editor, Japan Academy of Business Management, Chikura Publishing Co., 1974.	(LDA)	15–15	listed mfg., paired sampling	n.a.	5	3	Year 1—93% Year 2—90% Year 3—83% (original analysis sample)	No test sample results; small sample problem.
Itoh Mitsui Knowledge Industry (1977)	"The Practice of Corporate Evaluation and Business Prediction By Computer," Daiichi, Hoki Co., Tokyo, 1977.	LDA	48–54	second class listed firms and non-listed	n.a.	8	3	n.a.	Bankrupt vs. well performing firm analysis; abnormal values are eliminated; point estimate and rate of change variables.
Itoh Mitsui Knowledge Industry (1977)	same as above	LDA.	100–70	non-listed and listed mfg. and retail firms; small and medium size	1975–1976	8	2	n.a.	Qualitative and quantitative variables, e.g., employee morale, leadership at top and business policy; model used by several statistical analysis firms.

Source	Reference	Method	Sample	Firm type	Years			Accuracy	Comments
Nikkei—*Japan Economic Journal* (1978)	"A Performance Evaluation Model," *Japan Economic Journal*, January 1978.	LDA	50–50	n.a.	n.a.	6	5	n.a.	Selection of firms by journalists, well vs. poor performing firms; data modified to cash basis; value added measures and rate of change; proprietary firm model.
Tanaka and Wakagi from Tokyo Science University and Tokyo Policy Service and Company.	"Bankruptcy Prediction of Corporations and Considerations on Bankruptcy Aversion," *Japan Academy of Managerial Science*, Spring 1978 Conference (May).	multiple regression (ordinary least squares)	n.a.	listed and large-size firms	n.a.	8	10	$R^2 = 0.99$	Attempt to predict remaining years in business (dependent variable), analyzed firms industry by industry, remedial actions specified; no test analysis.
Nakinamura, *Nikkei Business* (1978)	"Z-Score—There Are 90 Corporations Whose Score Was Below 1.0," *Nikkei Business*, June 5, 1978	test of Altman (1968) model on Japanese firms	980 firms all existing	listed mfg., large and medium size	1976	5	1	n.a.	Modified ratios to reflect differences in debt ratios, profitability and retained earnings, 9% had failing firm profile, no follow-up tests.
Ohta Toshiba University Commerce (1978)	"A Failure Prediction Model," *Journal of Chiba Commerce University*, Vol. 16, No. 3, December 1978.	LDA	21–21	listed and mfg.	1964–1977	4	5	n.a.	No empirical results available, no adjustments made to data.
K. Takahashi K. Kurokawa K. Watase (Keio Business School) (1979)	*The Prediction of Corporate Bankruptcy Based On Financial Statement Data*, Monograph Series No. 1, Keio Business Society, Keio Business School, November 1979.	LDA and quadratic analysis	36–36 4–40 (holdout)	listed and mfg. firms	1962–1976	8	3	94.4% (original) 81.2% (split sample)	Utilized various cost of errors to estimate error rates, adjusted data in several ways; qualitative evaluation of auditor adjustments; very small holdout sample of failed firms; combined three years of data, cash basis.

(Continued)

Table 12-6 (*Continued*)

Author/ Researcher (Year)	Publication	Statistical Methodology	Sample Variables						Accuracy Rate	Comments
			Number of Firms Bankrupt—Nonbankrupt	Type of Firms	Sample Period	Number of Variables	Number of Years			
B. Yamada (Japan Development Bank, 1980)	*Business Analysis in the Information Era*, by C. Okuno and B. Yamada. Society of Tokyo University, 2nd Edition, March, 1980.	LDA	37–37	listed and mfg.	1961–1965	8	5		95.9% (original) 93% (secondary test)	Profitable and unprofitable samples, model contains data from several years for same firm.
M. Ozeki and T. Ohno (Waseda University, 1980)	"Bankruptcy Classification Based on Time Series Criterion with Data From Small and Middle Sized Firms," *Japan Academy of Managerial Science* (Spring 1980)	LDA, principal component and cluster analysis	46–23	unlisted, small and medium-size firms	1966–1978	5	n.a.		n.a.	Four different models: time series and trend analysis components.
Nikkei-Japan Economic Journal (1979)	Performance Evaluation Model (2), *Japan Economic Journal*, August 25, 1979.	LDA and principal component analysis	81–77	general population	n.a.	13 to 4 groups	5		n.a.	Firms selected by 200 journalists, well performing vs. poor performing firms; four groups of ratios made up final model; no test or follow-up analysis.
M. Murakami Japan Development Bank	"Operations Research of Corporate Bankruptcy," *Operations Research*, November, 1979.	LDA	61–305	mfg., listed and nonlisted	1961–1977	7	4		94.2% (analysis sample and original)	Abnormal data eliminated; no test sample results available, large nonfailed, random sample.

322

Author	Title	Method	Sample	Firm type	Years			Accuracy	Comments
O. Igarashi (1979)	"Discriminant Analysis on Corporate Evaluation—An Approach To Bankruptcy Prediction," *Operations Research*, December 1979	LDA	38–57	small and medium-size firms	1974–1977	14	n.a.	n.a.	Bankrupt, poor performing and well performing firms, three-group discriminant model; no adjustments to data.
J. Ko (NYU) (1982)	Predicting Bankruptcies of Japanese firms, NYU master's thesis (1982)	LDA (tested quadratic); assessed factor analysis format	41–41	listed mfg. firms	1960–1980	5	5	90.8% (analysis sample) and 82.9% (test sample)	Assessed several forms of model including linear (with and without interaction terms) and quadratic. Considered all past studies, both Japanese and other countries'.

last ratio was the standard deviation of net income over four periods. The final standardized coefficient model is of the form

$$Z_j = 0.868X_1 + 0.198X_2 - .048X_3 + 0.436X_4 + 0.115X_5$$

where,

X_1 = EBIT/sales,

X_2 = inventory turnover two years prior/inventory turnover three years prior,

X_3 = standard error of net income (four years),

X_4 = working capital/total debt,

X_5 = market value equity/total debt, and

Z_j = Z-score (Japanese model).

The standardized form results in a zero cutoff score; that is, any score greater than zero indicates a healthy situation, with probability of classification of bankruptcy less than 0.5, and probabilities greater than 0.5 for negative scores.

Other Japanese Studies

At a recent conference in Keio Graduate School of Business Administration, a summary of most of the efforts to date to build a Japanese bankruptcy classification model was presented (Takahashi and Altman, 1981). Table 12-6 illustrates and expands upon this summary. I am impressed at the serious attention given to this subject in Japan. This research represents efforts by university professors and practitioners, and at least two of those models are presently being tested or marketed by Japanese firms.

All but one of the models utilize discriminant analysis as the statistical classification technique. The other utilizes regression and principal component analyses. A few of the studies were concerend with smaller, non-listed firms although the majority included only listed companies whose data are more easily available. Despite these many efforts, the research in the bankruptcy area is likely to continue, especially if the Japanese domestic economy suffers a serious recession and the number of failures increases dramatically.

WEST GERMANY AND SWITZERLAND

During the 1970s, West Germany enjoyed exceptional economic growth. Even during these prosperous times, the number of business failures was relatively high, reflecting a highly competitive environment. The year 1980 brought significant economic pressures to the overall economy and with it the number of failures increased by more than 15% to over 9,160 companies. Preliminary estimates for 1981 show bankruptcies up over 2% from 1980 to 11,653 firms (10 months). The expected losses to creditors also increased by 2.3 billion Deutschmarks, over 1979, to DM 6.6 billion (Fischer, 1981). Table 12-7 compares the recent bankruptcy rates for West Germany and the United States. Just as we discovered in the comparison of Japanese and U.S. rates, the West German/U.S. ratios are quite similar. In recent years the ratio of bankruptcies to population in both countries was about 0.00014 and the ratio of bankruptcies to GNP was about 0.000011.

An Early Bankruptcy Classification Study (Switzerland)

While bankruptcy classification and its many implications have interested researchers in Germany for many years, the earliest major work published in German was performed in Switzerland by Weibel (1973). He constructed a sample of 36 failed Swiss firms from 1960 to 1971 and matched them to a like number of nonfailed firms in terms of age, size, and line of business. Using univariate statistical parametric and nonparametric tests, Weibel analyzed ratios of these two groups in much the same way that Beaver (1967) did. He found that many of the individual ratios were nonnormal and so he abandoned multivariate tests. [We have often referred (Altman *et al.*, 1977) to the nonnormality problem which exists in many economic and financial data sets but we prefer to test the robustness of models using such data rather than abandoning the tests. We do observe that some European researchers have found multivariate studies suspect due to the nonnormality properties of financial measures.]

Out of 41 original ratios, Weibel selected 20 for dichotomous comparisons. He utilized cluster analysis to reduce collinearity and arrived at the conclusion that six ratios were especially effective in discriminating among the paired groups. Three ratios were types of liquidity measures with one (near monetary resource assets—current liabilities/operating expenditures prior to depreciation) performing best. He also found that inventory turnover and debt/asset ratios were good individual predictors. He examined the overlapping range of individual ratios for the two groups and presented some *ad hoc* rules for identifying failures. He then divided the observations into three risk groups. The low-risk group had all six ratios in the interdecile range of good firms; high-risk firms had at least three ratios in the interdecile range of failed companies; and a final category was identified where the firm does not fall into either of the other two groupings. Weibel's results were quite accurate in the classification

Table 12-7 Relative Business Bankruptcy Rates, the United States and West Germany (1976–1980).

	Bankruptcies			Population (Millions)			Gross National Product ($ Billions)		
	United States	Germany	Ratio	United States	Germany	Ratio	United States	Germany	Ratio
1976	35,201	9,362	3.76	215.1	61.5	3.50	1706.5	446.9	3.82
1977	32,189	9,562	3.37	216.8	61.4	3.53	1889.6	515.7	3.66
1978	30,528	8,722	3.50	217.0	61.3	3.54	2127.6	641.1	3.32
1979	29,500	8,139	3.55	218.2	61.4	3.55	2368.8	761.0	3.11
1980	36,411	9,560	3.80	226.5	61.5	3.68	2730.6		

Sources: Annual Report of the Director of the Administrative Office of the U.S. Courts; Statistical Abstract of the United States. Statistisches Jahrbuch der Bundesrepublik Deutschland 1980.

stage; we have no documentation on how his "model" performed on hold-out tests and what has been the evolution of models in Switzerland since his original work.

German Studies

Many studies in Germany have investigated the causes and problems of insolvencies, especially for financial organizations, for instance, von Stein (1968). Beermann (1976) published one of the first German statistical classification models for insolvency analysis. He examined matched groups of 21 firms which operated or failed in 1966 through 1971. Applying dichotomous and linear discriminant tests, he analyzed 10 ratios encompassing profitability, cash flow, fixed asset growth, leverage, and turnover. His results, using the difference in means dichotomous test, were mixed, with one ratio type (profitability) yielding quite respectable results. The other ratios were far less impressive on a univariate basis. Beermann advocates using discriminant analysis, and his 10-ratio model yielded classification error rates of 9.5%, 19.0%, 28.6%, and 38.1% for the four years prior to failure. He does not indicate which model to use, and the coefficients of each measure were quite unstable in the four different year models. Also, we are given no indication of holdout test results or predictive accuracy and, due to the small sample, we do not have confirming evidence of the model(s) reliability.

Weinrich's (1978) book, from his dissertation, attempted to construct risk classes in order to predict insolvency. His sample of failed firms was considerably larger (44) than Beermann's, concentrating on small and intermediate-size firms, with average sales of DM 4 million (less than $2 million), that failed from 1969 through 1975. Weinrich considered three consecutive annual financial statements (Years 2 through 4 prior to failure) but did not utilize the one statement closest to insolvency. This is a marked difference from most of the other models we have studied.

 Weinrich abandoned the use of parametric classification techniques because of his feeling that many assumptions were violated (normality, variance homogeneity of groups, and high correlation amongst the variables). His linear discriminant models were quite good in terms of classification accuracy (11% error for Year 2, 15.7% and 21.9% for Years 3 and 4, respectively).

Weinrich did use factor analysis and found the technique useful, indicating at least six different factors that explained 80% of the variance of the ratios. He then devised a model of creditworthiness that contained eight relatively independent ratios and utilized both univariate and multivariate methods. A point evaluation system was devised based on quartile values of good and bad firms. His point system for the eight ratios is given in Table 12-8. For example, a net worth/debt ratio over 43.3% receives the best (lowest) point value. A firm with significant insolvency potential is one with 24 points or more (an average of three for each of the eight ratios). This arbitrary point system correctly classified over 90% of the failed firms two years prior to failure, but was only 60% accurate three years prior. The Type II error rate was quite high, averaging well over 20% in each year. Weinrich advocated the use of trend analysis of the point system as well as the point estimate.

Gebhardt (1980) compared dichotomous and multivariate classification tests of samples of failed and nonfailed firms based on models constructed before and after the 1965 Financial Statement Reform Law. The earlier model contained 13 matched pairs of industrial firms and the post-1965 model contained 28 pairs. He utilized a very large number of possible financial indicators which were reduced to 41 ratios for the dichotomous tests. He also incorporated crude measures of misclassification costs and tested his results with the Lachenbruch (1967) holdout test procedure. Gebhardt, like others, felt that the nonnormality of some ratios implied the use of nonparametric procedures but found those results unsatisfactory. The multivariate results were far superior. Gebhardt concluded that the pre-1965 models' results were actually better than the ones following the reform law.

Fischer's (1981) recent work concentrates on nonnumerical data for forecasting failure. His is particularly interested in methods of credit evaluation for suppliers who do not have the ability or the data to perform comprehensive conventional analysis on their existing and potential customers. He advocates an electronic data processing system which can retrieve and analyze such nonnumerical information as reports from newspapers, magazines, inquiry agencies, and credit information from other sellers. Unfortunately, according to Fischer, commercial rating agencies and banks are constrained as to how honest and revealing they choose to be with regard to their reports. In addition, the information provided may be outdated and certainly contains subjective elements. More than one source of credit information is therefore desirable.

Fischer advocates combining the permanent and transitory information on enterprises with microeconomic and sociopolitical data. Five arbitrary rating categories are devised based on nonnumerical data and the delphi technique (numerous experts in various areas) is also recommended. Each characteristic is rated over time into the five categories. The sum of development patterns from varying sources of information builds the basis for a final classification. Clustering techniques are also used by Fischer to clarify information types.

Table 12-8 Weinrich's Financial Statement Evaluation.

Ratio	Point Value 1	2	3	4	5
1	> 43.3	43.3 to 12.1	12.0 to 8.5	8.4 to -4.7	< -4.7
2	> 7.5	7.5 to 2.0	1.9 to 0.9	0.8 to 0.2	< 0.2
3	> -8.8	-8.8 to -29.3	-29.4 to -46.2	-46.3 to -89.9	< -89.9
4	> 21.3	21.3 to 7.2	7.1 to 4.3	4.2 to 0.9	< 0.9
5	> 257.4	257.4 to 200.7	200.6 to 90.7	90.6 to 62.1	< 62.1
6	< 284.9	284.9 to 1210.3	1210.4 to 1451.7	1451.8 to 9989.9	> 9989.9
7	< 165.3	165.3 to 1168.3	1168.4 to 1231.2	1231.3 to 9989.9	> 9989.9
8	< 9.7	9.7 to 27.8	27.9 to 47.9	48.0 to 79.9	> 79.9

Source: Weinrich (1978).

Note: The stated intervals in the pointing system are related to the quartile values of the samples of good and bad firms. *Ratio definitions:* (1) net worth/borrowed capital; (2) liquid means/borrowed capital; (3) soon available monetary resources—current liabilities/operating expenditure prior to depreciation; (4) profit + interest on borrowed capital/total capital; (5) turnover/total capital; (6) borrowed capital/cash flow; (7) borrowed capital—soon available monetary resources/net operating revenues; and (8) supplier debt + debt bills/goods bought.

The most recent and one of the most ambitious attempts is by von Stein (1981), but it is still incomplete. It involves over 115 insolvent firms and over 300 solvent entities for four financial statements prior to failure. The failure dates covered the years from 1971 through 1978. Univariate procedures proved unsuccessful in classifying firms, and von Stein switched to several nonparametric techniques as well as linear and quadratic discriminant analysis. He has tentatively concluded that the nonparametric tests were superior with classification accuracy 95% one year prior and as high as 87% three years prior. His Type II error was about 16%. He did not use a paired sample approach. Von Stein claims that the results are achieved under conditions close to those of a commercial bank operation. We await more information on this study.

BRAZIL

Brazil is an example of an economy where the end result of a series of economic setbacks would put severe pressure on private enterprises. For example, tightening of credit for all firms—especially smaller ones—can jeopardize financial institutions and undermine government efforts to promote economic development. Most observers would agree that action to detect and avoid critical pressures of this type is highly desirable.

Evolving Brazilian Financial Pressures

The Brazilian economy has enjoyed extraordinary growth in the last decade despite persistently high rates of inflation. The so-called "Brazilian miracle," however, is generally believed to be abating—at least temporarily. There have been several troublesome statistics and trends in the last few years and these trends are expected to continue—even to worsen. Brazilian firms in general, both national and multinational, operate with fairly high leverage ratios. These high leverage figures mean, of course, increasing fixed financial expenses which, in Brazil's case, are cash outflows subject to monetary correction. From 1974 through 1980, interest and related financial expenses have been growing faster than earnings available to cover these expenses. The margin of safety is diminishing dramatically and, with this drop, the overall risk dimensions of the average Brazilian firm are a cause of concern to managers, financial institutions, government officials, and other interested parties.

If one adds to the picture a relatively tight monetary policy that was adopted in the late 1970s to combat inflation, diminishing profit margins, a woefully inadequate capital market—especially the lack of debt capital sources even for the strongest firms—the result is a situation of increasing firm pressures. The huge international debt that has been accumulated in Brazil further exacerbates the situation.

Methodological Plan

Altman, Baidya, and Ribeiro-Dias (1979) examined two *a priori* groups of firms categorized as serious-problem (SP) and no-problem (NP) companies. A small number of variables were then calculated for each observation (firm) in each of the two samples. Data covered the period from one to three annual reporting statements prior to the problem date. The data from one year prior (and the corresponding year for the control sample) were then analyzed through the use of linear discriminant analysis.

The serious-problem firms were defined as those filing formal petitions for court-supervised liquidations (*falencias*), legal reorganizations in bankruptcy (*concordatas*), and out-of-court manifestations of serious problems. In all but two of the 23 serious-problem cases, the problem became manifest during the 30 months from January 1975 to June 1977. Industry categories represented include textiles, furniture, pulp and paper, retail stores, plastics, metallurgy, and others. The average asset size of the serious-problem firms was surprisingly high at 323 million *cruzeiros* (U.S. $25-30 million). Therefore, the model, if accurate, has relevance over a wide range of companies in terms of size. The control (or no-problem) sample was actually somewhat smaller, with an average size of just under 300 million *cruzeiros* and a median size of about 200 million *cruzeiros*.

One or two firms were selected for the control sample from each of the same industrial categories as those represented by the serious-problem group, and data were gathered from the year corresponding to the year prior to the problem date. Since there were more than 30 industrial categories to choose from, the number of firms in each industrial group was often quite small. Whenever possible, privately owned, domestic companies were selected since we felt that a state-owned or multinational affiliation reduced, in general, the possibility of failure.

The classification procedure used in this study is based on the failure model developed in the United States (Altman 1968), with modifications that allow for consideration of Brazilian standards and reporting practices. In this Brazilian study, the same variables were utilized (see p. 4), but X_2 and X_4 were modified. With respect to X_2, the retained earnings account on U.S. balance sheets reflects the cumulative profits of a firm less any cash dividends paid out and stock dividends. In most instances, the small, young firm will be discriminated against because it has not had time to accumulate its earnings. In Brazil, however, due to different financial reporting practices and adjustments for inflation, there is no exact equivalent to retained earnings. The nearest translation to retained earnings is *"lucros suspensos,"* which refers to those earnings retained in the business after distribution of dividends. This amount is usually transferred, however, within a short time (perhaps two years) through stock dividends to the account known as capital.

In addition, reserves which were created to adjust for monetary correction on fixed assets and the maintenance of working capital were deducted from profits and thereby decrease those earnings which are reported to be retained in the firm. These reserves, however, increase both the assets and the firms equity and they too are transferred to capital. In essence, then, that amount of capital which represents funds contributed by the owners of the firm is the only part of equity that is not considered in the Brazilian equivalent to retained earnings. X_2 was calculated as:

$$\frac{\text{total equity—capital contributed by shareholders (CCS)}}{\text{total assets}}$$

A more precise expression of the numerator would be the cumulative yearly retained earnings plus the cumulative reserves created over the life of the firm, but this information is very difficult to obtain outside the firm and was not available to the authors.

Since most Brazilian firms' equity is not traded, there cannot be a variable which measures the market value of equity (number of shares outstanding times the latest market price). To derive the new values for X_4, the book value of equity *(patrimonio liquido)* was substituted and divided by the total liabilities. The remaining three variables were not adjusted, although we are aware of the fact that certain financial expenses are also adjusted for inflation in Brazilian accounting.

Empirical Results

The empirical results will be discussed in terms of two separate but quite similar models. The first model, referred to as Z_1, includes variables X_2 to X_5 (four measures) of the original Z-Score model (Chapter 3). Model Z_1 does not include X_1 because the stepwise discriminant program indicated that it did not add any explanatory power to the model and the sign of the coefficient was contrary to intuitive logic. Once again, as so often is found in multivariate failure classification studies, the liquidity variable is not found to be particularly important. The second model, referred to as Z_2, does not include X_2 because X_2 is quite difficult to derive with just one set of financial statements and it is similar to X_4. Model Z_2 can therefore be applied without supplementary data.

The models are as follows:

$$Z_1 = 1.44 + 4.03 \ X_2 + 2.25 \ X_3 + 0.14 \ X_4 + 0.42 \ X_5$$

$$Z_2 = 1.84 - 0.51 \ X_1 + 6.23 \ X_3 + 0.71 \ X_4 + 0.56 \ X_5$$

In both cases, the critical cutoff score is zero. That is, any firm with a score greater than zero is classified as having a multivariate profile similar to that of continuing entities and those with a score less than zero are classified as having characteristics similar to those of entities which experienced serious problems.

Results from the two models are essentially identical based on one year prior data. Model Z_1 performed better for Years 2 and 3; therefore, only the results of that model are discussed. Of the 58 firms in the combined two samples, seven are misclassified, yielding an overall accuracy of 88%. The Type I error (that of classifying a serious-problem firm as a continuing entity) was 13% (three out of 23 misclassified) and the Type II error (that of misclassifying a continuing entity) was slightly lower at 11.4% (four of 35). These results are impressive since they indicate that published financial data in Brazil, when correctly interpreted and rigorously analyzed, do indeed possess important information content.

Due to the potential upward bias involved in original sample classification results, further tests of the models were performed with several types of holdout or validation samples. The accuracy of the SP sample is unchanged after applying the Lachenbruch test. Several replication tests also showed high accuracy levels. Finally, the accuracy of the model is examined as the data become more remote from the serious problem date. The SP sample results, as expected, show a drop in the accuracy of the models. We utilized the weights from the model constructed with Year 1 data and inserted the variable measures for Years 2 and 3 prior to the SP date. Year 2 data provided accuracy of 84.2% (16 of 19 correct). Year 3 data provided lower accuracy of 77.8% (14 of 18 correct) classifications. Therefore, in only four cases were errors observed in classification based on data from three (or more in some cases) years prior to the SP date.

Implications of Results for Brazil

The implications and applications of models designed for assessing the potential for serious financial problems in firms are many. This is especially true in a developing country, where an epidemic of business failures could have drastic effects on the strength of the private sector and on the economy as a whole. Most observers of the Brazilian situation would agree on the merit of preserving an equilibrium among private enterprises, state-owned firms, and multinationals. Such equilibrium would be jeopardized if the domestic private sector were weakened by an escalation of liquidations. If a model such as the one suggested is used to identify potential problems, then in many cases preventive or rehabilitative action can be taken. This should involve a conscious internal effort, by the firms themselves, to prevent critical situations as soon as a potential problem is detected. Besides internal efforts, a program of financial and managerial assistance—more than likely from official external sources—is a potential outcome.

Many economists, including this writer, have argued that significant government assistance for the private sector is an unwise policy except where the system itself is jeopardized. One can rationalize government agencies' attempts to stabilize those industries where a significant public presence or national security is involved, for instance, commercial and savings banks or a steel industry. In developing countries, the distinction between high public interest sectors and the fragile private sector is more difficult to make, and limited early assistance is advocated.

Applying Models in Developing versus Developed Economies

We are fully aware of the problems that the wholesale and unqualified use of failure models could cause. Obviously, if a firm demonstrates a profile similar to those of past serious-problem entities and the model is used by all or most of those organizations providing credit to firms, the model's "prediction" will become a self-fulfilling prophecy. While some firms "deserve" to cease their operations due to inefficiency, we advocate using such prognostications to help rebuild and restructure a temporarily faltering operation. Recently in the United States a chief executive of a concern listed on the American Stock Exchange managed to bring the firm back to financial health, (Chapter 6). In any event, the model should not be construed as either infallible (the results show clearly that it is not) or as a type of "black-box" solution to problems.

AUSTRALIA

Australia has certain unique characteristics, with huge development potential (like Brazil) but with an already established industrial base. While the influence of multinational firms is quite important, the local corporate structure is large enough to support a fairly substantial capital market.

Table 12-9 Liquidations—New South Wales (1949–1978).

Year	Total Number of Liquidations	Total Number of Companies on Register	Liquidations per 10,000 Companies on Register
1949	166	15,478	107
1950	130	16,624	78
1951	48	18,240	26
1952	119	19,562	61
1953	155	21,130	73
1954	72	23,518	31
1955	146	26,414	55
1956	203	29,144	70
1957	141	32,587	43
1958	162	36,999	44
1959	201	42,164	48
1960	170	48,965	35
1961	206	54,116	38
1962	314	59,000	53
1963	268	60,483	44
1964	485	63,729	76
1965	509	66,372	77
1966	424	69,564	61
1967	478	73,470	65
1968	569	78,988	72
1969	506	85,640	71
1970	573	97,062	59
1971	537	107,606	50
1972	894	118,288	76
1973	1,058	128,286	82
1974	1,155	133,784	86
1975	1,349	133,595	101
1976	1,178	140,428	84
1977	1,542	148,031	104
1978	1,566	155,707	101

Sources: Parliament of N.S.W., *Report of the Working of the Companies Act.* Corporate Affairs Commission, Annual Reports. Prepared by Izan, Australian Graduate School of Management, Sydney, 1981.

The various types of financial and accounting organizations present have grown in parallel with the corporate register. One of the characteristics of a dynamic capitalistic economy is the flow of firms into and out of the system. Despite strong growth characteristics, Australia also has experienced a relatively high business failure rate which we estimate to be perhaps two or three times higher than that of the United States. Table 12-9 lists the business liquidation rate per 10,000 registered firms in the State of New South Wales, by far the largest state in terms of gross domestic product and industrialized activity. Compared to the recent range in the United States (22 to 61 per 10,000 firms) the rate of 100 per 10,000 firms (about 1%) appears quite high. In actuality, the Australian liquidation figures are inflated due to the inclusion of voluntary "winding ups" on the part of firms which are not the result of financial distress. We estimate (Altman and Izan, 1981) that the "true" failure figures from 1978 through 1980 were in the vicinity of 45 to 60 per 10,000 registered firms. In 1978 there were 57 voluntary liquidations, most of them not associated with distress. In any event, the *annual* failure rate is less than 1% of the population.

Castagna and Matolcsy

The active financial environment in Australia is a motivation for rigorous individual firm analysis. A series of studies by A. Castagna and Z. Matolcsy (C&M) culminating in their published work (1981) have analyzed the failure prediction potential in Australia and have concluded that there is a strong potential for models like those developed in the United States to assist analysts and managers.

Research Design

One of the difficult requirements for failure analysis found in just about every country in the world outside the United States is assembling a data base of failed companies large enough to perform a reliable discriminant analysis model. Despite a relatively large number of liquidations, Australian data on failed firms are quite restricted. C&M were able to assemble a sample of only 21 industrial companies (the number of firms would have been much larger if mining companies were included). The failure dates spanned the years from 1963 through 1977, with the date determined by the appointment of a liquidator or receiver. An alternative criterion date might have been the time of delisting from the stock exchange or the liquidation/receiver date, whichever comes first. For every failed company in the sample, there is a randomly selected surviving quoted industrial firm from the same period. Industries represented include retailers, manufacturers, builders, and service firms.

(a)

$Z = -1.4723 - 0.0023 \times V1 + 0.4512 \times V2$
$\quad - 0.7574 \times V3 + 2.2905 \times V4 + 1.0999 \times V5$
$\quad - 0.0360 \times V6 + 0.0972 \times V7 - 0.0572 \times V8$
$\quad + 0.0659 \times V9 - 0.4014 \times V10$

Decision Rule:
Classify in the failed group if $Z \geq 0$
Classify in the surviving group if $Z < 0$

(b)

$Z = -6.2453 - 10.695 \times V2 + 10.466 \times V3 - 9.8824 \times V4$
$\quad - 0.8250 \times V7 + 9.622 \times V10 + 1.6145 \times (V2)^2$
$\quad - 3.2968 \times V2 \times V3 + 0.5363 \times V2 \times V4$
$\quad - 0.0015 \times V2 \times V7 - 0.2256 \times V2 \times V10 + 1.6473 \times (V3)^2$
$\quad - 0.2316 \times V3 \times V4 - 0.0177 \times V3 \times V7 + 0.0552 \times V3 \times V10$
$\quad - 0.9133 \times (V4)^2 + 0.0594 \times V4 \times V7$
$\quad + 3.8704 \times V4 \times V10 - 0.0105 \times (V7)^2$
$\quad + 0.0488 \times V7 \times V10 + 0.79 \times (V10)^2$

Decision Rule:
Classify in the failed group if $Z \leq -5.7884$
Classify in the surviving group if $Z > -5.7884$

V_1 = returns on shareholder's funds (%)
V_2 = EBIT/total asset (%)
V_3 = operating income/operating assets (%)
V_4 = quick ratio (x)
V_5 = current ratio (x)
V_6 = gross cash flow/total debt (%)
V_7 = total debt/total assets (%)
V_8 = working capital/total assets (%)
V_9 = retained earnings/total assets (%)
V_{10} = market capitalization/total debt (x)

Source: A. D. Castagna & Z. Matolcsy (1981).

Figure 12-1 (a) *Specification of the Linear: A Temporal Model with the 10-Variable Set Using Equal Priors.* (b) *Specification of the Quadratic: A Temporal Model with the Five-Variable Set Using Unequal Priors.*

Empirical Results

Prior studies by C&M (1975, 1979) reduced the number of potential discriminating variables to 10 which were then analyzed in a linear and quadratic discriminant structure. The authors also attempted to test their results for various *a priori* group membership probabilities. The results suggest that it is difficult to identify a unique model to predict corporate failures and that some specification of user preferences is desirable. Still, they do indicate a 10-variable linear and five-variable quadratic classification models, which are specified in Fig. 12-1.

As noted, the results of C&M's work are not definitive. For example, if one is concerned with minimizing the misclassification of failed companies, then the linear model using equal priors outperforms all other models tried. This model also had the best overall results, except in the fourth year prior to failure. However, the linear model does not perform better than other models in the classification of surviving companies. A stepwise procedure indicated that a five-variable model did not perform as well as the models based on the ten-ratio set in the overall classification tests. All of their comparisons are based on the Lachenbruch validation tests.

The C&M study does not address prediction accuracy *per se*. All of the tests are on the original sample of 21 firms. In order for the tests to be predictive in nature, their model(s) should be applied to subsequent firm performance in Australia. The authors do note that they expect to monitor their findings on samples of continuing companies listed on the Australian Stock Exchange.

A New Model in Progress

Altman and Izan (1982), in a subsequent attempt to address the failure classification problem in Australia, analyzed a larger (50-firm) sample of failed companies and an equal number of nonfailed entities. Perhaps the most distinctive aspect of their model is the attempt to standardize the ratios by the respective firms' industry medians. The results (not complete) from this industry relative approach will then be compared with a similar model using only the "raw" ratios. The reason for this attempt to standardize by industry is the heterogeneous nature of the failed firms and the feeling that raw ratios compiled from a sample of firms representing such diverse industries as textiles, light and heavy manufacturers, service firms, retailers, builders and contractors, and finance companies could not be applied with any degree of confidence unless the ratios were somehow comparable. In addition, Australian accounting convention, as is the case in every country outside the United States, does not require the capitalization of financial leases. Hence, direct ratio comparison is potentially misleading, especially between firms in an industry that tends to utilize leases a great deal and another where direct ownership of assets is the rule. Industry relative data will not, however, adjust for intraindustry comparisons where lease utilization differs significantly.

ENGLAND

The British financial environment is probably the most similar to the United States system in terms of the amount and quality of financial information available to analysts of individual corporate entities. The number and rate of business failures in the United Kingdom are perhaps the highest in the world, especially in the late 1970s and early 1980s when relatively tight monetary policy and recessionary periods wracked the economy. The number of bankruptcies in 1981 was 14,210, a 26% increase over 1980. Table 12-10 shows that the failure rate in England over the last decade has averaged over twice that of the United States, and, based on earlier comparisons, is significantly higher than the rates of Japan, West Germany, and Australia. As such, it is understandable that attempts have been made in the United Kingdom to analyze the information content of reported data for assessing firm performance and failure potential.

The work of Taffler and Tisshaw (1977) follows the methodology and objectives of that which was reported earlier. They have approached the problem primarily from the viewpoint of security analysis and adaptations of their work, and that of Taffler and Houston (1980) and Taffler (1976), is currently being used by practitioners for investment selection purposes. They also indicate that their model is relevant for accounting firms to assess the going concern capability of clients and in their work as receivers and liquidators of firms that have already failed.

Table 12-10   Business Failure Rates, the United States and the United Kingdom, (1971–1980).

	Percent of Firms Registered or Covered	
Year	United States[a]	United Kingdom[b]
1971	0.42	0.69
1972	0.38	0.59
1973	0.36	0.44
1974	0.38	0.64
1975	0.43	0.94
1976	0.35	0.99
1977	0.28	0.96
1978	0.24	0.77
1979	0.28	0.65
1980	0.42	0.95

[a]Based on Dun & Bradstreet's business failure rate; the percentage of firms followed by D&B (converted from the number per 10,000 firms to a percent); from the *Failure Record*, N.Y., annually.

[b]Company liquidations in the United Kingdom as a percentage of registered companies. *Source: Annual Abstract of Statistics*, London, 1981 and the *Annual Report of the NIDC*, 1979.

Research Design—Taffler and Tisshaw

To construct their solvency model, Taffler and Tisshaw (T&T) utilized linear discriminant analysis on a sample of 46 failed firms and 46 financially sound manufacturing companies. The latter sample was matched to the failed sample by size and industry (no information on these characteristics available), from period 1969 through 1975. Failed firms were those entering into receivership, creditors' voluntary liquidation, compulsory winding up by order of the court, or government action (bailouts) undertaken as an alternative to the other unfortunate fates. Eighty different ratios were examined for the two samples with a resulting model utilizing only four measures. These four were

X_1 = profit before tax/current liabilities,

X_2 = current assets/total liabilities,

X_3 = current liabilities/total assets, and

X_4 = no-credit interval.

The first three ratios are taken from the balance sheet and measure profitability, liquidity, and a type of leverage, respectively. The no-credit interval, based on a measure first derived by Sorter and Benston (1960), is the time for which the company can finance its continuing operations from its immediate assets if all other sources of short term finance are cut off. More directly it is defined as immediate assets–current liabilities/operating costs excluding depreciation. T&T state that the no-credit interval is "something akin to the acid-test ratio" (p. 52).

Empirical Results

Both the model described above and an "unquoted model" (for nonlisted companies) appeared to be quite accurate in classifying correctly over 97% of all observations. Another model by Taffler (1976), supposedly the one being used by practitioners in the U.K. investment community, had accuracies of 96%, 70%, 61%, and 35% for the four years prior to failure.

The nearly perfect one-year-prior accuracy that T&T observe utilizing their model contrasts sharply with the relatively small percentage of quoted and unquoted firms that were assessed to have a going concern problem by their auditors. In fact, T&T report that just 22% of the 46 quoted firms (and none of the 31 unquoted manufacturing bankrupt firms) had been qualified on going concern grounds prior to failure. An earlier study by Altman and McGough (1974) found a similar differential between the Z-score model and U.S. accounting auditors' going concern qualifications.

Implications

The dropoff in accuracy is quite noticeable as earlier year data are applied, although, for investment purposes, one needs less of a lead time before failure in order to disinvest without losing a major amount of his investment. It is fair to say, however, that as failure approaches, stock prices tend to move downward in a rather continuous manner. Taffler and Houston (1980) indicated that 12% of large quoted industrial firms had Z-scores indicating high failure risk. This is a comparable figure to results we observed utilizing our own ZETA model (Altman, Haldeman, and Narayanan, 1977) in the United States (Chapter 4).

The authors also point out that their experience shows that about 15 to 20% of those firms which display a profile similar to failed companies will actually fail. In addition, the British government appeared to them to be keeping many ailing firms alive. Although this type of paternalism is less common in the United States, examples like Lockheed and Chrysler Corp. periodically crop up.

Finally, T&T conclude that accountants are too defensive when it comes to considering the value of conventional published historic statements. When several measures of a firm, described from a set of accounts, are considered together the value of the information derived is enhanced dramatically. Essentially, T&T advocate a multivariate approach to financial analysis, and I certainly agree. It is unfortunate that they did not share with readers a more complete description of their findings and the data used in their analysis. Their results are certainly provocative and appear to be of some practical use in England.

In his latest attempt to revise the company failure discriminant model (Taffler, 1981), a smaller sample of 23 failed companies (1968–73) and 45 nonfailed entities displaying financially healthy profiles were examined first within a principal component analysis framework. A large list of almost 150 potential variables was reduced to just five. These five are

earnings before interest and taxes/total assets$_{t-1}$,

total liabilities/net capital employed,

quick assets/total assets,

working capital/net worth, and

stockturn.

The variables were discussed in terms of their discriminant standardized coefficients, and other relative measures of contribution, but no function weights were provided. Taffler did utilize prior probability and cost-of-error estimates in his classification procedures. He concludes that such an approach is best used in an operational context as a means of identifying a short list of firms which might experience financial distress (p. 15). Another conclusion is that the actual bankruptcy event is essentially determined by the actions of the financial institutions and other creditors and cannot strictly be predicted by using a model approach.

Other U.K. Studies

A recent attempt by Marais (1979), carried out while on a short-term assignment for the Industrial Finance Unit of the Bank of England, also utilized discriminant analysis to quantify relative firm performance. He too concentrated on U.K. industrials and incorporated flow of funds variables with conventional balance sheet and income statement measures. Using a sample of 38 failed and 53 nonfailed companies (1974–1977), he tested several previously published models from the United States and the United Kingdom using both univariate and multivariate techniques.

He then went on to develop his own model, of which space does not permit a full discussion. His model included the following variables:

X_1 = current assets/gross total assets,

X_2 = 1/gross total assets,

X_3 = cash flow/current liabilities, and

X_4 = funds generated from operations minus net change in working capital to total debt.

His results were considered "satisfactory" and his conclusions modest. He mainly advocated that firms whose scores fell below a certain cutoff point should be regarded as possible future problems, "that all Z-scores can hope to do is act as a sophisticated screening device to those firms most urgently in need of analysis" (p. 29).

A later work, by Earl and Marais (1982), expanded upon this work with more enthusiastically reported results and implications. Classification results of 93%, 87%, and 84% respectively for the three years prior to failure are reported. The authors felt that funds flow data improved their classification accuracy. The single ratio of cash flow/current liabilities was a successful discriminator. Subsequent tests on failures and nonfailures in 1978 revealed a very low Type I error but an unacceptably high Type II error assessment.

IRELAND

In Ireland, Cahill (1981) presents some exploratory work on a small sample of 11 bankrupt, listed companies covering the period from 1970 through 1980. Three primary issues are explored: (1) identification of those ratios which showed a significant deterioration as failure approaches, (2) whether the auditors' reports expressed any reservations or uncertainty about the continuance of the firms as going concerns, and (3) whether there were any other unique aspects of the failed companies' conditions.

Cahill's analysis revealed a number of ratios indicating clear distress signals one year prior to failure. These ratios compared unfavorably with aggregate norms and ratios for the comparable industrial sector. Although several measures continued to show differences in earlier years, the signals were less clear in Year 2 prior and it was difficult to detect strong signals from ratios prior to Year 2.

Only one of the 11 auditors' reports was qualified on the basis of going concern. Five other less serious qualifications were present in the auditor's reports. Cahill speculates that the low frequency of auditor qualifications on a going concern basis was due to auditor reluctance and accounting convention in Ireland as well as their feeling of being part of a "small society." We observed similar circumstances in Australia. Still, according to Cahill, since deterioration was quite apparent, those close to the situation should have been aware of the seriousness and earlier remedial action taken or qualification given.

Unsuccessful merger activity and significant investment and asset expansion financed by debt were the major causes of Irish failures. Several of the firms continued to pay dividends right up to the year prior to failure. On the other hand, only one company actually made payments to unsecured creditors after insolvency, indicating that asset value had deteriorated beyond repair and only then was failure declared.

CANADA

Canada, like Australia, is a relatively small country in terms of business population, yet it too is concerned with the performance assessment of individual entities. The economy is very much tied to the fortunes of the United States and its financial reporting standards are often derived from the same accounting principles. Like so many environments that we looked at earlier, the key constraint in Canada is the availability of a large and reliable data base of failed companies. This requires both a sufficient number of failures and publicly available data on those firms. Both attributes do exist in Canada, but just barely.

Knight (1979) analyzed the records of a large number of small business failures as well as conducting interviews with the key persons involved. The author contends that his study supplies information "to answer the question, why do small businesses fail in Canada and also generates certain guidelines as to how the failure rate in Canada may be decreased from its recent increasing level." Not surprisingly, Knight finds that a firm usually fails early in its life (50% of all failed firms do so within four years and 70% within six) and that some type of managerial incompetence accounts for almost all failures.

Knight also attempted to classify failure using a discriminant analysis model. He amassed a fairly large sample of 72 failed small firms with average sales and assets of about $100,000. A five-variable discriminant function realized disappointing results, however. Only 64% of the original sample of 36 failed and 36 nonfailed firms and 54% of the test sample of a like number of firms were correctly classified. He concluded that the discriminant analysis procedure was not successful. Knight did combine firms in many different industries, including manufacturing, service, retail, and construction and this will contribute to estimation problems, especially if the data are not adjusted to take into consideration industry differences and/or accounting differences, for instance, lease capitalization. We discussed this industry effect at length earlier in the Australian situation.

Altman and Lavallee's Work

The results of Altman and Lavallee (1981) were more accurate when manufacturing and retailing firms are combined but they do not advocate a single model for both sectors. Indeed, the holdout tests of this study indicate that nonmanufacturers cannot be confidently measured when the model contains variables which are industry sensitive.

The Altman and Lavallee (A&L) study was based on a sample of 54 publicly traded firms, half failed and half continuing entities. The failures took place during the ten years 1970–1979 and the average tangible asset size of these 27 failures was $12.6 million at one statement date prior to failure (average lag was 16 months). Manufacturers and retailer-wholesalers were combined although the data did not enable them to adjust assets and liabilities for lease capitalization. The continuing firms were stratified by industry, size, and data period and had average assets of $15.6 million. One can observe, therefore, that the Canadian model for the 1970s decade consisted of firms with asset sizes similar to those of the previously reported early U.S. models (e.g. Altman, 1968) constructed from the 1950s and 1960s data period.

A&L examined just 11 ratios, and their resulting model contained five based on a forward stepwise selection procedure. The model for Canada (Z_c) is

$$Z = -1.626 + 0.234 \, (X_1) - 0.531 \, (X_2) + 1.002 \, (X_3)$$
$$+ \, 0.972 \, (X_4) + 0.612 \, (X_5)$$

where

Z_c = Canadian Z-score,

X_1 = sales/total assets,

X_2 = total debt/total assets,

X_3 = current assets/current liabilities,

X_4 = net profits after tax/total debt, and

X_5 = rate of growth of equity − rate of asset growth.

Classification Results

The overall classification accuracy of the Z_c model on the original 54-firm sample was 83.3%, which is quite high, although not as impressive as that reported in some of the other economic environments. Practically speaking, classification criteria are based on a zero cutoff score with positive scores indicating a nonfailed classification and negative scores a failed assignment. Reliability, or holdout tests, included Lachenbruch (1967) test replications, the original sample broken into randomly chosen classification and test samples, and testing the model on prior years data, for example Years 2 through 4 before failure. The Lachenbruch and replication holdout results showed accuracies very similar to those of the original sample results and the prior year accuracies were 73% (Year 2), 53% (Year 3), and only 50% (Year 4). Therefore, the model appears reasonably accurate for up to two statements prior to failure but not accurate for earlier periods. These findings are quite similar to those of Altman's (1968) model and we can suggest that the similarities in accuracies are partially related to the similarities of the data quality and the somewhat diverse industries represented in the sample.

A&L also simulated their results for various assumptions of prior probabilities of group membership and costs of error. Their findings were that Type I errors could be reduced, even eliminated, but that the resulting Type II error was unacceptably high and vice versa for eliminating the Type II error. The Z_c model's results were also compared to a naive classification strategy of assigning all observations to the nonbankrupt category or assuming that the resulting errors would be realized in proportion to the actual experience of bankrupts and nonbankrupts [proportional chance model; see Joy and Tollefson (1975)]. They concluded that, in every case, the Canadian Z_c model was more efficient; that is, it had a lower expected cost than a naive model.

Finally, A&L observe that the industry affiliations of the misclassified firms were predominantly retailers amongst the failed group and manufacturers among the nonfailed. It appeared that one of the variables, sales/assets (X_1), was particularly sensitive to industry effects, with the misclassified failed retailers all having high asset turnovers and the misclassified manufacturers all with low turnovers.

Implications

A&L attempted to reestimate the model without the sales/assets variable, but the results actually were worse. One can conclude that the Canadian investigations are at an early stage and follow-up work is needed in subdividing a larger sample into manufacturers and retailers-wholesalers and/or improving the information on critical industry differences, such as lease usage and capitalization. Only additional time will permit analysts to construct models with sufficiently large samples or to witness an improvement in the quality of reported data. We are aware of a move with the Canadian government to set up an early warning system to identify potential large publicly traded firm crisis situations, for instance, Massey-Ferguson. Authorities are currently considering available models such as Altman (1968) and A&L (1980) as alternatives to building their own model.

THE NETHERLANDS

Another relatively small country which has received attention from financial researchers of distress prediction is The Netherlands. Business failures soared to 7,268 for the first 10 months of 1981, an increase of 42% over 1980. Several recent Dutch studies have attempted to apply classification techniques to failure early warning systems. The main problem that Abrahamse and van Frederikslust (1975), Bilderbeek (1977, 1979), and van Frederikslust (1978) encountered was small sample size of bankrupt firms. Still, their works were carefully performed and added evidence that financial ratios can indeed convey a great deal of information. It is likely that the number of observations will rise with the increase in failures in the early 1980s.

Bilderbeek

Bilderbeek (1977) analyzed a sample of 38 firms which went bankrupt from 1950 through 1974 and 59 ongoing companies, but found that only 85 firms had sufficient data for analysis. Bilderbeek analyzed 20 ratios within a stepwise discriminant framework and arrived at a five-variable model of the form

$$Z_{NB} = 0.45 - 5.03X_1 - 1.57X_2 + 4.55X_3 + 0.17X_4 + 0.15X_5$$

where

Z_{NB} = Z-score (Netherlands, Bilderbeek),
X_1 = retained earnings/total assets,
X_2 = added value/total assets,
X_3 = accounts payable/sales,
X_4 = sales/total assets, and
X_5 = net profit/equity.

Two of the five signs (coefficients), X_4 and X_5, are positive and contrary to expectations since, for this model, negative scores indicate a healthy situation and positive scores indicate a failure classification. His model was based on observations over five reporting periods prior to failure and is not based on one-year intervals. His results were only mildly impressive, with accuracies ranging from 70 to 80% for one year prior and remaining surprisingly stable over a five-year period prior to failure. He explains in his book (1979) that the stability is due to the facts that there are no liquidity variables and the stable role of the value added measure. Subsequent tests of Bilderbeek's model have been quite accurate (80% over five years). Apparently, several institutions are now using his model for practical purposes.

Van Frederikslust

Van Frederikslust's (1978) model included tests on a sample of 20 failed and a matched nonfailed sample of observations for 1954 through 1974. All firms were quoted on the Netherlands Stock Exchange. In addition to the now traditional research structure, that is, linear discriminant, single-year ratio, equal *a priori* probability of group membership assumptions, the author performed several other tests. Those included (1) looking at the development of ratios over time (temporal model) as well as analyzing ratio levels, (2) varying the *a priori* assumption of group membership likelihood to conform with a specific user of the model (e.g., lending officer), and (3) varying the expected costs of the models, taking into consideration the specific user's utility for losses.

Van Frederikslust attempts to provide a theoretical discussion for his choice of variables. He concludes that traditional measures of firm performance, that is, liquidity, profitability, solvency, and variability of several

of these categories, are the correct indicators to look at. Industry affiliation and general economic variables are also thought to be important but
are not included in his model. In fact, the primary model only contained
two variables representing liquidity and profitability.

Van Frederikslust's primary model analyzed level of ratios. His definition of failure included many different types of juridical mechanisms but
essentially involved the failure to pay fixed obligations. His sample included textile, metal processing, machinery, construction, retailing, and
miscellaneous firms. The nonfailed group (20) were randomly selected
from the same industries, size categories (assets), and time periods as was
the failed group. His first model was

$$Z_{NF} = 0.5293 + 0.4488X_1 + 0.2863X_2$$

where

Z_{NF} = Z-score (Netherlands, Frederikslust),
X_1 = liquidity ratio (external coverage), and
X_2 = profitability ratio (rate of return on equity).

The author distinguishes between the *internal coverage* ratio (cash balance + resources earned in the period/short-term debt) and the *external
coverage* ratio [short-term debt in period t plus available short-term debt
$(t - 1)$]. The external coverage measures what can be expected from the
renewal of debt and additional debt. "Failure at moment (t) is completely
determined by the values of internal and external coverage at that moment" (p. 35). Van Frederikslust uses only the external coverage measure
in his "simple" model.

Separate models are developed for each year, as Deakin did (1972). The
arguments for this are that a separate model is necessary to assess failure
probabilities for different time periods and that the distributions of ratios
vary over time. While we do not necessarily agree that separate models
are desirable—indeed, they could be confusing—the discussion on timing
of failure prediction is a useful one. The classification program utilized
was actually a 0, 1 multiple regression structure and not the discriminant
analysis model used in most other studies. Fisher (1936) has shown that
the coefficients of these structures are proportional when dealing with a
two-group model.

The results for the one-period model indicate that the estimated
chances of misclassification into the two groups are 5% for the failed
group and 10% for the nonfailed group. The expected accuracy falls as

time prior to failure increases. For example, the error rates are 15% and 20% respectively for two years prior.

A revised model, analyzing the development of ratios over time, yielded an equation which utilized the liquidity ratio in the latest year before failure, the profitability ratio two years prior, the coefficient of variation of the liquidity ratio over a seven-year period, and the prediction error of the profitability ratio in the latest year before failure. Again, separate models were developed for each year prior to failure. Using Lachenbruch's procedure for estimating error rates, the results were quite similar to those of the first set of equations based on the two variable, "levels" ratios. Accuracies for earlier years did show slight improvements.

FRANCE

In France, the business failure rate increased dramatically in 1981 to 20,895 firms, a jump of 20% over 1980. Altman *et al.* (1973) first attempted to apply credit scoring techniques to problem firms, many of which filed for bankruptcy (*faillite*). Working with a sample of textile firms and data provided by Banque de France, this study applied principal component analysis to a large number of financial indicators and proceeded to utilize the most important ones in a linear discriminant model. Their results were at best mediocre on test samples and, while the model did provide insights into that troublesome sector, it was not implemented on a practical basis.

A more recent study by Bontemps (1981), using a large sample of industrial companies and data from the Centrale de bilans of Credit National (supplier of long-term debt capital to French firms), achieved high accuracy on original and holdout tests. His results are quite interesting in that as little as three variables were found to be useful indicators. Bontemps combined both the univariate technique developed by Beaver (1967) with arbitrary, qualitative weightings of the three most effective measures to classify correctly as much as 87% of his holdout sample of 34 failed and 34 nonfailed firms. The original function was built based on a matched (by industry, size, and year) sample of 50 failed and nonfailed entities from 1974 through 1979. At this time, the results are being evaluated and, of course, they are confidential.

Collongues (1977), Mader (1975, 1979, and 1981) also have attempted to combine financial ratios with data from failed and nonfailed French firms. Mader's studies were descriptive of firms in difficulty and the utility of ratios as risk measures. Collongues did utilize discriminant analysis in his analysis of small and medium-size firms with some success.

The application of statistical credit scoring techniques in the French environment appears to be problematic, but the potential remains. One problem usually is the quality of data and the representativeness of them. But this is a problem in all countries and is not unique to France. It would appear that the new economic plan being put forth by the Socialist government in France in 1981 and 1982 could very well utilize a well-constructed and reliable model. The government has gone on record as intending not to keep hopelessly insolvent firms alive artificially but to try to assist those ailing firms prior to total collapse. An accurate performance predictor model could very well help in this endeavor.

INTERNATIONAL COMPARISON OF RATIOS

In putting together this chapter, an interesting issue arose as to the similarities among ratios of failed and nonfailed firms across national boundaries. Since many of the studies reviewed earlier utilized the same or similar variable profiles, it was possible to examine average ratios in different countries.

The comparative average ratio results for four different countries (five samples of firms since we examined two separate studies from the United States) are listed in Table 12-11. In addition to the United States, these countries include Canada, Brazil, and Australia. We do not have any *a priori* economic hypothesis as to expected ratio similarities across countries but, due to financial reporting standards unique to local conditions and different political-economic interrelationships, we do not expect a great deal of similarity. Indeed, we do find large differences in average ratios for our failed groups and somewhat smaller differences across nonfailed groups. Since we did not have the actual distributions of firm ratios for most of our samples, it was not possible to do any significance tests across samples.

With the exception of my early study (1968), we observed that the data are derived from essentially similar time periods for the other four samples. Most involved data from the decade 1970 through 1979. Therefore, we cannot explain ratio mean differences on temporal grounds. We observe fairly large cross-country differentials in all ratios for the failed groups and, with the exception of the asset turnover, all of the failed groups' ratio averages were "better" than the earlier 1968 study. Cross-ranking of averages for individual ratios does not reveal consistent country rankings for either the failed or nonfailed groupings. We conclude, therefore, that ratio averages are not "country sensitive" in a consistent manner.

Table 12-11   International Comparisons of Average Group Ratios.

				Failed Groups		
Ratio Name	United States Altman (1968)	United States Altman et al. (1977)	Australia Castagna and Matolcsy (1981)	Brazil Altman et al. (1979)	Canada Altman and Lavallee (1981)	Japan Ko (1981)
Working capital/ total assets	−0.061	0.150	0.062	−0.120	0.100	−0.181
Retained earnings/ total assets	−0.626	−0.406	−0.038	0.010	n.a.	−0.163
EBIT/total assets	−0.318	−0.005	0.002	0.050	−0.120	−0.007
Market value equity/ total liabilities	0.401	0.611	0.800	0.350	n.a.	0.533
Sales/total assets	1.500	1.310	1.200	0.880	1.480	1.052
Average Z-score	−0.266	1.271	1.707	1.124	n.a.	0.667
			Nonfailed Groups			
Working capital/ total assets	0.414	0.309	0.187	0.230	0.300	0.107
Retained earnings/ total assets	0.355	0.294	0.022	0.240	n.a.	0.154
EBIT/total assets	0.153	0.112	0.086	0.160	0.040	0.063
Market value equity/ total liabilities	2.477	1.845	3.110	1.140	n.a.	0.878
Sales/total assets	1.900	1.620	n.a.	1.230	2.310	0.988
Average Z-score	4.883	3.878	4.003	3.053	n.a.	2.070

Sources: Various articles; see reference section.

We also can compare the average ratios for the two U.S. samples (1968 and 1977). In every ratio case for the *nonfailed group,* the later figures (1977) show a deterioration in the average ratio. Two reasons could account for this. One, there has been a general deterioration since the 1960s in the financial performance of U.S. corporations and financial risk has increased. Second, the 1977 data are adjusted for capitalization of leases, thereby increasing the asset base. With a larger denominator in each of the ratios, we observe lower *positive* ratios and "higher" *negative* ratios.

This is confirmed by the failed group averages; for negative ratios, the averages are higher in the 1977 period. The only exception to the lease capitalization and financial deterioration theses is the somewhat higher average in 1977 for the market value of equity/total liabilities ratio for failed firms. We find it difficult to explain this, especially since the non-failed group showed the opposite ranking.

We have also calculated, in Table 12-11, average Z-scores for the bankrupt and nonbankrupt groups in four countries (for five samples if we include the two from the United States). It appears that the original Z-score (1968) sample had the greatest dispersion with the highest average nonbankrupt and the lowest average bankrupt firm score. The distribution is tightest for Ko's Japanese sample. Interestingly enough, the lowest nonbankrupt group's average score (i.e., Japan's 2.07) is greater than the highest bankrupt group's rating (Australia's 1.50).

We were also a bit surprised to find that the average bankrupt firm for the ZETA (1977) sample was considerably higher than the earlier 1968 sample (1.27 vs. -0.27). A good deal of this difference is caused by our adjustments to the data in the later sample (primarily the capitalization of leases). The larger asset base tends to increase the negative ratios, particularly X_2 (retained earnings/total assets) and X_3 (EBIT/total assets). This is consistent with the lower average positive score for the nonbankrupt group in the ZETA sample than in the earlier sample.

It is particularly interesting to compare the average ratios from the two U.S. samples of nonfailing firms (columns 1 and 2 in Table 12-11) with the Japanese sample. As we noted earlier, Japanese firms will probably have lower Z-scores due to lower retained earnings, profits, and higher leverage as well as higher asset totals per dollar (yen) of profits and sales. In fact, every ratio for the two U.S. samples is greater than its Japanese counterpart. Note, however, that while this is true for the nonfailed sample, which we expect is fairly representative for the population of firms, the distinction is not as clear for the failed sample.

SUMMARY AND A FEW CONCLUSIONS

We have attempted to review and compare a relatively large number of empirical failure classification models from ten countries. Much of the material is derived from little-known or unknown sources and as such we hope that the study will stimulate a greater transnational discussion. Indeed, as financial institutions and government agencies in countries such as Canada, the United States, Brazil, France, and England wrestle with the specter of large firm failures in the future, the knowledge that prior work has been done with respect to early warning models may help obviate the consequences or reduce the number of these failures.

I expect that the quality and reliability of models constructed in many of the aforementioned countries to improve (1) as the quality of information on companies is expanded and refined, (2) as the number of business failures increase, thereby providing more data points for empirical analysis, and (3) as researchers and practitioners become more aware of the problems and potential of such models. Where sufficient data do not exist for specific sector models, for instance, manufacturing, retailing, and service firms, the application of industry relative measures can perhaps provide a satisfactory framework for meaningful analysis. Of course, this requires that government or private agencies build reliable industry data bases for comparison purposes.

References

Abate, R.P. "Numerical Scoring Systems for Commercial Loans" *Bankers Monthly*, January 1969.

Abrahams, A. and van Frederikslust, "Discriminant Analysis and the Prediction of Corporate Failure," *European Finance Association 1975 Proceedings*, edited by R. Brealey & G. Rankine, Amsterdam: North Holland, 1976.

Adams, W., "Merging Sick Giants," *New York Times*, August 8, 1978.

Almon, S., "A Distributed Lag Between Capital Appropriations and Expenditures," *Econometrica*, January 1965.

Aharony, J., C. Jones, & I. Swary, "An Analysis of Risk and Return Characteristics of Corporate Bankruptcy Using Capital Market Data," *Journal of Finance*, September 1980.

Altman, E.I., "Financial Ratios, Discriminant Analysis and the Prediction of Corporate Bankruptcy," *Journal of Finance*, September 1968.

Altman, E.I., "Bankrupt Firms' Equity Securities As An Investment Alternative," *Financial Analysts Journal*, 1969.

Altman, E. I., "Corporate Bankruptcy Prediction and Its Implications for Commercial Loan Evaluation," *The Journal of Commercial Bank Lending*, 1970.

Altman, E. I., *Corporate Bankruptcy in America*. Lexington, MA: Lexington Books, 1971.

Altman, E.I., "Predicting Railroad Bankruptcies in America." *Bell Journal of Economics and Management Science*, Spring 1973.

Altman, E.I., "A Financial Early Warning System for Over-the-Counter Broker Dealers." *Journal of Finance*, September 1976.

Altman, E.I., "Bankruptcy Identification: Virtue or Necessity?" *Journal of Portfolio Management*, Spring 1977.

Altman, E. I., "Predicting Performance in the Savings & Loan Association Industry," *Journal of Monetary Economics*, October 1977.

Altman, E.I., "Commercial Bank Lending: Process, Credit Scoring and Costs of Errors in Lending," *Journal of Financial & Quantitative Analysis*, November 1980.

Altman, E.I., "Examining Moyer's Re-examination of Forecasting Financial Failure," *Financial Management*, Winter 1978.

Altman, E.I., "A Further Empirical Investigation of the Bankruptcy Cost Question," *Journal of Finance*, September, 1984.

Altman, E.I., R. Avery, R. Eisenbeis, & J. Sinkey, *Application of Classification Techniques in Business, Banking & Finance*, JAI Press, 1981.

Altman, E.I., T. Baidya, and L. M. Riberio-Dias, "Assessing Potential Financial Problems of Firms in Brazil," *Journal of International Business Studies*, Fall 1979.

Altman, E., and M. Brenner, "Information Effects and Stock Market Response to Signs of Firm Deterioration," *JFQA*, March 1981.

Altman, E.I.; R. Eisenbeis. "Financial Applications of Discriminant Analysis: A Clarification." *Journal of Financial and Quantitative Analysis*, March 1978.

Altman, E.I., and L. Goodman, "An Economic and Statistical Analysis of the Failing Company Doctrine," *NYU Working Paper*, 1980.

Altman, E. I.; R. Haldeman, and P. Narayanan. "ZETA Analysis: A New Model to Identify Bankruptcy Risk of Corporations." *Journal of Banking and Finance*, June 1977.

Altman, E. I., and Izan, "Identifying Corporate Distress In Australia: An Industry Relative Analysis" Australian Graduate School of Management, Sydney, 1982.

Altman, E. I., and Izan, "Identifying Corporate Distress In Australia: An Industry Relative Analysis," Australian Graduate School of Management, Sydney, 1982.

Altman, E.I., and M. Lavallee, "Business Failure Classification in Canada," *Journal of Business Administration*, Summer 1981.

Altman, E.I., Margaine, M., Schlosser, M., and P. Vernimmen, "Statistical Credit Analysis in the Textile Industry: A French Experience," *Journal of Financial and Quantitative Analysis*, March 1974.

Altman, E.I., and T. McGough, "Evaluation of a Company as a Going Concern," *Journal of Accountancy*, December 1974.

Altman, E.I. and A. Sametz, *Financial Crises: Institutions and Markets in a Fragile Environment*. New York: J. Wiley, 1977.

Anderson, T. W., *An Introduction to Multivariate Statistical Analysis*. New York: Wiley, 1962.

Argenti, J., *Corporate Collapse*, New York: McGraw-Hill, 1976.

Ball, M., "Z-Factor: Rescue by the Numbers," *Inc. Magazine*, December 1980.

Ball, R., and Brown, P., "An Empirical Evaluation of Accounting Income Numbers," *Journal of Accounting Research*, Autumn 1968.

Bankruptcy Reform Act of 1978, *Bankruptcy Law Reports*, No. 389 (October 25, 1978), Part II. Chicago: *Commerce Clearing House*.

Bankruptcy Tax Bill of 1980 (H.R. 5043), Chicago: *Commerce Clearing House*.

Bates, T., "An Econometric Analysis of Lending to Black Businessmen." *Review of Economics and Statistics*, August 1973.

Bauman, J.K., "The Impact of the Failing Company Doctrine in the FTC's Premerger Clearance Program," *Syracuse Law Review*, Vol. 19 (1965).

Baxter, N., "Leverage, Risk of Ruin and the Cost of Capital," *The Journal of Finance*, September 1967.

Beaver, W. "Financial Ratios as Predictors of Failures," in *Empirical Research in Accounting*, selected studies, 1966 in supplement to the *Journal of Accounting Research*, January 1967.

Beaver, W., "Alternative Accounting Measures as Predictors of Failure," *Accounting Review*, January 1968.

Beermann, K., *Possible Ways to Predict Capital Losses with Annual Financial Statements*. Dusseldorf: 1976.

Bettinger, C., "Bankruptcy Prediction as a Tool for Commercial Bankers," *Journal of Commercial Bank Lending*, July 1981.

Bilderbeek, J., "An Empirical Study of the Predictive Ability of Financial Ratios in the Netherlands," *Zeitschrift fur Betriebswirtschaft,* May 1979, No. 5 (in English).

Blum, Mark P., "The Failing Company Doctrine," *Boston College Industrial and Commercial Review,* Vol. 16 (1974a).

Blum, Mark P., "Failing Company Discriminant Analysis," *Journal of Accounting Research,* Vol. 12, No. 1 (Spring 1974b).

Blum, Marc P., "Discussion of Failure Models for Non-financial Institutions," in Altman and Sametz, *Financial Crises.* New York: Wiley, 1977.

Bock, Betty, "The Failing 'Failing' Company Justification for a Merger," *The Conference Board,* No. 25 (1969).

Bontemps, P.O., "La Notation du Risque de Credit," (Credit Scoring for Risk), Paris: Credit National, 1981.

Box, G.E.P., "A General Distribution Theory for a Class of Likelihood Criteria," *Biometrika 36,* 1949.

Brigham, E., *Financial Management: Theory & Practice,* 3rd ed. Dryden Press, Hinsdale, Ill., 1982.

Cahill, E., "Irish Listed Company Failure Financial Ratios, Accounts and Auditors' Opinions," *Journal of Irish Business and Administrative Research,* April 1981.

Carmichael, D.R., "The Auditor's Reporting Obligation—The Meaning and Implementation of the Fourth Standard of Reporting," in *Auditing Research Monograph No. 1.* New York: AICPA, 1972.

Casey, C., "The Effect of Accounting Information Load on Bank Loan Officers' Predictions of Bankruptcy," *Journal of Commercial Bank Lending,* August (1978).

A.D. Castagna and Z.P. Matolcsy, "An Examination of Company Deaths: A Comparative Study of the Financial Profiles of Acquired and Failed Companies," *Research Paper #1,* Centre for Securities Industries Studies, Kuring-gai College of Advanced Education, Sydney, Australia, 1977.

A.D. Castagna and Z.P. Matolcsy, "The Prediction of Corporate Failure: Testing the Australian Experience," *Australian Journal of Management,* June 1981.

Cohen, M., The Commission on Auditors Responsibilities, *Report Conclusions and Recommendations,* New York, 1978.

Cohen, I.J., T.C. Gilmore, and F. A. Singer, "Bank Procedures for Analyzing Business Loan Applications," in *Analytical Methods in Banking,* K.J. Cohen and F. S. Hammer (eds.). Homewood, Ill.: R.D. Irwin (1966).

Collier on Bankruptcy, 15th ed. New York: Bender, 1980.

Collongues, Yves, "Ratios Financiers et Prevision des Faillites des Petites et Moyennes Entreprises" (Financial Ratios and Forecasting Failures of Small and Medium Size Enterprises), *Review Banque,* No. 365, 1977.

Cooley, P. and P. Lohnes, *Multivariate Procedures for the Behavioral Sciences,* New York: Wiley, 1962.

Cumming, C., and K. Saini, "The Macroeconomic Determinants of Corporate Bankruptcies in Japan and the U.K.," Federal Reserve Bank of New York, Research Paper, December 1981.

DeAngelo, II., and R. Masulis, "Optimal Capital Structure Under Taxation," *Journal of Financial Economics,* Vol. 8, (1980).

Deakin, E.B., "A Discriminant Analysis of Predictors of Business Failure," *Journal of Accounting Research*, March, 1972.

Deakin, E., "Business Failure Prediction: An Empirical Analysis," in E. Altman and A. Sametz, eds., *Financial Crises: Institutions and Markets in a Fragile Environment.* New York: Wiley, 1977.

Dun and Bradstreet, *The Failure Record*, New York, 1976.

Dun's Review, "How to Tell Who's Going Bankrupt," October 1975.

Dietrich, J., and R. Kaplan, "Empirical Analysis of the Commercial Loan Classification Decision," *Accounting Review*, January 1982.

Earl, M.J., and David Marais, "Predicting Corporate Failure in the U.K. Using Discriminant Analysis," *Accounting & Business Research*, forthcoming, 1982.

Edmister, R.O., "Financial Ratios and Credit Scoring for Small Business Loans," *Journal of Commercial Bank Lending*, September 1971.

Eisenbeis, R.A., "Pitfalls in the Application of Discriminant Analysis in Business, Finance, and Economics," *Journal of Finance*, September 1977.

Eisenbeis, Robert A., and Robert B. Avery, *Discriminant Analysis and Classification Procedures: Theory and Applications*, Lexington, Mass.: D.C. Heath and Co., 1972.

Fama, E.G., Fisher, L., Jensen, M.C., and Roll, R., "The Adjustment of Stock Prices to New Information," *International Economic Review*, February 1969.

Fischer, J., "Forecasting Company Failure by the Use of Non-Numerical Data," paper presented at the EIASM Workshop on Bank Planning Models, Brussels, April, 6, 7, 1981.

Fisher, R.A., "The Use of Multiple Measurements in Taxonomic Problems," *Annuals of Eugenics*, No. 7, September 1976.

Fisher, L., "Determinants of Risk Premiums on Corporate Bonds," *Journal of Political Economy*, June 1959.

Frank, R., W. Massy, and G. Morrison, "Bias in Multiple Discriminant Analysis," *Journal of Marketing Research*, August 1965.

Gebhardt, G., "Insolvency Prediction Based on Annual Financial Statements According to the Company Law—An Assessment of the Reform of Annual Statements by the Law of 1965 from the view of External Addresses," *Bochumer Beitrage zur Unternehmungs and Unternehmens-forschung*, ed. by H. Besters et al., Vol. 22, Wiesbaden, 1980.

Gonedes, N.J., "Capital Market Equilibrium and Annual Accounting Numbers: Empirical Evidence," *Journal of Accounting Research*, Spring 1974.

Haugen, R., L. Senbet, "The Insignificance of Bankruptcy Costs to the Theory of Optimal Capital Structure," *Journal of Finance*, May 1978.

Heath, Loyd C., "Financial Reporting and the Evaluation of Solvency," in *Accounting Research Monograph No. 3.* New York: AICPA, 1978.

Hickman, W.B., *Corporate Bond Quality and Investor Experience*. Princeton: Princeton University Press, 1958.

Hill, Henry P., "Reporting on Uncertainties by Independent Auditors," *Journal of Accountancy*, January 1973.

Hofer, C., "Turnaround Strategies," *Journal of Business Strategy*, Summer 1980.

Jaffe, J.F., "Special Information and Insider Trading," *Journal of Business*, July 1974.

Johnson, C.G., "Ratio Analysis and the Prediction of Firm Failure," *Journal of Finance*, December 1970.

Joy, O.M., and J. Tollefson, "On the Financial Applications of Discriminant Analysis," *Journal of Financial & Quantitative Analysis*, Vol. 10, No. 5 (December 1975).

Kaplan, R. and G. Urwitz, "Statistical Models of Bond Ratings: A Methodological Inquiry," *Journal of Business*, April 1979.

Kida, Thomas, "Investigation into Auditors' Continuity and Related Qualification Judgements," *Journal of Accounting Research*, Autumn 1980.

Kim, E. H., "A Mean-Variance Theory of Optimal Capital Structure and Corporate Debt Capacity," *Journal of Finance*, March 1978.

Knight, R.M., "The Determinants of Failure in Canadian Firms," ASA Meetings of Canada, Saskatoon, May 28–30, 1979, University of Western Ontario Working Paper, May, 1979.

Ko, C.J., *A Delineation of Corporate Appraisal Models and Classification of Bankrupt Firms in Japan*, New York University Thesis, 1982.

Korobow, L., and Stuhr, D.P., and Martin D., "A Probabilistic Approach to Early Warning of Changes in Bank Financial Condition," *Monthly Review*, Federal Reserve Bank of New York, July 1976.

Lachenbruch, Peter A., "An Almost Unbiased Method of Obtaining Confidence Intervals for the Probability of Misclassification in Discriminant Analysis," *Biometrics*, 23, 1967.

Langbein, J., and Posner, R., "Market Funds and Trust Investment Law," *American Bar Foundation Research Journal*, December 1975.

Libby, R., "Accounting Ratios and the Prediction of Failure: Some Behavioral Evidence," *Journal of Accounting Research*, March 1975.

Mader, F., "Les Ratios et l'Analyse du Risque" (Ratios and the Analysis of Risk), *Analyse Financiere*, 2eme trimestre 1975.

Mader, F., "Un Enchantillon d'Entreprises en Difficulte" (A Sample of Enterprises in Difficulty,) *Journee des Centrales de Bilan*, 1979.

Marais. D.A.J., "A Method of Quantifying Companies Relative Financial Strength," *Bank of England*, Working Paper No. 4, 1979.

Martin, D., "Early Warning of Bank Failure: A Logit Regression Approach," *Journal of Banking and Finance*, November 1979.

Merwin, C., *Financing Small Corporations*. New York: National Bureau of Economic Research, 1942.

Metz, R., "Marketplace: Avoiding the Stock of Shaky Companies," *New York Times*, November 18, 1976.

Miller, M., "Debt and Taxes," *Journal of Finance*, May 1977.

Moriarity, S., "Communicating Financial Information through Multidimensional Graphics," *Journal of Accounting Research*, Spring 1979.

Mosteller, F., and D.F. Wallace, "Inference in the Authorship Problem," *Journal of the American Statistical Association*, June 1963.

Moyer, C.R., "Forecasting Financial Failure: A Re-Examination," *Financial Management*, Summer 1977.

Neter, J., "Discussion of Financial Ratios as Predictors of Failure," *Empirical Research in Accounting: Selected Studies 1966, Journal of Accounting Research*, Supplement to Volume 4, 1967.

Noto, N.A. and D. Zimmerman, "A Comparison of Failure and Liability Trends and Implications for Business Assistance," Report No. 81-36 E, *Congressional Research Service, January 30, 1981*.

Orgler, Y.E., "A Credit Scoring Model for Commercial Loans," *Journal of Money, Credit and Banking*, November 1970.

Orgler, Y.E., *Analytical Methods in Loan Evaluation,* Lexington, MA.: Lexington Books, 1975.

Scott, J., "A Theory of Optimal Capital Structure," *Bell Journal of Economics,* Spring 1977.

Scott, J., "The Probability of Bankruptcy: A Comparison of Empirical Predictions and Theoretical Models," *Journal of Banking and Finance,* September 1981.

Seligson, Charles, "Major Problems for Considerations by the Commission on Bankruptcy Laws of the United States," *American Bankruptcy Law Journal,* Winter 1977.

Shindledecker, MC., "Going Concern Reports," NYU, 1980.

Sinkey, J., *Problem and Failed Institutions in the Commercial Banking Industry,* JAI Press, Greenwich, Conn., 1979.

Sinkey, J., "A Multivariate Statistical Analysis of the Characteristics of Problem Banks," *Journal of Finance,* March 1975.

Smith, R., and A. Winakor, *Changes in Financial Structure of Unsuccessful Corporations.* University of Illinois, Bureau of Business Research, 1935.

Sorter, G., and G. Benston, "Appraising the Defensive Position of a Firm: The Interval Measure," *Accounting Review,* October 1960.

Spivack, J., "A Comparison of the Value Line Relative Financial System with the Zeta Model," NYU Working Paper, June 1982.

Taffler, R., "Finding Those Firms in Danger," *Accountancy Age,* July 16, 1976.

Taffler, R., and Houston, "How to Identify Failing Companies Before It Is Too Late," *Professional Administration,* April 1980.

Taffler, R., and H. Tisshaw, "Going, Going, Gone—Four Factors Which Predict," *Accountancy,* March 1977.

Takahashi, K., K. Kurokawa and K. Watese, "Predicting Corporate Bankruptcy through Financial Statements," *Society of Management Science of Keio University,* November 1979.

Takahashi, K., and E. Altman, "Conference on the State of the Art in Bankruptcy Classification Models," Keio Graduate School of Business, Yokohama, Japan, June 25, 1981.

Tamari, M., "Financial Ratios as a Means of Forecasting Bankruptcy," *Management International Review,* Vol. 4 (1966).

Van Frederikslust, R.A.I., *Predictability of Corporate Failure.* Leiden: Martinus Nijhoff Social Science Division, 1978.

Vance, S.C., "Penn-Central—A Lesson for Bank Boards and One Bank Holding Companies," *The Bankers Magazine,* Winter 1971.

Van Horne, J., *Financial Management and Policy,* 5th Edition. Englewood Cliffs, N.J.: Prentice-Hall, 1981.

von Stein, J.H., *Identifying Endangered Firms.* Hohenheim University, 1981.

Walter, James, "Determination of Technical Insolvency," *Journal of Business,* January 1957.

Warner, Jerold, "Bankruptcy Costs, Some Empirical Evidence," *Journal of Finance,* May 1977.

Weibel, P.F., *The Value of Criteria to Judge Credit Worthiness in the Lending of Banks.* Bern: 1973.

Weinrich, G., *Prediction of Credit Worthiness, Direction of Credit Operations by Risk Classes.* Gabler Wiesbaden: 1978.

Weintraub, B., *What Every Credit Executive Should Know about Chapter 11 of the Bankruptcy Code,* New York: National Association of Credit Management, 1980.

Westerfield, R.W., "Assessment of Bankruptcy Risk," *Rodney L. White Center for Financial Research,* Working Paper No. 71–1, University of Pennsylvania, February 1971.

Weston, J., and E. Brigham, *Managerial Finance,* 7th Edition. New York: Holt, Rinehart and Winston, 1981.

White, M., "Bankruptcy Costs: Theory and Evidence," NYU Working Paper, July 1981.

Wilcox, J.W., "A Gambler's Ruin Prediction of Business Failure Using Accounting Data," *Sloan Management Review* Vol. 12 (September 1971).

Wilcox, J.W., "The Gambler's Ruin Approach to Business Risk," *Sloan Management Review,* March 1976.

Wilcox, J.W., "A Prediction of Business Failure Using Accounting Data," *Journal of Accounting Research,* Vol. 11 (1973).

Index

363